THE HATOYAMA DYNASTY

THE HATOYAMA DYNASTY

JAPANESE POLITICAL LEADERSHIP THROUGH THE GENERATIONS

MAYUMI ITOH

First published 2003 by
PALGRAVE MACMILLAN™
175 Fifth Avenue, New York, N.Y. 10010 and
Houndmills, Basingstoke, Hampshire, England RG21 6XS.
Companies and representatives throughout the world.

PALGRAVE MACMILLAN is the global academic imprint of the
Palgrave Macmillan division of St. Martin's Press, LLC and of
Palgrave Macmillan Ltd. Macmillan® is a registered trademark in the
United States, United Kingdom and other countries. Palgrave
is a registered trademark in the European Union and other countries.

ISBN 1–4039–6331–2 hardback

Library of Congress Cataloging-in-Publication Data

Itoh, Mayumi, 1954–
    The Hatoyama dynasty : Japanese political leadership through
    the generations / Mayumi Itoh.
        p. cm.
    Includes bibliographical references.
    ISBN 1–4039–6331–2
        1. Japan—Politics and government—1868– 2. Hatoyama
    family I. Title.

    DS881.9.I775 2003
    929.7'0952—dc21   2003040543

A catalogue record for this book is available from the British Library.

Design by Newgen Imaging Systems (P) Ltd., Chennai, India.

First edition: November, 2003
10 9 8 7 6 5 4 3 2 1

Printed in the United States of America.

For my parents and Megumi

CONTENTS

Acknowledgments

I acknowledge with gratitude the advice and assistance that I have received during the course of completing the first draft manuscript from Greg Rewoldt and graduate assistants Deogratius Mshigeni, Amanda Ringelberg, and Marshall Smith. I am also grateful to the University of Nevada, Las Vegas (UNLV) for granting me a sabbatical leave for the year 2000–2001, which enabled me to go back to Japan and work on the manuscript.

Earlier versions of parts of this book were published previously. Part of chapter 7 was originally published in "Hatoyama Kunio and Political Leadership in Japan: A Political Case Study," *Asian Survey*, Vol. XXXIX, No. 5, September–October 1999, pp. 720–735. Part of chapter 8 appeared in "Fallen Political Leadership in Japan: Will a New Party Eventually Emerge?" Japan Policy Research Institute (JPRI) Working Paper, No. 49, September 1998, pp. 1–6; "Japanese Constitutional Revision: A Neoliberal Proposal for Article 9 in Comparative Perspective," *Asian Survey*, Vol. XLI, No. 2, March–April 2001, pp. 310–327; and "Japan's Neo-Nationalism: The Role of the Hinomaru and Kimigayo Legislation," JPRI Working Paper, No. 79, July 2001, pp. 1–6. I would like to thank the following institutions for permission to reproduce these articles: the Regents of the University of California for *Asian Survey* and Japan Policy Research Institute for JPRI Working Paper.

I would also like to thank members of the Hatoyama family, as well as Kawate Shoichiro and Otake Nori of Hatoyama Hall, for their generosity in providing the pictures used in this book and on the book jacket. All the portrait photographs were provided by the Hatoyama Hall with the permission of the Hatoyama family members. The Hatoyama Hall is open to the public and houses memorabilia of the Hatoyama family. For information, contact: Hatoyama Hall, 1-7-1, Otowa, Bunkyo-ku, Tokyo, 112–0013 Japan; tel: 03–5976–2800; fax: 03–5976–1800; home page: http://www.hatoyamakaikan.com.

Finally, I would like to express my deepest appreciation to Gerald L. Curtis, Steven C. Clemons, Chalmers Johnson, and Donald S. Zagoria for their valuable comments on the draft manuscript; to Toby Wahl, Jennifer Yoon, Ian Steinberg, and Mukesh V. S. for their herculean editorial work; and to my parents Ito Shigeru and Asako and to my sister Ito Yayoi, for their continuous help in sending materials from Japan. This book is dedicated to my parents and my daughter Megumi who endured the whole period of writing this book.

This is not an "authorized biography." The Hatoyama family has provided no inputs to this book other than the photographs used (for which I thank them sincerely). Although the publication of this book was not possible without the help of the people mentioned here, all responsibility for its contents rests with me.

Mayumi Itoh

NOTES ON THE TEXT

The English translations of the Japanese sources were made by the author. The English translations were made in such a way that they best make sense in English or were paraphrased from the original Japanese. Translation of Japanese words, such as names of political parties in the prewar period, was generally modeled after Robert A. Scalapino, *Democracy and the Party Movement in Prewar Japan: The Failure of the First Attempt*, Berkeley, Calif.: University of California Press, 1962.

Romanization of Japanese words in this book is based on the Hepburn style (*New Japanese English Dictionary*, Tokyo: *Kenkyusha*, 17th ed., 1988, appendix). The guidelines for the Hepburn style stipulate that diacritical marks indicating long vowels are usually omitted when Romanized Japanese words are used in English sentences (*New Crown 1* [English textbook for junior high school first grade, authorized by the Ministry of Education], Tokyo: *Sanseido*, 1996, appendix). With numerous Japanese words and names being cited in the text, the addition of such signs could be confusing and could affect the smooth flow of the text. Therefore, Romanized Japanese words are shown without diacritical marks in this book.

Japanese names are cited with surnames first and then followed by given names as they appear in Japanese literature. However, for the second citing and afterward, first names are used to refer to members of the Hatoyama family in the text, as many members of the family appear, whereas surnames are used to refer to others. Strictly speaking, the word "Japan" is an inactive noun referring to a nation. Unless specified otherwise, however, this book uses the term as an active noun referring to the members of public policy decision-making groups that make up the Japanese government. For positions and titles of the people cited in the text, the book uses those held at the time of the event or situation in which the person is cited, instead of the present one, unless specified otherwise.

Reference numbers are normally placed at the end of each paragraph in the text. This book does not cover all the political events during which the four generations of the Hatoyama family lived. For background information, the relevant literature is cited in the notes of each chapter. This book's citations include Hatoyama family members' writings, such as Hatoyama Ichiro's autobiography, diary, and memoirs. Such sources might be construed as subjective because of self-interest and should be taken with a grain of salt. However, in Ichiro's case, his own account can be considered credible for the most part, because he was known to be overly outspoken to the extent that he had offended the Japanese wartime military and the U.S. occupation forces' personnel, endangering his political career. In fact, he writes with candor, often admitting his own mistakes. His writing provides important facts and insight that were not revealed elsewhere, therefore constituting an essential source of information for this study.

List of Acronyms

ARF	Association of Southeast Asian Nations Regional Forum
ASEAN	Association of Southeast Asian Nations
CIE	Civil Information and Education
CGP	Clean Government Party
CP	Conservative Party
DPJ	Democratic Party of Japan
DSP	Democratic Socialist Party
G2	Counterintelligence Section
GHQ	General Headquarters
GS	Government Section
HC	House of Councilors
HP	House of Peers
HR	House of Representatives
JCP	Japan Communist Party
JNP	Japan New Party
JSP	Japan Socialist Party
JTU	Japan Teachers' Unions
LDP	Liberal Democratic Party
LP	Liberal Party
MITI	Ministry of International Trade and Industry
MOE	Ministry of Education
MOF	Ministry of Finance
MOFA	Ministry of Foreign Affairs
NFP	New Frontier Party
NLC	New Liberal Club
NPS	New Party *Sakigake* (Pioneers)
PARC	Policy Affairs Research Council
SCAP	Supreme Commander of Allied Powers
SDF	Social Democratic Federation
SDFs	Self-Defense Forces
SDPJ	Social Democratic Party of Japan
TIT	Tokyo Institute of Technology
UNPKOs	United Nations Peacekeeping Operations

LIST OF FIGURES

LIST OF TABLES

Portrait photograph of the late Dr. Hatoyama Kazuo

Portrait photograph of the late Mrs. Hatoyama Haruko

Portrait photograph of the late Mr. Hatoyama Ichiro

Portrait photograph of the late Mrs. Hatoyama Kaoru

Portrait photograph of the late Mr. Hatoyama Iichiro

Portrait photograph of Mrs. Hatoyama Yasuko

Portrait photograph of Dr. Hatoyama Yukio

Portrait photograph of Mrs. Hatoyama Miyuki

Portrait photograph of Mr. Hatoyama Kunio

Portrait photograph of Mrs. Hatoyama Emily

CHAPTER 1
INTRODUCTION

The Hatoyama family is arguably the most prominent political family in modern Japan. The Hatoyama Dynasty has produced six Diet (parliament) members in four generations from 1856 to the present. Each of them led distinguished political careers, holding positions such as prime minister, foreign minister, house speaker, and political party president. What is common among the six Hatoyama politicians is that all went to Tokyo University (or its prototypes), the oldest national university in Japan, which has created leaders in almost every sector, from education, law, government, to business, for more than 130 years. In addition to political leaders, the Hatoyama family includes several renowned educators and scholars. In all, the name Hatoyama is synonymous with being the brightest in Japan. As political writer Sato Tomoyasu notes, the Hatoyama Dynasty has constituted the roots of both Japan's modern academism and its modern politics (see figure 1.1).[1]

Kazuo (1856–1911), of the first generation, was the first recipient of an LL.D (doctor of laws) in Japan and taught at Tokyo Imperial University. He was elected to the House of Representatives (HR) of the Japanese imperial parliament at its second session in 1892 and kept that seat until his death. Among the many positions he held, Kazuo served as house speaker and deputy foreign minister. Ichiro (1883–1959), of the second generation, became a member of the HR in 1915 and held the seat until his death. He was prime minister from 1954 to 1956 and created the *Jiyu Minshuto* (the Liberal Democratic Party, LDP) that has dominated Japanese politics from its inception in 1955 to this day. His younger brother, Hideo (1884–1946), became a member of the HR in 1932 after teaching law at Tokyo Imperial University.

Iichiro (1918–1993), of the third generation, was administrative vice minister of finance, the pinnacle of the bureaucratic pyramid. After his retirement from the Ministry of Finance (MOF), Iichiro became a member of the House of Councilors (HC), the nominal upper house of the Diet. He was foreign minister in the first Fukuda cabinet (1976–1977).

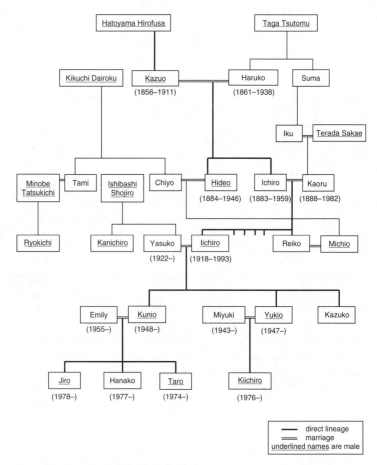

Figure 1.1 Genealogy of the Hatoyama Dynasty.
Sources: Ito Hirotoshi, *Hatoyama ichizoku* (Hatoyama Dynasty), Tokyo: Pipurusha, 1996 and Sato Tomoyasu, *Keibatsu* (Clans by marriage), Tokyo: *Tachikaze shobo*, 1994.

Finally, Yukio (1947–) and Kunio (1948–) make up the fourth genera-tion. Kunio, the younger brother, has been an HR member since 1976. Yukio taught engineering at Tokyo Institute of Technology (TIT) and then became a member of the HR in 1986. Both were originally members of the LDP; however, they left the party and created the *Nihon Minshuto* (the Democratic Party of Japan, DPJ) in 1996. Due to the family's political legacy, the brothers were often likened to the Kennedy family in American politics.

Sato writes, even in the age of the so-called *seshu giin* (hereditary Diet members) where they occupy a significant portion of the Japanese parliament, it is "exceptionally exceptional" that one family has produced Diet members in its direct lineage for four successive generations (see later). Moreover, they were not just rank-and-file legislators but were political leaders. Sato summarizes, "the footsteps of the Hatoyama family's political careers are essentially synonymous with the history of Japan's entire modern politics and its parliamentary history."[2]

Rationale for Studying the Hatoyama Dynasty

Despite the great significance of the Hatoyama family to modern Japanese politics, there is no comprehensive study of the members of the family available in English. The only work in English that exclusively studied Ichiro is by Donald Hellmann (1969). However, the book examines one specific policy—Japan's restoration of diplomatic relations with the Soviet Union in 1956 that Ichiro formulated—and does not cover Ichiro's entire political career. No book in English has been written about the other members of the Hatoyama Dynasty although they have made important contributions to Japanese politics.[3]

The scarcity of studies of the Hatoyama Dynasty is primarily attributable to the dominance of the bureaucratic model for the study of Japanese politics. The Western literature on Japanese politics has focused on institutional analysis and has largely ignored the role of individual leaders. A few notable exceptions are the study of Yoshida Shigeru (prime minister, 1946–1954) by John W. Dower (1979), the study of Tanaka Kakuei (prime minister, 1972–1974) by Chalmers Johnson (1995), and the study of Hirohito (emperor, 1926–1989) by Herbert P. Bix (2000). Institutional policy studies make the decision-makers faceless automatons acting upon the dictates of rational choices. While the Japanese preference for a consensus-building decision-making style in an entrenched bureaucracy gives political leaders less maneuverability and makes them less visible, their role in policy-making should not be dismissed. In a recent case, Kan Naoto of the DPJ displayed political leadership in 1996 against deep-rooted bureaucratic inertia when he was minister of public health and welfare.[4]

Ichiro: The Forgotten Japanese Leader

There is another reason why the study of Ichiro, "probably the best educated of all postwar prime ministers in the political culture of democracy[,]"[5] was neglected. Despite his long career, which extended over five decades from the Meiji to the Showa eras, Ichiro was ignored because the "Yoshida school" became the orthodoxy in postwar Japanese politics. Ichiro's ill-fated purge deprived him of the opportunity to form the first democratically chosen cabinet in postwar Japan. As Dower points out, "Had Hatoyama not been unexpectedly purged, he rather than Yoshida in all likelihood would have become the dominant political figure of Japan's first postwar decade."[6] Yoshida agreed to be Ichiro's proxy and took power. Yoshida adopted the stance of "subservient independence" vis-à-vis the United States, which was in line with General MacArthur's "peace constitution" (see chapter 5).

In contrast, Ichiro advocated Japan's *jishu* (self-reliant) constitution and national defense policy in order to restore Japan's real independence. Although Ichiro only proposed small self-defense capabilities and recognized the need for maintaining the U.S.–Japan Security Treaty, he was labeled as Gaullist and revisionist. In fact, U.S. officials, such as John Foster Dulles, secretary of state of the Eisenhower administration, criticized Ichiro for not trying hard enough to rearm Japan. In retrospect, it seems hardly militaristic to propose a constitutional revision in order to maintain minimal national self-defense forces (SDFs). However, given the "peace constitution," Ichiro's position was premature for its time (see chapter 5).

Kataoka Tetsuya argues that Edwin O. Reischauer, historian at Harvard University and U.S. ambassador to Japan (1961–1966), supported the MacArthur–Yoshida policy line. According to Kataoka, Reischauer counseled "Washington to moderate its demands for rearmament by echoing Yoshida's argument that that would arouse the 'underground militarists.' " These "underground militarists" refer to the purged *shokugyo seijika* (career politicians based on political parties). Ichiro, with whom Dulles, then special envoy of President Truman, secretly met in 1951, was one of them. As a result, the study of the "Yoshida school," composed of *kanryo seijika* (bureaucrats-turned-politicians), became the orthodoxy of Japanology in the United States and buried the legacy of Ichiro.[7]

Kataoka also argues that Ichiro's agenda for the revision of the election law is an integral part of the history of the Japanese constitution and is politically as important as the revision of the U.S.–Japan Security Treaty. Nevertheless, few scholars have studied Ichiro's aborted bill to introduce the single-member districts. The agenda took four decades to materialize in the revision of the election law in 1994 (see chapter 7). Kataoka states that this is so because the orthodox Japanese history made this agenda an "extreme taboo" and created an unwritten law to keep secret everything Ichiro had done. Consequently, even the fact that Ichiro was the LDP's

first president, and Japan's first prime minister from this party, is forgotten. It is widely but incorrectly assumed that Yoshida founded the LDP.[8]

Under these circumstances, this book examines Ichiro, the forgotten
Japanese leader, and attempts to make a fair assessment of his political
leadership. It also analyzes in-depth the process of Ichiro's purge and
depurging. By so doing, this book sheds new light on early postwar
Japanese politics.

The Contemporary Significance of the Study of Ichiro

The study of Ichiro also has great contemporary significance. In fact, it
is key to understanding Yukio's complex political philosophy that is
reflected in the DPJ's platforms. The liberal belief system established by
Kazuo runs in the Hatoyama Dynasty. Ichiro was ostracized as a liberalist, but stood up and helplessly fought the military regime in the prewar
and wartime periods. Ichiro was identified as conservative in postwar
Japan because the center of the spectrum of ideology had drastically
shifted toward the Left due to the legalization of Communism. This
ideological heritage explains the unique fusion of conservatism and
liberalism in Yukio's "neo-liberalism." The recently rekindled debate on
the constitutional revision and Yukio's support of the revision in favor of
acknowledging the SDFs as constitutional armed forces, suggest that
time has finally caught up with Ichiro. Ichiro's agenda, which was unat-
tainable in his time, has been revived by Yukio. This agenda, which
concerns restoring the true sovereignty of Japan, as well as the identity
of the Japanese, has come full circle (see chapter 8).

The Surge in Hereditary Diet Members

The study of the Hatoyama Dynasty is all the more relevant to the study
of contemporary political leadership, given the recent surge in the
hereditary Diet members in Japan. As many as 29 percent, or 137 out
of 480 seats contested in the June 2000 HR general elections, were
hereditary Diet members. In comparison, 17 percent, or 20 out of 121
seats contested in the July 2001 HC general elections (half of its total
delegation), were hereditary Diet members. In addition to the *nisei*
(second generation) hereditary Diet members, even the *sansei* (third
generation) hereditary Diet members are on the rise. In this context,
the Hatoyama Dynasty is the pioneer of hereditary Diet members with the
yonsei (fourth generation) hereditary Diet members. In addition to the
Adams, Roosevelt, and the Kennedy dynasties, the emergence of the Bush

dynasty in the United States also testifies to the phenomenal eminence of the political heritage of one family. Therefore, it would be of interest for American readers to see how the political heritage of one family is passed down from one generation to the next. This study shows the making of hereditary Diet members through the case of the Hatoyama Dynasty.[9]

The Genealogy of Japanese Political Parties

Beyond understanding political leadership, this book shows the evolution of the political party system in Japan. In fact, the genealogy of the Hatoyama Dynasty is none other than that of democratic political parties in Japan from the 1880s to present. For instance, Kazuo joined Okuma Shigenobu in creating the *Shimpoto* (the Progressive Party), one of the two oldest democratic parties, along with the *Jiyuto* (the Liberal Party) of Itagaki Taisuke. Kazuo was also instrumental in creating the *Kenseito* (the Constitutional Government Party), which enabled Okuma to form the first democratic cabinet in Japan (see figure 1.2).

In turn, Ichiro created three major conservative parties in postwar Japan: the *Nihon Jiyuto* (the Japan Liberal Party, thesis); the *Nihon Minshuto* (the Japan Democratic Party, antithesis); and the LDP (synthesis). The first two are offsprings of the original Liberals and the Progressives of the Meiji era. Therefore, the oldest two democratic parties are united and survive in the LDP. For the current generation, Yukio and Kunio left the LDP during the 1993 political reformation and created the DPJ in 1996 in order to challenge the LDP (see figures 1.3 and 1.4).

Accordingly, this book illustrates the overall picture of the genesis and evolution of major political parties (except those on the Left) in Japan. In addition, it examines numerous cases of cabinet formation and thereby shows the intricate process of alliance formation among political parties and its breakup. Specifically, this study analyzes the late 1890s in which Kazuo's Constitutional Government Party formed the first democratic cabinet in Japanese history; the mid-1950s in which Ichiro created the LDP; and the post-1993 era in which Yukio and Kunio created the DPJ. The analysis of the three periods over a century provides insight into the nature of Japanese party politics.

The present Japanese electorates are tired of constant changes in coalition cabinets, formed by alliances with mutually irreconcilable political parties. As a result, the majority of Japanese do not support any political party. This widespread political apathy signals the loss of credibility of the ruling LDP and the lack thereof the opposition parties. Against this setting, this study assesses the DPJ as an alternative to the LDP.

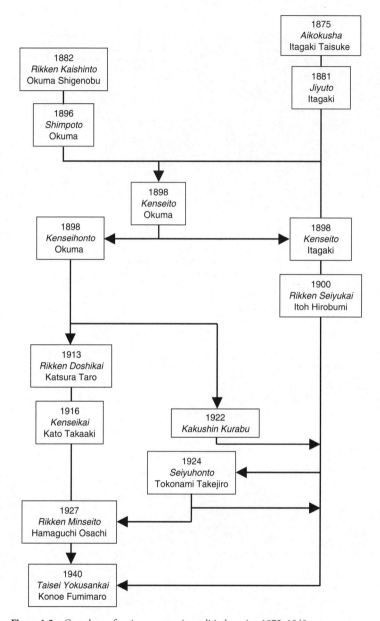

Figure 1.2   Genealogy of major conservative political parties, 1875–1940.
Source: Inoue Mitsusada, Kasahara Kazuo, Kodama Kota, *Nihonshi* (Japanese history), Tokyo: Yamakawa shuppansha, 1977.

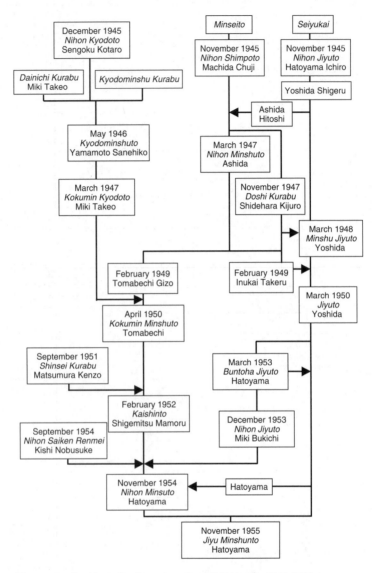

Figure 1.3 Genealogy of major conservative political parties, 1945–1955.
Source: Kataoka Tetsuya, ed., *Creating Single-Party Democracy: Japan's Postwar Political System*, Stanford, Calif.: Hoover Institution Press, 1992, p. 9.

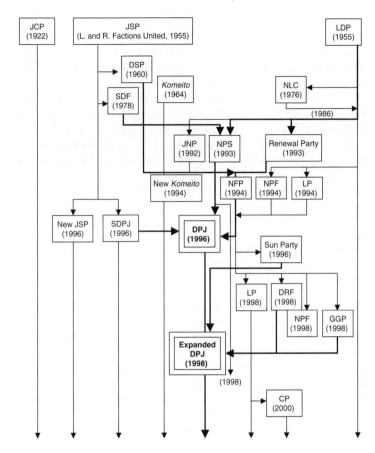

Figure 1.4 Genealogy of the Democratic Party of Japan (DPJ), 1955–2002.
Source: "*Umaretewa kie . . . seito neminguko*" (Born and disappear: a thought on naming political parties), *Chunichi Shimbun*, January 26, 1998.

Theoretical Inquiry on Political Leadership

Theoretically, this book asks the fundamental question: what makes a great leader? For years this question has occupied the minds of many scholars of history, politics, psychology, and sociology. It is a complex subject, encompassing innumerable factors. Defining the term "political leadership" presents the multifaceted nature of the subject. The definition varies depending on which aspect of political leadership one wishes to emphasize. Many social scientists have attempted this difficult task of defining the term political leadership.

Robert Elgie states outright that leadership is an unidentifiable concept, having no physical manifestation and closely resembling other related abstract concepts, such as power, influence, authority, and control. Contemporary scholars' definitions vary widely. James MacGregor Burns defines political leadership as a product of personal drives, social influences, political motivations, job skills, and the structure of career possibilities. Robert Tucker defines leadership as a process of human interaction in which some individuals exert a determining influence upon others. Harold Lasswell sees political leadership as a pattern of leader–follower interactions, which involves the ways that human beings affect each other. After careful examinations of the past studies on leadership, Elgie identifies political leadership as a "product of the interaction between leaders and the leadership environment with which they are faced." Elgie's definition is concise and yet grasps the totality of political leadership.[10]

The "Great-Man" Theory of Leadership

A literature review of the study of political leadership is useful. The first generation of the study of political leadership focused on the personal attributes of political leaders and analyzed the characteristics necessary for being a political leader. This is the "great-man" theory of leadership. It assumes that there are certain individuals whose innate superiority in one way or another stamps them as natural leaders. Thomas Carlyle represented this great-man school. He argues that great leaders were endowed with such special personal qualities that they were able to change the course of history.[11]

In this regard, Lasswell lists a range of personality studies in order to clarify the place of psychocultural factors in politics. They include studies of the following:

- to account for politically oriented personalities and to identify predispositions that facilitate the performance of one role rather than another;
- to describe the style of political behavior that occurs and to relate the style to psychocultural factors;
- to identify the styles of leadership characteristic of each personality and to isolate the factor combinations that account for the results;
- to discover the significance of a leader's main political role in the context of his whole personality system; and

- to identify the relevance of the prevailing distribution of personality systems in the structure.[12]

The "Cultural Determinist" School

The second school of thought in political leadership is the "cultural determinist" school. It is represented by Herbert Spencer who argues that the course of history is determined by the impersonal interplay of social and cultural forces over which individuals have little control. Robert Tucker also examines leadership in the context of political culture. Tucker defines culture as "a society's customary way of life, comprising both accepted modes of thought and belief and accepted patterns of conduct." Tucker then defines political culture as "a culture that pertains to government and politics."[13]

Tucker places the study of leadership as one of two schools of thought in politics: the power school and the leadership school. The power school defines politics in terms of the pursuit of power. Tucker criticizes this school as ignoring the ulterior purposes for which power is desired. He points out that some leaders rise above power politics and some people become political leaders without possessing power. By contrast, the leadership school takes a Platonic position that equates politics with leadership, defined as "an activity with utility for the polis, the activity of giving direction to the community of citizens in management of their common affairs, or the directive function in the state." Tucker is not fully in agreement with Plato's normative proposition (the philosopher as the ideal leader to realize an ideal polity in *The Republic*). Instead, Tucker posits leadership as a value-neutral phenomenon because leadership is not an ideal form of political rule and it takes many forms: effective and ineffective; wise and unwise; and constructive and destructive.[14]

The "Situationist" Approach

The next generation saw political leadership from a completely different perspective. Scholars such as C. A. Gibbs and R. M. Stogdill argue that it is not the personality but the situation that makes the great leader. The "situationist" approach postulates that the nature of a group's situation determines which of its members will emerge as a group leader.[15] Among other scholars, Gibbs emerged as a major advocate of this school of thought by stating:

> Leadership has usually been thought of as a specific attribute of personality, a personality trait, that some persons possess and others do not, or at least that some achieve in high degree and others scarcely at all.

The search for leaders has often been directed toward finding those persons who have this trait well developed. The truth would seem, however, to be quite different. In fact, viewed in relation to the individual, leadership is not an attribute of the personality but a quality of his role within a particular and specified social system. Viewed in relation to the group, leadership is a quality of its structure.[16]

Thus, Gibbs argues that leadership is a social role, not a personal attribute. Gibbs states that the adoption of a leadership role is dependent upon the specific situation and that the same individual in the same group may alternate between the roles of leader and follower as the group goals change. Gibbs further maintains that the three most important principles of leadership are: leadership is always relative to the situation—leadership flourishes only in a problem situation; the nature of the leadership role is determined by the goal of the group; and leadership is a process of mutual stimulation—a social interactional phenomenon in which the attitudes, ideals, and aspirations of the followers play as important a determining role as does the personality of the leader. In a similar vein, Stogdill writes, "[l]eadership is not a matter of passive status, or of the mere possession of some combinations of traits. It appears rather to be a working relationship among members of a group[.]"[17]

In refuting the great-man theory, situationists minimize the role of personal attributes. Nevertheless, Gibbs himself admits the role of personality when he states, "successful adaptation of [the specific situation] depends upon a complex of abilities and traits[;] . . . [m]ost frequently the individual is propelled into a position of leadership by virtue of his capacity for interpersonal contribution in the specific situation[;]" and "the person of all-round superiority is more frequently in situations in which he is able to make a contribution." Similarly, Stogdill acknowledges that "intelligence, alertness to the needs and motives of others, and insight into situations, further reinforced by such habits as responsibility, initiative, persistence, and self confidence" are necessary qualifications for the capacity to organize and expedite cooperative effort. He also states, "the leader acquires status through active participation and demonstration of his capacity for carrying cooperative tasks through to completion."[18]

These capacities that Gibbs and Stogdill mention are nothing but personal attributes of leadership. What the situationists seem to suggest is that a specific attribute of leadership—the interactive capability of a potential leader to the group and the situation—is essential for exercising leadership. In summary, the situationist approach made a significant contribution to the study of political leadership by shedding light on the importance of the situation and the interactive nature of political leadership.

The "Leader–Follower Interaction" Approach

Burns also pays attention to the interactive aspect of political leadership between leaders and followers and argues that leadership and follower-ship are the two essentials of power. He refutes the conventional defin-itions of leadership such as "leaders making followers do what *followers* would not otherwise do" and "leaders making followers do what the *leaders* want them to do." Instead, Burns defines leaders as those who induce followers to act toward certain goals that represent the values and the motivations—the wants and needs, the aspirations, and the expectations—*of both leaders and followers.* In Burns's words, "the genius of leadership lies in the manner in which leaders see and act on their own and their followers' values and motivations."[19]

Based on these premises, Burns makes a comprehensive study of the causal factors of political leadership. These independent variables consist of "origins of personal drives," "sources of political socialization," and "reasons for political motivations." Origins of personal drives include psychological effects on personality formation and the formation of motive bases—such as wants, needs, motives, expectations, attitudes, and values. Sources of political socialization comprise influences of the family, political schooling, peer group, and the society. Finally, reasons for political motivations include the need to satisfy ambition, recogni-tion, self-esteem, and gratification. In addition, Burns studies different types of political leadership, which range from "transforming leader-ship" (intellectual, reform, and revolutionary) to "transactional leader-ship" (opinion, group, party, legislative, and executive leadership).[20]

The "Interactionist" Approach

Burns's study led to a more organized and refined "interactionist" approach; referring to interaction between the leader and the environment. Elgie emphasizes that political leadership operates within the confines of a system and postulates that political leadership is the product of the inter-action between leaders and the leadership environment they face. Elgie argues that attributes of political leaders (such as their ambitions, personal-ity, and certain behavioral modes) are measured against environmental constraints (such as institutional structures, the long-term historical and social conditions, as well as the short-term social, economic, and political demands, and the needs of the society). In other words, attributes of political leaders and attributes of the leadership environment influence each other. Leaders can shape their environment but the environment also shapes their ambitions and behavior. Elgie states that the extent to which, and the ways in which, the one shapes the other is dependent on the nature of the interaction process, specifically on institutional structures.[21]

The interactionist approach seems to offer a most comprehensive framework for studying political leadership.

The "Middle-Ground" Approach: Personality Revisited

In reviewing the development of theories of political leadership, Tucker wrote in 1981 that the dominant school of thought is neither the great-man theory of leadership nor the situationist approach. Instead, Tucker states that currently scholars take a "middle-ground" approach that "recognizes the existence of certain general leadership qualities—intelligence, alertness to the needs and motives of others, insight into situation, initiative, persistence, and self-confidence—along with the variability of leadership traits according to the demands of group situations." Tucker has a reservation about Gibbs's finding that leadership flourishes only in problem situations, and questions if it is true in real-life situations involving large groups. In addition, Tucker notes that there is a three-fold task of leadership: diagnosing the situation authoritatively; devising a course of action designed to resolve or alleviate the problem; and mobilizing the political community's support for the leaders' definition of the situation and their prescribed policy response.[22]

The foregoing literature review suggests that both leaders' personal attributes and the environment are an integral part of political leadership. On the one hand, a person without leadership attributes cannot utilize the opportunity presented in a given environment. On the other hand, a person with leadership qualities cannot exercise leadership without the opportune environment. In conclusion, it is impossible to study political leadership in isolation and it is necessary to take a comprehensive approach, entailing the study of leaders' qualities, their environment, and leader–environment interactions.[23]

Theoretical Framework

In light of the literature review, this book employs a theoretical framework based on the middle-ground approach. This book defines personal attributes as being primary requirements ("independent variables") for political leadership, whereas the environment/opportunities are secondary requirements ("intervening variables") for the outcomes: political leadership ("dependent variables"). Whether potential political leaders exercise leadership successfully or not depends on how the independent variables (personal attributes) and intervening variables (the environment/ opportunities) interact with each other.

Personal Attributes

This book categorizes personal attributes into two different sets of traits: those related to political motivation and those related to capability. The personal attributes concerning political motivation are the aspirations and needs that potential political leaders want to fulfill. They include the desire to rule, the desire for fame or esteem, the need for self-actualization, and concern for the public good. Political leaders must possess at least some of these traits, if not all. For the Japanese case, as Ike Nobutaka notes, a family's expectation and pressure on its male heir-apparent to succeed to its trade and tradition play an important role in self-actualization. Although the relative importance of each factor in exercising successful political leadership may vary in each case, these motivational factors are powerful spurs to leadership.[24]

In addition to aspirational and motivational needs, potential political leaders must have the capabilities to actually exercise power, such as long-term vision, leadership skills, ability to exploit opportunities, as well as fundraising, organization, and support systems. In this regard, John Kenneth Galbraith argues that personality, property, and organization are three key sources of power. The latter two sources play an ever-more important role in present-day politics where political campaigns involve big money and large networks. In essence, potential political leaders must exhibit long-term vision for the public good, and must possess a variety of political skills, as well as funds and organization, to turn their political agenda into reality. However, even if potential political leaders possess all of these attributes and assets, they are not able to exercise political leadership effectively without being in a favorable environment.[25]

The Political Environment

Political leaders cannot exercise leadership without a suitable environment. The extent to which they can exercise leadership is confined by the given environment. Therefore, leaders must apply their personal attributes carefully to the constraints posed by the political environment. Political environments comprise such elements as political structure, the needs of the society, extraordinary opportunities, and good fortune. As Burns notes, leaders' goals are determined by the reality of the structures of political opportunity around them. This political context—the structure, risk, and opportunity of various offices—shapes the outcome of their ambition.[26]

The Interactions Between Personal Attributes and the Environment
In summary, potential political leaders must possess personal attributes, both motivational and those related to capabilities, and must apply these traits in the confines of the political environment, including political structure and societal needs, as well as the opportunities presented at a given time. The degree to which potential leaders successfully exercise political leadership depends on the strength of each factor and on the way the two forces (attributes and environment) interact with each other. Given the numerous dependent and intervening variables inter-acting with each other simultaneously, the relative importance of a given variable varies as does its relative effect on the outcome.

Based on the theoretical framework established here, this book exam-ines Japanese political leadership for the case of the Hatoyama Dynasty, the "exemplar" of modern Japanese politics for 150 years. Specifically, this book identifies personal attributes of the Hatoyama family members, examines the environment in which they have applied their attributes, and analyzes interactions between the two factors. In summary, through the use of a theoretical framework on political lead-ership, this book makes the first comprehensive study of the Hatoyama Dynasty in English.

CHAPTER 2

THE FIRST GENERATION: KAZUO AND THE MEIJI GOVERNMENT

Born at the Dawn of the Meiji Era

The Hatoyama Dynasty's political lineage begins with Kazuo. Kazuo was born in Edo (present Tokyo) in April 1856. Japan was in the midst of the political turmoil that shook the foundations of the Tokugawa shogunate government. Only three years earlier, the American Commodore Matthew C. Perry had made his first visit to Japan in order to open trade with that country, which had been under *sakoku* (seclusion) since 1633. Perry's second visit to Japan the following year resulted in the U.S.–Japan Treaty of Amity (the Kanagawa Treaty). Japan concluded similar treaties with England, Russia, and the Netherlands, thereby ending the seclusion. Japan's *kaikoku* (opening) weakened the shogunate's power. Civil wars erupted in various parts of Japan, between pro-shogunate groups and pro-emperor groups. The latter's eventual victory brought an end to the Tokugawa shogunate that had ruled Japan since 1603 and the restoration of power to the emperor in 1868: the so-called Meiji Restoration.[1]

Kazuo's father, Hatoyama Juemon Hirofusa, was a *samurai* (retainer) of Miura Bingo-no-kami, the lord of Katsuyama-*han* (province) in Mimasaka (northern part of the present Okayama-*ken*). Katsuyama was a small *han*, with 23,000 *goku* (approximately 3,220 tons) of rice. The power of each *han* was measured by the *horoku* (revenue, in the form of rice, that the shogun provided to each lord) and large *han* had more than 300,000 *goku*. Hirofusa was Lord Miura's *orusui-yaku* (a caretaker of a lord's residence in Edo during his absence). It was an important position. During the Tokugawa era, each lord was required to live in Edo periodically to pay allegiance to the shogun and the caretaker lived in the lord's residence as his representative in Edo. Hirofusa married Lord Miura's retainer's daughter, Miura Kikuko. Hirofusa's marrying a daughter of the Miura family, a higher-ranked family than the Hatoyama family in the Katsuyama-*han*, indicates his promise. In fact, Hirofusa was learned and a master of *kendo* (a Japanese martial art), while Kikuko was gentle and intelligent. The Hatoyama family's elite genealogy derives from this couple.[2]

Hirofusa had five sons, of whom Kazuo was fourth. Hirofusa kept the third son, Jutaro, the brightest among his sons, as his heir apparent, and the youngest son, Goro; and sent the other three sons for adoption. Adoption was common in the feudal system (the government abrogated a family and confiscated its property unless the family had an apparent male heir. A similar custom remained until 1945). Hirofusa himself had been adopted into the Hatoyama family from the Ogawa family. Kazuo was adopted by the Miura family, his mother's birth family. Jutaro was extremely bright and the only thing Kazuo could defeat him at was *sumo* wrestling; however, Jutaro died of pneumonia in 1868 at the age of 14. The eldest son Matazo, who was adopted by the Fujita family, soon died. As Hirofusa deeply grieved over Jutaro's death, young Kazuo told his father that he would make up for the loss of Jutaro.[3]

Maintaining the family honor was an important value in the feudal Japanese society and dishonoring the family name called for committing suicide. In addition to the desire to preserve the family honor, the need for self-actualization was an important motivational factor for Kazuo's decision to become a great man. In fact, the two aspirational factors are closely related with each other because individuals were identified with the family to which they belonged in the feudal society. Being the fourth son, Kazuo wanted to prove to his father that he could be the successor for the family. Kazuo's high ambition and extraordinary diligence stem from his pledge to his father at this time.[4]

Unlike Jutaro, Kazuo was robust and learned everything quickly from *kendo*, fishing, to kite flying. Later, Kazuo in fact succeeded to the Hatoyama name at Hirofusa's death in April 1877. Until then, Kazuo's legal surname had been Miura. Kazuo's childhood name (Japanese men changed their names from childhood to adulthood in the feudal system) was Tatsunosuke (meaning "dragon boy" as he was born in the Year of the Dragon in the Chinese zodiac). He changed his name to Kazuo ("a man of harmony") by himself when he learned a Confucian axiom, "time in the heaven is less valuable than prosperity on Earth. Prosperity on Earth is less valuable than harmony of men." This episode is indicative of his gentle character, which played a decisive role in his political career.[5]

The Youngest Student at *Daigaku Nanko*

Kazuo was 12 years old when Jutaro died in 1868. It was the first year of the Meiji era. In order to console his father's grief over Jutaro's death, Kazuo entered the *Kaiho-juku*, a traditional private school for Chinese literature. All the other students were between 17 and 20 years old. His classmates used Kazuo as an errand boy to buy snacks. Kazuo did not mind it at all and had them teach him in return. In October 1870, the Meiji government created an elite training school called the *Daigaku Nanko*, a prototype for Tokyo Imperial University founded in 1877. It was highly competitive. The government designated that it would admit one student from each small *han* (of less than 100,000 *goku*), two students from each middle *han* (of more than 100,000 *goku* and less than 300,000 *goku*), and three students from each large *han* (of more than 300,000 *goku*). The minimum age requirement was 15 years old. The school admitted only 300 students in total. All of them were *koshinsei* (scholarship students) and received generous stipends from the *han* that they came from. Kazuo was one year shy of the minimum age requirement but was accepted.[6]

Daigaku Nanko's 300 students were incorporated into 15 classes. Kazuo, the youngest, who had never studied English before, was incorporated into the lowest, Class 15. Kazuo studied diligently, staying up every night. Half of the students dropped out at the end of the first year. In the second year, in April 1872, Kazuo advanced to the highest, Class 1, along with Komura Jutaro and Saito Shuichiro. Kazuo majored in law when the school created its specialized-course college, *Kaisei Gakko*, in September 1873. Furuichi Kimitake, one of Kazuo's classmates, recalls that Kazuo was not only exceptionally bright but also was extremely diligent; therefore, he was second to none. Kazuo was at the top of Class 1 in the school's first comprehensive exam in February 1874. He kept the top position until he left for the United States in July 1875. Kazuo was determined to prove that a person from a small *han* could have a successful career. The school and his intelligence (defined as the capacity to do well academically) opened new opportunities for Kazuo's career.[7]

Kazuo realized that the traditional *Rangaku* ("the Dutch study") was outdated (the Japanese were gaining Western knowledge from the Dutch because the Netherlands was the only Western country with which the Japanese were allowed contact in the Tokugawa era). Kazuo petitioned the Ministry of Education (MOE) in 1875 to send students to the United States and Europe and argued that one day's delay meant one month's delay of Japan's modernization. Ichiro writes, "although my father was usually a calm and gentle person, he did bold things when he was determined." The ministry agreed and decided to conduct an exam to select students. The ministry announced that it would select 11 students in total, out of which three were to be law majors. Kazuo studied for the exam day and night without sleep for seven days. He passed the exam at the top, Komura was second, Kikuchi Takeo was third, and Saito was fourth. The ranking in the exam was exactly the same as that in class.[8]

An interesting episode involving this exam illustrates Kazuo's magnanimous character. Knowing Kazuo's superiority, Saito attempted to make Kazuo fail in the exam and mobilized students to petition the MOE. Saito knew a high-ranking official in the ministry. He wrote to the ministry that Kazuo was intelligent but was too young and *seken ni utoi* (unworldly). Saito claimed that it would be to Japan's shame if the ministry sent him abroad. Haraguchi Kaname, another classmate majoring in engineering, informed Kazuo of Saito's plot. Kazuo had no idea that Saito was writing a petition to fail him right next to his desk (Ichiro writes, "no wonder my father was unworldly"). However, Kazuo was nonchalant and ignored it. In the end, the ministry accepted four law majors by reducing the number of science majors from two to one. Thus, Saito was accepted in addition to Kazuo, Komura, and Kikuchi, as law majors. Saito later apologized to Kazuo but Kazuo just smiled and acted as if nothing had happened. The ministry officially announced 11 students as its first scholarship students to study abroad in June 1875. Nine students were assigned to go to the United States and two to Europe (France and Germany). Kazuo, the youngest, was 19 years old. Kazuo was concerned whether his father would approve his decision because he had already lost two sons. Hirofusa reluctantly approved it. Kazuo never saw his father again after he left Japan.[9]

Historical writer Toyoda Jo notes that despite his minor background, Kazuo actually had opportunities to advance his career in the initial Meiji period. It was an opportune time for young aspiring *samurai*, especially those from small *han*. They took advantage of the chaotic situation and courted the influential to get positions in the government. However, Kazuo was a man of integrity. He disliked playing among the influential and disliked being an opportunist. Kazuo was more interested in learning new knowledge from the United States and applying that knowledge to the modernization of Japan.[10]

Three Degrees in Five Years in the United States

Kazuo received an official letter of appointment from the MOE and left Yokohama to study at Columbia University in July 1875. Kazuo chose Columbia University in order to avoid competition with his Japanese classmates. Komura had chosen Harvard University and Kikuchi and Saito had chosen Boston University. If Kazuo had gone to the same university, he would be forced to compete with them, and Kazuo wanted to avoid such competition. Kazuo might have been mindful of Saito's earlier scheme. Being modest and the youngest, Kazuo deferred to his colleagues.[11]

Kazuo majored in law at Columbia University with emphasis on British common law. He studied intensively and extensively so that he knew the exact location of every article, book, and document in the library. He passed his qualifying exam with a perfect score, graduating at the top of his class in May 1877. Kazuo received a Bachelor of Arts at the commencement without knowing of his father's death in April. He grieved over Hirofusa's death when he learned about it. His new landlady Mrs. Abbot, a minister's widow, was kind and encouraged him not to abandon his goals. Kazuo overcame his sorrow and applied to the postgraduate school of Yale University. He studied French and Latin intensively to pass the admission exam. He entered the graduate school in September 1877. At Yale Kazuo studied as hard as ever. Dean Baldwin of the Yale Law School, a renowned scholar, enjoyed Kazuo's questions and even corrected his own views based on Kazuo's questions. Kazuo received a Master of Arts in June 1878 and an LL.D (Doctor of Laws) in July 1880.[12]

Kazuo graduated from the Yale Law School with the highest grade in his class. At Yale it is customary that the student who wrote the best dissertation of the year gives a speech at the commencement. Kazuo made his speech in English in front of an audience of more than 5,000. His dissertation was entitled "A Comparison of Family Systems between Japan and Rome." Kazuo's speech was so well received that the *Atlantic Monthly*, which did not usually pay attention to student writings, printed his speech in its entirety. Two decades later in October 1901, Dean Baldwin invited Kazuo to the bicentennial anniversary of Yale University and awarded him an honorary doctoral degree. After five years of study in the United States, Kazuo went back to Japan in August 1880 with three degrees in hand and full of ambitions. He was 24 years old. Kazuo was promised a role as a leader of the Meiji government that was eager to modernize its nation and catch up with the West under the banner of *Fukoku Kyohei* ("Rich Nation, Strong Army").[13]

Kazuo's Three Career Goals

Upon returning home, Kazuo did not seek a position in the government, but decided to use his recently acquired knowledge to construct a democratic civil society in Japan. Kazuo set three goals for his career: (1) to establish lawyers' status; (2) to create private universities in order to liberalize education; and (3) to institutionalize a constitutional government. First, at that time in Japan, there was no such profession as lawyer. Official recognition of lawyer as a profession was not established until 1893. Prior to this, practitioners of law were called *daigen-nin* (attorney). They were not licensed and their titles were publicly traded. They were regarded as "confidence men" for the wealthy and had low social status. The government initiated a qualifying exam for *daigen-nin* only in February 1876, modeled after the French laws. When Kazuo took the qualifying exam for *daigen-nin* in December 1881, people doubted his decision. They questioned why a person who had studied in the United States and could speak English wanted to become a *daigen-nin*. His friends said that his degrees would be dishonored. However, that was exactly why Kazuo wanted to establish lawyers' status. Kazuo hoped his achievement would improve the status of *daigen-nin*.[14]

Kazuo had experienced the pleasure of helping troubled and unfortunate people by practicing law in the United States. His first experience was helping his landlady, Mrs. Abbot. She was poor and she was making a living by providing room and board to students at Yale. Kazuo wondered about her poverty because the biography of Napoleon Bonaparte that her deceased husband had written was still selling well. Kazuo's investigation revealed that the publisher had not paid her royalties. As a law-major graduate of Columbia University, Kazuo was qualified to practice law and sued the publisher. Kazuo won and the publisher paid Mrs. Abbot a sizable amount of money. The widow was so grateful that Kazuo decided to practice law. Ichiro writes, "my father believed that making actual contributions to the society was most important thing to do in life, and carried out his belief in earnest."[15]

With regard to the second goal, Japan's imperial national universities, the *kangaku* (governmental schools), were authoritative and authoritarian. There were few good private universities when Kazuo returned to Japan. The notable exception was the *Keio Gijuku* (a prototype for Keio University), founded by Fukuzawa Yukichi (1835–1901) in 1868 to teach Western learning. Having studied in reputable private universities in the United States, Kazuo thought it unreasonable that children of wealthy families should go to low-tuitioned prestigious governmental schools, while children of the poor should go to expensive and less reputable private schools. Kazuo believed that education was the foundation for nation-building and that it would be a disservice to the well-being of the people to leave education as a monopoly of the government (see later).[16]

The Meiji Government: *Hambatsu* Politics

Regarding his third goal, the Meiji government had adopted a Bismarckian oligarchic political system, comprised of former lower-rank young *samurai* from the four *han*: Satsuma (western part of Kagoshima-*ken*), Choshu (northwestern part of Yamaguchi-*ken*), Tosa (Kochi-*ken*), and Hizen (parts of Saga-*ken* and Nagasaki-*ken*). This four-province oligarchy is referred to as the *hambatsu* (provincial clique) rule. *Sangi* (state councilors) from Satsuma and Choshu, such as Okubo Toshimichi (1830–1878) and Ito Hirobumi (1841–1909), were particularly influential in the government. The *Satcho-batsu* (Satsuma–Choshu clique) took a conservative and gradual approach to Japan's modernization and enforced the centralization of power of the Meiji government in the name of the emperor. The government undertook the sweeping *haihan chiken* (to abolish *han* and install *ken*; a national reorganization of local administrative districts) in July 1871. Meanwhile, the four cliques began an intense internal power struggle within the government. Their power struggle culminated in the *Seinan* war of 1877, in which Saigo Takamori (1827–1877, from Satsuma) was defeated. Then, Okubo was assassinated in 1878.[17]

After Okubo's assassination, Okuma Shigenobu, a state councilor from Hizen (Saga) of "iconoclastic temperament" (1838–1922), gained power in the government. In turn, Itagaki Taisuke (1837–1919), a state councilor from Tosa, left the government (he sided with Saigo's aborted "Korean campaign" in 1873), then launched a radical liberal movement, the so-called *Jiyu minken undo* (freedom and popular rights movement) in 1874, and created the *Jiyuto* (the Liberal Party) in 1881. In response, Okuma called for immediate creation of a British-style parliament in 1881. Okuma's conservative colleagues in the government, most notably Ito, did not like Okuma's political bandwagon with Itagaki's "popular rights" and ousted Okuma from the government in 1881. In exchange, Ito promised to establish a parliament in 1890. Ito's masterful bloodless purge of his rival is called the "Meiji 14's *seihen* (political change in 1881)." It established the dominance of the conservative *Satcho* clique, against the more radical *Tohi* (Tosa–Hizen) clique, in the *hambatsu* government. Ito formed his first cabinet (1885–1888) and also formed three more cabinets (1892–1896, 1898, and 1900–1901).[18]

In 1882, after the purge, Okuma created his own party, *Rikken Kaishinto* (the Constitutional Progressive Party, generally referred to as the *Kaishinto* in Japanese literature), with his followers such as Inukai

Tsuyoshi (1855–1932) and Ozaki Yukio (1859–1954). Although Itagaki and Okuma lost the power struggle in the central government, their contributions to the development of the democratic political system were arguably greater than those of the *Satcho* clique who stayed in the government. Itagaki and Okuma created the two powerful *minto* (people's party) against the *rito* (government's party) formed by the *hambatsu* government. Itagaki's Liberals and Okuma's Progressives remained two major political streams in Japan—through frequent disbandment, merger, renaming, and reorganization—and they eventually merged in 1955 and became the LDP.[19]

Kazuo returned to Japan in the midst of these political storms. The political situation was volatile and everything was in disorder. Japan was still a feudalistic state in many respects and former *samurai* were rebelling against the government. There was not even a constitution or parliament. Political parties began to emerge but political parties in the absence of a parliament were odd things. Moreover, the government suppressed Itagaki's Liberal Party and tried to split the party. Itagaki was stabbed during his speech in Gifu city in April 1882, when he made the famous statement, "Itagaki might die but the 'popular rights' will not." The Liberal Party was in fact split and Itagaki was obliged to disband the party in October 1884. Ichiro writes, "having observed the American democracy, my father must have been dismayed at the state of politics in Japan." Kazuo believed that a democratic parliament, based on a two-party system, would better serve the people. Witnessing the enormous gap between the American political system and that of Japan, Kazuo's determination to establish a constitutional democracy grew stronger. This conviction led Kazuo to pursue a political career.[20]

Teaching at Tokyo Imperial University

Kazuo's career took off immediately. Kazuo became a lecturer (equivalent to assistant professor) in the Faculty of Law at Tokyo Imperial University in August 1880. Kazuo was a very young teacher and one of his students was older than Kazuo. Kato Takaaki (1860–1926, from Aichi-*ken*, prime minister, 1924–1926) was one of his students. Kazuo treated his students as if they were his colleagues. They liked Kazuo's friendly approach and were impressed with his vast knowledge of law. Nevertheless, Kazuo was dismissed the next year because of his commencement speech. The university officials asked Kazuo to make a speech at the commencement in July 1881. Kazuo replied that he was not well informed of the current state of the nation and that he might say something inappropriate. The university officials agreed that he could say anything he wanted. Kazuo made a speech, entitled "The Effect of Law," at the commencement where members of the imperial family and other dignitaries were among the audience.[21]

In the speech, Kazuo stated that education was the first priority of nation-building and that Japan's educational institutions were extremely poor. He also stated that the government must spend more on education and held the MOF, as well as the MOE, responsible for Japan's poor budget for education. Ichiro writes in 1951, "such an argument is not unusual nowadays but just criticizing the government was a provocative thing to do back then." Kazuo's speech angered Finance Minister Sato Tsunetami. Coming from Saga-*batsu* like Okuma, Sato was an influential member of the government and demanded Kazuo's dismissal. The MOE tried to calm down Sato but in vain. The ministry dismissed Kazuo: the so-called Hatoyama speech incident. However, the ministry did not want to lose him, and unofficially allowed him to continue teaching as a lecturer and commissioned him to translate *Ancient Laws* so that he could make a living. Kazuo's reputation actually rose because of the incident. Thus, Kazuo took the first step toward his first goal: liberalizing Japanese college education (his larger progress toward this goal came later).[22]

After the dismissal, Kazuo took his qualifying exam for *daigen-nin* (attorney) in December 1881. Kazuo also married Taga Haruko in November 1881. Kazuo was 25 years old. Haruko was 20 years old.

Marriage with Taga Haruko: A Perfect Match

Taga Haruko was born in March 1861. She was the youngest of seven children of Watanabe Tsutomu, a *samurai* of Matsudaira Tambano-kami of Matsumoto-*han* (present Nagano-*ken*), with 60,000 *goku*. Watanabe was the lord's *orusui-yaku* (a caretaker in Edo) and devoted himself to preserving the Matsumoto-*han* during the final stage of the shogunate era, going back and forth between Edo (the shogunate) and Kyoto (the emperor's residence). Watanabe's wisdom to take the emperor's side saved the Matsumoto-*han*; however, he took the responsibility for turning against the shogunate government and subjected himself to house seclusion and changed his name to Taga. With the Meiji restoration, Taga was exonerated and was appointed *daisanji* (senior councilor) of the new Matsumoto-*ken* and later *daisanji* of Ishinomaki, Miyagi-*ken*.[23]

Being the youngest, Haruko was Taga's favorite child. Haruko was exceptionally bright, diligent, and outgoing. She studied Chinese literature from several former *samurai* who had returned from Edo with the Meiji restoration. Teachers taught students in the order in which the students arrived. Haruko woke up early in the morning when it was still dark and went to the teacher's residence before eating breakfast. She was always the first to arrive throughout the year, although it snows heavily in winter in Matsumoto (where the Japanese Alps are located). She was also the only female student. Taga tested his daughter's knowledge of Chinese literature and she passed. In March 1874, at the age of 13, Taga sent her to Tokyo Women's College in Takehashi, the oldest and the only public women's school then. It was rare for a girl to leave her parents' house to study in Tokyo. Therefore, Taga secretly sent Haruko in a *kago* (palanquin) without letting her mother see Haruko off. He feared that her mother would cry too much if she saw her leave.[24]

Tokyo Women's College was one of the most liberal schools for girls. It had Western female teachers and an English class in its curriculum. Haruko had never studied English before but she was *makezugirai* (no quitter). Taga bought her an expensive Japanese–English dictionary written by Dr. Hepburn, which cost 11 *yen* (about $550 at present). Although there were many wealthy families' daughters at the school, few had the dictionary. To meet her father's expectation, Haruko studied English intensively. When she felt sleepy, she pricked her feet with a needle to stay awake and continued to study, and became one of the top students in her class. However, the MOE abruptly closed the school in March 1877 due to the objection of the former *samurai* clan, who argued that Japanese girls should not study English. Haruko transferred to Tokyo Women's Teachers College in Ochanomizu and enrolled in its special English program, created for the displaced Tokyo Women's College students.[25]

Haruko despaired because there was no Western teacher at Tokyo Women's Teachers College. Nevertheless, she persevered and studied Chinese and English diligently. She graduated at the top of the class from the special English program in April 1878 and then enrolled in the general program. Haruko was selected by the MOE to study in the United States in 1878. Only three students were chosen from the school and Haruko was the youngest. In May 1879, the ministry officially assigned Haruko to study at Philadelphia Women's Teachers College. Haruko left the dormitory and made preparations for her departure from Yokohama in July. Then, the ministry abruptly canceled the program at the last minute, due to some cabinet members' objection to

Japanese girls getting an American education. Deprived of a chance of a lifetime, Haruko was devastated.[26]

Haruko went back to the teachers college's general program; however, it was difficult to catch up with her study. The other two students whose trips were also canceled were two years ahead of Haruko and they had already finished the hardest part of the program. In contrast, Haruko left in the middle of the program and had to cope with the hardest study period in a depressed state of mind. However, thinking of her father, who was even more heartbroken than Haruko, she studied even harder. After the dormitory's light was extinguished, she hid in a closet and continued to study, using candlelight. She even studied in the bathroom, the only place light was allowed. With these extraordinary efforts, she graduated from the general program of Tokyo Women's Teachers College in July 1881 and began teaching at her alma mater that August.[27]

Meanwhile, Haruko was introduced to Kazuo, who came back from the United States, in an *omiai* (meeting for a traditional arranged marriage) in fall 1880. Kazuo proposed to Haruko right away through a go-between. They were originally scheduled to marry just after her graduation in July 1881; however, Kazuo's dismissal from Tokyo Imperial University that month and his resultant decision to take a qualifying exam for *daigen-nin* delayed their marriage until November 1881. They did not see each other at all for almost a year, from their *omiai* meeting to the day of their wedding. Before the wedding, Haruko had dinner with her parents alone, and saw her father (who was an authoritarian stern parent) cry for the first time. Although Kazuo and Haruko hardly knew each other when they got married, their marriage fared well as Kazuo was gentle and liberal. They were a perfect match in terms of their intelligence and diligence. They broke with Japanese tradition and held a big reception, separate from the wedding ceremony. They became a renowned couple and pioneered many things. In hindsight, had Haruko gone to the United States as scheduled, she would not have met Kazuo. Ichiro writes, "even if my mother was a competent person, she would not have developed her potential as much as she did, had she not married Kazuo. It must have been fate."[28]

Fulfilling His First Goal

Kazuo passed the *daigen-nin*'s qualifying exam in December 1881 and opened a law firm in January 1882. It was the first *daigen-nin*'s office. People were surprised that a *daigen-nin* had opened a professional office, and soon his office became a model for other *daigen-nin*. His law firm prospered because it was unprecedented for a teacher at Tokyo Imperial University to become *daigen-nin*. Kazuo was elected to be president of the Tokyo *Daigen-nin* Union (a prototype of the Tokyo Lawyers Association) in March 1882. He was 25 years old. He traveled all over the country to help troubled people. In one case in Nagasaki, he saved a defendant, who was sentenced to the death penalty by the lower court, by finding out that one of the critical witnesses was disqualified. The sentence was repealed. In another case in Sendai, people heard of his reputation and came to hear his defense. However, they were disappointed because his defense was brief. They thought that Kazuo's statement was only an introduction to his defense, but that was his entire defense. Even the defendant's side was angry with Kazuo and cursed him; however they were elated in the end because the judge ruled the defendant innocent.[29]

Kazuo's defense was concise and focused. In an extreme instance, Kazuo stated only one phrase but the defendant was found innocent. The defendant was so glad that he paid Kazuo 100 *yen* (about $5,000 at present). It was an enormous amount of money in 1890 and newspapers reported, "100 *yen* for only one phrase!" His reputation soared. Nevertheless, making money by practicing law was the furthest thing from Kazuo's mind. He was indifferent to charging fees. Haruko writes that Kazuo dealt with many cases for which he could have charged enormous amounts of money. However, he was nonchalant about money and applied *jippishugi* (charging only the actual costs), leaving matters of remuneration in the hands of the clients. Haruko also writes that Kazuo was generous and gave, instead of lending, money to his friends when they were in need. When he did loan money, he did not bother to collect the loans because he did not want to jeopardize the friendship.[30]

In May 1910, he was elected to be president of the Tokyo Lawyers Association. Although he was already ill, he accepted the position and undertook the monumental task of building the Tokyo Lawyers Hall. He engaged in fundraising and skillfully brought the much protracted plan into reality in a short period of time. The construction began in May 1910 and was completed in January 1911. The opening ceremony was grand. It became his last contribution to establishing lawyers' status.[31]

Entering Politics: The Tokyo-*fu* Assembly

In October 1881 the Meiji government announced plans to create a parliament in February 1890. Kazuo was not in a hurry to enter politics. Kazuo had already launched two of his three career goals within two years of returning to Japan. He felt that he could wait until the creation of the first parliament to pursue his third goal. However, just after he opened his law firm, elections for Tokyo-*fu* (county) assembly were scheduled in February 1882. One of his avid supporters solicited him to run and volunteered to give campaign expenses. After careful consideration, Kazuo agreed. Kazuo won at the top with 1,572 votes. He was 25 years old. Kazuo was startled to find that there were no bylaws for the assembly. He quickly wrote bylaws, consisting of 225 articles modeled after American and English parliamentary procedures, and circulated them in May 1882. This pamphlet of bylaws immediately became a model for other local assemblies. His colleagues in the Tokyo-*fu* assembly included such promising politicians as Inukai and Ozaki who joined Okuma's Progressive Party.[32]

Kazuo soon exhibited his remarkable leadership at the assembly. He presided over the assembly in July 1882 when the session was paralyzed concerning the election of the speaker. The assembly was split into two factions and they were shouting at each other. Kazuo, the first-term and youngest member of the assembly, suddenly stood up and announced that he would preside over the session as acting chair. All the assemblymen present were stunned but followed his instructions. Kazuo succeeded in normalizing the session and executed the vote for the speaker. Kazuo also became famous for his "*bento* (lunch) speech." He humorously defeated a bill to reduce the lunch allowance for its assemblymen from 15 *sen* (the old monetary unit; 100 *sen* = 1 *yen*; about $7.50 at present) to 12 *sen*. He argued that assemblymen needed to have nutritious food (the Japanese diet was extremely poor) to work better for their county residents, and stated that the assemblyman who had submitted the bill must have been eating poor food. His sense of humor worked and the bill was defeated. Kazuo also successfully defeated a bill to reduce the expense for prisoners' meals out of its already small penitentiary budget of 16,500 *yen* (about $825,000 at present). He was reelected to the assembly and then, in April 1884, he was elected as the speaker of the assembly's county chamber. Kazuo had successfully launched his political career.[33]

Back to Tokyo Imperial University

In 1884, at the request of the MOE, Kazuo officially returned to Tokyo Imperial University. The university wanted a person like Kazuo for his unsurpassed knowledge of law and his reputation for independent thought and action. Thus, within four years after he started his career, Kazuo was wearing three hats: as a lawyer; an assemblyman; and a university lecturer. Kazuo was fulfilling his three career goals in earnest. Kazuo was promoted to be a professor at Tokyo Imperial University in 1886; though only to resign the position the following year. As he had begun working at the Ministry of Foreign Affairs (MOFA) in 1885, it became impossible to hold four fulltime jobs. Education Minister Mori Arinori (1847–1889, from Satsuma, assassinated by a reactionary for his pro-Westernization policy) begged Kazuo to come back to the university but Kazuo declined. Mori asked Prime Minister Ito to convince Kazuo to return. Ito wrote a polite letter to Kazuo and Kazuo was obliged to return to the university for the second time in 1887. Kazuo was promoted to be Dean of the Faculty of Law of the university in 1887, at the age of 31. Then, he became the first recipient of an LL.D (doctor of laws) in Japan in 1888. Kazuo's career was already well established in his early thirties.[34]

Service at the MOFA

Coming from a small *han*, Kazuo kept his distance from the *hambatsu* government, which was dominated by the *Satcho* clique. However, Foreign Minister Inoue Kaoru (1835–1915, from Choshu), of the first Ito cabinet, asked Kazuo to work for the MOFA in 1885. Kazuo was appointed *gondai shokikan* (senior secretary) and then became the director general of the Investigation Bureau. Kazuo was also appointed as director-general of the Translation Bureau in 1886, and held both the positions. Kazuo perfectly fit the needs of the ministry with his impeccable command of law and English, as well as superior negotiation skills. At that time, the ministry was struggling to revise the unequal treaties Japan had concluded with foreign governments at the end of the Tokugawa era. For instance, the government neither had judicial rights toward foreigners residing in Japan (the rights were held by the consul generals of the respective countries), nor did it have the right to impose tariffs on foreign imports.[35]

In 1887, Inoue resigned the foreign ministerial post due to the reactionaries' strong opposition to his pro-Westernization stance. Thereafter Prime Minister Ito held the foreign ministerial position; then Okuma succeeded to the post in 1888. In all, Kazuo served three foreign ministers: Inoue, Ito, and Okuma, from 1885 to 1889. Therefore, despite his lack of connections to the *hambatsu*, Kazuo acquired high positions in the government. In this sense, Kazuo overcame his disadvantaged background with his exceptional intelligence and extraordinary diligence. Kazuo had higher expectations and aspirations for his role opportunities than the social context warranted. In turn, his aspirations and the resulting actions modified the structure of the social opportunities.[36]

Kazuo sympathized with Okuma's challenge to the *hambatsu* oligarchy, as a moderate liberal, rather than Itagaki's radical liberal. Kazuo had a wholesome skepticism about the drastic transformation of Itagaki, who had supported Saigo's "Korean campaign" but after its defeat launched the radical "freedom and popular rights movement." Itagaki was later conciliated by Ito (who gave him the status of a count and the post of interior minister in his second cabinet) and was abandoned by the "popular rights" group. However, Okuma was bombed by a member of the right-wing group, *Genyosha*, and lost his right leg in October 1889. This *Okuma sonan* (accident) obliged Okuma to resign the foreign ministerial post. Following Okuma, Kazuo resigned from the ministry in January 1890 although Prime Minister Yamagata Aritomo (1838–1922, a general from Choshu) solicited him to stay. Yamagata even told Kazuo that he could go to any ministry he liked if he did not want to stay in the MOFA. Yamagata sent his messengers to Kazuo's house every day; however, Kazuo did not return.[37]

Haruko writes that she deeply deplored the Okuma accident (he could have lost his life). However, she thought that Kazuo did not have to resign from the ministry along with Okuma. It was customary that the minister's secretary resigned along with the minister. Neither the vice minister nor the director generals resigned. Moreover, Kazuo was not obligated to resign because he did not owe his position to Okuma. It was Inoue (foreign minister in 1885) and Ito (prime minister in 1885 and also foreign minister in 1887) who recommended Kazuo to the ministry. Kazuo did not resign from the ministry when they resigned the ministerial post. Nevertheless, Kazuo resigned with Okuma. At a loss, Haruko blamed herself for Kazuo's resignation. She felt that Kazuo was tired of her excessive sorrow for Okuma and had resigned.[38]

However, it was not Haruko's fault. Kazuo resigned from the ministry because of his loyalty toward Okuma. Kazuo felt the limits of working for the government ruled by the *hambatsu* and decided to work with Okuma to create a strong political party.

Principal of *Tokyo Senmon Gakko*

Okuma rewarded Kazuo's loyalty. In July 1890, Okuma made Kazuo a principal of a private university called the *Tokyo Senmon Gakko* that he created in 1882. Kazuo resigned the deanship of the Tokyo Imperial University, the most prestigious university, and became the third

principal of a new, small private university. In stark contrast to the authoritarian government university, the liberal atmosphere of a private university
fit Kazuo's creeds of freedom and democracy. Kazuo took his responsibilities at the *Tokyo Senmon Gakko* seriously and grew to have a strong attachment to it. Kazuo expanded the school's enrollment from 600 to 3,000 in
1902, when the school changed its name to Waseda University. The enrollment later doubled to over 6,000 in 1907, when he was obliged to resign
after 18 years of dedicated service. Waseda University grew to be one of the
two most prestigious private universities, and is known for its liberal creed,
whereas Keio University is known for its conservative creed. Waseda owes
its tradition of liberalism to Okuma and Kazuo.[39]

By 1890, it had become obvious that Kazuo did not wish to pursue a
career in the bureaucracy or in the national university. Having observed
the American democracy firsthand, Kazuo's reservations with the
hambatsu government grew. Kazuo was too idealistic and active to remain
in the government establishment. Kazuo had a long-term vision. Kazuo
identified creating a strong democratic political party as the prerequisite
for his ultimate goal of establishing a constitutional democracy. For this
goal, Kazuo abandoned high positions in the MOFA and the deanship of
the Tokyo Imperial University. This decision to align himself with the
opposition to the *hambatsu* government, rather than being part of the
nomenclature, was the most critical decision Kazuo made in his career.[40]

Political writer Ito Hirotoshi argues that this choice, to leave the
government and to challenge its rule, was dictated by his disadvanta-
geous background and ultimately prevented him from working at the
core of the Meiji government. Yet, it is questionable whether Kazuo's
decision was entirely dictated by his background. Kazuo did obtain high
positions in the government despite his inferior origin. He could have
stayed in the government and worked at its core if he had wished. It
seems that Kazuo's education in the United States and his idealism
shaped his career more than his origin.[41]

The year 1890 also marked a watershed in Japan's history.

Imperial Japan's First Parliament

With the promulgation of the imperial constitution in February 1889,
the first general elections for the HR of the imperial parliament were
held in July 1890. The Liberals obtained 130 seats and the Progressives
obtained 41. Thus, the two *minto* (people's party) had the majority out
of 300 seats, whereas the *rito* (government's party) had 84 seats, and
45 seats were independents. However, the *minto* could not form a

cabinet. The nascent parliament was far from democratic. First, the suffrage for the HR was limited to males over 25 years old who paid direct taxes over 15 *yen*, which constituted only 1.1 percent of the entire population. The House of Peers (HP), the upper house, was not elected. The Meiji government had instituted the peerage system in 1884 and the emperor appointed his relatives and other peers to the HP. More importantly, the HR elections did not matter in reality: the cabinet was not formed by the majority party in the HR but was run by the *Satcho* clique, as in the oligarchic rule prior to 1890. The imperial parliament was essentially a sham democracy. Prime Minister Kuroda Kiyotaka (1840–1890, from Satsuma) formed the so-called *chozen naikaku* ("transcendental cabinet" that "transcends" the majority party in the HR and claims nonpartisan authority "on the premise that the administration derived all its power from the Throne and hence could not presume to represent any less than all the Emperor's subjects").[42]

Elected to the HR and as House Speaker

Kazuo felt that it was premature for him to run for the HR; however, his supporters nominated him as a candidate without his consent. Kazuo was obliged to run, and ran as an independent. Kazuo's district, Tokyo District 9, comprised three *ku* (wards) out of a total of 35 wards in Tokyo city: Koishikawa (presently part of Bunkyo-*ku*), Ushigome (presently part of Shinjuku-*ku*), and Yotsuya (presently part of Shinjuku-*ku*). Kazuo was expected to win. Kazuo was nonchalant about the election and did not campaign. Haruko writes that Kazuo felt that campaigning for himself was not an honorable thing for a gentleman to do. During the campaign period, Kazuo was engaged in his law practice as usual, meeting with his clients and going to court. Even on election day he was out of town, on a trip to Sendai to defend a case. Meanwhile, the government suppressed nongovernment party candidates and, in total, 25 people died and 388 people were injured nationwide in election riots. On the eve of the election, Kazuo's influential supporters were threatened by his rival candidate's supporters, and were forced to hide in rice chests or under the *shinto* altars in their homes. They could neither campaign for Kazuo nor vote for him. Kazuo lost the election by as few as 15 votes, out of several thousand votes cast. Haruko writes that Kazuo was nonchalant about the loss.[43]

The two "transcendental cabinets" of the first session of the imperial parliament, led by Yamagata (above) and Matsukata Masayoshi (1835–1924, from Satsuma) each lasted only a little over one year. Prime Minister Matsukata grew tired of the people's parties' opposition and dissolved the HR. As a result, the second HR general elections were held in February 1892. Kazuo ran again from Tokyo District 9, as an independent. Despite severe interference from the government, Kazuo won in first place in the district this time. Thus, Kazuo became a member of the HR of the imperial parliament at its second session. Afterwards, Kazuo won HR elections nine times consecutively and continued to hold his seat until his death in 1911.[44]

Kazuo had a strong support system. Haruko managed his campaign funds. As Kazuo was nonchalant about money, Haruko saved money as much as she could, wearing old *kimonos*. She even saved money that Kazuo gave her on the strict condition that she order a new *kimono* (she later regrets it). Haruko writes that preparing campaign funds every four years (or more frequently when the HR was dissolved) was the hardest thing to do. Haruko was also Kazuo's campaign manager and took care of campaign staff and supporters while Kazuo was busy with the law firm. Haruko writes that Kazuo strictly told her not to bring election matters into law practice. He never used the staff at his law firm for his campaigns, although it was a common practice. He was a man of integrity, while Haruko was a strongwilled woman. Haruko was the first Japanese woman to appear in her husband's political campaigns when women were not supposed to make public appearances. The Japanese women did not have suffrage until 1945. Newspapers criticized Haruko as impertinent and shameless, and her life was threatened by right-wing people. Her elder brother begged her to stop campaigning; however, she never did. Because of her devotion to her husband and her sons, Haruko lost weight by a third (see chapter 3). Kazuo had many avid supporters, who admired his competence, intelligence, and integrity.[45]

Ito succeeded Matsukata (Ito's second cabinet, 1892–1896). Unlike Yamagata and Matsukata, Ito realized that he could not ignore the people's parties and tried to conciliate them. He co-opted Itagaki as his interior minister and tried to co-opt Okuma as foreign minister; however, it was in vain due to Itagaki's opposition. Ito's second cabinet lasted for an unprecedented four years and one month. Kazuo was elected to be the speaker of the HR, in his third term, in December 1896. He was 40 years old. His colleagues regarded Kazuo highly as house speaker. Kazuo's long-time deputy speaker Motoda Hajime noted that Kazuo was not a shrewd speaker in the sense that he did not use cunning techniques to manipulate discussions. Instead, Kazuo relied on his thorough knowledge of law, presided over the HR with integrity, and made clear-cut and fair judgments. Hayashida Kametaro, the chief secretary of the HR, stated that Kazuo did not object to anybody's opinion, but was open to any opinion. His well-rounded attitude and harmonizing skills were flawless.[46]

Kazuo was an enthusiastic debater and an eloquent speaker. Haruko writes that although Kazuo never spoke ill of a person or found fault with a person, he did not budge an inch and expressed strong opinions when it came to political debate. Kazuo fiercely confronted incumbent ministers at the parliament and proved himself to be a formidable opponent. Haruko writes that he did so because of his commitment to overthrowing the *hambatsu* and establishing a constitutional democracy. Kazuo's political career at the national level was in full bloom at the age of 40.[47]

The Challenge to *Hambatsu* Rule

It was still a formative age of democracy. The emperor was the ruler and all the political institutions, including the constitution, the parliament, and the bureaucracy, were serving the emperor. Although the HR was popularly elected (albeit with extremely limited suffrage), the cabinet was not formed by the majority party in the HR. Therefore, Kazuo began a challenge to the *hambatsu* in earnest. In December 1896 Kazuo helped Okuma to create his second party, the *Shimpoto* (translated as the Progressive Party as in his first party). Then, Kazuo successfully negotiated with the Liberals, and with the Progressives, to merge and create a new party in June 1898: the *Kenseito* (the Constitutional Government Party). It was Okuma's third party. Kazuo named the party, modeled after American democracy. With the cooperation of Itagaki, the new party obtained the majority standing in the HR, obliging Ito's cabinet (his third) to resign *en masse* (it lasted five months). The *Waihan* (an acronym of Okuma and Itagaki in Chinese pronunciation) cabinet, with Okuma as prime minister and Itagaki as interior minister, was the first cabinet formed by the majority party of the HR. It took eight years from the establishment of the first parliament for this to occur. Kazuo was instrumental to this historic achievement.[48]

Unreasonable Appointment as Vice Foreign Minister

Given Kazuo's contribution to the creation of the Constitutional Government Party and to the birth of the *Waihan* cabinet, Kazuo was expected to become the cabinet's foreign minister in June 1898. Nevertheless, Okuma made Kazuo vice foreign minister. People in the political circles felt this appointment to be unreasonable. It turned out that Prime Minister Okuma himself assumed the foreign ministerial position. The real reason for Okuma not giving Kazuo the ministerial position has not been established. There are several speculative explanations, ranging from "Okuma apparently did not know how instrumental Kazuo was to the creation of the Constitutional Government Party," "Kazuo was too young (42 years old) and did not have seniority in the party," to "Okuma offered the post to Kazuo but Kazuo declined because he did not want to get involved in the fight over the post." One undeniable factor was the fact that the old factional divisions remained strong within the Constitutional Government Party, and the intra-party rivalry over the ministerial posts became intense.[49]

Initially, the two groups had apparently agreed that the former Progressives would get 60 percent and the former Liberals would get 40 percent of the cabinet posts. However, the Liberals grew angry when Okuma gave them three ministerial posts (Itagaki, Matsuda Masahisa, and Hayashi Yuzo), whereas he gave the Progressives four posts (would-be Kazuo, Ozaki, Oishi Masami, and Ohigashi Yoshitetsu). "Itagaki was also disgruntled that only two of his henchmen were in the cabinet, as compared to four of Okuma's." Ichiro writes that at the formation of the *Waihan* cabinet, everybody expected that Kazuo would become foreign minister. However, Okuma decided not to finalize the post until Hoshi Toru (1850–1901, from Tokyo, an influential member of the Liberal Party and then Japan's minister to the United States) returned. Okuma was known to be a sentimental person and was easily swayed by *jojitsu* (personal affairs). Therefore, Okuma held the two positions (prime minister and foreign minister) until Hoshi's return.[50]

The first roster of the *Waihan* cabinet in June 1898 had Komura (who went to Harvard University, with the MOE's scholarship, at the same time as Kazuo) as vice foreign minister, whereas Kazuo's post was still up in the air. Okuma then changed the roster in September 1898, and made Kazuo vice foreign minister. This change suggests that there was still a possibility for Kazuo to become foreign minister. Meanwhile, Hoshi suddenly came back from Washington D.C. in August, expecting that he would get the foreign ministerial position. Okuma rejected Hoshi's request. A vacant position created by the unexpected resignation of Education Minister Ozaki in October 1898 (for the so-called republic speech that August, in which he allegedly proposed the creation of a republic in opposition to the imperial reign), made matters worse. With Ozaki's resignation, Itagaki tried to replace Ozaki with Hoshi as education minister and to make Kazuo foreign minister. However, Okuma replaced Ozaki with Inukai (Progressive), and kept the foreign minister's position for himself. This angered Hoshi, and resulted in the Constitutional Government Party's breakup.[51]

Kazuo lost a once in a lifetime chance of becoming foreign minister in the first democratic cabinet formed in Japan. Ichiro considers this the fatal misfortune of Kazuo's political career. Ichiro writes that even if Itagaki (Liberal) was willing to make Kazuo foreign minister, Okuma, Kazuo's mentor, hesitated for unclear reasons. Had Kazuo been a self-promoting person, he would have demanded the position, as Hoshi did. However, Kazuo did not hold any grudges. He accepted the position of vice foreign minister and did the actual job of foreign minister for Okuma. Okuma might have had an attachment to the foreign ministerial post because he was obliged to resign the post in 1889 due to the bombing accident. Prime Minister Ito, Okuma's rival, also held the two posts in 1887. Ichiro writes that it was unfortunate that Kazuo did not have a good *oyabun* (boss) who would take care of his followers. Okuma did not duly reward Kazuo for his contribution in making Okuma prime minister. Ichiro writes, "Had my father worked for Ito, his political career would have been several times glorious."[52]

In this regard, Haruko believes that had Kazuo not resigned the MOFA with Okuma (in 1889), he could have become foreign minister in 1898. Had Kazuo stayed in the ministry, he most likely would have advanced to the rank of vice foreign minister in the meantime; therefore, Okuma would have been compelled to make Kazuo foreign minister in 1898. This assumption seems plausible because the post of vice foreign minister was only one rank higher than the positions Kazuo had already held in 1886. Whatever the true reasons might have been, Kazuo's modesty and his loyalty to Okuma were partly accountable for his missed chance.[53]

Haruko admits that both Kazuo and herself had a certain unworldliness and lacked *shoseijutsu* (art of living). Kazuo regarded flattery and selfishness as sins. Kazuo and Haruko did not visit the residences of Ito and Inoue even when they recommended Kazuo for the MOFA; because paying courtesy calls to seniors' residence could be misconstrued as currying favor with them. Despite their close political partnership, Kazuo did not visit Okuma's residence unless there were important matters to be discussed. Haruko states that even so some people thought that Kazuo was currying favor with Okuma. Kazuo believed that the right way to express his gratitude toward his seniors was to do the best work for the nation. Ichiro writes that Kazuo was not the type of person who sought opportunities for himself. Rather, Kazuo waited for opportunities to come to him. When an opportunity came to him, he considered it. His decision on whether to accept the offer was solely based on *shingi* (loyalty) toward the person who offered the position. Once he accepted the offer, he performed his duties in earnest. Although Kazuo held many high positions over three decades, it was not because he was intent on getting high positions for the sake of the positions themselves, but rather in order to fulfill his high ideals.[54]

The Collapse of the *Waihan* Cabinet

In 1898, with the Constitutional Government Party's breakup, the former Liberals, led by Hoshi, chased away the former Progressives from the party headquarters and claimed themselves to be the Constitutional Government Party. Consequently, Okuma created yet another new party, the *Kenseihonto* (the Orthodox Constitutional Government Party), and requested the Meiji emperor to allow a reshuffling of the cabinet. The emperor did not respond. Having lost its majority standing in the HR, the *Waihan* cabinet resigned *en masse* in October. The *Waihan* cabinet lasted only for four months. Ironically, in addition to Ozaki's republic speech, the fight over Kazuo's would-be post was a major cause of the breakdown of the *Waihan* cabinet.[55]

The second Yamagata cabinet succeeded the *Waihan* cabinet in November 1898. Prime Minister Yamagata suppressed the power of political parties and enacted the *Chian keisatsuho* (Public Peace Police Law). Ito felt vindicated by the collapse of the *Waihan* cabinet and found it amusing that, despite its ideal claim to be a liberal democratic cabinet, the cabinet broke up due to the petty fight over a cabinet post. However, Ito opposed the reactionary stance of Yamagata and began laying the groundwork for his fourth cabinet.[56]

The Creation of the *Seiyukai*

With the collapse of the *Waihan* cabinet, Kazuo returned to his law practice and management of the *Tokyo Senmon Gakko* (Waseda University in 1902). Meanwhile, Ito created a political party called the *Rikken Seiyukai* (Friends of Constitutional Government Association, referred to as the *Seiyukai*) in September 1900, with his confidante Prince Saionji Kimmochi (1849–1940, a descendant of the aristocratic Fujiwara family, the rulers in the ancient Heian period). The party was essentially Ito's *goyo seito* ("kept party") and was a mixture of the *hambatsu* (provincial clique) and *minto* (people's party) in that he recruited many bureaucrats as well as members of the breakaway Constitutional Government Party (former Liberals), led by Hoshi. Thus, the elements of Itagaki's Liberals survived in the *Seiyukai*.[57]

Ito also asked Kazuo to join the *Seiyukai* but he declined. Haruko writes, when Ito tried to recruit Kazuo into the *Seiyukai* at its inception, his messenger asked Kazuo to specify the place for their secret meeting because Kazuo was still a member of the Orthodox Constitutional Government Party. However, Kazuo told the messenger that politicians should not have any secrets in their deeds and that he would visit Ito's residence. Ito agreed and they met in Ito's residence. During their meeting, Ito told Kazuo that Okuma was a horrible person, who had not even made Kazuo foreign minister, and that Ito would not be able to work with Okuma. Realizing that Ito and Okuma could not reconcile with each other, Kazuo declined Ito's request. Thus, despite Okuma's poor treatment, Kazuo remained loyal to Okuma. Ito was not offended; however, Haruko writes that many people misunderstood Kazuo because of his rigid integrity and independence. Kazuo detested *hyori* (hypocrisy) and secrets. He loathed manipulation. In the world of politics, people were doing the opposite.[58]

As the *Seiyukai* acquired the majority standing in the HR, the second Yamagata cabinet resigned *en masse* and Ito formed his fourth cabinet. Then, in October 1901, Kazuo and Ito were invited to Yale University's bicentennial anniversary to receive honorary doctoral degrees. Without notes, Kazuo gave a long speech, entitled "Comparisons and Critiques of French Laws and English Laws." As his English was flawless, one of the audience commented that the Japanese no longer needed English teachers. Kazuo also gave special intensive lectures for ten days at the law school. This was just after the assassination of President McKinley. Many American dignitaries, including President Theodore Roosevelt and the first lady welcomed Kazuo and Haruko enthusiastically. The first family invited the couple to the White House and extended exceptional hospitality toward them. In addition, Kazuo was given a first-class decoration from the Ch'ing dynasty in September 1899. It was an unusual acknowledgment. Kazuo was recognized by foreign governments, if not by his own government.[59]

The Move to Ito's *Seiyukai*

Ito and Yamagata made a secret deal to alternate power between *Seiyukai*'s Saionji and Yamagata's protégé, Katsura Taro (1847–1913, a general from Choshu) in 1906, as Ito and Yamagata themselves had done earlier. In total, Katsura formed a cabinet three times (1901–1906, 1908–1911, and 1912–1913) while Saionji did so twice (1906–1908 and 1911–1912). The years of the alternating Katsura and Saionji cabinets from 1906 to 1913 are referred to as the *Keien* (an acronym of

Katsura and Saionji in Chinese pronunciation) age. Consequently, the *raison d'être* of Okuma's Orthodox Constitutional Government Party, as an opposition party against the ruling *Seiyukai*, weakened. The division within that party grew deeper, and Okuma resigned the party presidency in 1907. Nevertheless, only when the party was reduced to a skeleton, after Okuma's departure, did Kazuo leave the party and join the *Seiyukai* in January 1908. Haruko was surprised by Kazuo's move but Kazuo simply explained that he had joined the *Seiyukai* because creating a strong political party for the sake of a democratic parliament was his ultimate goal.[60]

Haruko adds that Kazuo never complained about his affairs to her. As in this case, Kazuo usually made up his mind by himself. He seldom bothered other people about decisions he had to make because he felt that asking for another's opinion on his personal affairs was an imposition. When Kazuo did ask for advice, he followed that advice in order to honor the adviser. Had Kazuo joined the *Seiyukai* earlier in 1900 (at Ito's request), he could potentially have obtained a ministerial post in Ito's fourth cabinet or the subsequent *Seiyukai* cabinets. However, Kazuo remained loyal to Okuma and stayed in the moribund Orthodox Constitutional Government Party until 1908.[61]

The Dismissal from Waseda University

When Okuma resigned the Orthodox Constitutional Government Party's presidency in 1907, he abruptly abolished the post of the principal of Waseda University and assumed the presidency of the university himself. Accordingly, Kazuo was dismissed from the principal's position despite his enormous contribution to the growth of the university for nearly two decades. Haruko writes, it must have been painful for Kazuo to have to leave Waseda. He had dedicated himself to the university and had a strong attachment to it. Haruko felt that Okuma's cruel dismissal made Kazuo finally decide to join Ito's *Seiyukai*. Kazuo had been loyal to Okuma throughout their political partnership. Kazuo made his obligation toward Okuma his first priority. Kazuo had declined a number of offers of political appointments from prime ministers, such as Ito, Matsukata, and Yamagaka, because of his responsibility toward Waseda. Nevertheless, Haruko writes, Kazuo never complained about the dismissal. Instead, he tried to console Haruko, by saying that she should think he was liberated from the obligation.[62]

Although Kazuo made Waseda University one of the two most prestigious private universities, his contribution to the university is largely forgotten and few associate Kazuo with Waseda at present.

The Final Stage of Political Career

After joining the *Seiyukai*, Kazuo continued to win HR elections. The senior party leader Okazaki Kunisuke commented that there was nobody like Kazuo in the party. Being a lawyer, scholar, and educator, Kazuo could have served as minister of justice, education, foreign affairs, or anything else. As speaker, he was second to none in solving problems. He had the remarkable ability to turn complex issues into simple ones and solve them in a harmonious fashion. In fact, Kazuo was expected to be foreign minister in the late stage of the first Saionji cabinet. However, he narrowly lost that chance to Kato Takaaki (his former student at Tokyo Imperial University). Kazuo was then elected as chairman of the HR's budget committee in 1909 during the second Katsura cabinet, and was expected to become a state minister in the near future. Ichiro writes that the three and a half years at the *Seiyukai*, until his death in October 1911, were Kazuo's last "glorious" days. During that short period of time, Kazuo served as the party's majority leader for the HR, chaired the party's Policy Affairs Research Council's first section (in charge of foreign affairs, justice, and education), the HR's budget committee, the HR's commerce laws revision committee, and so on. Ichiro writes, "my father kept working and engaged in negotiations until late at night without having dinner. He tied up his hunger by eating snacks and drinking *sake*. No wonder, his health deteriorated."[63]

Kazuo was also elected to be president of the Tokyo Lawyers Association in May 1910. Kazuo was at the pinnacle of his career. As for his private life, Kazuo had two promising sons. Ichiro was married in September 1908 and Hideo was married in May 1910. It might have been the happiest time of Kazuo's life. However, he developed cancer in the esophagus. He was calm when he realized it. Kazuo often told Haruko at that time, "I am happy. I had a happy life." Kazuo contracted malarial fever in June 1911 and died on October 3, 1911. He was 55 years old.[64]

Haruko recounts the day before Kazuo died. Kazuo told her, "I dreamed that Mr. Ito (he became the first resident-general of the Protectorate of Korea in 1905 and was assassinated by a Korean nationalist in Harbin, northeast China, in 1909) was calling me from the other side of the river bank (a river dividing the real world and the world of the dead in Buddhism). I was trying to swim across the river but the water was getting deeper and deeper. Then I woke up. I was anxious to see Mr. Ito." Haruko believed that Ito had come from heaven to take Kazuo away. Although Haruko was a strong person, she was devastated by Kazuo's death and tried to follow him. She writes, "I felt that Kazuo would be happy if I followed him. I begged Ichiro to forgive me for doing so. Ichiro told me that, now that they (her two sons) had lost one parent and felt deprived of half of their hope, how could they have hope if they lost another parent. I realized my mistake and decided to devote my life to women's education." Her friends also tried to console her by advising her to think that Kazuo's early death would mean early success for Ichiro's political career.[65]

Although he was from a *samurai* clan that traditionally subscribed to Buddhism, Kazuo was a Shintoist, the religion the imperial family and aristocracy subscribed to. People speculated that Kazuo might be a Christian because he was unusually gentle and even saintly. They found out that Kazuo was a Shintoist when his funeral service was conducted in the rare Shinto style. Such dignitaries as Prime Minister Saionji, Interior Minister Hara Takashi, Justice Minister Matsuda, gave eulogies. Hara said "his political activities thus far were only preliminaries to his future activities. I was expecting him to further materialize his visions into politics. I am very sad that he could not accomplish this." Other eulogies included "a man of extraordinary character, a great loss to Japan," "a man of belief; adhered to his belief in openness; expressed his belief openly without fear, yet, was open to others' opinions and, therefore, did not antagonize anybody," "not only intelligent but also warm, like spring." Members of the *Seiyukai* and the Japan Lawyers' Association, officials of Waseda University, and more than 1,000 students at Waseda attended the service (the university was officially closed for the service). The total number of participants was 3,500. The road from his house to the Yanaka cemetery was closed. Kazuo was buried that evening. It was a beautiful full-moon night. Japan lost a "man of exceptional talent of the Meiji era."[66]

A Comparative Assessment with Kazuo's Contemporaries

It is useful to compare Kazuo's career with those of his contemporaries who were also from small *han*, such as Komura Jutaro (1855–1911), Hara Takashi (1856–1921), Inukai Tsuyoshi (1855–1932), and Ozaki Yukio (1859–1954), in order to assess the effect of their origins on their careers.

Komura Jutaro
Kazuo and Komura had many things in common. Komura was born in 1855, a year before Kazuo, and was also from a lesser *han* (Hyuga-obi, part of Miyazaki-*ken*). He ranked second after Kazuo in the qualifying exam to go abroad and went to Harvard University. Therefore, they had almost identical environments, intelligence, and opportunities. However, upon returning from the United States, Komura chose the

career of a diplomat. Komura steadily advanced in his career in the MOFA and was instrumental in concluding the Anglo-Japanese Alliance (1902). He was an ambassador extraordinary and plenipotentiary to the peace treaty conference that ended the Russo-Japanese War in Portsmouth, New Hampshire in 1905. After dealing with the annexation of Korea in 1910, Komura became foreign minister of the second Katsura cabinet in 1911 and revised the unequal treaties on tariffs with foreign governments. He died in 1911, the same year as Kazuo. Although Komura was from a small *han*, he had a successful career in the government, became foreign minister, and left a name in history. Komura was a pragmatist and pursued a solid path. Komura's case seems to indicate the importance of personal attributes more than that of the environment in shaping a person's career.[67]

In contrast, Kazuo was an idealist. He spread his energy too widely, because of his exceptional talent and his ideals, and did not leave as big a footprint as Komura, at least concerning name recognition. At present, the Japanese know of Komura as the Meiji's foreign minister who concluded the Portsmouth Treaty, with the good offices of American President Theodore Roosevelt, whereas they know of Kazuo primarily as Ichiro's father. Komura's rank at the MOFA suggests the likelihood of Kazuo's having become foreign minister in 1898 had he stayed in the ministry. Komura was deputy director-general of the Translation Bureau when Kazuo was its director-general in 1886. In this sense, Haruko's perception was right; however, positions were not important to Kazuo.[68]

Hara Takashi

Hara was born in Nambu-*han* (Morioka, Iwate-*ken*) in 1856, two months earlier than Kazuo. Nambu-*han* was a traitor to the Meiji government because it had sided with the shogunate. Hara personally resented the *hambatsu* rule because he was a son of a *karo* (*han*'s high-ranking minister). He looked down on Meiji's *genro* (elder statesmen) because they were originally low-rank *samurai* of Satsuma and Choshu. Hara attended a law school attached to the Justice Department, worked at the *Yubin Hochi Shimbun* (newspaper), and then became a politician. Hara was the interior minister of the second Saionji cabinet when Kazuo died. He became president of the *Seiyukai* and then formed a cabinet in September 1918. He was hailed as the *heimin* (commoner) prime minister because he was the first premier of non-*hambatsu* and non-peer origin. He was even referred to as "Lenin of the west, Hara of the east." However, contrary to the expectations of the people, the Hara cabinet was indifferent to social movements and opposed to the introduction of universal (male) suffrage. Toyoda writes that Hara was essentially a shrewd machiavellian and a forceful politician. He was assassinated in November 1921.[69]

Ichiro also notes that Hara was a ruthless and forcible person but thinks that Hara was an ingenious politician. Ichiro personally admired Hara for his ability to unite the hodgepodge *Seiyukai* and to consecutively win elections. Ichiro dubbed his father's would-have-been successes (had he lived longer) in Hara's actual successes. Yet, Ichiro realized the difference between the two and writes, "both Hara and my father went to *hanko* (province school), studied law, and become politicians in the early Meiji period. However, their characters and orientations were different. My father was intrinsically a scholar, while Hara was a born politician."[70]

Inukai Tsuyoshi and Ozaki Yukio

Inukai (from Okayama-*ken*) and Ozaki (from Kanagawa-*ken*), Kazuo's colleagues in the Tokyo-*fu* assembly, the HR, and in Okuma's successive parties, accomplished remarkable political careers and left their imprints in politics. Inukai was a HR member since the first parliament, led two opposition parties, became president of the *Seiyukai* (1929) and was prime minister (1931–1932). Ozaki was also a HR member since the first parliament, became education minister of the *Waihan* cabinet (1898), was mayor of Tokyo city (1903–1912), and was justice minister of the second Okuma cabinet (1914–1916). He holds the world record for continuous membership (64 years) in an elected assembly. Ozaki is known for his independent stance and is referred to as the "god of constitutional government" in Japan. Inukai and Ozaki launched the movement to overthrow the third Katsura cabinet in 1912 under the banner of "overthrow the cliques and defend the constitution." This was the so-called *Daiichiji goken undo* (the first movement to defend the constitution). Katsura tried to resist the movement by forming the *Rikken Doshikai* (the Constitutional Fellow Thinkers' Association). However, the party failed to obtain a majority in the parliament and the Katsura cabinet resigned *en masse* in 1913. This incident is called the *Taisho no seihen* (political change of the Taisho), named after the new imperial reign.[71]

The critical difference is that Inukai and Ozaki consistently pursued political careers, whereas Kazuo spread himself too thin, being heavily engaged in education. Haruko writes, "Kazuo was an ingenious scholar and did everything very fast; however, he was too active merely to be a professor. He worked extremely hard and spared no time probably because he was destined to have a short life." By maintaining three careers, Kazuo burned himself out.[72]

An Overall Assessment of Kazuo's Political Leadership

In the overall assessment, Kazuo's gentle nature did not lend itself to being a powerful leader. His family members recall how undomineering Kazuo was (atypical for men in the Meiji era). Haruko writes that Kazuo never dictated or raised his voice to anybody, even to his sons, servants, or students (many students lived in his house as political apprentices). Kazuo looked at people's positive aspects and overlooked their short-comings. Haruko points to his magnanimous heart by saying, "I was enlightened by his generosity and consulted about everything with him." Ichiro writes, "There is nothing easy about being kind. Although it appears to be easy to be kind; in reality it is most difficult to be truly kind. Yet, my father was truly kind. It is no exaggeration to call him the 'god of kindness.' He was warm to the bottom of his heart. We (his two sons) have never seen him raise his voice or scold for 28 years during which we lived together. He used to say that it is unpleasant to scold people, so he did not. I have no memory of my father yelling at us. It is understandable for my brother because he was a quiet boy, but I was wild. I remember only one occasion when he punished me. When I was three or four years old, I did something naughty and he took me to a bathroom and poured water on my head. Even at that time, he did not yell at me. Few people could take such a calm attitude."[73]

Ichiro's brother Hideo recalls that Kazuo's nature was gentle and even saintly. Kazuo cherished justice and freedom and adhered to these values. He respected others' opinions. Hideo writes, "My father never imposed his orders on me. He neither opposed my decision to be christened nor did he oppose my decision to stay at Tokyo Imperial University to become a scholar. He only expressed his hope that I would enter the real world (rather than staying in the ivory tower) and make actual contributions to the society. Yet, he consented when I said I was suited to study. I respect him as a person, more than as our father. Yet, he was our father."[74]

With regard to Kazuo's personal character, little information suggests any negative aspects. Both Toyoda and Ito, who made comprehensive studies of the Hatoyama Dynasty, note that all the materials they read attest to Kazuo's gentle and peaceful character. The only negative remark (by modern standards) was that both Kazuo and Haruko liked to smoke. Haruko writes that she acquired the habit of smoking during

Kazuo's first campaign for the HR. Kazuo's constituents felt akin to him and Haruko when they smoked with them. Although they knew that smoking was bad for their health, they did not make serious efforts to stop smoking. When Kazuo was forced to stop smoking due to his illness, Haruko stopped smoking as well. In addition, Haruko's ambiguous confession that she had been *fumei* (unwise) for not making new *kimono* and for not wearing fashionable clothes (in order to save money for Kazuo's campaigns) might seem to imply that Kazuo might have had extramarital affairs. It is just speculation by this author, but it is plausible because it was common for established Japanese men to have mistresses. It was not customary to write about such affairs in biographies.[75]

In summary, Kazuo had strong aspirations to become a political leader: to establish a constitutional democracy. However, unlike Okuma and Itagaki, Kazuo lacked one important motivational attribute for a political leader: the desire for power. In regard to his capabilities, Kazuo had the long-term vision and the realistic political wisdom to place himself in a moderate liberal position, instead of radicalism. He also had considerable political leadership competency. Kazuo had a thorough knowledge of law, superb negotiation skills, and an impeccable ability to make fair and objective judgments. He was also an enthusiastic debater and an eloquent speaker. Nonetheless, Kazuo was not a man with the caliber of a great leader. Kazuo was too principled to be a shrewd politician. He was generous and modest to the extent that he was unworldly. Kazuo's peaceful and saintly character was not necessarily an asset for a strong political leader. His integrity and modesty worked against achieving higher political positions.

Toyoda thinks that three of Kazuo's personal attributes were important in shaping his career: (1) he was diligent and liked to study; (2) he was gentle and respected harmony among people; and (3) he believed in justice and wanted to bring justice into the society. These attributes were distilled into his three career goals. Kazuo was a first-class scholar of law; however, his political ideals and vitality did not keep him in his study room.[76]

Toyoda argues that Kazuo had the capacity to be a state minister (such as foreign minister, justice minister, or education minister), if not prime minister. However, in order to control the political circles at that time, it was necessary to have connections with the *hambatsu*, as well as such capabilities as (1) the organizational skill of Okubo Toshimichi (carried out the centralization of the Meiji government, assassinated); (2) the machiavellianism of Hoshi Toru (house speaker, a Liberal Party's leader, assassinated) and of Hara Takashi (*Seiyukai* president, prime minister, assassinated); (3) the reconciliatory ability of Ito Hirobumi (the first and four-time prime minister, tactfully balanced the *hambatsu* politics and constitutional democracy, assassinated); and (4) the grand strategy of Saigo Takamori (military chief of staff, carried out the peaceful transfer of power from the shogun to the emperor, committed suicide). Kazuo was weak in these particular political capabilities. Toyoda concludes that Kazuo was intrinsically a scholar and a conscientious humanist.[77]

With regard to interactions between personal attributes and the environment, Kazuo's personal attributes played a more important role for his political career than the environment. His diligence and intelligence surpassed his disadvantaged background. However, he chose not to seek an opportunistic route in the government and instead chose a path to become an educator and a lawyer. As a politician, Kazuo joined an opposition party to challenge the *hambatsu* rule. These choices are largely attributable to his personal character and beliefs, more than his undistinguished origin. Similarly, the subsequent successes (and the failures) of his political career were dictated by his personal attributes and his ideals more than by the environment.

Conclusion

In conclusion, Kazuo did not leave as big a name as his exceptional intelligence and extraordinary diligence seem to have warranted. Kazuo would probably have become foreign minister had he stayed in the ministry. Kazuo would have become president of Tokyo Imperial University had he stayed in the university. However, he abandoned these prestigious government positions for his higher ideals. Had Kazuo lived longer, he might have become foreign minister in the Katsura or Saionji cabinets or in the second Okuma cabinet. However, leaving a name in history was not as important to him as pursuing his ideals, and he worked to exhaustion.[78]

While Kazuo did not leave as big a name as some of his contemporaries, his contributions to the modernization of Japan should not be underestimated. Kazuo was a member of the Tokyo-*fu* assembly and Tokyo city assembly. He was a member of the HR since its second session. He held important positions in the HR, such as house speaker and budget committee chair. He was also vice foreign minister. Kazuo created the Constitutional Government Party for Okuma; the first people's party that obtained the majority in the HR, leading to the first democratic cabinet. Kazuo was indeed one of the founding fathers of Japanese democracy. Kazuo was also president of the Tokyo Lawyers Association. He was principal of Waseda University. Toyoda writes that as a lawyer, an educator, and a politician, Kazuo contributed enormously, much more than the corrupt politicians of the *hambatsu* and the radical democrats of the "people's rights." The extraordinary time of the Meiji era needed an extraordinary person. Kazuo perfectly filled its needs. Kazuo responded to the call of the times and dedicated his life to establishing a civil society.[79]

Kazuo grew up in the revolutionary age at the end of the shogunate era and lived through numerous turbulent political upheavals during the Meiji era. Had Kazuo lived longer, he would have further contributed to his grand cause. However, the age of militarism was encroaching upon Japan when Kazuo died. As Japan annexed Korea in 1910, militarism gained momentum. In this political atmosphere, liberal politicians, even moderate ones, were regarded as "traitors." Hara was assassinated in 1921. Inukai was assassinated on May 15, 1932. This "5·15 incident" ended the practice of forming a party-based cabinet and replaced it with a military regime. For good or bad, Kazuo died without witnessing the escalation of militarism and its disastrous end. It was Ichiro's turn to undertake Kazuo's mission in the dark age of militarism.[80]

Chapter 3

The Second Generation: Ichiro
and Prewar Politics

Growing Up in an Elite Family

Ichiro was born in Tokyo on January 1, 1883. His brother Hideo was born in February 1884. Ichiro was born into a renowned family, with a father who was referred to as an "exceptional talent of the Meiji era" and a mother who was a pioneering women's educator. Haruko resumed teaching English at her alma mater, Tokyo Women's Teacher's College, when Hideo was four months old. It was extremely rare for a Japanese married woman to have a career then. She created the Kyoritsu Women's Training School (a prototype of Kyoritsu Women's College) in March 1886, as one of its founding board members. She became its sixth president in 1922 and taught there until her death in 1938. Scholars take note of Ichiro's exceptional background. In the words of Masuda Hiroshi, no one fits the description "an elite in the political circles" better than Ichiro. Kataoka Tetsuya describes Ichiro as "perhaps the best educated of all postwar prime ministers in the political culture of democracy." As the elder son of an elite family, Ichiro was expected to succeed to his father's career and achieve an equal level of success. Haruko entrusted to Ichiro her dream that Kazuo did not fulfill (of becoming a state minister). According to Matsumoto Seicho, Ichiro did not suffer from the heavy pressure because he was bright and a born optimist. Ichiro was an *obotchan* (silver-spoon boy), conscious of his family reputation. He accepted the responsibility and fulfilled it.[1]

Ichiro's parents, especially his mother, provided indispensable help to his self-actualization. Haruko's determination to make her son a political leader was such that she read biographies of world leaders in English to Ichiro while she was pregnant with him (*taikyo*, uterus education, to teach a baby during pregnancy). Ichiro writes of his parents with great affection and appreciation. It was an unusually candid acknowledgment since such personal feelings were rarely expressed in Japanese writing.

Ichiro describes them as "a gentle father and a stern mother," as opposed to the norm of the Japanese traditional family that had "a stern father and a gentle mother."[2]

A Spartan Mother: "Godmother of the Hatoyama Family"

During elementary and middle-school years, Haruko educated Ichiro, more than the schools. Haruko sent Ichiro and Hideo to bed early and made them study early in the morning. Haruko woke them up at half past three in the morning, and made them study mathematics, English, and Chinese for two hours before they went to school. She was so enthusiastic about their education that she did everything from making up math quizzes to sharpening pencils for them. When they woke up, they first answered the math quizzes she had prepared. When they finished the math quizzes, Haruko taught them English and Chinese herself. On Sundays and holidays, she let them wake up half an hour later at four o'clock. She never allowed them to break this routine in summer. As they were always learning one to two years ahead of the school curriculum, they had no difficulty with school exams. No sooner had his teacher finished writing down questions on the blackboard than Ichiro turned his answers in. Haruko also made Ichiro read biographies of world leaders, such as Disraeli, Gladstone, Pitt senior, and Pitt junior, hoping to inspire Ichiro to become a politician.[3]

Ichiro was a *yancha* (wild) boy, while Hideo was a quiet boy. Ichiro was bright but did not like to study as much as Hideo, who maintained the highest academic standing throughout his school years. When Kazuo told Hideo to study less and play more, Hideo told his father, "I have the freedom to study as much as I please." Ichiro writes, "My mother was worried about me because I did not like to study. She used to say that she had to force us to study until we developed our own will to study, and that she would not interfere once we developed such a will. I developed a desire to study only when I began preparation for the entrance exam for *Ichiko* (the best high school under the old education system, which combined the high school level education and the general course level of the university). Unless my mother forced me to study, I would have been left behind my peers and become a loser." Ichiro adds that Haruko sat up late until eleven o'clock at night, waiting for Kazuo to come home. To fulfill dual obligations—as the wife of a lawyer, politician, and university principal, and as the mother of two sons—Haruko worked to exhaustion. Haruko was also running a women's college. As she continued this hard schedule, she lost weight, from 12–13 *kan*

(99–107 lb) to 8.5 *kan* (70 lb). Haruko's devotion to her sons' education was exceptional. Ichiro writes, "it must have been an enormous burden and pain on her part. I am deeply indebted to my mother."[4]

As expected, both Ichiro and Hideo went to the *Ichiko* in September 1900 and September 1901 respectively. Ichiro entered the *Ichiko* in the twenty-third place out of 51 students (the acceptance rate was 10 percent) but gradually improved his standing to eighth in his class at his graduation in June 1904. Ichiro's GPA was 82.2 out of 100, when getting more than 90.0 was regarded as almost impossible. Then, Ichiro moved to the British law faculty of Tokyo Imperial University, which was right next to *Ichiko*, and graduated from the university as the third highest in his class. Meanwhile, Hideo maintained the top standing throughout *Ichiko*, where he was privileged to learn English from Natsume Soseki (famous writer), and graduated with a GPA of 91.7. He exceeded the impossible threshold and was called the best in the history of the *Ichiko*. However, he was physically weak and his score in physical education was 77.6. Had Hideo been healthier, his GPA would have been phenomenal. Hideo went to the German law faculty of Tokyo Imperial University and graduated at the top. Ichiro wrote, "I could never beat my younger brother in academic scores except for P.E."[5]

Haruko's efforts paid off. While Ichiro actually excelled in math and science, and his teachers advised him to become an engineer, he had no hesitation in choosing a political career. Ichiro writes, "It was a rule for a son to carry out his father's mission. My parents also educated me hoping for just that. After I entered *Ichiko* and Tokyo Imperial University, I set my mind to becoming a lawyer and a politician and studied hard." Haruko's regret over Kazuo's death turned her into a strong promoter of Ichiro's political career. She wrote a letter to Hara Takashi (then a *Seiyukai* leader), asking him to take Ichiro under his tutelage. Haruko also actively participated in Ichiro's campaigns at times when Japanese women did not have suffrage. For her extraordinary devotion to make a political leader out of Ichiro, Haruko is dubbed the "godmother of the Hatoyama family."[6]

A Gentle Father: "God and Friend"

In contrast, Kazuo was a "god and friend" to his sons. Kazuo encouraged free spirit and played games with his sons when Japanese society regarded play as a vice. Ichiro writes, "despite his hard schedule, my father closed his law firm on Sundays and played with us. He played *sumo* and tennis with us to build up our physical strength. We also flew kites, went to the zoo, walked in the woods, and did gardening on fine days, and played ping pong, *go*, and *shogi* on rainy days. Through this play, he taught us the importance of honesty (fair play) and of concentrating on one thing at a time." However, Kazuo was not only interested in playing with his sons. Kazuo gave his sons an American liberal education based on the motto, "study hard and play hard," whereas the Japanese norm was "study hard and no play." In fact, it was Kazuo's idea to make his sons study in the morning and read English books. Haruko writes, "although Kazuo was not spartan, he believed that the brain was clear in the morning and made our sons to wake up at half past three and study for two hours." Ichiro thought of his parents as "a gentle father and a stern mother" because his mother was executing his father's decisions.[7]

In summary, Ichiro grew up in a protected environment and was given an elite education. He was referred to as an *obotchan* (silver-spoon boy) because of his *junsui baiyo* (pure breed) upbringing. Ichiro writes, "I was criticized that I was *seken ni utoi* (unworldly) and that I did not know hardships; however, I could not help it because my parents gave me the best environment and unlimited affection." In addition to his upbringing, his unworldliness derives from his father who was also referred to as such. Shaped by the nature and the nurture, Ichiro had a certain aspect of naïveté, being excessively honest, idealistic, and open. Responding to his parents' wish, Ichiro decided to devote himself entirely to politics. He writes, "as my father spread himself too thin and thereby failed to leave as big footsteps in politics as he could have, I decided to devote myself solely to politics. Once I made up my mind to become a politician, I thought day and night about how to establish a true democratic parliament." This is the making of a born *shokugyo seijika* (career politician).[8]

Marriage with Terada Kaoru

After graduating from Tokyo Imperial University in July 1907, Ichiro began working at Kazuo's law firm in August, became a lecturer at Waseda University in April 1908, and then married Terada Kaoru in September. Ichiro was 25 years old and Kaoru was 20 years old. Kaoru was born in 1888 in Yokohama. Her father, Terada Sakae, was a *samurai* of Kuroda-*han* (Fukuoka-*ken*) and became a bureaucrat (justice of the Yokohama and Tokyo local courts, and chief secretary of the HR). He later became a member of the HP. Kaoru's mother, Iku, was Haruko's niece (her elder sister, Suma's daughter). Iku died early at the age of 35 in 1902 and Kaoru, the eldest among five children, helped her father (who did not remarry) to take care of her three sisters and a brother. Kaoru was beautiful, bright, and strong. Without her knowledge, Kaoru was adopted by the Hatoyama family when she was 18 years old. Haruko handpicked her grandniece as a potential bride for Ichiro and trained her firsthand to be a politician's wife. Haruko was aware of possible genetic defects caused by intermarriages. However, Kaoru's exceptional merits outweighed such concern. Ichiro, a graduate of Tokyo Imperial University and the first son of a former speaker of the HR, was inundated with marriage proposals, but he chose Kaoru. The mass media widely covered the famed family's son's wedding. The famous couple, who would have an enormous impact on the political and educational circles, was born.[9]

After the marriage, Kaoru dutifully observed Haruko's teachings. As Haruko did, Kaoru wore three hats: politician's wife, mother of a son and five daughters, and a principal of the Kyoritsu Women's College. Soon after their wedding, Haruko took Kaoru to Ichiro's campaigns. Wherever they went, a huge crowd gathered to see the beautiful young wife of the renowned family. An American analogue would be a scene of Rose and Jacqueline Kennedy campaigning for John F. Kennedy. Haruko and Kaoru energetically visited constituents individually by foot so much so that their *zori* (Japanese sandal) straps cut into their feet. Miki Bukichi, Ichiro's opponent in the same district, complained that he was a greater politician than Ichiro but he could not defeat Ichiro in elections because of the two women behind him. Kaoru met Haruko's high expectations and took good care of Ichiro's constituents. With her dedication, Ichiro never lost his seat in the HR. Kaoru also surprised Ichiro by making her voice extend throughout a huge hall in a campaign. She took lessons in *yokyoku* (Japanese classical poem chanting) in order to develop her voice. Her reserved but stately demeanor later earned her the reputation of being an exemplary "Japanese first lady."[10]

Succeeding to Kazuo's Mission

Ichiro started his political career at the age of 29 when he ran for the Tokyo city assembly in February 1912. Ichiro ran from the *Seiyukai* (to which Kazuo had belonged) and was elected. Ichiro writes, "My father was a member of the HR as well as of the Tokyo city (formerly Tokyo-*fu*) assembly, as it was allowed to serve in two assemblies simultaneously back then. When my father passed away, I was 28 years old and was not eligible for the HR (its candidacy eligibility age was 30 years), whereas the Tokyo city assembly's eligibility age was 25 years. I won the supplementary election for the Tokyo city assembly to fill his vacancy. Three years later in March 1915, I won the general election for the HR. I was 32 years old."[11]

Ironically, this was during the second Okuma cabinet (April 1914–October 1916). Okuma was no longer a fighter for freedom and popular rights, but had been conciliated by Ito who gave Okuma the status of count. Okuma had no power base in a political party (all the parties he had created no longer existed) at that time. Okuma was merely brought in by *genro* (elder statesmen) kingmakers as a counterweight against the dominant *Seiyukai* in the HR. Okuma's cabinet consisted mainly of members of the HP and had to rely on the weak *Kenseikai* (the Constitutional Government Association); a new name for the *Rikken Doshikai* (the Constitutional Fellow Thinkers' Association) created by Prime Minister Katsura in 1913. Okuma's former protégé Inukai, the president of the *Rikken Kokuminto* (Constitutional Nationalist Party), declined to join the cabinet, whereas another protégé Ozaki (a member of the *Seiyukai*) accepted the justice minister's position and was criticized in political circles. During the March 1915 HR election campaigns, the mass media wrote that Ichiro dared to challenge the Okuma cabinet in spite of his father's close association with Okuma, running from the opposition party *Seiyukai*. Ichiro won and succeeded to Kazuo's election district, called then the Ushigome District. Ichiro won 15 times consecutively and retained a seat in the HR until his death in March 1959.[12]

The Early Years in the Tokyo City Assembly

Ichiro soon began displaying political leadership in the Tokyo city assembly. Ichiro was elected deputy speaker of the assembly in December 1918. At that time, the bill increase by Tokyo Gas was a big issue in the assembly and Ichiro fought well against it. Ichiro felt it necessary to establish himself in the city assembly in order to win the HR elections. He created an intra-assembly group, named *Tokiwakai*, in order to control the assembly. Ichiro lost the election for assembly speaker in 1920; however, he allied himself with a neutral intra-assembly group, called *Jichikai*, and made its leader, Yanagisawa Yasutoshi, the speaker. As his deputy, Ichiro controlled Yanagisawa and gained power in the assembly. Then, Miki Bukichi (1884–1956, from Kagawa-*ken*, the Constitutional Government Association) and Ono Bamboku

(1890–1964, from Gifu-*ken*, *Seiyukai's ingaidan* [outer-parliament group]) were elected to the Tokyo city assembly in 1922. Miki had been Ichiro's rival since the HR elections in 1915. Miki lost to Ichiro then, but both won in the next HR elections in 1917. Although Ichiro and Miki belonged to rival parties and fought as political opponents, they liked each other and often found themselves allied in the Tokyo city assembly. In turn, Ono supported Ichiro from his first campaign for the HR. When Ichiro became chief secretary of the Tanaka cabinet in 1927, Ichiro made Ono his first private secretary.[13]

As Miki became Ichiro's number-one confidante and chief of staff of his cabinet in the postwar era, it is useful to review his background. Miki was born into the family of a Confucian scholar in Matsudaira-*han* (present Takamatsu city). With the Meiji restoration, his father became unemployed, ran an antique shop, and lived in poverty. Miki was a stubborn and wild boy. While at the prestigious Takamatsu middle school, one of his classmates Kuwajima Shukei pronounced "knew" as [knju:], without knowing "k" was silent. Their English teacher and classmates burst into laughter. However, Miki defended Kuwajima by saying "He is right. Since there is 'k' it should be pronounced [knju:]." They burst into laughter again. Kuwajima, who later became ambassador to Brazil, did not forget this event. Miki was then expelled from the school. One of his classmates ate in a noodle shop, and ran out without paying. While the shop owner was chasing this student, others also ran out without paying. The owner testified that one of them was called Miki (Miki denied that he was there) and he was expelled from the school with three other students.[14]

Miki was then enrolled in Doshisha middle school in Kyoto, where he exerted himself too much in study and *kendo* and became ill. After rehabilitation in his hometown, Miki planned to practice law and went to Tokyo to work at Hoshi Toru's law firm as an apprentice in 1901; however, Hoshi was assassinated the day before Miki was scheduled to begin working at his firm. At a loss, he entered Tokyo *Senmon Gakko* (Waseda University) and immersed himself in Okuma's anti-*hambatsu* politics. Miki went to Prime Minister Yamagata's (count and *genro*) residence every night and agitated against his cabinet in front of the entrance gate. The police tried to stop him but he continued, arguing that it was not illegal to speak in the public street. Although Yamagata's residence was huge (it has become a famous wedding reception hall, "Chinzanso"), he was able to hear Miki's agitation in his living room.[15]

Miki is indebted to Ichiro's family for his early career (before he passed the bar exam). Suzuki Kisaburo, Ichiro's brother-in-law, taught criminal law at Waseda and found Miki a job at the Bank of Japan (equivalent to the U.S. Federal Reserve Bank). However, Miki was fired nine months later because he made a public speech against the Katsura cabinet regarding the Portsmouth Peace Treaty (to end the Russo-Japanese War). Then, Suzuki asked Terada, Ichiro's father-in-law, to hire him at the HR secretariat. It is said that Suzuki, on his deathbed, asked Miki to take care of Ichiro. In this sense, the strong thread between Ichiro and Miki in the postwar era was already tied during Miki's Waseda years. While Ichiro became a leader of the *Seiyukai*, Miki became secretary general of the Constitutional Government Association at the age of 38 and worked for Prime Ministers Kato Takaaki and Hamaguchi Osachi.[16]

The Early Years in the HR

Ichiro was reelected to the HR in 1917. Ichiro was feisty and was nicknamed *yaji shogun* (a hooting general) at the HR. Following is an episode illustrative of young politician Ichiro. Suzuki Fujiya, a HR member from the Constitutional Government Association, used to live at Ichiro's house as one of Kazuo's apprentices. Suzuki grew resentful toward Ichiro, who was flattered by Kazuo's servants and apprentices. Becoming a HR member himself, Suzuki felt that he was finally on par with Ichiro. In February 1922, Suzuki attacked Ichiro by falsely accusing him of involvement in the Tokyo Gas scandal at the parliament. Suzuki even yelled at Ichiro, "*Sokono kozo* (a young brat over there)" during the session. When Ichiro found Suzuki in the smoking room during a break, Ichiro hit Suzuki, breaking his glasses and injuring his face. Suzuki accused Ichiro at the prosecutor's office and submitted a motion in the HR to reprimand Ichiro. However, HR speaker Oku Shigesaburo (*Seiyukai*) considered Suzuki also to blame for his abusive remarks and did not take up the motion. The prosecutor's office did not take the matter seriously either. Ono writes that Suzuki, who owed his political career to Ichiro's father— receiving everything from living and college expenses to campaign funds—was in no position to take such an attitude toward Ichiro. Through experiencing such incidents, Ichiro matured as a politician.[17]

Despite this episode, Ichiro was actually amiable and likable. A couple of prewar episodes illustrate this side of Ichiro. According to Ono, Ichiro's constituents asked him to oppose a plan to build Keio University Hospital in his district (merchants in the district feared that the hospital would be in the way of their businesses). Ichiro was obliged to do so. Kitazato Shibasaburo ("Japanese Pasteur") of Keio University was upset and said that he would mobilize the Japan Medical Association to defeat Ichiro in the next elections. Ono acted as an intermediary and asked Kitazato to meet Ichiro. At their meeting, Ichiro explained to Kitazato that politicians could not ignore constituents' requests and succeeded in removing Kitazato's anger. Kitazato told Ono that he liked Ichiro. On another occasion, a jobless Chinese was agitating against Ichiro as a greenhouse-grown elite who did not know people's suffering. Ono suggested to him that he go to see Ichiro, but he insisted that Ichiro come to see him. Ichiro did not mind going to see this Chinese man when the Chinese were considered the third-class citizens in Japan (other politicians would have simply ignored him). Ichiro was also generous and gave him a bottle of *sake*, sent by Chang Tso-lin, which Ichiro had kept for a special occasion. The Chinese was impressed with Ichiro's visit and became his fan. Ono writes that Ichiro's personal gift of making people like him was a real political asset. His amiable character—generous, open, and trusting—attracted people and made his opponents his friends. Ono adds that because of this nature, Ichiro was often deceived and manipulated.[18]

The Secretary-General of *Seiyukai*

Ichiro soon became a leading member of the *Seiyukai*. Hara Takashi was president of the *Seiyukai* when Ichiro became a HR member in 1915. Hara formed a cabinet in September 1918 but was assassinated in November 1921. Takahashi Korekiyo (*Seiyukai*, 1854–1936) succeeded Hara as party president and prime minister; however, he was unsuccessful at maintaining unity within the party and resigned in 1922. Three "transcendental cabinets"—of Kato Tomosaburo, Yamamoto Gombei, and Kiyoura Keigo—emerged between 1922 and 1924. Then, the *Seiyukai* split in January 1924 concerning the Kiyoura cabinet that was backed by the HP. Ichiro moved to its liberal break-away *Seiyuhonto* (the Orthodox *Seiyukai*), led by Tokonami Takejiro; however, he returned to the *Seiyukai* in February 1926, as Tokonami was conciliated by the Constitutional Government Association. Ichiro was also elected to be speaker of the Tokyo city assembly in December 1924 and was elected *Seiyukai*'s secretary general in March 1926. Ichiro was in his early forties and his political career was in full bloom. A year after the 1923 great Kanto earthquake, Ichiro rebuilt a house in the 1,400-*tsubo* (1.14 acre) lot in Otowa that he had inherited from Kazuo (Kazuo owned the 2,000-*tsubo* property but Hideo inherited 600-*tsubo*). The new two-story Western-style house is dubbed the "*Otowa goten* (palace)."[19]

The Constitutional Government Association vs. the *Seiyukai*

The Constitutional Government Association, the Orthodox *Seiyukai*, and the *Kakushin Kurabu* (Reform Club) launched *Dainiji goken undo* (the second movement to defend the constitution) in 1924, demanding universal (male) suffrage and reforms of the HP. As a result, Prime Minister Kiyoura resigned and Kato Takaaki (1860–1926, Constitutional Government Association) formed a three-party coalition in May 1924. The Kato coalition cabinet enacted in 1925 the universal suffrage law that gave suffrage to all males over 25 years old without property requirements. However, the enactment was a package deal with the enactment of the notorious *Chian ijiho* (Peace Preservation Law). Wakatsuki Reijiro (1866–1949, Constitutional Government Association) formed a cabinet after Kato's death (he had been sick) in 1926. Later, Miki stated that had Hara and Kato lived longer, Japan would not have been driven into total war. In turn, the *Seiyukai* brought in Tanaka Giichi (1863–1929, former army general from Choshu) as its president, incorporated the Reform Club in 1925, and overthrew the Wakatsuki cabinet. It was a custom of the imperial government since its inception that unless the army chose an army minister of its liking, a cabinet could not be formed (there was no such thing as civilian control). At this time of encroaching militarism, political parties needed increasing cooperation from the military to form a cabinet. With the formation of the Tanaka cabinet in April 1927, the *Seiyukai* took power back from the Constitutional Government Association.[20]

The Chief Secretary of the Tanaka Cabinet

Ichiro became *shokikancho* (chief secretary) of the Tanaka cabinet because he had seniority in the *Seiyukai*, having already won the HR election five times. However, he was not allowed to attend cabinet meetings. Ichiro had a reputation for being candid and open. Other cabinet members, dominated by the military, feared that Ichiro might leak military secrets to the press (the press liked Ichiro). Ichiro's brother-in-law, Suzuki Kisaburo (1867–1940, former attorney general), became interior minister. Suzuki was married to Kazuko, Kazuo's daughter and Ichiro's half sister. Kazuo was adopted by the Miura family, he married the family's daughter (a common practice), and Kazuko was born. Little is written about Kazuo's first marriage and the birth of his daughter Kazuko. Ichiro writes that Kazuko was his half sister and was brought up in his family for a certain period of time until she married Suzuki, who was the third son of Kawashima Tomiemon and was adopted by Suzuki Yoshitaka. Suzuki and Kazuko were married in April 1894. Ichiro called Suzuki *oyaji* (dad) because he was 16 years older than Ichiro. Suzuki became the *Seiyukai* president in May 1932 and supported Ichiro throughout his political career.[21]

Prime Minister Tanaka held the foreign ministerial post himself. He also created a new ministry, *Takumusho* (Ministry of Frontier Development), and he held this ministerial post too. Tanaka thereby supported the military's plan to advance into the Chinese continent in order to protect Japan's interests, obtained through victories in the Sino-Japanese War (1894) and the Russo-Japanese War (1904–1905): the so-called Tanaka's positive policy. Tanaka sympathized with the high echelons of the Kwantung Army (Japanese army in charge of Manchuria), which considered it necessary to create a buffer zone in Manchuria in order to repel communist Russia and to absorb Japan's increasing population. From 1927 to 1928 Tanaka sent troops three times against the Chiang Kaishek's Kuomintang (the Nationalist Party, KMT), which was trying to unify China. The Kwantung Army assisted an influential Manchurian warlord, Chang Tso-lin (1875–1928), who had helped the Japanese military during the Russo-Japanese War. However, Chang was no longer a yes man of the Kwantung Army and began obstructing the Manchurian Railroad, the army's lifeline. The Kwantung Army bombed Chang to death in June 1928. Ichiro was shocked to hear the news; it was a top military secret and even the cabinet chief secretary (Ichiro) was not informed (the truth was not disclosed until Japan's defeat in 1945). However, the rumor spread that it was Kwantung Army's sabotage, and Emperor Hirohito asked *genro* Saionji Kimmochi to investigate and find out the truth. Emperor Hirohito summoned Tanaka but Tanaka denied the rumor. In the end, the emperor became fed up with Tanaka and the Tanaka cabinet resigned *en masse* in July 1929. Consequently, the *Seiyukai* fell apart.[22]

Japan entered a turbulent and uncertain age. Communism began to rise with the creation of the Japan Communist Party (JCP), as a branch of the Comintern (Communist International or the Third International) in 1922. With the rise of the communists, the Tanaka cabinet revised the Peace Preservation Law (adding the death sentence for punishment) and arrested communists in March 1928. Ichiro was saddened by the sudden death of Akutagawa Ryunosuke (1892–1927), a writer from Ichiro's alma mater. This genius committed suicide because of a nervous breakdown and "ambiguous anxieties." The uncertainty of the state of the nation might partly account for his death.[23]

The Constitutional Democratic Government Party

After the breakdown of the Tanaka cabinet, the *Rikken Minseito*
(Constitutional Democratic Government Party created by the merger of
the Constitutional Government Association and the Orthodox *Seiyukai*
in July 1927) formed two cabinets: the Hamaguchi Osachi (1870–1931)
cabinet and the second Wakatsuki cabinet. However, they were short-
lived. Prime Minister Hamaguchi was shot by a right-wing nationalist in
1930 and died in 1931. Then, the military ignored the second Wakatsuki
cabinet's decision not to expand Japan's occupation of China. In order to
create a pretext to invade and annex Manchuria, the Kwantung Army
bombed the Manchurian Railroad in September 1931, alleging that
Chang Hsueh-liang, Chang Tso-lin's successor, was the culprit. The truth
about the "Manchurian Incident" was not disclosed until 1945.[24]

Without knowing the truth, the mass media and the general public
supported the military. The *Seiyukai*, as the opposition party, criticized the
Wakatsuki cabinet's Foreign Minister Shidehara Kijuro (1872–1951) as
"weak-kneed." Japan was isolated by the Western powers' protectionist
policies, restricting foreign access to their markets. Japan was also humili-
ated by the "Three-nation Intervention" (Russia, France, and Germany),
by which Japan was forced to concede the spoils of war of the Sino-
Japanese War. Given Japan's scarce natural resources, these Western
powers' moves accentuated the Japanese drive for territorial expansion. In
that setting, Ichiro joined the nationwide anti-Shidehara diplomacy
bandwagon. Ichiro was also influenced by his colleague, Mori Tsutomu
(1882–1932), who had worked at the Shanghai branch of the *Mitsui
Bussan* (a large general trading company). Mori had connections with the
military and supported Tanaka's "positive policy." Ichiro later severed
relations with Mori and declared his antimilitary stance when the military
waged total war on China. However, his anti-Shidehara bandwagon at this
time cost him dearly in the postwar period. In the aftermath of the
Manchurian Incident, the second Wakatsuki cabinet resigned *en masse* in
December 1931.[25]

The Education Minister of the Inukai Cabinet

Inukai, president of the *Seiyukai*, formed a new cabinet in December
1931. Ichiro became education minister of the Inukai cabinet. Suzuki
became justice minister. However, the Inukai cabinet was ill-fated. The
Kwantung Army declared the creation of *Manchukuo* in March 1932,
with P'u-yi (1905–1967), the last Ch'ing dynasty emperor, as its
puppet. The military's action triggered strong international protest,

especially from the United States. Inukai was hesitant to approve the *Manchukuo* and was shot in the prime minister's public residence by junior navy officers on May 15, 1932 (a complex internal feud within the military was behind the *coup d'état*); the so-called 5·15 incident. The impact of the 5·15 incident on politics was enormous. Party-based career politicians were silenced and the practice of the "transcendental cabinet" resumed, led by the military. The next party-based cabinet was not formed until 1946.[26]

The Saito Transcendental Cabinet

Prince Saionji, the only surviving *genro* and kingmaker, did not take the military seriously even if Inukai, his long-time political opponent and colleague, was assassinated in broad daylight. He likened the military to a group of children and thought that they would be happy if they were given a decoration. It was the nobility's naïveté. Saionji changed his initial and logical idea to make Suzuki succeed Inukai (interior minister, the post Suzuki had held, was equivalent to vice premier) and recommended Saito Makoto (1858–1936, navy general) as prime minister. However, even a navy general needed the cooperation of political parties in order to manage the parliament. Therefore, Saito appeased them and agreed to accept three ministers from the *Seiyukai* and two from the Constitutional Democratic Government Party. Ichiro was chosen as one of the three from the *Seiyukai*. Suzuki became president of the *Seiyukai*. It seems odd for Ichiro, being a genuine party politician, to join the Saito transcendental cabinet. Ichiro writes that he had no intention of becoming a member of the Saito cabinet; however, Ando Masazumi, his colleague at the *Seiyukai* and vice education minister at the Inukai cabinet, urged him to stay on as education minister for the sake of Japan's education. Ichiro responded that he would stay if Ando would stay as vice education minister. Ando refused the offer, saying that if he stayed with Ichiro it would be construed that he persuaded Ichiro to stay in order for him to stay in the cabinet. Ichiro writes that as his name implies (Masazumi means "genuine purity"), he was a man of integrity.[27]

Under these circumstances, Ichiro remained education minister in the Saito cabinet. It proved to be fatal to his postwar career. Soon, he met crises. Ichiro was frustrated because Suzuki did not become prime minister and became ill. The military controlled the cabinet. Ichiro had severed relations with Mori. He was the youngest member of the Saito cabinet and had no friends there. In September 1932, the Saito cabinet approved the *Manchukuo*. In protest to the Lytton investigation committee's report and the League of Nations resolution to disapprove the creation of *Manchukuo*, Japan withdrew from the League of Nations in March 1933. As Ichiro was isolated in the cabinet, Japan was isolated in the international community.[28]

The "Takigawa Incident"

Ichiro then encountered pressure from the HP to purge communist professors in national universities. In March 1933, the parliament passed a resolution to control educational circles. Along this line, the Interior Ministry banned two textbooks on criminal laws written by Takigawa Yukitoki of Kyoto Imperial University, as inappropriate to Japan's *kokutai* (national policy). The following month, the MOE requested that Konishi Shigenao, president of Kyoto University, dismiss Professor Takigawa. Konishi rejected the request. Pressured by the military and the nationalists in the parliament and the bureaucracy, Ichiro, in the capacity of education minister, suspended Takigawa from the university. This measure triggered a strong protest; all of the 39 faculty members of the Faculty of Law of Kyoto University resigned, students boycotted classes, and communist sympathizers organized a protest movement. This is the so-called Takigawa incident of April 1933. The MOE suppressed the movement by firing Konishi. In addition, during Ichiro's term as education minister, the Nagano-*ken* governor dismissed a number of elementary school teachers as having "dangerous thoughts." These events came to be construed as "evidence" of Ichiro being militarist and ultranationalist in 1946.[29]

The "Teijin Incident"

In February 1934, Ichiro was falsely implicated in the bribery of Teijin, a major synthetic silk manufacturer. A don of the right-wing, Hiranuma Kiichiro (1867–1952, later prime minister), was deputy speaker of the Privy Council and wanted to become its speaker. Emperor Hirohito was concerned with the shift to right-wing politics since the 5·15 incident and Saionji did not recommend Hiranuma to the speaker's post. As a reprisal, Hiranuma attempted to breakdown the incumbent Saito cabinet and made *Jiji Shimpo*, a newspaper run by his group, fabricate bribery scandals involving the financial circles that supported the Saito cabinet. As a result, Teijin's president and officials of the MOF were indicted; the so-called Teijin incident. This was a frame-up, motivated by Hiranuma's personal vendetta; however, their innocence was not proven until October 1937, and the Saito cabinet resigned *en masse* in July 1934.[30]

Ichiro was implicated but not indicted because he had already resigned the ministerial post in March 1934. Ichiro was tired of being a minister. He was interrogated both at the HP and the HR on the fabricated scandal. The military was running the cabinet. Ichiro could not see any significance in being a minister. He felt that he was made education minister of the Inukai cabinet merely because his parents were renowned educators. He was regarded as Suzuki's puppet in the Saito cabinet. He was even attacked by his colleagues in the *Seiyukai* because he had severed relations with his pro-military colleague Mori. Prime Minister Saito asked Ichiro not to answer questions in the HP regarding the Teijin incident because Ichiro had a reputation of making candid statements. Ichiro felt that if he did not answer questions, he would appear suspicious, and asked Saito to allow him to speak in the HP. This resulted in his famous *meikyo shisui* statement.[31]

The *meikyo shisui* Statement

In answering questions in the HP regarding the Teijin incident, Ichiro stated that he would deal with the incident with a mind of *meikyo shisui* (clear mirror, still water). The phrase is taken from the ancient Chinese writings of Confucius and Suntzu. The word *meikyo* (from Suntzu) means that only clear mirror can reflect the truth. The word *shisui* (from Confucius) means that only still water can reflect the truth. Together, the phrase refers to a wise man's completely unclouded state of mind. By this statement, Ichiro meant that he would make the matter as transparent as possible, and had no intention of resigning. However, newspapers reported that he was resigning. Tiring of attacks in the parliament and by the mass media and isolated in the cabinet, Ichiro resigned. The phrase *meikyo shisui* became famous in expressing the politician's *tabula rasa* (blank slate) state of mind and was frequently referred to for some time.[32]

The Acting President of the *Seiyukai*

Okada Keisuke (1868–1952), Saito's protégé in the navy, formed a cabinet in July 1934, succeeding the Saito cabinet. Saionji, the kingmaker, felt that if he recommended a party-based cabinet, the military would rebel, and tried to appease the military once again by bringing in an old navy admiral. The *Seiyukai* members were uneasy because they could not form a cabinet of their own again, despite the fact that they held an overwhelming majority of 300 seats in the HR. Then, Prime Minister Okada dissolved the HR in January 1936. The *Seiyukai* lost to the Constitutional Democratic Government Party in the HR general elections, with 171 and 205 seats respectively. Worse, Suzuki (who was sick) lost the election in spite of being the *Seiyukai* president. It was unprecedented for a party president to lose in a HR election. Ichiro won in Tokyo District 2 in third place; however he was discouraged by Suzuki's loss. Consequently, the *Seiyukai* did not elect a new president, and instead appointed four acting presidents, including Ichiro. The quadruple leadership soon split into two factions and Ichiro became one of the faction leaders. Ichiro reached an apex of leadership of one of the two major political parties, and was considered a likely prime minister for the future. However, the military, which already controlled politics, suppressed political parties. Ichiro was labeled as a "liberalist" and was estranged from the political circles as a *persona non grata*.[33]

The "2·26 Incident"

Saionji's idea to buy time by co-opting an old navy admiral (Okada) in the cabinet again turned out to be naive. On February 26, 1936, 1,400 soldiers, led by junior army officers, attacked the prime minister's official residence, the police headquarters, and elsewhere, and assassinated political leaders, including Finance Minister Takahashi Korekiyo (former prime minister), Interior Minister (*Naidaijin*) Saito Makoto (former prime minister), and Army General Watanabe Jutaro. This came to be known as the "2·26 incident." Prime Minister Okada managed to escape and his brother-in-law, Colonel Matsuo Denzo, was assassinated instead. In the aftermath of the incident the military's political power was strengthened under the pretext of disciplining the army. From this time, junior army officers in effect controlled the cabinet by screening candidates for all cabinet posts. The subsequent eight cabinets—of Hirota Koki (1878–1948, a politician from the right-wing political association *Genyosha*), Hayashi Senjuro (1876–1943, army general), the first of Prince Konoe Fumimaro (1891–1945), Hiranuma Kiichiro, Abe Nobuyuki (1875–1953, army officer), Yonai Mitsumasa (1880–1948, navy general), the second and third of Konoe—were formed in this way until the emergence of Tojo Hideki (1884–1948) in October 1941. These prime ministers were robots of the military. The Hirota cabinet launched a campaign to expel liberalists in March 1936, and concluded an anticommunist defense agreement with Germany in November 1936. Then, the first Konoe cabinet sanctioned the invasion of China and signed the tripartite defense agreement against communism with Germany and Italy in July 1937 (the formation of the Axis Alliance). Thus, Japan entered a dark age.[34]

The Resistance Against Fascism

After Ichiro resigned as education minister of the Saito cabinet in March 1934, he withdrew from the frontlines of politics and spent more time contemplating politics. Ichiro was filled with anger against right-wing politics and with despair for the failing political parties and constitutional democracy. Ichiro opposed the military by means of political writing. Ichiro wrote in a leading monthly magazine *Chuokoron* in January 1936, "I feel as if I am a bystander of politics. Liberalism and parliamentarianism are being pushed back by dictatorial forces. It might be advantageous for politicians to go along with the current trend, rather than challenging it; however, I cannot ingratiate myself with the military as others do. I believe in the philosophy that one should realize self-actualization according to self-imposed rules, rejecting intervention from others . . . It is very dangerous for the Japanese to try to imitate Hitler and Mussolini. It is human nature to seek freedom and it is a mistake to oppress it." This article was published before the 2·26 incident, and reads as though it had predicted the *coup d'état*.[35]

Ichiro later wrote, "I was certainly *mukomizu* (reckless) and *yoryo no warui* (unwise) to have written an anti-military article just before the 2·26 incident. A smarter person would have kept quiet and stayed low-key; however, I could not help speaking out. As a result, the military intensified its suppression of me. That's why I was still referred to as an *obotchan* (silver-spoon boy) even though I was over fifty years old." Yet, Ichiro was not ashamed of his naïveté. He wrote, "as my father taught me in deeds, I would rather be the deceived than be the deceiver. I would not like to be a petty machiavellian. I would like to adhere to the spirit of fair play even if I were criticized as naive and unworldly. Like my father, I would like to promote an ideal for the sake of the growth and welfare of the people."[36]

Ichiro also wrote in another monthly magazine *Kaizo* in December 1936, "the forces of fascism are suppressing party politics, limiting the power of the parliament, and rejecting the cabinet formed by political parties. All three cabinets—of Inukai, Saito, and Okada—were overthrown by such forces. The Inukai and Okada cabinets were obviously directly overthrown by fascists (bloody *coups d'état*), whereas the Saito cabinet was overthrown by the fascists' conspiracy. Although fascists might not have been directly involved in the overthrow of the Saito cabinet, it is a public knowledge that they were behind it. Nevertheless, party politics is not dead and will reemerge . . . Hitler and Mussolini are dictatorial utopians of the right wing, whereas Stalin is a dictatorial utopian of the left wing."[37]

It took enormous courage to write antimilitary articles at that time. Those who expressed opposition to the military were in danger of assassination. However, in May 1937, Ichiro again spoke out at the *Seiyukai's* general assembly and tried to impeach the incumbent Hayashi cabinet (February–June 1937). His speech stunned the political and military circles. Ichiro was further estranged from the political mainstream.[38]

The Trip to Europe

Ichiro and Kaoru went to Europe from July 1937 to February 1938. The official purpose was to attend the International Congress of Parliamentarians Alliance in Paris, as acting president of the *Seiyukai*. Ichiro writes that as he had little to do with politics those days, he thought it might be a good time to make a trip abroad. His father used to say that it was important to see the world if he wanted to become a politician, but he had never been able to go while his brother studied in Germany. The military invaded China just before his scheduled departure. Ichiro thought that he should cancel the trip; however, Prime Minister Konoe assured Ichiro that he would not expand the war effort and that it would end shortly. With Konoe's assurance, Ichiro went to Europe. The military in China ignored Konoe's instruction not to expand the war front. When Ichiro came back in February 1938, the military had already occupied Nanjing. During this trip, Ichiro saw Yoshida Shigeru (1878–1967), then ambassador to England, and they exchanged concerns over the Fascists' moves in Europe and in Asia. They did not know at the time that they would fight over the premier's post for years later.[39]

During this trip, Ichiro met British Prime Minister Neville Chamberlain. Ichiro could not meet his elder brother Austin, who had received the Nobel peace prize for his effort to conclude the Locarno Treaty of 1925 (the nonwar treaty within Europe), as he had died in March 1937. Chamberlain asked Ichiro about anti–Anglo-American rallies in Japan. Ichiro replied that only fools were joining such rallies. His comments were reported in Japan and it was feared that upon his return his landing at Yokohama port might be obstructed. In fact, a right-wing member thrust a threatening letter on Ichiro when he returned. At Konoe's request, Ichiro also met Adolf Hitler and Benito Mussolini, Japan's Axis Alliance partners. A journal of his trip to Europe became important material to purge Ichiro in 1946.[40]

The *Seiyukai* Split

Meanwhile, the intra-party fight within the *Seiyukai* escalated. The four acting presidents split into two factions. Three acting presidents— Nakajima Chikuhei (airplane manufacturer), Maeda Yonezo, and Shimada Toshio—formed a group with Nakajima as its president, in April 1939. In response, a month later, Ichiro formed a group with Kuhara Fusanosuke as its president. The pro-military Nakajima group called itself *kakushinha* (the progressive faction), whereas the liberal Kuhara group was called *seitoha* (the orthodox faction). A younger *Seiyukai* member Kono Ichiro (1898–1965, from Kanagawa-*ken*) felt that the pro-military Nakajima was undesirable as party president and sided with Ichiro. Kono, a graduate of Waseda University, worked as a reporter for the *Asahi Shimbun* for nine years and became a HR member in 1932. Since then, Kono became Ichiro's loyalist. Nakajima's progressive group took over the *Seiyukai* party headquarters in April 1939. In hindsight, Ichiro felt that the party's breakup was actually good as the intra-party feud had distracted him from fighting the real enemy: the military.[41]

Konoe's Imperial Rule Assistance Association

Japanese militarism escalated with the invasion of China in July 1937. The first Konoe cabinet enacted the National Mobilization Law in April 1938, whereby the government obtained the right to control the national economy and all aspects of peoples' lives without approval by the parliament. Ichiro and his colleagues vehemently opposed the bill, denouncing it as a precursor to total war. Nevertheless the bill was passed. The second Konoe cabinet signed the Tripartite Pact with Germany and Italy in September 1940, despite the fact that Germany had betrayed Japan (notwithstanding the anticommunist defense agreement between Germany and Japan of July 1936, Germany had concluded the Non-Aggression Pact with the Soviet Union in August 1939). The Konoe cabinet also disbanded all political parties, including both factions of the *Seiyukai*, in July 1940 and incorporated them into the new political organization called the *Taisei Yokusankai* (the Imperial Rule Assistance Association) in October 1940.[42]

The nature of the Imperial Rule Assistance Association, with Prime Minister Konoe as president, was ambiguous. Questioned by Ichiro and other politicians who were against the association in the HR, Konoe argued that the association was not a political party but merely a national organization to deal with the war situation. Interior Minister Hiranuma (former prime minister) insisted that it was an association to carry out public projects and that it would not engage in political activities. However, in reality it was created in order to suppress political parties that were opposing the military's policy. The Imperial Rule Assistance Association absorbed major political parties that had been disbanded earlier, along with other organizations such as unions and women's associations. The parliament in the absence of political parties lost its *raison d'être*.[43]

All the parliamentary members were forcibly incorporated into the Imperial Rule Assistance Association. In order to challenge the pro-Imperial Rule Assistance Association parliamentary alliance formed in September 1941, Ichiro formed an intra-HR political group called *Dokokai*, with 36 colleagues that November. The *Dokokai* included Ando Masazumi, Ozaki Yukio, and Katayama Tetsu (later president of the Japan Socialist Party, JSP). Ichiro's group was fighting against the Imperial Rule Assistance Association from within and the military intensified oppression of Ichiro's group.[44]

Tojo's Imperial Rule Assistance Political Association

In April 1942 the Tojo cabinet formed a political party called the *Yokusan Seijikai* (the Imperial Rule Assistance Political Association) and banned all other parties. The cabinet also enforced a recommendatory election system for the HR under the banner of the *yokusan senkyo* (the imperial rule assistance elections). The cabinet endorsed only candidates who were recommended by its own screening committee and severely suppressed voluntary candidates. Ichiro's group members ran without the committee's recommendation and suffered blatant campaign obstruction by the authorities. The HR elections resulted in an absolute majority for those with recommendation, with 381 seats, while those without recommendation obtained 85 seats, nine of whom were members of Ichiro's *Dokokai*. All the HR members elected were forcibly registered in the Imperial Rule Assistance Political Association, the only legal party.[45]

Ichiro writes of the unprecedented HR elections, "it was an outright government-run election and a dictatorship in the disguise of a parliamentary democracy." Ichiro was ordered to stop his public speeches and was taken to the police station. Several hundreds of Ichiro's supporters were detained for many days. The authorities repeatedly asked Ono, Ichiro's close aide, to run as an Imperial Rule Assistance Political Association's candidate and told him that if he severed relations with Ichiro he would be elected. Ono refused, ran as non-recommended, and lost the election. Ono's supporters blamed Ichiro for his loss; however Ono's mother said that she was glad that he lost the election. Had he betrayed Ichiro and run with the cabinet's recommendation, she would have disowned him. In retrospect, Ono feels that the loss actually saved his political career; he escaped the postwar purge because of this loss, and became an influential member of the Yoshida cabinet.[46]

The Imperial Rule Assistance Political Association reduced the parliament to a mere rubber-stamp legislature of the military-run cabinet. It also intensified suppression of freedom of speech. The *kanken* (government police) infiltrated the basement of Ichiro's house. They also confiscated his letters and other documents. For example, Ichiro's diary, published in 1999, covers the period February 1938 to June 1951; however, the entire 1943 and 1944 sections and the first half of the 1945 section are missing. During that period, Ichiro rarely attended the parliament. Instead, he spent most of his time at his summer house in Karuizawa (eastern part of Nagano-*ken*) and engaged in farming for food self-sufficiency.[47]

The Helpless Resistance Against the Tojo Cabinet

Nevertheless, Ichiro did not give up fighting against the Tojo cabinet. When the Tojo cabinet submitted a bill to revise the Wartime Special Criminal Law in February 1943, Ichiro returned to Tokyo and tried to defeat the bill; but his efforts were in vain. The legislation was aimed at strengthening Tojo's dictatorship by allowing the government police to punish those who might gravely affect its regime. Only Ichiro, Miki, and Nakano Seigo (1986–1943, the Constitutional Democratic Government Party, former *Asahi Shimbun* reporter) spoke out, and few dared to oppose the bill.[48]

Once again, in June 1943, Ichiro fought against the Tojo cabinet bills regarding an increase in the military budget, streamlining industry, and increasing food production, but in vain. These bills would essentially minimize the food rations and threaten the people with starvation. The Tojo cabinet tried to pass these bills in three days. The 82nd session of the parliament had only three days, and the deliberations at the HR had only one day. Ichiro hurried back to Tokyo and formed the so-called *Sansha rengo* (Tripartite Alliance) with Miki and Nakano to fight the bills. They were at the forefront of the resistance against the military and were ridiculed as the "Three Men of Non-recommendation" (because they were elected without the cabinet's recommendation). Ichiro eloquently argued in the HR that these bills would directly affect people's life and that it was necessary to deliberate on them judiciously and sufficiently. His speech was of a "prime minister's caliber" and had a great impact on the floor. The courage of the three politicians exhibited the essence of true statesmanship and impressed the HR members who were present. However, the officials refused to extend the session. Their high-handed attitude infuriated Nakano and he made a fiery speech, which triggered a shouting match. The three politicians argued well but they were helpless in front of the monolithic pro-Imperial Rule Assistance Political Association members. The parliament passed the bills in three days as scheduled.[49]

Ichiro was struck by the unusually strong manner in which Nakano made his speech. Nakano was from Fukuoka, Kyushu. Men from Kyushu had a reputation of being high-blooded, as in the case of Saigo Takamori. Even so, Ichiro felt that there was something unusual about Nakano's rage. It showed Nakano's determination and, in fact, it became his last speech. After the showdown in the HR the "Three Men of Non-recommendation" resigned the Imperial Rule Assistance Political Association. They were totally isolated; their colleagues in the HR did not even speak to them for fear of being associated with them. The government police were following them and it was dangerous for them to stay in Tokyo. Ichiro decided to return to Karuizawa and Miki to Shodoshima, a small island near his hometown in Kagawa-*ken*. However, Nakano remained in Tokyo and contemplated ways to overthrow the Tojo cabinet. Four months later, in October 1943, Nakano was arrested by the government police and committed suicide the day he was released. The cause of his death was called *funshi* (death by indignation). The general public was not informed of this intense resistance against the Tojo cabinet because of the strict censorship.[50]

The Pledge with Miki and Political Exile

In December 1943, Ichiro met Miki for the last time in the compound of the HP and talked about the future of Japan. Ichiro asked Miki, "Japan will be burnt down because of Konoe's *hiasobi* (fire play) with Tojo. Will you help me to clean up Japan afterwards?" He agreed and said, "You will be prime minister." I said to him, "Then, you will be speaker of the HR." After making this pledge, they left Tokyo. They did not see each other again until after the war. Since then, Ichiro lived in political exile in Karuizawa, farming on fine days and reading on rainy days. Ichiro took farming seriously. His only son, Iichiro, was conscripted into the navy and was at the war front. His son-in-law Furusawa Junichi (who was married to his eldest daughter, Yuriko) was also at the war front. Therefore, his grandchildren helped with the farming. His eldest grandson Koichi (13 years old) spent summer school recesses in Karuizawa. Koichi weeded all day and cried because the basket full of weeds on his back was heavy, but Ichiro and Kaoru did not help him. His granddaughters picked up cow's dung as fertilizer. Looking at these small grandchildren working hard at the farm, Ichiro told himself that he would reinstate constitutional democracy in Japan.[51]

Koichi writes, "there was no rice (Japanese staple) and no sugar. People turned grass yards into farms. Even *koyashi* (human waste fertilizer) was a precious commodity and people were not willing to give their *koyashi* to others. My grandfather's farm had 3,000 *tsubo* (2.45 acres). He worked at the farm from 9 o'clock in the morning until 6 or 7 o'clock in the evening every day. His farm was so well taken care of that it was called a 'model farm.'" Koichi recounts the first day when he accompanied Ichiro to his farm. "When I woke up, my grandfather had already finished breakfast and was reading Mencius. We spent all day weeding. It was hard work. All the dirt on my feet was hardened with sweat, but I felt good. This was my first day as a farmer. I did not think of the air raids (in Tokyo) at all. However, fertilizing was another thing. It was truly a gruesome task. We carried a bucket of *koyashi* 600 times to fertilize the entire field. I felt my grandfather could be anything he wanted to be."[52]

Coudenhove's Revolution for Fraternity

Among other books he read in Karuizawa, Ichiro was struck by *The Totalitarian State Against Man* by Count Richard Nicholas Coudenhove-Kalergi, an Austrian economist (1894–1972). Coudenhove is well known as a "father of the European Community." He was born in Tokyo as the second son of Count Heinrich Coudenhove-Kalergi, an Austro-Hungarian diplomat, and Aoyama Mitsuko, a commoner. Heinrich met Mitsuko when he was *charge d'affaires* in Tokyo. They were one of the first international couples joining a Westerner and a Japanese. They had four sons and three daughters. The Coudenhove family was originally Flemish. The founder of its Austrian branch settled in Bohemia centuries ago and his descendants were long prominent in the service of the House of Hapsburg. Richard Coudenhove proposed Pan-europeanism in 1923 at the age of 29. From his family background, "it is not surprising that his mind should show traces of Flemish persistence, Greek lucidity, and Japanese talent for synthetic expression." Nor is it surprising that he conceived of such an idea as Paneuropeanism. Coudenhove himself writes, "Born of a European father and a Japanese mother, I have been accustomed since my childhood to interest myself in questions which transcend all differences of civilization and race and men and humanity . . . As founder and leader of the movement which aims at a federation of the States of Europe I have had to grapple for a decade and a half with all the problems which are to-day uniting or dividing human beings."[53]

Coudenhove's writings are simple and yet profound. For instance, "Man is a creature of God. The State is a creature of man . . . Man is an end and not a means. The State is a means and not an end . . . " "The state is useful like a machine and dangerous like a machine: Man is a being, and the State is his tool—for good or for evil." Coudenhove was both anticommunist and antifascist, opposing totalitarianism both of the Left and the Right. He wrote, "for whatever the difference between bolshevism, national socialism, and fascism, they have a common meeting-ground in the cult and the omnipotence of the state on the one hand and the degradation and impotence of the individual on the other." Coudenhove also stated that there have been revolutions for freedom and equality but there has not been a revolution for fraternity. A revolution for fraternity is essential for democracy to succeed: freedom without fraternity would lead to autocracy, whereas equality without fraternity would lead to anarchism. Noting the struggle among liberalism, fascism, and communism, he proposed a revolution for fraternity to transcend the framework of the state.[54]

Coudenhove escaped Nazi prosecution and went to the United States where he taught economics at New York University. His Paneuropeanism culminated in the European Parliamentary Union in 1946 and the European Economic Community in 1958: prototypes of the European Union. He was nominated for the Nobel Peace Prize several times, but never won due to objections from the Soviet Union.[55]

Coudenhove's book strengthened Ichiro's convictions on freedom and democracy. By reading and contemplating on politics, Ichiro endured his "first age of winter" and engaged in further self-actualization. Little did he know that his "second age of winter" would follow in 1946. Meanwhile, the war situation had worsened. Germany betrayed Japan again. Japan had concluded a Neutrality Pact with the Soviet Union in April 1941, through the good offices of Germany. Japan did so in order to buy time to rectify its deteriorating relations with the United States regarding China; however, Germany invaded the Soviet Union in June 1941. In December 1941, Japan failed to ameliorate its relations with the United States and took a collision course with the United States. The rest is the history of the Pacific War. Japan's darkest age coincided with Ichiro's darkest age, both in his political career and personal life. Ichiro lost his mother in 1938, his brother-in-law Suzuki (his "dad") in 1940, and his brother Hideo in January 1946.[56]

Hideo was physically weak and died at the age of 61. Against Kazuo's wish, Hideo became a law professor in Tokyo Imperial University, received a degree of LL.D in 1917, and wrote a dozen books on *saikenho* (credit law). However, Hideo resigned from the university and opened a law firm in 1926, and became a HR member in 1932. Hideo then wrote, "Now I am happy and satisfied because I was able to follow my father's words to work for the real society. He was great. I regret that I could not reach my father's greatness." Hideo was also actively involved in the League of the Nations, as a member of the Japanese delegation, and also taught at Nihon University.[57]

Prince Konoe Fumimaro: A Tragic Young Premier

Ichiro had a surprise visitor in Karuizawa in April 1945. It was Prince Konoe. The Konoe family is the highest-ranked family among the five *Sekke* (families of regent); the descendants of the Fujiwara family that controlled the emperor during the Heian era. By comparison, Prince Saionji was from one of the nine lower-ranked *Seiga-ke*. Saionji was obligated to Konoe's father, Atsumaro, and wanted to repay his debt to Atsumaro by making his son prime minister. Therefore, he made Konoe his protégé. First, Saionji asked Konoe to become prime minister after the 2·26 incident in 1936. Konoe appeared to be a perfect choice because he was close to the emperor and had ties with the army, but Konoe declined. The old Saionji told the young Konoe that he could not make his weak physical condition an excuse and recommended Konoe to Emperor Hirohito. Notwithstanding Hirohito's solicitation, Konoe declined. After the two short Hirota and Hayashi cabinets,

Konoe finally accepted the post of prime minister in June 1937. He was 46 years old, and was referred to as *seinen saisho* (a young premier).[58]

Contrary to the expectations of the party politicians, Konoe proved to be too weak to resist the demands of the military and allowed the escalation of militarism. During his first cabinet, Konoe announced the creation of the "New Order in East Asia" and resigned in January 1939 after having failed to end the war with China. Konoe formed two more cabinets in July 1940 and June 1941. His second cabinet created the Imperial Rule Assistance Association. Ichiro had often expressed his opinions to Konoe, however, being preoccupied with creating his new regime Konoe did not listen to a *Seiyukai* "has-been." His third cabinet failed in the negotiations with the United States regarding China. Konoe's mentor, Saionji, being gravely concerned with Japan's future, died in November 1940. Konoe was isolated and came to see Ichiro only after Japan's defeat had become imminent.[59]

Under these circumstances, Ichiro was hesitant to talk to Konoe when the latter visited him in April 1945. Konoe apologized to Ichiro by saying that he had not intended to suppress the power of the parliament by the Imperial Rule Assistance Association, but that he was trying to suppress the power of the military. Ichiro put the past behind them for the sake of bringing peace to Japan. They discussed how to end the war and whether Japan should first negotiate with the Soviet Union or the United States. Konoe was willing to go to Moscow to negotiate with Joseph Stalin and to Washington to negotiate with Franklin D. Roosevelt. Ichiro was against negotiation with the Soviet Union. They had no idea that Stalin had already agreed with Roosevelt and Winston Churchill to join the war against Japan at the secret Yalta summit conference in February 1945. When Ichiro walked him to his villa, Konoe snuck into his house through a hole in the fence (Konoe had visited Ichiro in secret to deceive his guards). There was still snow on the ground in April. Ichiro felt there was something unusual about Konoe's sad demeanor when he saw him off. In December 1945, Konoe committed suicide just before his incarceration as a war criminal. Ichiro then recalled Konoe's sad appearance when they had met that spring.[60]

The war ended, and the time that Ichiro had anxiously waited for had finally come.

Chapter 4
The U.S. Occupation and Ichiro's Purge

Notwithstanding the fact that Ichiro fought against the Tojo cabinet and was oppressed by the military, the U.S. occupation authorities purged Ichiro as "militarist and ultranationalist" in May 1946. His purge was unexpected and was surrounded with mysteries. Based on a new study by a diplomatic historian and Ichiro's newly published diary and other materials, this chapter examines Ichiro's purge in-depth. By analyzing two American purge officers' views and several Japanese specialists' views, this chapter makes a comprehensive assessment of Ichiro's purge and sheds new light on the U.S. occupation policy in Japan.

The U.S. Occupation

With Emperor Hirohito's acceptance of the Potsdam Declaration in August 1945, Japan was occupied by U.S. military forces representing the Allied Powers. The General Headquarters (GHQ) of the Supreme Commander of the Allied Powers (SCAP), General Douglas MacArthur, was instituted in Tokyo in September. Soon, the title of the general, the SCAP, became the name for the entire command. Although the SCAP was charged with indirect control of Japan, in reality it enforced direct control. Prince Higashikuni Naruhiko formed the first postwar cabinet two days after Japan's surrender; however, the cabinet was forced to resign *en masse* in October 1945 as it tried to preserve the *ancien régime*. MacArthur then chose the old Shidehara Kijuro (four-time foreign minister in the prewar period) to be prime minister because he spoke English.[1]

The GHQ-SCAP undertook the ambitious mission of reinventing Japan. It set two goals for Japan: demilitarization and democratization. However, the GHQ was bitterly factionalized between the Government Section (the GS), led by Brigadier General Courtney Whitney, and the

Counterintelligence Section (referred to as the G2), led by Major General Charles A. Willoughby. Whitney was a conservative Republican and MacArthur's friend—one of the so-called Bataan Gang in the Philippines. Whitney was uninterested in the democratization of Japan. He delegated the day-to-day business of planning and execution to his deputy, Colonel Charles L. Kades, who refers to himself as a "thorough New Dealer." In turn, Willoughby—another of the Bataan Gang who joined MacArthur's Joint Chiefs of Staff—was skeptical of drastic democratization of Japan. With MacArthur's personal preference for drastic reforms of Japan (as he wanted to leave his name in history), the GS dominated the first phase of the occupation.[2]

According to Lieutenant Milton J. Esman, in charge of public administration in the GS, Colonel Kades engineered sweeping reforms in Japan in order to root out all the vestiges of wartime Japan. Esman states, "Colonel Kades was a man of tremendous talent, tremendous charm. I believe that he was able to persuade General Whitney to go along with the number of reforms that Whitney might be skeptical of because he was a profoundly conservative person." Kades collaborated with Japanese Communists, who had been in jail during the wartime and were free of responsibility for the war. The GHQ legalized the JCP that had earlier been banned. Kades spoke fondly of Nosaka Sanzo, a member of the JCP's central committee (later the committee chair), in an interview. Kades stated, "we were liberating the Japanese from the subjugation that they had been subjected to." GHQ's reforms were so drastic that an aspiring politician Nakasone Yasuhiro (prime minister 1982–1987) "could not understand the nature of MacArthur's occupation policy and felt that MacArthur was trying to destroy Japan by the poison of communism."[3]

One of the unfortunate aspects of the reforms was that few of the GHQ personnel, including MacArthur, had knowledge of or expertise on Japan. Kades admits his ignorance of Japan by saying, "I had *zero* knowledge of Japan. I had *no* knowledge of Japan other than what we gleaned from daily newspapers about Japan." The GHQ personnel were not experienced in administrative tasks either. According to Matsumoto Seichio, in his in-depth study of Japanese prime ministers, the Truman administration sent low-ranking New Dealers to Japan, in contrast to its enthusiasm to help rebuild Europe. These New Dealers saw Japan as a virgin land; they applied their utopian concepts to Japan without knowing its domestic situation, and conducted an experiment impossible in the United States. Japan's new course was in the hands of these personnel.[4]

In order to realize its two goals in Japan, the GHQ first undertook the revision of the constitution. MacArthur rejected the Shidehara cabinet's draft revision (the Matsumoto draft), which retained the sovereignty of the emperor, and ordered the GS to draft constitutional revisions in six days in February 1946 (the MacArthur draft). When Lieutenant Esman expressed his objection to the haste and secrecy of the process, he was suddenly given a five-day "rest and recreation" order. When he came back from a trip to Nikko, the draft was almost finished. None of the 24 authors of the MacArthur draft had any constitutional expertise. Navy Lieutenant Richard Poole was assigned to write the article concerning the status of the emperor only because his birthday fell on the same day as the emperor's. The MacArthur draft provided Article 1 to demote the emperor's status from a divinity to a mere "symbol of the state" and Article 9 to deprive Japan of any military capabilities. The GHQ considered retaining an imperial role to be necessary to control Japan effectively. Therefore, it allowed Japan to preserve the imperial system (albeit demoting the emperor's status) in exchange for Japan's acceptance of Article 9. The GHQ gave the Shidehara cabinet a 48-hour ultimatum to accept the MacArthur draft, with U.S. airplanes circling above the prime minister's residence. The Shidehara cabinet announced the draft as its own in order to preempt opposition in the Diet. The Diet adopted the MacArthur draft as Japan's new constitution; it was promulgated in November 1946 and went into force in May 1947. This is the origin of the so-called MacArthur constitution or peace constitution.[5]

The Creation of the Japan Liberal Party

Ichiro left Karuizawa and returned to Tokyo in August 1945. Since his house in Otowa was damaged by the massive air raids of March 1945, he stayed at Ishibashi Shojiro's (his son Iichiro's father-in-law and a founder of the Bridgestone Tire Company) house in Azabu. Ichiro's colleagues in the prewar *Seiyukai*, specifically the members of the *Dokokai*, who rebelled against Tojo's Imperial Rule Assistance Political Association, gathered at Ishibashi's residence and debated about the creation of a new party. They asked Ichiro to be the president of a new party but he was not enthusiastic at first. After having experienced the rise of militarism, Ichiro was resigned to the idea that a party based on creed, rather than greed, would not grow in Japan. He felt it would take time for Japan to recover. Only after persistent requests from his colleagues did he agree to be a party president. At first Ichiro tried to form a liberal progressive party that encompassed a wide range of groups from the prewar proletarian forces, intellectuals, to businessmen. Ichiro gave up the idea, realizing the unbridgeable difference between Ichiro's group and the Socialists. He then turned to Miki Bukichi, an influential member of the prewar *Minseito* (Democratic Government Party). Although Miki was an outsider to Ichiro's group, Miki eventually agreed to join Ichiro's new party. Miki did not forget his wartime pledge to Ichiro to help rebuild postwar Japan. The outcome was the creation of the *Nihon Jiyuto* (the Japan Liberal Party), in November 1945, with an antifascism and anti-controlled economy platform.[6]

With regard to fundraising, Ichiro did not have strong ties with the core of the financial circles, such as Mitsui and Mitsubishi. Ichiro writes, "I believed from the beginning (of my political career) that people in the financial circles should not interfere with politics." Therefore, Ishibashi, a new business entrepreneur, became Ichiro's primary financier. Ishibashi was taken by Ichiro's personality so much so that his daughter Yasuko married Ichiro's son. Ishibashi allowed Ichiro's family and his aides to stay in his house, which became the Japan Liberal Party's de facto office during its early stages. Even more, Ishibashi provided them with food that was in dire shortage. They survived by eating *satsumaimo* (sweet potatoes) because there was no rice. Ichiro writes, "the birth of the Japan Liberal Party is owed to Mr. Ishibashi and sweet potatoes." Similarly, Kodama Yoshio, the boss of a right-wing group, was taken by Ichiro's personality and financially helped to create the Japan Liberal Party. According to Kodama's autobiography, Ichiro frankly told Kodama that he could not accept his financial contribution if strings were attached. Kodama responded that he had no personal conditions and that his only request was to retain the imperial system. Ichiro agreed and accepted Kodama's contribution. Kodama was later indicted in the Lockheed bribery scandal in 1976.[7]

The Japan Liberal Party excluded those who had cooperated with the military regime and tried to infuse new life in Japanese politics. The 15 founding members included Ichiro, Miki, Kono Ichiro, Ashida Hitoshi (prime minister in 1948), Narahashi Wataru, and Ando Masazumi. Ono Bamboku, Ichiro's henchman from the Tokyo city assembly days, was not included because he had lost in the HR in the 1942 "Tojo elections." Ichiro became the first party president, Miki, *somu kaicho* (director general), and Kono, *kanjicho* (secretary general). Kono was 47 years old. Many members, including Ashida, who wanted to be secretary general, objected to Kono's appointment. They said that he was too young, but Miki supported Kono. Ichiro writes, "although Kono is the youngest in our group, he is already an influential politician. He is capable, sharp, and persistent. Few could win a debate with him. He also devoted to fundraising. Some people speak ill of him because they are jealous. Actually he is very soft and sentimental." Miki did not support Ashida because, while joining the Japan Liberal Party, he accepted the welfare minister's position in the Shidehara cabinet, which was a vestige of the wartime government. From this time forward, Miki and Kono became inseparable allies and the most loyal confidantes of Ichiro. In total, 43 incumbent HR members joined the Japan Liberal Party. Ichiro was 62 years old.[8]

In turn, former Democratic Government Party members, along with the pro-military Nakajima faction of the *Seiyukai*, created the *Nihon Shimpoto* (the Japan Progressive Party). A middle-of-the-roader was also formed under the name *Nihon Kyodoto* (the Japan Cooperative Party) that advocated cooperation between management and labor. On the Left, the JCP, which was banned in 1928, resumed its activities for the first time as a legal political party in October 1945. So did the JSP. The Soviet Union did not miss the opportunity and backed up the JCP. With the come-back of the JCP, along with the GHQ's radical reforms, the center of the spectrum of ideology shifted toward the Left. The Liberals and the Progressives were labeled conservative.[9]

When the 89th session of the Diet was convened in November 1945 with incumbent members from the 1942 elections, the Progressives had 274 members, whereas the Liberals had 43 members in the HR. With the passage of the revision of the election law in December 1945, the Shidehara cabinet announced HR elections the following month. Ichiro was confi-dent that the Liberals would win the first postwar HR general elections because his conservative rival Progressives largely consisted of those who had cooperated with the military regime, whereas the Liberals were composed of those who had resisted it. Ichiro campaigned extensively, traveling nationally from Tohoku in the north, to Kyushu in the south. The people were in a state of dire starvation at the end of 1945. Food, includ-ing rice, salt, sugar, and other basic materials, was rationed. Trains were overloaded with war veterans returning home, people who were going to rural areas for food hunting, and black market dealers. Even the president of the Japan Liberal Party could not get a seat on the train. At one time, Ichiro found himself being yelled at by a dealer when he was sleeping on a potato sac in an aisle. At another time, Ichiro found himself standing on the outside deck, covered with snow. Ichiro had never experienced such a difficult campaign. Ichiro developed pneumonia during his trip to Tohoku; however, he did not stop campaigning. Despite the doctor's order to stay in bed for three weeks, Ichiro went to Kyushu three days later.[10]

An episode in this period illustrates Ichiro's concern for public good and the strong will to fulfill it. Despite the massive starvation, the Truman administration decided not to aid Japan with food (it considered the problem to be Japan's responsibility [SWNCC150/4]). Notwithstanding the directive, Ichiro went to see General George C. Marshall, army chief of staff (who was acting for General Richard Sutherland during his leave), to request food imports from the United States at the GHQ on November 12, 1945. General Marshall was at first unwilling, saying that the American sentiments toward Japan were worsening. Nevertheless, Ichiro persisted and in the end Marshall agreed. Ichiro's conviction persuaded the U.S. authorities to change their policy.[11]

The "Purge from Public Office"

In January 1946, the GHQ abruptly directed the Shidehara cabinet to call off the HR general elections scheduled that month; instead they issued the purge directive. The GHQ instructed the Shidehara cabinet to set up a screening committee, so that unless one passed the screening, one could not obtain a position in the government. The GHQ screened several hundred thousand Japanese and purged between 210,000 and 260,000 military officers, politicians, businessmen, and other professionals, who were assumed to have played a part in the military regime, from public office (government and educational circles). The measure was officially entitled "The Removal and Exclusion of Undesirable Personnel from Public Office." It was one of the highest prerogatives of the GHQ. The GHQ identified seven categories of criteria: (A) those who were arrested as suspected war criminals unless released or acquitted; (B) all career officers of the Imperial Japanese Army and Navy; (C) leaders and influential members of ultranationalistic, terroristic, and secret patriotic societies; (D) leaders and influential members of the Imperial Rule Assistance Association and its affiliates; (E) officers of financial and development organizations who were involved in Japan's attempt to create the Greater East Asia Co-Prosperity Sphere; (F) governmental officials who had overseen the various outposts of the Japanese empire; and (G) a "catchall" criteria that encompassed any person who had played an active governmental part in Japan's acts of aggression or who had expressed himself as being an active exponent of military nationalism.[12]

According to Hans Baerwald, a purge officer in the GS, the seventh and final criterion was the most controversial. Criterion G gave a wide leeway of interpretation in determining purgees and "could be used to remove the political opponents of individuals empowered to administer the purge." According to Matsumoto, the GS used dubious information and did not scrutinize it well. Consequently, the purge was conducted in an arbitrary and random fashion and involved those who were merely "assumed" to have cooperated with the military. If one scrutinized the Japanese, most of them would be considered guilty because they were indoctrinated and mobilized to cooperate with the war effort in the name of the emperor. Worse, once a person was identified as a purgee, the person could not appeal. To appeal GHQ's decision was considered treason. Matsumoto writes, "while the purge liquidated militarists and ultranationalists and helped to raise an atmosphere of democratic revolution, it wrongly purged a number of experienced politicians."[13]

The GHQ tried to eradicate any pro-military elements from partaking in a new Diet and implemented the purge before the general elections, rescheduled for April 1946. All the HR candidates were doubly screened and scrutinized. The GHQ purged all the "recommended members" of the HR, who had run with the endorsement of the Tojo cabinet in 1942, in recourse to the catchall category G. Although he was a "non-recommended member," Ichiro was also screened. Ichiro writes in his diary that he reported to the GHQ on November 25, 1945, accompanying Ando, Yamamoto Katsuichi, and Matsumoto Takizo (as an interpreter). Three GHQ officers, including Major General P. E. Ruestow (of the GS), asked many questions. However, Ichiro was not purged.[14]

In total, as many as 83 percent of the incumbent HR members were purged and lost candidacy to run for the HR. All political parties were affected by the purge, with the exception of the JCP. The extremity of the purge was such that the GHQ even purged socialists. A prime example was the case of Ichikawa Fusae, the legendary female HR member, who had fought for women's rights throughout her life (1893–1981). This pioneering socialist was purged because she was a board member of an association attached to the Imperial Rule Assistance Association (all the labor and women's associations were forcibly incorporated into the Association in 1940). The damage to the party leadership was immeasurable. The purge affected 260 out of 274 Progressives in the HR, 30 out of 43 Liberals, 21 out of 23 Cooperatives, and 10 out of 17 Socialists. The Liberals were not as affected as the Progressives (all of its leaders were purged); however, the Liberals were reduced to only 13 in the HR. Also, the purge of Ichiro's aides, such as Ando, was a blow to Ichiro. As a result, each party recruited new candidates in a hurry and desperately campaigned for the elections.[15]

The Liberals' Victory and the Unexpected Purge

The first postwar HR general elections were held on April 10, 1946. Because of the sweeping purge that eradicated veteran politicians, the elections were chaotic and extremely competitive. Phenomenally, 2,770 candidates (out of which, 2,624 were first-time runners), from 363 political parties, fought for 466 seats. As expected, the Liberals won the elections, with 142 seats, while the Progressives came in second, with 94 seats, and the JSP was third, with 92 seats. The Cooperatives took 14 seats and the JCP took five seats. Although the Liberals did not obtain an absolute majority, it defeated the Progressives by a wide margin. Therefore, Ichiro was expected to become prime minister and succeed the Shidehara cabinet. Nevertheless, Emperor Hirohito's *taimei koka* (imperial approval) to appoint Ichiro as prime minister did not come through immediately after the elections. The new constitution did not come into force until May 1947 and, according to the old Meiji constitution, a cabinet could not be reshuffled unless the incumbent prime minister resigned *en masse* and recommended his successor to the emperor.[16]

Ichiro received conflicting speculations. According to an *Asahi Shimbun* reporter, once Ichiro became prime minister, it would be difficult for the GHQ to purge him; therefore, he should keep quiet and not offend the GHQ until he assumed the premiership. In contrast, Shirasu Jiro, deputy director of the Central Liaison Office (between the GHQ and the Japanese government) and an aide to Foreign Minister Yoshida of the Shidehara cabinet, gathered that if Ichiro became prime minister he would be purged. Instead, if Ichiro gave up the premier's post and became a state minister in the prospective second Shidehara cabinet, he would not be purged. His confidantes asked Ichiro what he would do. Ichiro said that he would follow the verdict of the people and that he could not become a minister in someone else's cabinet for the sake of escaping the purge. In hindsight, Shirasu was right, although it is difficult to speculate whether the GHQ would have still tried to purge Ichiro after he had assumed the premiership. Shirasu's information came from General Willoughby of the G2 and Colonel H.I.T. Creswell also of the G2, who sensed that the GS was going to purge Ichiro and warned Shirasu and Yoshida. Ichiro did not know at the time that his unusual determination would oblige him to live more than five years under purge.[17]

Prime Minister Shidehara finally recommended Ichiro to the emperor on May 3 and Ichiro was going to announce his cabinet the following day, upon the receipt of the imperial approval. However, on the morning of May 4, Ichiro received a letter from the GHQ instead. The contents of the letter were ambiguous, saying that Ichiro would be "checked" from attending the Diet. It was the directive of his purge. It meant that Ichiro was deprived of his qualification as a HR member and therefore of his competency to form a cabinet. The first postwar democratic cabinet chosen by the people was aborted a few hours before its formation.[18]

Ichiro notes the crucial two days in his diary as follows:

May 3   Prime Minister Shidehara visited the imperial palace to recommend me as his successor. Shidehara also reported that he would inquire this decision with the GHQ. The press installed dozens of phone lines at Ishibashi's residence in anticipation of the imperial approval.

May 4   Visited Mr Minobe (Tatsukichi, 1873–1948 constitutional scholar; to ask him to join the cabinet). Had decided on the roster of the cabinet. When I returned home, I was told of a sudden change in the situation. My purge became official around 11 a.m. The contents of the directive were outrageous. I was expelled from the Diet that I had served in for more than 30 years and missed forming a cabinet, without given a chance to defend myself. Attended the party's HR-member meeting after 5 p.m. I did not know what to say in front of crying party members.[19]

Japan Liberal Party members could not understand why Ichiro was identified as "militarist and ultranationalist" and purged. Ichiro writes that the official of the MOFA delivered the GHQ's directive in such a hurry that it was not translated into Japanese. It was not even signed by General MacArthur. The reporters, who had been standing by for the imperial approval, were astounded. In addition, more than a dozen foreign reporters demanded Ichiro's comments. Ichiro was at a loss because he did not have the Japanese translation of the directive and also had to respond to them in English. Ichiro wrote, "Kono was no help when it comes to English. The news of my purge caused an uproar bigger than (the supposed) formation of my cabinet." The fact that the directive was not signed by MacArthur indicates that the GHQ issued the order in a great hurry so that it would appear to have preceded the Shidehara's recommendation to the emperor (details later).[20]

The way Kaoru reacted at that time impressed Miki. When the GHQ directive was delivered to Ishibashi's house, Miki saw it first. Ichiro's aides were in a festive mood, preparing for the announcement of his cabinet. Miki said that it was a dirty trick. Suddenly, the atmosphere became that of a wake. However, Kaoru appeared unaffected and quietly began preparations for withdrawal of Ichiro's cabinet formation.

Miki felt that she might have been stoic as she had already gone through hardships before (such as the military's oppression) or that she was trying to emulate Haruko who would have acted in the same way. Miki was awestruck by her stately manner and felt that he must make Ichiro prime minister on behalf of this great lady, as well.[21]

The GHQ issued Ichiro a special memorandum, entitled "Removal and Exclusion of Diet Member," SCAPIN (SCAP Instruction) 919, May 3, 1946 (see appendix). Hence, Ichiro's purge was referred to as the "special memorandum case" and it was the first of such cases. Because of the unexpectedness (he was an anti-militarist and was not purged in January 1946), the enormous impact (he was prime minister-to-be), and the abruptness (the day of his cabinet formation), Ichiro's purge shook Japan. Ichiro had just come out of a long internal exile and was forced to go back to an even longer one. Ichiro's purge is surrounded by mysteries. Why did the GHQ purge Ichiro, who was stigmatized as a liberalist by the military? Why did it take almost a month after the HR elections for Shidehara to recommend Ichiro to the Emperor? Why did the GHQ issue the special memorandum to purge Ichiro? In order to unravel the mystery, it is necessary to examine SCAPIN 919.

SCAPIN 919

Ichiro was chief secretary of the Tanaka cabinet that revised the Peace Preservation Law in 1928 in order to control Communist activities. The SCAPIN 919 Section a. states that since Ichiro was the cabinet's chief secretary, he "necessarily shares responsibility" for the legislation. It does not mention the fact that the Tanaka cabinet was controlled by the military to the extent that Ichiro was not permitted to attend cabinet meetings. Similarly, the SCAPIN 919 Section b. holds Ichiro responsible for suppression of Communist teachers, including the "Takigawa incident" (see chapter 3), because it took place when he was education minister in the Saito cabinet. It does not mention the fact that Ichiro was isolated in the military-led cabinet and that he resigned the ministerial post spontaneously. Harry Emerson Wildes, an officer of the GS, argues that the charge against Ichiro concerning the Takigawa incident "may have been unjust" because Ichiro "had been called upon to fire Takigawa but had demurred, and eventually signed the order only under instructions from the Cabinet." Wildes also argues that the incident did not "give momentum to the spiritual mobilization of Japan . . . into war" as alleged in the directive. A massive suppression of Communism began in 1931 prior to Ichiro's assumption of the post of education minister. Wildes writes, "It was neither begun nor notably furthered by Hatoyama." Wildes concludes, "[r]eliance upon the incident to purge Hatoyama suggested that the case against him was weak."[22]

In turn, the SCAPIN 919 Section c. accuses Ichiro of endorsing Hitlerite totalitarian mobilization of labor. It refers to passages from the book, *Sekai no kao* (Face of the world). The book was based on a journal of Ichiro's trip to Europe. However, Baerwald, a purge officer, states that "[h]is admiration for Hitler's labor policy is really irrelevant" to the purge criteria and that "the case against Hatoyama leaves much to be desired." The same holds true for the SCAPIN 919 Section d., which refers to passages from the same book. It is important that even if Baerwald took the book at its face value, he thinks that the passage of the book is irrelevant to the purge criteria (more on the book later).[23]

Finally, the SCAPIN 919 Section e. claims that Ichiro "has posed as an anti-militarist." In reality, it was hardly possible to pose as an anti-militarist. The military regime's control was such that once one uttered an anti-militarist remark, one had an immediate reaction. In that situation, one could not "pose" as an anti-militarist. It was easier and safer to pose as a pro-militarist, as most of Ichiro's colleagues in the HR did. Ichiro's campaign address for the 1942 elections, quoted as the evidence of Ichiro's support for the military, was written under the strict censorship of the Tojo cabinet (more on this later).[24]

In summary, that Ichiro was part of the two military-run cabinets that suppressed communism during the late 1920s and early 1930s, as well as his writings in the late 1930s and early 1940s when strict censorship was enforced, constituted the official reasons for his purge. Two GS officers (Baerwald and Wildes) published their views that the evidence against Ichiro was either irrelevant or weak. The real reason for his purge lay somewhere else.

The Anti-Atomic Bombing Statement

In the *Asahi Shimbun* article entitled "*Shinto kessei no koso*" ("a plan to form a new party," actually written by its reporter Wakamiya Shotaro) dated September 15, 1945, Ichiro criticized the use of atomic bombs on Hiroshima and Nagasaki as genocide and an act of war crime equivalent to the use of gas chambers. Ichiro argued that the Americans should be aware of their responsibility and help rebuild Japan. It took enormous courage for a Japanese to publicly criticize the United States in general, and its action to end the war with Japan in particular. Not surprisingly, his article infuriated the GHQ. The GHQ summoned Hosokawa

Takamoto, the editor-in-chief of the *Asahi Shimbun*, and scolded him for denouncing the United States. The newspaper was banned for two days. This incident led to the GHQ's controversial censorship of the Japanese media.[25]

This article offended the conservative personnel of the GHQ, who had favorable views of Ichiro. However, they still did not consider Ichiro as *persona non grata* for a new democratic Japan. The stronger impetus for Ichiro's purge came from the leftist faction within the GHQ. The New Dealers in the GS, run by its deputy, Colonel Kades, considered most of the noncommunist politicians war criminals. *The Chicago Sun* reporter Mark Gayn writes, "the GHQ knew that the top level of the JSP, with a few exceptions, is loaded with war criminals—not with conservative nationalists like Yoshida and Hatoyama—but with intelligent and aggressive National Socialists, who before and during the war were on intimate terms with the young army fanatics." Shirasu, the deputy director of the Central Liaison Office, heard the rumor that the leftist faction of the GS was trying to purge Ichiro and directed the Shidehara cabinet to review his case. He went to the conservative G2 to protest the GS's move. In January 1946 the Shidehara cabinet cleared Ichiro's case and the GS failed to purge Ichiro.[26]

The Proposal for an Anticommunist League

Ichiro then infuriated the leftists within the GHQ, who already considered Ichiro a war criminal. Japan was stricken by hunger and poverty and Ichiro saw the condition as a seed for the rise of communism. Ichiro felt that it would not be so difficult for communists to start a revolution in Japan because few Japanese youth would confront it. This observation led him to a conviction that Japan must be equipped with its own defense capability; not a big one, but capability sufficient to deter a Communist takeover. Ichiro advocated anticommunism and the need for self-defense forces in his nationwide campaigns for the HR elections. Ichiro's conviction culminated in a proposal for the creation of an anticommunism league on February 22, 1946. He argued that Japan was in danger of falling to the ultraleft-wing forces just after it was controlled by the ultraright-wing fascism; the Japanese should support moderate and conservative democratic parties in order to build a truly democratic society. His proposal infuriated the Soviet Union. Ichiro heard that Moscow Broadcasting criticized his statement and that the Soviet representative to the Allied Council for Japan vehemently protested it. Ichiro writes, "this proposal offended the JCP, backed by the Soviet Union, and the leftist group at the GHQ, and thereby created a momentum for my purge."[27]

Ichiro made this bold proposal because he believed that the consolidation of power of the conservatives was the only way to offset the damage caused by the massive purge of politicians. Yoshida, who became prime minister because of Ichiro's purge, cynically stated that he might be partly to blame for Ichiro's purge because he had encouraged Ichiro to propose the anticommunist league.[28]

While the GS's New Dealers, infuriated by Ichiro's anticommunist statement, decided to take up Ichiro's case again, some politicians took advantage of the situation for their own political gain. Prime Minister Shidehara was one of them.

Prime Minister Shidehara

Hearing the rumor that the GHQ might purge Ichiro, Prime Minister Shidehara tried to stay in power despite the Liberals' victory in the HR elections. Shidehara hesitated to recommend Ichiro to Emperor Hirohito and instead attempted to form his second cabinet with the Progressives. Shidehara's hesitation might be also attributable to Ichiro's behavior in the prewar period. Shidehara was bitter about Ichiro's anti-Shidehara diplomacy bandwagon. Hoshijima Niro, a Japan Liberal Party member, thinks that "it was Shidehara who did him in." Hoshijima states, "Not only did they differ on policy, but, [they] did not get along well at all . . . There was a kind of negative side to Shidehara, and he probably did not feel happy about Hatoyama's running." While this might not be a decisive reason for Ichiro's purge, it explains Shidehara's hesitation.[29]

Just after the HR elections, Shidehara summoned Ichiro to the prime minister's residence. Ichiro did not understand Shidehara's intention. Matsuno Tsuruhei and Ichiro's other aides, suggested that he go. Only Kono did not. Ichiro went to see Shidehara. At the meeting, Shidehara told Ichiro that he would not give power to Ichiro. Shidehara even tried to conciliate Ichiro by inviting him to join his new cabinet. Ichiro later regretted this meeting as the "biggest mistake in my life." Shidehara's ultimatum enabled him to prolong his cabinet and thereby bought time for the GHQ to prepare for Ichiro's purge. Had Shidehara resigned earlier, Ichiro might not have been purged. After the assumption of power, it would have been difficult for the GHQ to purge Ichiro, a legitimate prime minister of Japan, chosen by the people and sanctioned by the emperor. Ichiro writes, "I should not have gone to see Shidehara because I had won the HR elections. Shidehara had no power to tell me what to do. To make such a mistake meant that I was not ready to be prime minister and the heavens gave me a lesson to learn."[30]

The Progressives took advantage of Ichiro's predicament and co-opted Shidehara as its president. Shidehara tried to form a cabinet by a coalition with the JSP and independents. In response, Miki and Kono organized a four-party coalition to overthrow the Shidehara cabinet with the Cooperatives, the JSP (the faction that turned down Shidehara's call), and the JCP. They voted for a resolution to call for the immediate resignation of the Shidehara cabinet. The general public was in favor of a prospective Hatoyama cabinet as they expected from it a new Japan. Overwhelmed by the anti-Shidehara four-party coalition, encompassing the whole range of the spectrum of ideology, and the public support for it, the GHQ suggested that Shidehara resign. The Shidehara cabinet finally resigned on April 22, 1946. However, it was too late.[31]

Interior Minister Mitsuchi

Interior Minister Mitsuchi Chuzo might be partly accountable for Ichiro's purge. Mitsuchi was twelve years older than Ichiro and was also a member of the *Seiyukai*. Ichiro writes that one of the primary reasons for his purge was neglect on the part of the Shidehara cabinet. The Shidehara cabinet did not take any political action vis-à-vis the GHQ despite the latter's request to reexamine his case in April 1946. Later Ichiro found out that the Interior Ministry had in fact issued a document stating that there was no reason to purge Ichiro. Ichiro also found that the MOE had issued a document, which stated that the dismissal of Professor Takigawa was reasonable at that time and therefore did not constitute a reason for Ichiro's purge. However, Mitsuchi allegedly kept the two documents in his desk and did not submit them to the GHQ. In the world of politics, Ichiro writes, people do such unconscionable things. Mitsuchi did so because he wanted to be prime minister. He allegedly shouted at Shidehara to resign right away and demanded that he be his successor. However, Mitsuchi's dream was not realized as he was also purged.[32]

Chief Cabinet Secretary Narahashi

Narahashi Wataru, chief secretary of the Shidehara cabinet, also tried to undermine Ichiro. While Narahashi was one of the founding members of the Japan Liberal Party, without hesitation he accepted the post of director general of the law enforcement bureau of the Shidehara cabinet. He later became the cabinet chief secretary. Narahashi believed that if Ichiro were purged, it would be possible to form the second Shidehara cabinet with a coalition of the Liberals and the Progressives. Thus, Narahashi, along with members of the JCP, allegedly provided materials to facilitate Ichiro's purge with the GHQ's Civil Information and Education (CIE) Section. It was not difficult to find fault with wartime Diet members and purge them; all of them had been members of the Imperial Rule Assistance Political Association. Narahashi even made up a rumor that the Truman administration, rather than the GHQ, directly ordered the purge of Ichiro.[33]

Ichiro's purge not only involved a power struggle among the Japanese politicians but also involved a factional feud within the GHQ, entangled with ideological rivalry. Baerwald writes in 2002 that Willoughby and Whitney were engaged in a feud over basic occupation policy and which of them would become MacArthur's closest advisor on Japanese politics. With the choice of the GS as a primary funnel for daily contacts between the GHQ and the Japanese government, Willoughby, out of jealousy, spread rumors that the GS was a haven for "New Dealers," "pinkos," and other radicals. Meanwhile, an American, who was in close contact with Colonel Kades of the GS, was building up the case against Ichiro. The American was Mark Gayn of *The Chicago Sun*, a "sympathetic left-wing American journalist" in the words of John Dower.[34]

Mark Gayn

Gayn orchestrated a fatal "prelude" to Ichiro's purge. On April 4, 1946, several days before the HR elections, foreign correspondents organized a dinner meeting at the Press Club with four party representatives: Ichiro, Nagai Kan of the Japan Progressive Party, Matsuoka Komakichi of the JSP, and Nosaka Sanzo of the JCP. First, they were asked to make a brief statement of their party platforms. At that time, Ichiro naïvely said that he thought that Karl Marx was a greater threat than William Pitt. Then, Ichiro was singled out for the rest of the meeting and was bombarded with questions for hours. Ichiro writes, "I was invited by Burton Crane of *The New York Times* to the Press Club. I accepted the invitation without much thought because Crane had written favorably of me. When I arrived there, there was a big commotion. Crane, the host, was trying to defend me but they told him to shut up. They already had an English translation of my book *Sekai no kao* (Face of the world) and attacked me on its content, picking out the passages that supported Japan's militarism. I did not remember the content of the book well and explained that the overall tone of the book was in defense of democracy; however, they did not listen. They finished the meeting by passing a resolution in favor of my purge. American leftist correspondents, such as Mark Gayn and Bill Costello of CBS, planned my purge and held the press conference. In fact, I was purged one month later. Gayn himself admits this in his *Nippon nikki* (Japan Diary)."[35]

Gayn's *Japan Diary* states, "Before dinner I had organized a political probe. The suspect was Hatoyama. It may be that correspondents have no business to engage in politics. But I thought this was a legitimate undertaking in every possible way. As an American I wanted to help rid Japan of a ranking war criminal—a man made doubly dangerous by the fact that he is scheduled to be the next prime minister. As a newspaperman, I looked forward to a front-page story." Gayn obtained the translation of *Sekai no kao* from GHQ officers. The book contained passages that "did not sound well from the lips of a prospective premier in a democratic Japan." The GHQ officers had tried in vain to purge Ichiro by using the book and passed the book on to Gayn. Gayn "tore the book into half a dozen sections and farmed them out to interested correspondents, Chinese, English, and American." Reporters questioned Ichiro, quoting passages of the book, such as a praise of the efficiency of Nazi system and a remark on the resemblance between German Nazism and Japanese *bushido* (way of samurai). "As the probes closed in, Hatoyama became confused . . . [and] became a rattled old man, unable to think fast enough to cope with the hunters. Hatoyama answered that he could not remember anything but later said that he had lied in his book. Reporters nailed him down when they asked if he would confess in front of the people that he had lied eight years ago and whether he could assure that he would not lie again." More than five hours had passed when they finished questioning Ichiro. Gayn himself describes the probe as a "savage" performance.[36]

What had promised to be a happy dinner turned out to be a probe to accuse Ichiro of being a fascist. Gayn finishes that day's diary by saying he was looking forward to the reactions of GHQ and the Japanese government, that had cleared Ichiro, and to tomorrow's news headlines. The following day, the U.S. military gazette *Stars and Stripes* said that "reporters grilled former pro-Nazi candidate." It also said that Ichiro had failed to report the book to the Japanese government's screening committee. The GS cited the omission of the book as a "grave violation" of the SCAPIN 550 directive (to report all past records).

According to Wildes, "[f]ollowing publication of reports of this grilling—an ordeal which Occupation chiefs sedulously avoided—Whitney changed suddenly to implacable opposition" and demanded that the Japanese government reexamine Ichiro's record. The government replied that reexamination was unnecessary since everything, including *Face of the world*, had been investigated and found innocuous. Whitney reiterated his demand and stated, "the general [MacArthur] would not intervene unless or until the Japanese government takes necessary measures." The government correctly interpreted it as an order for Ichiro's purge.[37]

Gayn writes on April 23, 1946 (the day after Shidehara's resignation) that when he and Robert Cochrane (*The Baltimore Sun*) saw Ichiro the previous night, he "beamed at us as if we were his warmest friends, and said he was now preparing the roster of a new cabinet." Gayn already knew by that time that Ichiro would be purged. Gayn did not forget to push the case against Ichiro at the GHQ after the press conference and writes, "Hatoyama might be disappointed as the GHQ has not gotten over the press disclosures of his past." On May 3 (correctly, May 4) 1946, Gayn writes, "A few hours before Hatoyama was to be officially designated by the Emperor as the new premier, General MacArthur ordered the Japanese government to remove him from the Diet. The special memorandum listed Hatoyama's sins as a war criminal—including the evidence brought out at that tumultuous meeting at the Press Club."[38]

To recapitulate, the Shidehara cabinet had cleared Ichiro and the GS's initial attempt to purge Ichiro had failed. Ichiro's Japan Liberal Party won the HR elections and Prime Minister Shidehara recommended Ichiro to the emperor as his successor. Therefore, had Gayn not picked up Ichiro's case, Ichiro would not have been purged. The question is then why did Gayn target Ichiro.

Gayn identifies Ichiro as a "ranking war criminal." Gayn even likens Ichiro to Tojo and describes him as "on a smaller scale . . . equally culpable[.]" Gayn denounces the Japan Liberal Party's platform as "rest[ing] solidly on two planks—war on communism and support of the Emperor." He describes the party as being "as illiberal as the Progressives are unprogressive. The only difference between the two is that the Liberals won the Diet seats without an official endorsement from Tojo's iniquitous Imperial Rule Assistance [Political] Association." Gayn overlooks the crucial difference between running with the endorsement of the Tojo cabinet and running without it for the 1942 HR elections. In addition, the Liberals and the Progressives have their origin in the Meiji period and their position in the spectrum of ideology must be judged in a historical context. Gayn himself recognized this point when he interviewed 87-year-old Ozaki Yukio on March 21, 1946 and found out that he was anachronistic. Gayn writes, "Once again I discovered that I, and many of my friends, had used a wrong set of yardsticks." Later when Gayn invited Ichiro to his house on December 9, 1946, Ichiro mentioned a book Crane (*The New York Times*) had given him; what he called "Burritt's *One Big Grobe*." Gayn writes, "The book that delighted Hatoyama and Yoshida was William Bullitt's [first American ambassador to the Soviet Union] *One Big Globe* . . . The book shows that communism and Russia are the common enemy of every democratic country."[39]

What is clear from these accounts is that Gayn targeted Ichiro because he was openly anti-communist. Therefore, Gayn ignored Ichiro's resistance to Konoe's Imperial Rule Assistance Association and Tojo's Imperial Rule Assistance Political Association. Even some of the GHQ officers felt that Gayn's persistence to purge Ichiro was extreme. On April 24, 1946, Gayn writes that he and Cochrane visited Colonel Creswell, chief of the Counterintelligence Corps, "to find out what had gone wrong with the screening of the war criminals who got into the Diet, including Hatoyama." Colonel Creswell told them that the records of those elected to the Diet were of no concern to the American press. Creswell further said, "You boys go around with a chip on your shoulder. All of you come down here and say Hatoyama is this, Hatoyama is that. Each one of you has a pet hate, but all of you together are ganging up on Hatoyama. I'll give you an example of the harm you're doing." Creswell referred to "Tokyo Rose" whom GHQ detained for months but could not find any evidence against. Creswell said that the GHQ nevertheless would not dare release her because "we know that you boys will promptly jump on our necks."[40]

In brief, Gayn targeted Ichiro because he was anti-Communist and prime minister-to-be. He also wanted a "scoop." Gayn was blacklisted as one of the "Dangerous Correspondents" by the Central Liaison Office and was sent home on December 21, 1946.[41]

The Publication of *Face of the World*

Now, it became clear who planned Ichiro's purge and why. However, a question remains: Why would Ichiro, who had denounced Hitler and Mussolini publicly in the article "*Jiyushugisha no techo*" ("a note of a liberalist") in January 1936, praise fascist leaders in *Sekai no kao* (Face of the world)? The answer is simple: Ichiro did not write the book. The book was actually written by Yamaura Kanichi, former reporter of *Jiji Shimpo*. Few English literature mentions this fact. Yamaura was Ichiro's speech writer and, among other things, wrote his campaign address for the 1942 "Tojo elections." Ichiro did not mention Yamaura's name at the press in order to protect him (the purge extended to the mass media circles). Ichiro states in his autobiography (1951) that he wrote his impressions of his trip in his diary as candidly as he had written the article in January 1936. For instance, Ichiro wrote in the diary that while there might be some merits of the Nazi system (such as the autobahn highways and hard-working people), he was not impressed with the totalitarian system even though he was bombarded with massive propaganda for the superiority of the system. He felt that the Germans were living in an age of madness. In contrast, Ichiro felt comfortable with the unchauvinistic attitudes of the American and British people. Ichiro jotted down his candid impressions, having no idea that his diary would be published.[42]

Yamaura told the truth about the book in a *Bungei Shunju* article in September 1950. When Yamaura saw Ichiro's diary, he had a hunch that it would sell and proposed the publication to Shimanaka Yusaku of *Chuokoronsha*, without Ichiro's consent. Shimanaka agreed and published it in 1938 with the title of *Gaiyu nikki sekai no kao* (Journal of trip abroad: Face of the world). Yamaura heavily edited Ichiro's diary in order to pass the government censorship. Yamaura realized that had he published Ichiro's diary as it was, it would not only be banned but also would cause enormous trouble for Ichiro. Ichiro had already been stigmatized as a "pro-Anglo-American liberalist" by the military. Ichiro had faced a possibility of obstruction of his landing at Yokohama port upon return from the trip. Therefore, Yamaura drastically wiped out the "color" of Ichiro. For example, he removed the passage in which Ichiro expressed his view to the Japanese minister to Austria that Japan should end its war with China immediately. Yamaura replaced Ichiro's personal views with praises of the militarism both at home and abroad in order to pass the censorship.[43]

Yamaura also wrote in the "editor's notes" of the book that "given that the original text was an individual's diary, it contained passages that were not suitable to be made public [referring to Ichiro's antimilitary views], and therefore, they were removed." Yamaura also declared in the book that "the editor [Yamaura] is solely responsible for the content." Nevertheless, these "preventive measures" did not help. Yamaura writes, "if read objectively within the political context at that time, the book did not contain any part in which Hatoyama could be misconstrued as an ultranationalist. The problem was that those who intended to purge Hatoyama picked up the smallest passages, out of context, and manipulated them as evidence to purge him."[44]

Yamaura further states that the same was true for Ichiro's campaign address for the 1942 elections that he had written for Ichiro. The censorship authorities repeatedly threatened Yamaura and made him rewrite the address a number of times until it passed. Yet, Yamaura tactfully managed to weave advocacy for liberalism and parliamentarianism into the address. Therefore, Yamaura contends that the address cannot misconstrue Ichiro as an ultranationalist in any way, but rather should be commended for its brave advocacy in the face of the military regime. Yet, the GHQ found fault with the particular passages, out of context, and accused Ichiro of supporting the Tojo policy and justifying the invasion of China (see appendix).[45]

Ichiro states that had the diary been published the way it was originally written, he would not have been involved in such an ordeal (grilling at the press club and the resulting purge). Yamaura felt all the more guilty because he had received all the royalties (the book sold 8,000 copies) and used them all, whereas Ichiro only received the trouble and not a penny from the book. Yamaura notes that if the author had been someone else, Yamaura would have been accused, but Ichiro was not the type of person to blame other people. In turn, Yoshida, who became the windfall prime minister, sarcastically called Yamaura *shukunsha* ([M]VP) of Ichiro's purge in their meeting. Yoshida enjoyed the paradox, whereas Yamaura was speechless.[46]

Now, it became clear that two out of the five accounts of the GHQ's directive (SCAPIN 919, Sections c. and d.) rely on the self-censored book, edited by Yamaura. Another account (SCAPIN 919, Section e.) relies on the heavily censored campaign address, written by Yamaura. The GHQ took the censored writings at face value. In order to make an objective assessment of Ichiro's purge, it is important to examine Baerwald's views because he was a purge officer, became a scholar, and wrote a pioneering study of the issue in 1959.

Baerwald's Views: An Assessment

Baerwald considers the criteria applied to Ichiro's purge "inappropriate." First, Baerwald argues that the objectives of GHQ's purge were twopronged: (1) to remove individuals who were tainted with war responsibility and (2) to remove those who are or may become antidemocratic.

He contends that insofar as the first (and original) objective remained primary, the purge was solidly founded; however, the introduction of the second objective, added by General MacArthur, made the overall objective of the purge ambiguous. Baerwald argues that the GHQ created the catchall criteria of category G, in order to satisfy the second objective, and that the adoption of this broad criteria caused confusion in the identification of purgees. Baerwald states that much of the acrimonious controversy surrounding the purge stems from the dichotomy of its objectives and that Ichiro's case became the *cause célèbre* of the controversies involving the catchall criteria of category G.[47] He writes:

> The phraseology supporting Hatoyama's purge illustrates the paradox of the objectives of the purge as a whole . . . From the viewpoint that the purge's objective was to remove those who had deceived and misled the people of Japan to embark on world conquest, the case against Hatoyama leaves much to be desired. It rests on two counts. First, he was an active participant in the government's policy to control dangerous thoughts. Again, he supported General Tanaka's "positive policy" vis-à-vis China. His admiration for Hitler's labor policy is really irrelevant to the purge criteria, though no doubt indicative of his general outlook. This is the crux of the matter. Had the other objective of the purge, that of clearing the decks of Japan's erstwhile leaders so that previously suppressed or younger leaders could come to the fore, been primary, a far more convincing case could have been constructed.[48]

Baerwald further states that Ichiro's case illustrates that a case could be made to support the purge of almost anyone of consequence on the basis of category G's broad criteria. Consequently, his case, along with several score controversial cases, led to the allegation that the purge was arbitrary and motivated by political considerations. Baerwald concludes that the purge was an unprecedented experiment to change the leadership of a nation by peaceful means; however, the purge as a concept was antithetical to the notion of liberal democracy and it suffered from weaknesses inherent in its unrealistic objectives. Therefore, it was far less successful in facilitating the development of a new, democratically inclined leadership in Japan. A successful execution of alternative programs for Japan's democratization, involving leadership change and reeducation, would have required a far greater degree of expert knowledge of Japanese society than the occupation personnel actually had.[49]

Wildes's Views

Wildes, another officer at the GS, published his view that the case against Ichiro was weak in 1954. Wildes acknowledges the fact that

Ichiro had appealed to General Ugaki Kazushige to halt the advance of militarism and that he had opposed the Tripartite Alliance with Nazi Germany and Italy, for which he had earned Tojo's hatred and had spent the war years in political exile. Wildes argues that Ichiro became "the prime Communist target" because he had showed a "notable Red phobia" and had received "the largest plurality of any candidate." Wildes writes that Ichiro's parliamentary record and the Liberals' platforms for responsible democratic government caused the GS initially to look upon him favorably. However, leftists retorted that the party platforms were mere window dressing and denounced Ichiro's advocacy of retaining the emperor system as feudalistic (despite the fact that it was with the proviso that the British-type monarch reign but not govern). According to Wildes, the GS was divided as to whether to purge Ichiro, through-out the winter of 1945 and 1946. "Realists, especially those familiar with prewar Japan, contended that, while his liberalism was outdated, his hatred of militarism and his very real devotion to parliamentarian-ism could, under wise Occupation guidance, lead to good government. Leftists, ardent for [a] quick and drastic change, considered him a symbol of past evils[.]"[50]

Wildes points out that the "Japanese press, then largely leftist, misrepresented Hatoyama, and foreigners who read the colorful and provocative statements attributed to him ignored his liberalism but scented insincerity, anti-Americanism, and hunger for revenge." Meanwhile, "Occupation officials who had talked with him were not deceived; both [the] Counterintelligence Corps and [the] Civil Intelligence Section reported that his record was clear." Leftist sympa-thizers, however, kept on his trail, found no mention of the book *Face of the world* in his file, and organized the press conference. Noting that Ichiro's case was entangled with the factional rivalry within the GHQ, Wildes considers Ichiro "unwise" in failing to keep on good terms with the GS. For example, "[a]fter a long succession of unnecessary inter-views with Whitney underlings" and "wearied by the constant summonses to Dai Ichi Building [where the GHQ was located]," Ichiro allegedly replied at yet another call that "If they want me, they know where to find me." A GS major took this as an insult and reported to Whitney that Ichiro was "undemocratic."[51]

In summary, it is significant that two insiders of the GS had published critical views of Ichiro's purge. It is time to examine Japanese observers' views in order to make a comprehensive assessment of Ichiro's purge.

Hanai's Views

Political scientist Hanai Hitoshi seems to think that Ichiro's purge was justifiable. Hanai considers Ichiro "a remnant of the Taisho democracy" (a period in which democratic movements flourished, such as the first movement to defend the constitution in 1912, and the second movement to defend the constitution in 1924. The period is referred to as such because it coincided with Emperor Taisho's reign, 1911–1926). Hanai notes that Ichiro became a HR member in 1915, advanced his career in the constitutional parliamentary system, and became an influential member of the *Seiyukai*. He also notes that Ichiro criticized the military-clique bureaucrats, opposed the legislation of the National Mobilization Law (1938) and the creation of the Imperial Rule Assistance Association (1940), and created an intra-parliamentary group (*Dokokai*), which was forcibly absorbed in the Imperial Rule Assistance Political Association (1942). After making an antigovernment speech at the pro–Imperial Rule Assistance Political Association Group's meeting in June 1943, Ichiro withdrew to Karuizawa. Hanai argues that Ichiro believed that he made his utmost effort to deter the huge tide of military politics, even if the odds were against him. Ichiro therefore believed that he was free of war responsibilities. Ichiro attributed the war responsibilities to the dominance of the military-clique bureaucrats and the pro–Imperial Rule Assistance Political Association politicians' bandwagon with the former. By so doing, Hanai argues, Ichiro ignored the responsibilities with the prewar politicians, who were preoccupied with a power struggle among themselves and gave the opportunity for the military-cliques to gain power. Hanai contends that since Ichiro was an influential politician during the prewar period, he is responsible for allowing the military-cliques to take control of politics; therefore, he is responsible for the war. Hanai however recognizes that Ichiro was not "militarist and ultranationalist." Hanai himself ends his analysis with the statement that his views might be too harsh on Ichiro.[52]

Kojima's Views

Political writer Kojima Noboru, in his in-depth and voluminous study of the San Francisco Peace Treaty, argues that Ichiro's purge was Gayn's conspiracy. Kojima characterizes the press conference as a "people's court." Kojima states that foreign reporters cross-examined Ichiro for the book that was published eight years ago. Ichiro was all the more confused because the questions were based on the unauthorized English translation of the book made by the CIE Section of the GHQ. Ichiro was also disadvantaged by the language because he spoke "labored English." The manner in which they questioned Ichiro was not that of a press conference but that of an impeachment trial. The other three party representatives were terrified and just kept silent. Ichiro had to endure censure for hours. Kojima concludes that Ichiro's purge was "*jittai no naimono* (without substance)." Kojima writes, guided by the idealistic mission of reforming Japan, not only the members of the GHQ but also American reporters were assuming the role of prosecutors in Japan and were putting politics and society into chaos.[53]

Masuda's Views

Diplomatic historian Masuda Hiroshi, in his latest study of the GHQ's purge, contends that Ichiro's purge was a conspiracy of the GS, entangled in the factional feud within the GHQ. According to Masuda, as of November 1945 when the GHQ personnel interviewed Ichiro, they had all the materials concerning Ichiro, including his meeting with Hitler in 1937. The Japanese government's screening committee cleared him and the GHQ, knowing that his record was innocuous, did not purge him in January 1946. However, as Ichiro further antagonized communists (his anticommunist league proposal in February 1946), the leftists in the GS again took up his case. Swayed by the dominance of the GS over purge matters, the Counterintelligence Corps (OCCIO) wrote two drafts concerning Ichiro in April 1946—one that supported purging Ichiro and another that did not support purging him. Colonel Creswell, the OCCIO's head, reported to the GS that the collected evidence indicated that Ichiro was "absolutely inapplicable" to the purge criteria; however, stated that it was questionable whether Ichiro would be suitable to be prime minister. Colonel Kades of the GS expanded part of the report that was instrumental in Ichiro's purge and ignored the rest. He came up with a strategy to claim that Ichiro committed a "grave violation" of the SCAPIN 550 directive by omitting the book *Sekai no kao* in his file, and demanded to reexamine his case.[54]

According to Masuda's interview with Baerwald in August 1986, the GS gathered every newspaper article that was critical of Ichiro, in cooperation with Nosaka and other JCP members. They did not leave any stone unturned. Now it makes sense why Ichiro wrote, "the content of the GHQ's directive for my purge was a carbon copy of the articles of the *Akahata* [Red Flag, the JCP's official gazette]. The directive for my purge was an English translation of *Akahata*." The JCP that had been persecuted by the military took advantage of the military's censorship this time and used Ichiro's censored writings.[55]

After a rigorous and thorough study of the GHQ-SCAP documents, Masuda contends, "the GS first decided to purge Ichiro and then gathered the evidence." Masuda found out that the GS fabricated the date of the directive for Ichiro's purge (SCAPIN 919)—backdated one day to May 3, 1946—so that it would appear to have preceded the time when Prime Minister Shidehara recommended Ichiro to Emperor Hirohito. Masuda notes that the GHQ tried to cover it up by sending a letter to Foreign Minister Yoshida. Whitney's letter to Yoshida superfluously insisted that the GHQ did not know of Shidehara's move and that they issued SCAPIN 919 prior to that time. It meant that the GHQ wanted to avoid purging Ichiro after the imperial sanction. The GHQ narrowly managed to do so and kept the disguise of indirect rule. Masuda concludes that there is no doubt that Ichiro's purge was a conspiracy of the GS. Being swayed by the radicals in the GS, the GHQ decided to purge Ichiro, in recourse to the catchall category G, and issued the first special memorandum. It took the form of the special memorandum because the GHQ overruled the Japanese screening committee's decision to clear Ichiro. Since then, the GHQ issued over 100 special memoranda and purged their *persona non grata*.[56]

The question still remains as to why the conservative upper echelon of the GHQ went along with the GS in purging Ichiro. Masuda argues that Ichiro's "over-confidence" was *the* fundamental cause for his purge. Ichiro believed that he had genuinely fought the Tojo cabinet and adhered to his belief in parliamentarianism. He became too optimistic after the GHQ initially cleared him. That he had escaped the massive purge of January 1946 put him and his colleagues in the Japan Liberal Party offguard. The knowledge that the G2 was supportive of him made Ichiro even more optimistic. As a result, Ichiro's group launched a public offensive against communism in earnest. It was a bold undertaking: ever since the GHQ legalized the JCP, no other party had dared to issue a statement critical of the party. In terms of international political setting, the Cold War between the two superpowers had not begun at least overtly in Asia in 1946. Narahashi later stated that Ichiro's proposal for the anti-Communist league was three years premature. In the words of Colonel Jack P. Napier, a purge officer in the GS, the GS upper echelon perceived Ichiro's confidence as "too proud." By denouncing Communism, Ichiro touched the pride of GHQ that legalized the JCP.[57]

Masuda thinks that the conspiracy theory of Mitsuchi and Narahashi, or of Yoshida for that matter, was not as strong a factor as was thought by the media then. Nevertheless, the fact that the Shidehara cabinet did not act positively in defense of Ichiro's case did not help. In summary, Masuda argues that in addition to the power struggle among the Japanese politicians, Ichiro's purge involved a higher stake: the power and prestige of the GHQ vis-à-vis the loser. Masuda concludes that Ichiro's case not only epitomizes the arbitrary nature of the GHQ's purge but also signifies the occupation forces' individual impeachment of the loser in the name of their power and prestige. The GHQ used Ichiro's case as a *miseshime* (to teach the Japanese a lesson).[58]

In this regard, Matsumoto argues that outspokenness was Ichiro's Achilles heel. Ichiro was purged primarily because he spoke out and offended communists and the GHQ. Wildes also writes that Ichiro was "too talkative and that cunning people trapped him into inconsistency in words and accused him of being double-tongued." In hindsight, Ichiro could have avoided the purge, had he kept silent. Masuda thinks that had Ichiro exerted prudence to form his own cabinet, he would not have been purged and would have been able to form his cabinet a little later. At least, he would not have had to wait for eight years and seven months to actually form his cabinet.[59]

Toyoda's Views

Historical writer Toyoda Jo argues that among many speculations concerning causes of Ichiro's purge, the conspiracy of the foreign correspondents is the strongest. Neither the Shidehara cabinet nor the GHQ found enough evidence to purge Ichiro and gave it up. However, Gayn took it up with missionary zeal and Gayn's plot became a *coup de grâce* for Ichiro's purge. In the overall analysis, Toyoda thinks that Ichiro was not without fault. Ichiro's own past deeds, such as his anti-Shidehara bandwagon during the prewar period, also contributed to his purge ("what goes around comes around"). His outspokenness not only offended the leftists in the GS, which was in charge of the purge, but also touched the pride of the GHQ. Ichiro's outspokenness cost him dearly, as it did in the wartime period. Yet, Toyoda states that one is hard-pressed to criticize Ichiro. Ichiro endured the suppression of the military for years and felt that his time had finally come (he was already 63 years old). His determination reflected the extent of the hardships he had endured. In addition, the idea to abandon the plan to form a cabinet for the sake of escaping a personal purge did not sit well with Ichiro. It was a matter of integrity. Ichiro could not make such a cowardly and unconscionable political bargain.[60]

The Purge of Ichiro's Confidantes

Subsequently, Ichiro's confidantes, Miki and Kono, were purged. Miki was unanimously voted in as speaker of the HR in May 1946; however, one week later, he was purged as a "militarist and ultranationalist" just before the inauguration of his post. It was on the second day of the Yoshida cabinet and twenty days after Ichiro's purge. Miki was told that if he would decline the post, he would not be purged. Miki flatly rejected the bargain, saying that the integrity of the parliament would be jeopardized if he declined the position for the sake of escaping his personal purge. Like Ichiro, Miki could not take such an unconscionable action. Masuda argues that Miki's purge was part of the same conspiracy as the one against Ichiro. As in the case of Ichiro, the Shidehara cabinet postponed recommending Miki (as house speaker) to the emperor and, in the meantime, the GHQ prepared the documents to justify his purge. Consequently, Miki again retired to his hometown in Shikoku as he did during the war. He spent five years and one month under purge. Miki lost the chance to become speaker of the first postwar popularly elected HR; and he never become speaker.[61]

Kono was also purged for the same pretext. Regarding the purge of Miki and Kono, Masuda writes, "given their records of anti-militarism, there is little rationality in their purge. The GHQ purged Miki and Kono, the two key men of the Japan Liberal Party, after Ichiro, in order to undermine the party." Masuda adds that Yoshida, assuming the dual position of prime minister and foreign minister, collaborated with the GHQ and purged his political enemies: the so-called Y (Yoshida) category purge.[62]

The Extremity of the Purge

Wildes writes, with Ichiro out of the way and the purge of national politicians effective, the GS expanded the scope of the purge to business circles and local governments. It was understandable to incarcerate war criminals; however, the Japanese were shocked by the indiscriminate nature of the purge. It extended to include heads of fire fighters' units of the smallest villages and turned Japanese society upside down. The massive purge changed the nature of the GHQ rule from indirect to, in effect, direct rule. In the words of Masuda, the degree of impact of the purge matched that of the 1929 Wall Street stock market crash on the American society. Masuda concludes that the SCAP set unrealistic goals in its reforms of Japan and the execution of its reforms was distorted by the factional feud within the GHQ.[63]

The GHQ's liberal reforms went too far to the extent that the Truman administration sent George F. Kennan, the "architect of the containment of communism," to Tokyo to reverse the course (see chapter 5). In retrospect, the GHQ ironically purged Ichiro, an anticommunist Japanese leader, with the advent of the Cold War.

Conclusions

The examination of a number of views—American and Japanese—suggests that Ichiro's purge was unreasonable in light of his prewar and wartime conduct and the GHQ's purge criteria. The GHQ exaggerated Ichiro's role in the two military-led cabinets. The GHQ found fault with Ichiro's censored writings. The GHQ overlooked Ichiro's resistance to militarism. Paradoxically, Ichiro, a *persona non grata* of the military regime, became a *persona non grata* of the GHQ. In conclusion, Gayn's impeachment campaign against Ichiro succeeded and Ichiro was abruptly purged on the day of his cabinet formation. Toyoda writes that for a politician, there can be nothing more cruel than being purged on the day of his cabinet formation. Hence, Ichiro was dubbed a "tragic politician."[64]

Ichiro's purge lasted for five years and three months from May 4, 1946 until August 5, 1951. It took an additional three years and four months for Ichiro to become prime minister on December 10, 1954. In total, more than eight years and seven months have passed since the day of his aborted cabinet. How Ichiro persevered during that period and eventually formed his cabinet is another intriguing chapter of postwar politics.

CHAPTER 5
ICHIRO AND POSTWAR POLITICS

Based on Ichiro's newly published diary and other materials, this chapter examines the process of Ichiro's depurging and his regaining power. By so doing, this chapter analyzes how and why the SCAP and the Yoshida cabinet obstructed Ichiro's depurging and sheds new light on early postwar Japanese politics.

The Aftermath of the Purge

The SCAP purged Ichiro on May 4, 1946, the day his cabinet was to be formed. Paradoxically, however, Ichiro's purge did not bring about what the SCAP had expected. According to Masuda Hiroshi, it was a miscalculation on the part of Colonel Kades of the GS. Considering Ichiro not liberal enough for postwar Japan, Kades was hoping to form a cabinet, based on the JSP. However, to Kades's surprise, the JSP formed an alliance with Ichiro's Japan Liberal Party in order to overthrow the Shidehara cabinet. Ichiro expeditiously chose his successor, Yoshida Shigeru, who then formed a Japan Liberal Party–led cabinet. SCAP's massive purges put the so-called *shokugyo seijika* (career politicians based on political parties), such as Ichiro, into semi-retirement and allowed the *kanryo seijika* (bureaucrats-turned-politicians) to rise to the occasion. Yoshida was a prime example. Masuda notes, afterwards, covert power struggles between the Yoshida cabinet, backed by the G2, and the JSP, backed by the GS, were fought. The aftermath of Ichiro's purge, as well as the process of his depurging, indicates the contradictions of the entire purge.[1]

Yoshida Shigeru

Ichiro needed to find a substitute to lead the Japan Liberal Party and form a cabinet immediately. After inquiring of a few candidates in vain (experienced politicians were either incarcerated or purged), Yoshida

(1878–1967, from Tosa [Kochi-*ken*]) agreed to form a caretaker cabinet for Ichiro. People from Tosa are referred to as *igosso* (obstinate character) and are known for their stubborn character. Yoshida's father Takenouchi Tsuna was a freedom fighter of the Tosa Liberal Party, led by Itagaki Taisuke. Yoshida was adopted by a wealthy trader in Yokohama at the age of two and spent a dissipated and vagarious life. After wandering among several middle schools, he graduated from Tokyo Imperial University in July 1906 at the age of 27 and became a career diplomat. In contrast, Ichiro advanced straight along his academic track and graduated from the university at the age of 24 in 1907. Although Ichiro was five years younger than Yoshida, Ichiro was ahead of Yoshida career-wise. When Yoshida was consul general at Mukden at the time of Marshal Chang Tso-lin's assassination, Ichiro was chief secretary of the Tanaka cabinet.[2]

Yoshida married a daughter of Makino Nobuaki (1861–1949, a son of Okubo Toshimichi, a diplomat-turned-politician, and advisor to Emperor Hirohito; attacked in the 2·26 *coup d'état*). The military disliked Yoshida's pro–Anglo-American stance and opposed his appointment in 1936 as foreign minister of the Hirota cabinet. Consequently, Yoshida was "exiled" to England, as ambassador, from April 1936 until March 1939. After Japan's defeat, Yoshida became foreign minister in Prince Higashikuni's cabinet (its original foreign minister Shigemitsu Mamoru was incarcerated as a class A war criminal in Sugamo Prison for a seven-year sentence) in September 1945 and then in the Shidehara cabinet in October of that year.[3]

With his unexpected purge, Ichiro handpicked Yoshida, an "unknown material" for a politician. On the surface it appears that Yoshida was more acceptable to the SCAP than Ichiro. Ichiro was an influential politician, whereas Yoshida was a bureaucrat. However, Yoshida and Ichiro shared the same values. Both were anticommunist and antifascist. Mark Gayn, who masterminded Ichiro's purge, correctly held the same animosity toward Yoshida as toward Ichiro and labeled both as "ultranationalists" and "war criminals." Gayn, nevertheless, did not target Yoshida because he was not a political leader and posed less "danger" to Japan. The SCAP did not purge Yoshida because it feared that purging another head of the Japan Liberal Party (the legitimate party to rule Japan chosen by the people), after Ichiro, could cause an uproar among the Japanese. Yoshida allegedly had a *menzaifu* (proof of acquittance) in hand as he was temporarily incarcerated by the gendarmerie for his participation in an unsuccessful "peace plot" (to negotiate an early surrender by Japan) in April 1945. His group was codified by the police as YOHANSEN (Yoshida *Hansen* [antiwar]).

However, it might have been a pretext (for not purging him) because Ichiro and Konoe were also involved in the plot. In hindsight, by purging Ichiro, the SCAP inadvertently created by far a more difficult Japanese prime minister to deal with. Kataoka Tetsuya argues that MacArthur knew how much Yoshida, an imperial royalist, loathed the new constitution. Also, Yoshida was a shrewd machiavellian and was known to be arrogant and perverse, whereas Ichiro was amiable, open, and somewhat naive.[4]

Yoshida's "Four-Point" Letter

Ichiro writes that Yoshida thrust a letter on him, containing four conditions, in exchange for his agreement to become president of the Japan Liberal Party and form a caretaker cabinet for Ichiro. The four points consist of:

(1) You (Ichiro) shall be fully in charge of the personnel selection of the party because I (Yoshida) do not have ties to the party;
(2) You shall control the party; however, you shall not interfere with the personnel selection of my cabinet;
(3) I do not have money (for political campaigns) and I cannot raise money. Therefore, you shall take care of money; and
(4) I can quit any time I want. I shall hand over the post to you upon your depurging.[5]

By contrast, Yoshida claimed that his letter contained only three points. Yoshida writes, "I put forward three conditions governing my acceptance of the post: first of which was that I had no money and did not intend to collect any for the party; the second that Mr. Hatoyama was to have no say in the selection of Ministers in the new Cabinet; and the third I was free to resign whenever I reached the conclusion that I had had enough of politics." Yoshida portrays himself as a victim of Ichiro's purge, rather than a beneficiary. He writes, "I myself was one of the victims of the resulting situation [of the SCAP's purge], since the elimination of Mr. Hatoyama from the public scene was the immediate cause of my casting my lot with a political party, something I had never previously contemplated, and being named its president."[6]

Ichiro trusted Yoshida and lost the letter. Ichiro regretted it later, as Yoshida refused to return power to Ichiro when he was depurged in August 1951. Kono Ichiro, Japan Liberal Party's secretary general, read Yoshida's "four-point" letter. He recalls that he was struck by Yoshida's arrogance and tactfulness in getting the best deal out of Ichiro's predicament. Yoshida told Nishio Suehiro, JSP secretary general, that he was a "mercenary prime minister." Thus, Yoshida was well aware of the nature of his premiership as being a proxy leader.[7]

The Advent of the Yoshida Years

Yoshida turned out to be a strong politician and formed an unprecedented five cabinets within the span of eight years. The Yoshida cabinets were as follows: (1) May 1946–May 1947, the Japan Liberal Party with the cooperation of the Japan Progressive Party; (2) October 1948–December 1948, solely of the *Minshu Jiyuto* (Democratic Liberal Party, generally referred to as the *Minjito* in Japanese literature); (3) February 1949–October 1952, Democratic Liberal Party with the *Nihon Minshuto* (the Japan Democratic Party, reorganized Progressives) (4) October 1952–March 1953, solely of Yoshida's new Liberal Party; and (5) April 1953–December 1954, Liberal Party with the cooperation of the *Kaishinto* (the Progressive Party, reorganized Progressives).[8]

Between the first and second Yoshida cabinets, there existed two short-lived coalition cabinets: (1) JSP's Katayama cabinet (May 1947–February 1948) with the Japan Democratic Party and the National Cooperative Party and (2) Japan Democratic Party's Ashida cabinet (March 1948–October 1948) with the rightist faction of the JSP and the Cooperatives. The Progressives had reorganized itself into the Japan Democratic Party in March 1947, with Ashida Hitoshi as its president and Shidehara as its honorary president. To challenge the Ashida cabinet, Yoshida merged with the Shidehara faction of the Japan Democratic Party and created the Democratic Liberal Party in March 1948. Then, Prime Minister Ashida was involved in the *Showa Denko* bribery scandal of June 1948 and resigned in October 1948 (he was arrested in that December). This led to the formation of the second Yoshida cabinet, solely of the Democratic Liberal Party, in October 1948. However, the Democratic Liberal Party lacked a majority in the HR and the HR subsequently passed a non confidence vote of the Yoshida cabinet in December 1948.[9]

The Third Yoshida Cabinet

The HR general elections of January 1949 brought the Democratic Liberal Party an absolute majority (264 out 466 seats) and Yoshida formed his third cabinet in February 1949. Yoshida surrounded himself with such bureaucrats-turned-politicians as Ikeda Hayato and Sato Eisaku, who later became prime ministers. This inner circle of Yoshida's protégés is referred to as the "Yoshida school." Despite the absolute majority standing,

Yoshida co-opted the Japan Democratic Party in order to preempt possible formation of an anti-Yoshida alliance of opposition parties. Yoshida's coalition with the Japan Democratic Party resulted in the breakup of the party into a pro-coalition faction, led by Inukai Takeru (son of Inukai Tsuyoshi), and an anti-coalition faction, led by Tomabechi Gizo. This breakup resulted in yet another merger of the Democratic Liberal Party and the pro-coalition faction of the Japan Democratic Party: the formation in March 1950 of a new *Jiyuto* (the Liberal Party), led by Yoshida. In retaliation, the Japan Democratic Party's anti-coalition faction formed a new party called the *Kokumin Minshuto* (the National Democratic Party) with the Cooperatives and others in April 1950. Then, the party reorganized itself as the *Kaishinto* (the Progressive Party), with Shigemitsu, who had just served his seven-year sentence, as president, in February 1952. The JSP also broke up into rightist and leftist factions in January 1950.[10]

Yoshida accepted the MacArthur constitution that deprived the emperor of sovereignty. Yoshida also undertook a policy of minimum armament for Japan, in recourse to the constitution. Yoshida took these conciliatory measures toward the SCAP for the following reasons. The SCAP was omnipotent and omnipresent and even Yoshida could not defy its authority. The Japanese general public accepted pacifism à la MacArthur and the Left, as a reaction to their wartime experiences and the atomic bombings of Hiroshima and Nagasaki. In addition, the minimum defense policy benefited Japan by enabling it to divert most of its energy to economic recovery; however, at the cost of perpetuating its dependence on the United States, the so-called "subordinate independence." Kataoka suspects that there was what he calls the "MacArthur–Yoshida compact," in which MacArthur coerced Yoshida to accept the SCAP's policy, even by hinting that he would be U.S. president.[11]

Reverse Course

The Truman administration felt that the SCAP's liberal reforms of Japan went too far. While the GS revised the constitution and eradicated noncommunist politicians, the Economic Science Section (ESS) engaged itself in the remaking of Japanese economy. By dissolving the *zaibatsu* (financial cliques), such as Mitsubishi and Mitsui, it deprived Japan of the backbone of its productivity. In turn, the Japanese communists were gaining power, and labor unions, legalized by the SCAP, were paralyzing Japan's production. The Japanese society was in anarchy. Matsumoto Seicho notes that the omnipotent SCAP was trying to reinvent Japan in its image without thinking of the consequences.

Kataoka writes that the paradox of SCAP's reforms was that there might have been "democratization" but there was no "democracy."[12]

Chalmers Johnson, in his in-depth study of the Matsukawa incident (the deadly sabotage of the Japan National Railroad in August 1949, in which communists, unions, and the U.S. military were implicated), writes that it is controversial "whether the Americans should have been quite so liberal in their definitions of political prisoners and in acting on their unquestioned beliefs that everything done by Japan's prewar and wartime governments was fascistic and against the public interests . . . What seems clear, however, is that the release of a large group of ideologically committed revolutionaries into a war-torn and defeated society without any efforts to rebuild the economic foundations of that society resembled less a prescription for 'democratization' or 'psychological disarmament' than one of revolution and counterrevolution."[13]

The Truman administration perceived the chaos in Japan as even more alarming, given the external situations. In China, the Chinese Communist Party (CCP), led by Mao Zedong, was launching a national campaign against Chang Kaishek's Nationalist Party (KMT). Meanwhile, Joseph Stalin was strengthening the bond of international communism by creating satellite countries in Eastern Europe and the Cominform (Communist Information Bureau) in October 1947. Having lost a mutual enemy—fascism—the United States and the Soviet Union were escalating their confrontation. Yet, Washington did not obtain precise and satisfactory information about what exactly the SCAP was doing in Japan. According to George F. Kennan of the State Department, it was not only because of "the geographical distance or devious governmental channels then available" but also because of "the psychological distance between the State Department and the SCAP." Kennan writes that General MacArthur "had a violent prejudice against the State Department," and resented any attempt by the department to interfere in the conduct of the occupation in Japan. General George C. Marshall, secretary of state, and General MacArthur did not get along personally, partly because of the frictions of the wartime competition between the Pacific and European theaters for supplies and support. General Marshall was reluctant to exchange views with General MacArthur personally.[14]

The Dispatch of George F. Kennan

In February 1948 Washington's growing distrust of MacArthur and the SCAP reformers prompted the Truman administration to dispatch Kennan to Japan. Kennan describes the liaison between the department and the SCAP as having been so distant and so full of distrust that he felt as if he were "an envoy charged with opening up communications and arranging the establishment of diplomatic relations with a hostile and suspicious foreign government." Kennan saw the weakness of Japan's economy as fertile soil for the growth of communism and felt that occupation policies had been devised for the specific purposes of rendering Japanese society vulnerable to communist political pressures and of paving the way for communism's takeover of Japan. However, General MacArthur told Kennan that communists were no menace in Japan. Regarding the charges concerning communist infiltration within the GHQ, MacArthur did not deny them and said, "We have probably got some of them. The War Department has some. So does the State Department. It doesn't mean very much."[15]

Kennan found "most serious" the situation created by the "wholesale" purging of people in government, in education, and in business. He writes,

> [The] SCAP had proceeded on a scale, and with a dogmatic, impersonal vindictiveness, for which there were few examples outside the totalitarian countries themselves. Seven hundred thousand people had already been involved, at the time of our visit, in the attendant screening. Just in the educational establishment alone, some 120,000 out of a half million teachers had been purged or had resigned to avoid purging. Nor was there any visible end to this process . . . All useful punitive psychological effect had been lost amid the confusion of ordinances, directives, and programs. The indiscriminate purging of whole categories of individuals, sickeningly similar to totalitarian practices, was in conflict with the civil rights provisions of the new constitution that we ourselves had imposed upon the Japanese. It had had the effect of barring from civil life many people who could not be regarded on any reasonable standards as exponents of militarism and whose only crime had been to serve their country faithfully in time of war. Important elements of Japanese society essential to its constructive development were being driven underground. Pressures were being engendered which, if not promptly relieved, were bound to come to the surface someday in extremely unhealthy ways . . . the policies of SCAP had brought Japanese life to a point of great turmoil and confusion, and had produced, momentarily at least, a serious degree of instability.[16]

Ichiro under purge did not meet Kennan during his visit to Japan. Upon returning home, Kennan proposed to end the occupation as a "sanction" against Japan and instead to help in the economic rehabilitation of Japan. Along this line, Kennan recommended halting reparations and stopping interference with Japan's internal matters, such as censorship, purges, and dissolution of the *zaibatsu*. His proposal officially became National Security Council directive 13/2 (NSC13/2) in October 1948. It signaled the beginning of the "reverse course." The Truman administration ordered General MacArthur to carry out the NSC13/2 directive, and MacArthur banned communism and damaged labor unions; the "red purge." Kennan considers his role in bringing about this change in Japan "the most significant constructive contribution I was ever able to make in government" after the Marshall Plan.[17]

MacArthur Sabotages Depurging

Ichiro had a few times requested the GHQ-SCAP to reexamine his purge and depurge him but in vain. According to his diary, on January 10, 1949, "Colton (GHQ officer) also urged me to request reexamination again; however, my case was not reexamined. The Yoshida cabinet was sabotaging my depurging." Yoshida justified this, stating that MacArthur told Yoshida in January 1949 to keep Ichiro's purge because of Soviet insistence. This episode also suggests a discord within the SCAP. With the enforcement of the "reverse course," the conservatives in SCAP took power and Colonel Kades and other New Dealers were recalled.[18]

Nevertheless, MacArthur did not fully implement the NSC13/2 directive. He depurged only about 10,000 purgees in October 1950. The announcement for depurging the rest of the purgees, including Ichiro, did not come through until June 1951. According to Kataoka, MacArthur obstructed the release of Ichiro and other political purgees for three years in order to keep the constitution intact. Navy Lieutenant Richard Poole, one of the constitutional drafting members at the GS, stated that it was MacArthur who insisted on the inclusion of the war-renouncing Article 9. Poole states, "It's very difficult to require a country to forever and a day forswear armed forces even in self-defense, so I raised the questions. Col. Kades looked at me and said, 'Poole do you know where the draft comes from?' I said, 'No, sir.' He said '*The General*,' and he said, 'Need I say anything more?' I said 'No, sir.'" Lieutenant Milton J. Esman, another constitutional drafting member at the GS, states, "MacArthur was concerned with his place in history. And wouldn't it be remarkable that a military man was able to induce a society like Japan to renounce arms?" According to Kataoka MacArthur had great pride in the constitution and was obsessed by the desire to perpetuate it. MacArthur favored socialists because he felt that only they would defend the constitution. MacArthur had succeeded in conciliating Yoshida, and Yoshida agreed to the terms of the San Francisco Peace Treaty and of the U.S.–Japan Security Treaty that were in line with Article 9: the United States shall remain a protector of Japan.[19]

Kataoka argues that MacArthur knew that Ichiro and other conservative politicians would be the enemies of his constitution. Had MacArthur released them, they would have opposed such terms in favor of according a greater degree of independence to Japan. Therefore, MacArthur carried out the "reverse course" only in the economic realm and sabotaged the depurging. As a result, Ichiro was obliged to be a bystander, while Yoshida was in the limelight at the signing of the Peace Treaty at the San Francisco Opera House in September 1951. Kataoka contends that MacArthur's sabotage was detrimental to Japan in terms of restoring real independence and that these politicians rightfully considered Yoshida a traitor. Ichiro died without knowing that MacArthur had sabotaged his depurging for three years.[20]

Japan officially regained full independence when the San Francisco Peace Treaty came into force in April 1952. However, it was "subordinate independence."

The "Second Age of Winter"

During the initial year of his purge Ichiro stayed at Atami, a spa resort near Mount Fuji, and spent his time translating Coudenhove's *Totalitarian State Against Man* that he had read during his wartime political exile. Ichiro obtained his permission to publish the book in Japanese, and published it as *Jiyu to Jinsei* (Liberty and Life) in 1953. In addition, he wrote four books concerning his political beliefs and his life, including his autobiography. Ichiro stayed in Karuizawa from the second year of his purge until the end of his purge in August 1951. He spent his days farming and reading as he had done before. He writes that he did not feel so miserable in those days, but rather enjoyed life in the country.[21]

Ichiro's life under purge was not as rustic and restful as it appeared. On occasions, police and prosecutors visited him in Karuizawa and searched his house, making a mess. When Ichiro traveled to Atami to play *go* (Japanese chess) with his friends, police followed his daily moves and checked his visitors—politicians and reporters. GHQ had banned playing *go* because the play is based on invading other's territories. Ichiro demonstrated *go* at the request of an officer of the GHQ's CIE Section, which resulted in lifting the ban on *go*. Ichiro writes that these trips were difficult. Due to his purging, Ichiro was deprived of the stipend and privileges of a Diet member, including the Japan National Railways free pass. He had to stand in line to purchase a ticket and traveled standing in the sardine-packed third-class train all day. During the wartime, when Ichiro was "purged" by the military regime, he was still a Diet member and was paid a stipend. Now, all the privileges were gone. Observing the war-torn cities from the train, as one of the standing crowd, Ichiro understood the hunger, poverty, and pain of the people.[22]

Ichiro Remained Influential Under Purge

Ichiro was not detached from the world of politics during the purge. The injunctions in the purge ordinance prohibited meetings between purgees and persons holding public office, but only if they were concerned with the handling of official affairs or political activities. Hans Baerwald writes that in the fall (actually, spring) of 1948 numerous reports circulated that Ichiro met with Liberal Party secretary general Ono Bamboku and Progressives at a hotel in Atami, owned by a local Liberal Party boss. Yoshida also journeyed to the same hotel to see Ichiro. These meetings coincided with rumors that a merger between the Liberal Party and a faction of the Japan Democratic Party was contemplated. However, the Special Investigation Bureau failed to substantiate the claim that "political" topics had featured in Ichiro's conversations with these politicians, and Ichiro was not indicted. Baerwald's account refers to the creation of the Democratic Liberal Party in March 1948. Ichiro was instrumental to the creation of this party, which produced the second Yoshida cabinet in October 1948.[23]

Gayn invited Ichiro for lunch at his house on December 9, 1946. He describes Ichiro as "just a well-fed, jovial, impeccably dressed old man" and as "a shrewd politician who well concealed any resentment he may have for me." Ichiro said in a friendly manner that he had come from his "exile" at Atami. The GHQ had told him to stay out of Tokyo and politics; they were keeping an eye on him, tapped his phone, and listened in every time he talked to Prime Minister Yoshida. Gayn writes, "The purged war criminals are so well entrenched in the business of policy-making that it has become one of the standing Japanese scandals. They functioned as the hidden government, flouting the power and authority of the United States . . . Hatoyama himself played host to a flock of Liberal Party bosses the night after the party's convention." This "amiable" man, purged from public life, has become the "hidden government" of Japan. Ichiro "reeled off the names of the cabinet ministers who had come to him to seek guidance. He said the trouble with all of them was they gave in too easily to the GHQ . . . " Gayn writes, "I regretted I could not fasten his words to a record, to be played every time Headquarters [GHQ] issued a statement on Yoshida's 'democratic ideals.' "[24]

At the same interview, Ichiro said, "at first I thought that the American army desired to dye Japan red. There were communists in the GHQ and they helped Japanese communists to take over the radio and the press. However, I realized that the occupation policy was to support the conservatives when General MacArthur and Mr. Acheson issued statements denouncing Communism in May and June 1946." Ichiro asked Gayn to keep their conversations off-the-record; however, Gayn disclosed the details of their conversations to Colonel Kades that night. In addition, Matsumoto notes that Yoshida was upset with Ichiro's reference to Yoshida as the Japan Liberal Party's proxy president, and obstructed Ichiro's depurging. Again, outspokenness was Ichiro's Achilles heel.[25]

A Tidal Change

Japan's geographical position became important to the U.S. global strategy with the outbreak of the Korean War in June 1950. The Truman administration requested the rearming of Japan notwithstanding the "peace constitution." Prime Minister Yoshida resisted the request in recourse to the constitution. Yoshida in the end gave in to U.S. pressure to create the *Kokka Keisatsu Yobitai* (National Police Reserve) in July 1950, which was reorganized into *Hoantai* (National Security Forces) in October 1952 and upgraded to *Jieitai* (Self Defense Forces, SDFs) in July 1954. The leftist parties denounced the SDFs as unconstitutional. Caught between the U.S. demand and the leftists' opposition, Yoshida resorted to sophism; saying that these forces were not armed forces, and therefore, they were not unconstitutional. Ever since the constitutionality of the SDFs became the most controversial issue in postwar politics.[26]

As a corollary to Yoshida's resistance to rearming Japan, Ichiro became a favorable choice for the U.S. government, as Japan's leader. Also, the general public grew tired of the autocratic Yoshida who was nicknamed *wanman* (one man, grand standing) prime minister. Yoshida kept creating new cabinet posts and reshuffling cabinet rosters. Over the course of his premiership, he appointed 79 individuals to cabinet posts, and did not remember many of their names.[27]

A Secret Meeting with Dulles

There was an important prelude to Ichiro's depurging. In Tokyo on February 6, 1951 Ichiro secretly met with John Foster Dulles, who visited Japan as a special envoy of President Truman. Ichiro disclosed the content of the so-called Dulles–Hatoyama Talk in his memoirs. Ichiro writes that Dulles wanted to see him but it had to be done in complete secrecy because the GHQ's MPs were following Dulles. In the meeting, Ichiro gave Dulles a letter describing issues confronting Japan. In the letter, Ichiro argued: (1) Japan should be equipped with enough defense capability to deter invasions by the communist countries; (2) democratic nations should form a strong unified front against them; (3) a militarily stronger Japan would be a good ally for the United States and other democratic nations. In order to realize these objectives, Ichiro urged the U.S. government to help reduce anti-U.S. sentiment among the Japanese people (communists were taking advantage of this sentiment); to end its occupation of Japan; and conclude a peace treaty as soon as possible. Ichiro also requested an end to the purge, arguing that if the purgees were left unemployed, they might become easy prey for communists. Many of the purgees did not understand why they had been purged to begin with. Depurging them would greatly contribute to creating pro-U.S. sentiment in Japan.[28]

This meeting was an eye-opener for Ichiro. He learned that there were differences in policy between the State Department and Yoshida; Dulles was looking for Yoshida's replacement; MacArthur tried to obstruct their meeting; and therefore, MacArthur was in league with Yoshida. It also indicates that the Truman administration considered Ichiro a prospective prime minister in post–peace treaty Japan. Regarding Ichiro and Yoshida, in a magazine article in May 1951, the senior politician Kojima Kazuo (a former HP member) commented that neither Ichiro nor Yoshida was yet mature as a politician. Only both of them together would have made a politician of the same stature as Hara Takashi. They were not as shrewd as Hara. Hara used cunning measures, but he had to deal with *genro* with extreme scruples. Now (in 1951), politicians do not have to worry about such things. In this sense, both Ichiro and Yoshida were not yet fully evolved politicians.[29]

Yoshida Obstructs Ichiro's Depurging

With the tidal change in the international environment, Ichiro's depurging seemed to be just a matter of time. However, he was confronted with another obstacle; this time, it was Ichiro's Japanese opponents. The Yoshida cabinet ignored the GHQ's instruction to reexamine Ichiro's case, insisting that the Japanese government had no authority on his case because it was a "special memorandum case," in which the GHQ overruled the Japanese government screening committee's decision and purged their *persona non grata*. Okazaki Katsuo, Yoshida's chief cabinet secretary and later foreign minister, ignored Ichiro's petition to repeal his case. Ichiro was excluded from the October 1950 depurging due to the alleged conspiracy of the members of the Yoshida group, such as Okazaki and Hirokawa Kozen (agricultural minister). Ichiro was then excluded from the February 1951 depurging. Ichiro writes, "many mysterious things happened regarding my depurging. Although the GHQ's directive included my case in the February 1951 depurging, I was not depurged. This was so despite the fact that I was told that General MacArthur himself had assured his friend Dr. Yamanouchi that my depurging would be among the first. On the contrary, my depurging ended up being among the last."[30]

President Truman dismissed MacArthur in April 1951 when he advocated the bombing of Manchuria during the Korean War. Dulles visited Japan again in that month, and finalized the terms for the peace treaty and the security treaty with Japan. Then, the GHQ announced the depurging of 73 memorandum cases, including that of Ichiro, in June 1951. In fact, about 3,000 people from political and business circles, such as Ishibashi Tanzan and Miki Bukichi, were depurged that month. Ichiro was expected to be depurged on June 7, 1951. Nevertheless, Ichiro was once again excluded. Ichiro went to visit a steel factory in Hirohata, near Osaka, with Nagano Shigeo (then president of Fuji Steel and later of New Japan Steel) on June 5, as scheduled. Ichiro noted in his diary, "Left Tokyo with Kaoru and Nagano, as a guide, by train. Arrived at Osaka and went to Hirohata by bus. More than a dozen press reporters accompanied us from Tokyo in anticipation of my release on June 7. We were bombarded by the press in Nagoya, Kyoto, and so on (stations in between Tokyo and Osaka)."[31]

Ichiro writes, "The press surrounded me as if I had already become prime minister and waited for the official announcement of my depurging (in Osaka). However, my depurging did not come through." The press was at a loss. Ichiro left to Osaka on June 7. He was again bombarded by the press when he arrived in Tokyo on June 8. This time they questioned Ichiro about yet another missed depurging. "What I heard upon arrival in Tokyo was the (Yoshida) cabinet obstructed my release in this way and that way. I heard this both from the GHQ and Japanese sources."[32]

Ichiro Suffers a Stroke

Ichiro vividly recalls the stroke he suffered in his residence on June 11, 1951. On a hot and steamy morning, Ichiro and his aides, such as Ando Masazumi and Miki (who were depurged in October 1950 and in

June 1951, respectively), were debating on how to take power back from Yoshida. Ando was in favor of Ichiro's returning to Yoshida's Liberal Party and then taking power back from within, whereas Miki was in favor of creating a new party and confronting Yoshida from outside. Miki saw through Yoshida and figured that Yoshida would not honor his promise to Ichiro. Ichiro agreed with Miki. When Ichiro went to the toilet in a lunch break, he suffered a stroke. This was his second tragedy, after the purge. Ichiro's diary on June 11, 1951 simply says, "Monday, fine (weather)." The simple account indicates his *munen* (regret). His speaking and thinking abilities were not damaged; however, his left hand and leg were paralyzed and he had to work on rehabilitation in Izu. The older members of the Liberal Party, who were anxiously waiting for Ichiro's depurging and his return to the party, were all heartbroken.[33]

Ichiro attributed the stroke to his immaturity. He wrote, "I was carried away with the imminence of my depurging and exerted myself too much in preparation for my political comeback. I was also indignant over Yoshida's obstruction. While there was nothing I could do about the purge, the stroke was attributable to my immature state of mind and I could have avoided the stroke . . . I learned to be thankful to everybody and everything and to maintain peace of mind. Attaining this state of mind helped my rehabilitation."[34]

The Final Depurging

Ichiro's depurging finally came through on August 5, 1951, two months after he had suffered a stroke. In summary, Ichiro's depurging was entangled in the power struggle between the SCAP, which enforced a drastic policy on Japan as a sanction, and the Truman administration, which implemented a reverse course in order to help rebuild Japan as a U.S. ally. In particular, General MacArthur's personal interest and pride in keeping the peace constitution intact collided with the policy of Truman administration officials, such as Dulles and Kennan, and delayed Hatoyama's depurging. The depurging was also part of the domestic power struggle within the conservative parties. Prime Minister Yoshida's personal stake, as well as that of his cabinet members, in retaining his cabinet further delayed Ichiro's depurging.

Ichiro was not strong enough to make campaign trips. He gave up an idea to create a new party and returned to Yoshida's Liberal Party, with Miki, Kono, and Ishibashi. Despite the Ichiro group's request that Yoshida should return the party presidency to Ichiro, Yoshida ignored it and said, "I cannot give power to a sick man." Yoshida writes, "with the

San Francisco peace conference scheduled to take place in September, it was out of the question for me to hand back the presidency of the ruling party to him as some members of the party apparently expected me to do."[35]

Yoshida's Surprise Dissolution of the HR

Yoshida then suddenly dissolved the HR in August 1952: the so-called *nukiuchi kaisan* (surprise dissolution). He convened the 14th temporary HR session in order to deceive HR members that there would be no dissolution of the HR in the near future, and then dissolved the session on its third day. In order to ensure the deception, Yoshida appointed one of his aides, Ono Bamboku, to be house speaker. Ono had been Ichiro's first aide since the Tokyo city assembly. Ichiro made Ono political vice home minister in the first Yoshida cabinet. As Yoshida appointed a bureaucrat to be home minister, Ichiro felt that a party politician should serve as his deputy. Ichiro also made Ono the Liberal Party's secretary general when Kono was purged. Ono dedicated himself to the Liberal Party and served Yoshida well because Yoshida was Ichiro's caretaker. He became a key member of the Liberal Party and was referred to as one of its *gosanke* (big three). Yoshida dissolved the HR session on its third day, without even holding a plenary session. The dissolution did not even have the required signatures of his cabinet members. Ono was ridiculed as the "three-day speaker."[36]

Ichiro writes, "not only my group but also most of the Liberal Party members were not informed of the dissolution. It was Yoshida's tactic to hold HR general elections before my group was able to prepare for the elections. In addition, Yoshida changed the party by-laws and suddenly expelled Kono and Ishibashi from the party." Miki was right. Only Yoshida's closest aides—Ikeda, Sato, and Okazaki—knew about the surprise dissolution. It astonished members of the Liberal Party itself and angered members of opposition parties. Public opinion criticized Yoshida's maneuver as unconstitutional, and the Progressives appealed to the supreme court. Consequently, the Liberal Party split into the Yoshida faction and the Hatoyama faction.[37]

The HR General Elections of October 1952

During the election campaign, Ichiro criticized Yoshida's position that "Japan possessed the National Security Forces but they were not armed forces" as being the same sophism as the ancient Chinese riddle, "a white horse is not a horse." In order to resolve the contradiction, Ichiro advocated constitutional revision and the normalization of relations with the Soviet Union. With the escalation of the Cold War, Ichiro felt that Japan should have self-defense forces, in addition to the collective security system with the United States. Ichiro also felt that Japan should normalize its relations with the Soviet Union lest the latter attack Japan, should a war between the United States and the Soviet Union break out (the Soviet Union was not a signatory to the San Francisco Peace Treaty). Ichiro writes that these two platforms were two sides of the same coin; both were designed to preserve Japan's national security.[38]

The Liberal Party won the HR general elections of October 1952 with 240 seats (out of 466 seats); however it lost 42 seats from the time of dissolution. The results included 85 seats for the Progressives, 57 for the rightist faction of the JSP, 54 for the leftist faction of the JSP, and 0 for the JCP. Although the Liberal Party obtained an absolute majority in the HR, it suffered from the intra-party rivalry between the Yoshida and the Hatoyama factions. At the beginning, the party appeared to be evenly split; however, the Ono faction decided to side with Yoshida, which determined the dominance of the Yoshida faction. Ono justifies his move by saying that he wanted to avoid the breakup of the Liberal Party, and, being caught between Yoshida and Ichiro, he tried to reach a compromise by forming another Yoshida cabinet first, and then transferring power to Ichiro.[39]

The Name-Calling Dissolution

Ichiro accepted the formation of the fourth Yoshida cabinet on three conditions: (1) the cabinet shall cooperate with opposition parties; (2) it shall democratize intra-party affairs; and (3) it shall rectify secrecy and dogmatism in diplomacy. Yoshida also agreed to reinstate Ishibashi and Kono. As a result, the fourth Yoshida cabinet was formed in October 1952. However, Yoshida ignored the three conditions. Yoshida did not even reinstate Ishibashi and Kono. As a result, the Liberal Party was again split into two factions. Ichiro formed an intra-party group called the *Minshuka domei* (Democratization Alliance, or *Mindo*) with fifty-some members within the Liberal Party.[40]

Although the Liberal Party had a majority, its power was dwindling due to the decline of Yoshida's popularity. Worse, Yoshida caused yet another dissolution of the HR, this time inadvertently. In February 1953, Yoshida was responding to the questions of Nishimura Eiichi of the rightist faction of the JSP regarding the international situation. As usual, Yoshida was obscuring his points and was merely quoting Truman and Dulles. Being frustrated, Nishimura said he was asking Yoshida's views, not the Americans'. Yoshida was offended and shouted, "*Bakayaro*" (bastard). The rightist JSP claimed that it was an insult to a Diet member and moved to discipline Yoshida. Miki advised Yoshida to apologize and settle the situation; however, he refused. In March, the unprecedented move to discipline the incumbent prime minister was passed in the HR plenary session. The Liberal Party's anti-Yoshida factions, such as the Hatoyama and Hirokawa groups (Yoshida's loyalist Hirokawa turned against Yoshida as Yoshida made Sato, instead of Hirokawa, party secretary general), were absent. Then, opposition parties—the Progressive Party and both factions of the JSP—submitted a bill for a non confidence vote for the cabinet. Miki advised Yoshida to resign and give power to Ichiro. Miki thought that this "bloodless revolution" would preempt giving unnecessary power to the Left, whereas dissolution of the HR might empower the Left. Yoshida refused again. The non confidence vote was passed in March 1953 (the Hatoyama group voted in favor this time). In reprisal, Yoshida dissolved the HR. Since this dissolution originated from Yoshida's insulting remark, it is referred to as the *Bakayaro kaisan* (the name-calling dissolution).[41]

The Creation of the Separatist Liberal Party

Miki was an ingenious *sakushi* (fixer). Miki did not miss the chance of bringing Hirokawa, the Liberal Party faction leader, on to Ichiro's side when Hirokawa severed relations with Yoshida, and succeeded in making Hirokawa's group leave the Liberal Party with Ichiro's group. This resulted in the creation of a breakaway party, *Buntoha Jiyuto* (Separatist Liberal Party, generally referred to as the *Bunjito* in Japanese literature). Kono confides, "Miki was the strongest advocate for defecting Yoshida's Liberal Party, while I was actually against it. However, I could not let people blame good old Miki. Therefore, I took the blame; people therefore think that I was the driving force for the Liberal Party's breakup. I am not actually an aggressive person. However, I was willing to be the 'villain' and get the blame for hardline actions for the sake of Hatoyama and Miki."[42]

The new party had 35 members and they thought that they could win as many as 100 seats in the general elections of April 1953. However, in the absence of any national organization, the new party had a hard time campaigning. Ichiro even suggested putting up his Otowa house as collateral to make a campaign fund. However, Miki and Kono rejected the idea. Ichiro also writes that during the campaign, Yoshida made a public pledge that should the Liberal Party obtain less than 200 seats, he would resign. The results were 199 seats for the Liberal Party, 76 for the Progressive Party, 72 for leftist JSP, 66 for rightist JSP, and 35 for the Separatist Liberal Party. The combined JSP increased by three times, from 46 to 138 seats. This was exactly what Miki had feared. Some original members of the Separatist Liberal Party, including Hirokawa, lost, but the total number remained the same for the party. Yoshida won the premier election over Shigemitsu, Progressive Party president. Thus, reneging his public pledge, Yoshida formed a minority cabinet solely by the Liberal Party: his fifth in May 1953.[43]

Ichiro Returns to the Liberal Party

In summer 1953, Ando, then home minister in the fifth Yoshida cabinet, asked Ichiro to return to the Liberal Party. Ishibashi Shojiro, a founder of the Bridgestone Tire Company, also met with influential members of the Separatist Liberal Party and tried to convince them to compromise with the Yoshida group. Concerned with the strike at Nissan (backed by the increased power of the leftist faction of the JSP), Ishibashi felt that conservative parties should not remain divided. Ishibashi and Ando often visited Ichiro, who was resting in Karuizawa. In contrast, Miki and Kono opposed the idea. They thought that should Ichiro return to the Liberal Party, he would only be betrayed by Yoshida again. In the end, Ichiro agreed to return to the Liberal Party on the condition that the party create a *kempo chosakai* (constitutional research council) and a *gaiko chosakai* (diplomatic research council). Immediately after hearing of Ichiro's consent, Yoshida suddenly visited Ichiro in Otowa. Yoshida went to Ichiro's study on the second floor without taking off his overcoat and shoes (against Japanese custom). He told Ichiro that only Ichiro needed to come back and that he did not need to bring anybody with him, and abruptly left. Instead of being offended, Ichiro felt sorry for Yoshida (for his arrogance and his desperate attempt to hang on to power).[44]

Ichiro writes, "Mr. Ishibashi and Mr. Ando were pestering me so much that I decided to return." According to Miki's biography, Yoshida used Ando and Ishibashi in order to convince Ichiro. Although Ando wanted to be education minister in the Yoshida cabinet, Yoshida made him home minister; his real assignment was "operations vis-à-vis Hatoyama." Yoshida also used the Ishibashi family. Due to the aftereffects of his stroke, Ichiro was dependent on Ishibashi's daughter Yasuko, Ichiro's daughter-in-law. Even Ishibashi's wife came to talk to Ichiro. In this regard, journalist Tomimori Eiji writes, "with Yoshida's persistent requests, Hatoyama returned to the Liberal Party and, thereby, betrayed Miki and Kono. An issue of money seems to have been involved in his return (the Separatist Liberal Party had enormous debts). Even so, his return disappointed Miki to the extent that he even thought of quitting politics."[45]

Money was involved. A biography of Sato Eisaku, based on his detailed diary, tells the true reason for Ichiro's return. Sato's diary was classified by the government. With the permission of his wife after his death, former *Asashi Shimbun* reporter Yamada Eizo wrote a biography, and published it in 1988 after her death. According to this biography, Yoshida offered to take on Ichiro's debts, incurred in the elections, and Sato delivered ¥20 million to Ichiro's aides. This is the focal point of the so-called *Zosen gigoku* (Shipbuilding scandal), which surfaced in 1954, in which a shipbuilding company, *Zosen kogyokai*, made a secret contribution of ¥20 million to Yoshida's Liberal Party. Yoshida's confidantes, Ikeda and Sato, were implicated. Sato was indicted and scheduled to be arrested. It is suspected that Yoshida used this money to induce Ichiro to return to the party; however, it is not established.[46]

Therefore, it was not the case that Ichiro betrayed Miki and Kono. Ichiro would not have returned to the Liberal Party without their consent. In fact, Ichiro went to see Miki on the day before his return to the Liberal Party. Miki told the crying Ichiro, "Don't worry. We can be together again soon. I cannot die before I make you prime minister." Kono, in tears, asked Ichiro "to return to the Liberal Party and wait for the right time to come. Miki and I will work together to realize the formation of the Hatoyama cabinet; then we will be united again." The Liberal Party vice president Ogata Taketora (1888–1956), of the mainstream Yoshida faction, ridiculed Ichiro's move as *detari haittari* (leaving and entering). The mass media picked it up but Ichiro writes, "Yoshida did the similar thing. So did British prime ministers such as Churchill, Disraeli, and Gladstone." Political scientist Ike Nobutaka notes that switching parties was a common practice then, and writes that politicians shifted from one party to another from time to time, usually between conservative parties, but sometimes between conservative and radical parties.[47]

The "Eight Angry *Samurai*"

In the end, 25 members of the Separatist Liberal Party (the party lost one member due to a death), led by Ichiro, returned to the Liberal Party in November 1953. The remaining eight members of the Separatist

Liberal Party, including Miki and Kono, did not go back. Miki told the others to follow Ichiro in order to support Ichiro, and said that he would follow them later. Kono and Ikeda Tadashi did not take Miki's words at face value and sensed that Miki had decided to quit politics. They knew that Miki's conscience would not allow him to join Yoshida. Yamamura Shinjiro, one of the eight, also said that if he had to give in to Yoshida, he would quit the Diet. Realizing Miki's unusual determination to sacrifice his political life to save Ichiro's face, the seven members of the Separatist Liberal Party decided to stay with Miki and formed the new *Nihon Jiyuto* (Japan Liberal Party).[48]

These eight politicians were referred to as the "Eight Angry *Samurai.*" They were "orphans" of the political circles and worked underground to create a new party for Ichiro. They had no money and decided to hold public meetings by charging admission fees. People gathered to hear fiery speeches by the Eight Angry *Samurai*, and they successfully launched nationwide campaigns. Their year-long ordeal resulted in the creation of the *Nihon Minshuto* (Japan Democratic Party) in November 1954, with Ichiro as president. Their story was dubbed the "Showa era's *Chushingura*" (a fact-based drama about 47 *samurai* who avenged their master in 1702). A famous theater company played its Showa-version parody, *Akai Jutan* ("Red Carpet," implying power struggle at the Diet). The play was popular.[49]

The Fall of the Yoshida Cabinet

Yoshida was elated. He won the premier's election over Shigemitsu and formed his fifth cabinet. Ichiro and 25 other defectors had returned to Yoshida's fold in infamy, and were treated with contempt by Yoshida. Although Yoshida formed the Constitutional Research Council, as he had agreed, he appointed Kishi Nobusuke, as chair, instead of Kita Reikichi, whom Ichiro recommended. Ichiro's confidantes, Miki and Kono, were forced to go underground. However, the Yoshida cabinet suffered from a series of bribery scandals, such as the Shipbuilding scandal. Fearing that the arrest of the incumbent party secretary general (Sato) might result in the overthrow of his cabinet, Yoshida made his justice minister Inukai intervene administratively. Inukai overrode Sato's arrest and resigned his post in April 1954 for taking the extrajudicial measure. Later, Ono and Kono tried to make Inukai a state minister in the reshuffled Kishi cabinet in June 1958; however, to Ono's dismay, Sato, who was deeply indebted to Inukai in 1954, strongly opposed it. It showed a difference between the career party politicians, who honored the sense of personal indebtedness, and the bureaucrats-turned-politicians, who ignored such personal factors. In response to Yoshida's 1954 maneuver, opposition parties submitted a bill for a non confidence vote in the cabinet to the HR. Due to the absence of 14 members of the Ashida faction and others in the Progressive Party, totaling 20 members, the non confidence vote failed (208 in favor and 228 opposed). However, the fall of Yoshida's reign was imminent.[50]

The Liberal Party's nonmainstream faction leaders, such as Kishi and Ishibashi Tanzan, and Progressive Party's leaders, such as Shigemitsu and Ashida, agreed to Miki's (now president of the new Japan Liberal Party) proposal to remove Yoshida's power and create a new party. All four had ambitions of succeeding Yoshida. Miki then managed to build a consensus among the pro–new party groups that the new party president should be Ichiro. Ichiro agreed to become a new party's president because Yoshida had done almost nothing he had promised after Ichiro had returned to the Liberal Party. In turn, Ono, the Liberal Party's director general, wanted to avoid a head-to-head confrontation between the Liberal Party and Miki's Japan Liberal Party. Ono felt that should Miki's attempt fail, the Liberal Party's mainstream leaders, such as Ogata, Ikeda, and Sato, would succeed Yoshida and Ichiro's chance would be lost forever. Ono, in tears, pleaded with Ichiro not to rebel against Yoshida. However, the time was ripe. Shigemitsu, the Progressive Party's honorary president, even said that he would be Ichiro's soldier.[51]

The Creation of the Japan Democratic Party

In November 1954, 35 members of the Liberal Party, including Ichiro, Kishi, Ando, and Ishibashi, left the party and created the Japan Democratic Party, with Shigemitsu's Progressive Party and Miki's Japan Liberal Party. Ichiro became president. The party executives included Shigemitsu, vice president; Kishi, secretary general; Miki, director general; and Ashida and Ishibashi, *saiko iin* (supreme officers). The party had 121 members in the HR, whereas the Liberal Party had 185 members. Combined with the two factions of the JSP, which abhorred Yoshida's oppressive stance, the Japan Democratic Party could muster a majority vote in the HR. Meanwhile, as a result of the formation of the Japan Democratic Party, the Liberal Party was divided into two groups: one in favor of the Yoshida cabinet's resigning *en masse* (peaceful power transfer to Ichiro) and the other in favor of dissolution of the HR for holding new general elections (head-to-head confrontation with the Japan Democratic Party). The former included Ogata (next party president-to-be) and Ono, whereas the latter included Ikeda and Sato, Yoshida's two exemplary protégés. Yoshida was hoping that the Liberal Party could still win the HR elections and yelled at Ikeda, "Fire Ogata." In the meantime, Kishi, along with the two factions of the JSP, agreed to submit a bill for a nonconfidence vote against the Yoshida cabinet on December 7, 1954. Yoshida refused to resign up to the last minute, but finally gave in on the day of the actual submission of the bill.[52]

However, the transfer of power to Ichiro was not easy. The Japan Democratic Party was still the second largest party. Again, it was Miki's turn. Miki and Kishi asked the two factions of the JSP for cooperation. Neither the leftist nor rightist faction of the JSP wanted to give power to Ogata, Yoshida's successor. They agreed to support Ichiro for prime minister on condition that Ichiro immediately dissolve the HR and hold general elections in order to hear the verdict of the people. In the showdown election for prime minister on December 9, 1954, Ichiro obtained 257 votes against Ogata's 191 votes in the HR, and 116 votes against 85 votes in the HC.[53]

Ichiro, Miki, and Kono could not stop crying. They had rebelled against the military regime, and yet all three were purged by the SCAP, and missed a chance to form the first democratic cabinet in postwar Japan. It was a long journey to power. The three were tied together by the liberalism of Waseda University; both Miki and Kono were graduates of the university to which Ichiro's father had dedicated himself (Ichiro also taught there before running for Tokyo city assembly). They were genuine career politicians. Ichiro writes, "more than the GHQ's purge and my sickness (stroke), Yoshida's obstruction was the hardest ordeal." Miki finally achieved his wartime pledge to Ichiro. The Eight Angry *Samurai*'s loyalty to Ichiro brought Yoshida's reign to an end and changed the course of politics. More than eight years and seven months had passed since Ichiro was purged. He was 71 years old.[54]

The First Hatoyama Cabinet

The first Hatoyama cabinet members included Shigemitsu (former Progressive), foreign minister and vice prime minister; Ando, education minister; Kono, agricultural minister; Ishibashi, trade minister; Miki Takeo (former Progressive and later prime minister, 1974–1976), transportation minister. Ichiro struck a delicate balance between his loyalists from the Liberal Party and former Progressives in allocating ministerial posts. Some party members objected to Ando's appointment, as he had served in the Yoshida cabinet. However, Ichiro kept Ando because he was one of his oldest aides and it was Ando's lifetime dream to become Ichiro's education minister (he was vice education minister when Ichiro was education minister in the Inukai cabinet). As for the party management, Kishi became secretary general and Miki director general. According to their wartime pledge, Miki was to be house speaker when Ichiro took power; however, Miki told Ichiro that he should stay behind the scenes. Miki was content with the formation of the Hatoyama cabinet.[55]

When Ichiro entered the prime minister's official residence in Nagata-*cho*, he was filled with emotions. He remembered the time when he was chief secretary of the Tanaka cabinet, and thought that he should have asked Frank Lloyd Wright to design in fewer stairs (now that he had to use a cane due to his stroke). Ichiro also thought of Prime Minister Saito, whom he had served as education minister and who was assassinated in this residence in the 2.26 *coup d'état* (as interior minister). He slowly walked around the residence, filled with memories of his predecessors and his early years.[56]

The Advent of the "Hatoyama Boom"

Ichiro, amiable and candid, was popular among the general public, who were tired of Yoshida's dogmatism and secrecy. Ichiro brought a new outlook in politics with his open style. Shortly after he took office, Ichiro issued an order to all government agencies forbidding civil servants from playing golf or mah-jongg with businessmen. Ichiro tried to break the collusion of power between the bureaucracy and business that was rampant in the Yoshida cabinet; however, it was a daunting task. Ike wrote in 1956, "[I]t is doubtful, given the nature of the relationship between government and interest groups, that Hatoyama's directive will have lasting results; but it did serve to focus official attention on certain unethical practices that had become rather conspicuous." This move shows Ichiro's clean stance, noted by other scholars such as Hellmann.[57]

Ichiro immediately prepared for general elections for the HR, as he had promised to the two wings of the JSP (a cunning politician would not honor such a promise once he obtained power). Ichiro dissolved the HR in January 1955 and held the general elections that February. Ichiro campaigned intensively, with Kaoru's support. The result was a victory for the Japan Democratic Party with 185 seats, 112 seats for the Liberal Party, 89 seats for the leftist faction of the JSP, and 67 seats for the rightist faction of the JSP. Although the Japan Democratic Party lacked an absolute majority, the party had increased by 64 seats and become the largest party. It was called the "Hatoyama boom." Ichiro formed his second cabinet in March 1955, with key cabinet members remaining the same as in his first (because the duration of the first cabinet was brief).[58]

The Second Hatoyama Cabinet

The second Hatoyama cabinet was far from stable. Given the minority status of the cabinet, Ichiro's premiership depended on his bipartisanship with the JSP. The two wings of the JSP together had obtained 156 seats, one third of the 466-seat HR. It meant that they could deter constitutional revisions; Ichiro's ultimate domestic agenda. Another problem was a more personal one but was important to Ichiro. Ichiro wanted to realize his wartime pledge to make Miki house speaker. Nevertheless, the defeated Liberal Party made a deal with the JSP to make its member house speaker in exchange for making a JSP's leftist faction member deputy speaker. Miki lost the election for house speaker. Ichiro apologized to Miki. Miki told Ichiro that he did not have to become house speaker insofar as his missions were realized: (1) for the Japan Democratic Party to become the largest party; (2) for Ichiro to become prime minister; and (3) more important, for the two conservative parties (the Liberal Party and the Japan Democratic Party) to merge for the sake of establishing a stable government that could formulate solid policy for rebuilding Japan. Miki had realized the first two. He was yet to fulfill his final mission: the so-called *hoshu godo* ("conservative merger").[59]

Grilled by Yoshida's Liberal Party

Although Yoshida had resigned as prime minister and president of the Liberal Party, he remained influential in the party. Yoshida used a strategy to grill Ichiro to exhaustion. Ichiro writes, "the Liberal Party summoned me every day to the plenary sessions of both the HR and the HC, as well as to every committee meeting and attacked me (the prime minister is required to report to the Diet sessions, similar to the British parliament's question and answer sessions). The sessions sometimes lasted from 10 o'clock in the morning to 10 or 11 o'clock at night. I was given less than 30 minutes' lunch time and was not allowed to drink water during the sessions or eat dinner. Later, I was told that they were hoping that, given my weak physical condition, I would die of exhaustion within a few months had they summoned me every day. During the sessions, they were waiting for me to make mistakes, found fault with my statements, and demanded an apology and retraction of my mistakes. Sometimes, I was made to apologize for not attending a session at the HC because I was attending a session at the HR that was held at the same time." Ichiro writes, "it was the hardest time in my very long political life."[60]

"The Conservative Merger"

Miki believed that the "conservative merger" was the only way for the conservatives to effectively control the Diet and confront the JSP. However, it was almost impossible, as the conservatives had been fighting among themselves as genuine rivals. It is the fate of politicians to have to fight with enemies within (among conservative parties in this case) and enemies outside (leftist parties) simultaneously. Miki made a bombastic statement in April 1955 in order to realize his last wish. He stated that the "conservative merger" was necessary for achieving political stability; the Hatoyama cabinet would resign and the Japan Democratic Party would break up if they were the obstacles to the merger. His statement startled the political circles and the general public because it came just after the formation of the second Hatoyama cabinet in March. It was the first step forward for the merger à la Miki. Miki had already laid the groundwork with Ogata, Liberal Party's president, via Kono. Kono was Ogata's junior at the *Asahi Shimbun*, and they were on good terms. Ogata also felt the need for the conservative merger in order to deal with the leftist parties; however, Yoshida refused. Ogata thought that even if the Liberal Party could overthrow the minority Hatoyama cabinet in cooperation with the socialists, the Liberal Party then would be obligated to the socialists and could be swayed by them. Ogata calculated that it would not be too late for him to become prime minister after the merger, by which the conservatives could deter the leftist opposition to their agenda.[61]

Miki was still confronted with strong opposition from both the Liberal Party and the Japan Democratic Party. Within the Liberal Party, Ikeda and Sato of the Yoshida faction, as well as Ono, opposed the merger insofar as there was a secret deal that Ichiro become the new party's first president and Ogata the second. Within the Japan Democratic Party, some of Ichiro's loyalists opposed the merger because they feared that Ogata or Shigemitsu might become the first party president. In turn, the former Progressives in the party opposed the merger because they did not like Ogata. Then, in May 1955, Kishi, party secretary general, made a surprise statement that he would not oppose breaking up the party in order to realize the merger. This was the second step forward for the merger à la Miki.[62]

Ichiro was concerned with the rivalry between Miki and Ono. Miki and Ono had been rivals for three decades during the prewar period. Miki (*Kenseikai*) went to Ono's (*Seiyukai*) constituency in Gifu-*ken* and campaigned against Ono, in Ono's presence, three times. During the postwar period, although initially both belonged to Ichiro's Japan Liberal Party, they once again became political rivals. Ono was sent to serve in Yoshida's cabinet and became the Liberal Party leader, while Miki left Yoshida's Liberal Party and created the Japan Democratic Party for Ichiro. Ono was called "*kaibutsu* (monster) of the conservatives," whereas Miki was referred to as "*odanuki* (big raccoon or deceiver) of the political circles." Insofar as the two fixers of the conservatives would not converge, the merger was not possible. In the end, Ono agreed to meet with Miki.[63]

Ono writes that he was convinced that Miki was trying to use him and Ogata in order to prolong the Hatoyama cabinet. Miki himself once said, "I lie with sincerity." In the "monster-raccoon" meeting, Ono was determined not to be deceived by Miki; however, as they began talking, he realized that Miki's goal was not at such a petty level but at the grand national level: to stabilize the power of the conservatives. Ono was touched by Miki's passion for the merger for the sake of Japan's future. Ono agreed to cooperate with the merger. It was the third step forward for the merger. Consequently, a quadripartite meeting among Miki, Kishi, Ono, and Ishii Kojiro (Liberal Party secretary general) was held in May 1955, which was followed by a Hatoyama–Ogata summit in June.[64]

While Miki had managed to get consent from the Liberal Party, a problem remained within the Japan Democratic Party. Former Progressives, such as Miki Takeo and Matsumura Kenzo, still opposed the merger and threatened to leave the party. It was a step backward for Miki's grand design. It was Kono's turn. Kono coordinated the difference between the two Mikis and conciliated Matsumura. Then, in August 1955, Kishi and Kono made a deal during their trip to Washington, accompanying Foreign Minister Shigemitsu for talks on defense contributions and the security treaty. The trip gave them a chance to get to know each other. Kono asked Kishi to support Ichiro as long as his cabinet lasted, and in turn promised Kishi that he would make every effort to make Kishi prime minister afterward. They agreed that the first new party president would be Ichiro and the second Ogata.[65]

Ichiro writes, after the trip Kishi became very cooperative with his group. Upon their return, however, Kono and Kishi found out that the Liberal Party's Ikeda and Sato insisted on having a public election for a new party president. They figured that the Liberal Party and the former Progressives in the Japan Democratic Party together could elect Ogata as the new president. Meanwhile, the two socialist parties succeeded in their merger in October 1955. Miki had no time to lose. Miki, Kono, and Kishi planned to pass a party resolution in both houses to form a preparatory committee for the new party creation, consisting of all the members of both the Liberal Party and the Japan Democratic Party. The Liberal Party was obliged to follow suit. Then, the quadripartite meeting (Miki, Kishi, Ono, and Ishii) came up with an ingenious compromise plan: (1) to leave the new president post vacant for the time being (because it was *the* barrier to the merger); (2) to hold the election for party president in spring 1956; and (3) to form the third Hatoyama cabinet. Ikeda and Sato still opposed it, but Ono and Ishii managed to have them acquiesce. The turbulent drama for the conservative merger ended in November 1955.[66]

The Creation of the LDP and the Third Hatoyama Cabinet

Miki realized his last wish. His determination was such that he was dubbed "incarnation of the conservative merger." The Liberal Democratic Party (LDP) was created with 299 HR members and 118 HC members in November 1955. Ichiro, Ogata, Miki, and Ono became acting presidents of the party, Kishi became secretary general, and Ishii became director general. Thus, the "1955 system" of the LDP reign was established. The architects of the merger, Miki, Kono, and Ono, did not fully fathom the significance of what they had created.[67]

As a result of the conservative merger, the second Hatoyama cabinet resigned *en masse* and Ichiro formed the third Hatoyama cabinet in November 1955. The party presidential election was scheduled in April 1956 and the Ogata group was expecting to win the election. However, Ogata suddenly died of a heart attack in January 1956 and Ichiro became the LDP's first party president. Ichiro deeply mourned Ogata's death because Ogata was a grand-scale politician. Ichiro also sympathized with Ogata because he himself suffered a mild heart attack when he was playing golf in January. A doctor diagnosed that Ichiro was sick but advised him not to resign the premier's position: should he resign, he would become a really sick man.[68]

Then, Miki died in July 1956. Miki did not seek a cabinet post for himself although he could have become vice prime minister or a state minister if he had desired. He was above the musical chairs game for ministerial posts and remained behind the scene in the party leadership. When Ichiro was pressed to reshuffle his cabinet in June 1956, Miki on his deathbed told him, "you are too soft and do not have the guts to fire your cabinet members. I would take care of everything if I were not sick, but I cannot now. Let's not reshuffle this time." Ichiro writes, "Miki's ability to persuade his opponents in a short period of time was remarkable, as he did toward Hirokawa (the creation of the Separatist Liberal Party) and Ono (the conservative merger). Skillful talk or congruence of interests alone cannot change people's minds the way Miki did. His deep convictions and genuine sincerity touched people's hearts and made them change their minds."[69]

Ichiro writes in his memoirs, "Miki was an extremely strong-willed man. I have been impressed with his ability ever since the Tokyo city Assembly time. We liked each other even though we were constantly fighting in the assembly. I felt that he could complement my weaknesses and that he could be my best supporter. During the Tojo cabinet, we promised to help each other in reconstructing Japan after the war. However, both of us were purged just before our goal was to be realized. I have endless memories of him." Ichiro also writes, "his death mask was great, indeed. It was a face of extremely strong will—a will to carry out anything without hesitation. It was a face that knows no fear. Looking at his face, I once again realized that he was a first-class politician. I kept mumbling to my wife, 'it is a great face.' " Ichiro dedicated his memoirs to Miki and Ando, whom Ichiro outlived.[70]

The Defense Issue

In his third cabinet, Ichiro embarked on tearing down the Yoshida legacy and tried to make politicians take control over the bureaucracy. Ichiro set up LDP platforms: (1) *jishu kempo* (self-reliant constitution)— to revise the constitution in order to possess constitutional self-defense forces; and (2) *jishu gaiko* (self-reliant diplomacy)—to restore relations with the Soviet Union and develop closer relations with China. Ichiro realized the need for having minimum self-defense capabilities as early as December 1945 and advocated constitutional revisions in order to fulfill the need. It was a risky undertaking when the general public subscribed to pacifism, backed by the leftist parties. The leftist parties had launched a massive international peace movement in protest of the U.S. nuclear tests in the Bikini Islands in 1954, in which Japanese fishermen became sick and one died of exposure. The two factions of the

JSP obtained one-third of the HR seats and merged in 1955. In these adverse conditions, Ichiro established the *Kokubo kaigi* (National Defense Council) and the *Kempo chosakai* (Constitutional Research Council) in March 1956. The Left denounced these moves as a "reverse course" and mobilized a peace movement, opposing the SDFs and the U.S.–Japan Security Treaty.[71]

The U.S. administration perceived Ichiro's stance as neutral and felt that Ichiro was not trying hard enough for Japan's rearmament. At the U.S.–Japan defense talks in Washington D.C. in August 1955, Shigemitsu made a big concession and proposed to deploy 180,000 army personnel by 1958. Yet, the Eisenhower administration requested that Japan deploy 350,000 army personnel. It was an unrealistic request, given Japan's economic power at that time. Such a move would only intensify protests by the Japanese public and empower the Left. Secretary of State Dulles also rejected Shigemitsu's request to reduce Japan's contribution to U.S.–Japan defense expenses. He was also indifferent to Japan's requests to revise the U.S.–Japan Security Treaty (to make its terms more equal), to return Okinawa, and to resume trade with China.[72]

The second agenda met with the rejection of the United States. Choosing a "subservient independence" path for Japan, Yoshida was indifferent to these diplomatic initiatives. In contrast, Ichiro tried to restore Japan's *jishusei* (self-reliance) and real independence. For this, Ichiro was dubbed Gaullist although he was not against the U.S.–Japan Security Treaty. Kataoka writes, Ichiro's group "collided with Yoshida and his double-pronged policy. They were concerned less with rearmament itself than with diplomatic equality and mutuality that went with rearmament, not with military hardware but with possible corruption of the body politic that may result from avoiding all international entanglements." However, the United States did not allow Japan to initiate its own diplomacy toward the Soviet Union and China.[73]

With the leftist opposition and the lack of support from the United States, Ichiro's agenda for constitutional revisions failed and the problems with the "subservient independence" have troubled U.S.–Japan relations to this day.

The "Hatomander Bill"

Ichiro also tried to legislate a *shosenkyoku-sei* ("small-size election district system") in order to marginalize the Left and create a two-party system. Ichiro proposed the revision of the election law for the HR in February 1956 and submitted the bill to the Diet in March. The HR election districts had consisted of single-vote multiple-seat districts: the so-called *chusenkyoku-sei* ("medium-size election district system"). The bill changed them to small-size districts (or single-member districts), which would be conducive to the creation of a two-party political system, such as that of the United States. The leftist parties, notably the JSP, opposed the bill and criticized it as the "Hatomander bill"; a pun on Hatoyama and "Gerrymander." The Diet was in turmoil in April. To compromise with the JSP, Ichiro submitted an amendment bill. It passed the HR in May but failed in the HC, and thus the bill was aborted. The LDP and the JSP had actually worked out a deal that the JSP would support and pass the amendment bill in the HR, in order to save the LDP's face, but it would oppose the bill in the HC.[74]

The agenda for the single-member district was revived in 1992 by Prime Minister Miyazawa Kiichi. After a series of political compromises, the revision of the election law, introducing the single-member district, passed in January 1994 under the Hosokawa coalition cabinet (see chapter 7).

The Fraternity Youth Society

Aside from politics, Ichiro was engaged in friendship movements. Ichiro founded *Yuai Seinen Doshikai* (Fraternity Youth Society) in 1953. Ichiro writes, "The idea initially occurred to me when I translated Coudenhove's *The Totalitarian State Against Man*. I was struck by his ideals and founded the society." The organization had a hard time propagating itself at a time when youth and students were not considered as such unless they were leftists. The members visited welfare facilities and rural areas to hold seminars and show movies. They also appealed for world peace, opposing atomic bomb testing. Although the society was politically neutral, leftists denounced the group as anticommunist, whereas the Liberals (Yoshida faction) called it "reds." However, the members painstakingly continued their activities. They left Tokyo with only one-way train tickets in their hands. They collected the membership fees from the new members who joined the society that day and used this income to pay for that night's accommodations and the next day's travel expenses. In this reckless way, they gradually propagated the spirit of fraternity nationwide. In the end, they established branches in every prefecture, with 240 branches and more than 16,000 members. All members are younger than 35 years old. Ichiro writes, "The society is planning to build 15 Youth Hostels. I am looking forward to singing the 'society song' with young people when they are built." The society built the first Youth Hostels in Japan that met international standards in 1959. Ichiro did not live to see the completion of the Youth Hostels or meet Coudenhove when he visited his "homeland" in 1967.[75]

World Friendship and Peace Movements

In March 1955 Cordell Hull, then commander of the U.N. Forces, and Osias, former president of the Filipino Senate, and other foreign dignitaries gathered at Ichiro's Otowa palace. The press were nervous about the objective of their visit because it was a time when the U.S.–Japan "defense burden sharing" and the Japan–Filipino war reparations were at issue. It turned out that they held a ceremony to promote Ichiro from the 33rd rank (the lowest) to the 31st rank of the Freemasons. Ichiro had joined the Freemasons in February 1951 because Coudenhove was a member. *The Mainichi Shimbun* reported that Ichiro had tears of joy when he was given the certificate of a master mason and stated, "my mother would be very happy had she known that a world peace-loving group had accepted me and celebrated my promotion."[76]

Ichiro was a Christian and supported other world friendship groups, such as Moral Rearmament (MRA). MRA was founded in 1938 by an American priest Frank Bookman (1878–1961), in order to confront Nazism by mobilizing moral and spiritual power. After the war, the group helped reconciliation between France and Germany and also helped to convince the former Allied Powers to sign the San Francisco Peace Treaty with Japan. The group's four principles are absolute honesty, purity, self-lessness, and love. Ichiro writes of the time when Bookman visited Japan in April 1956, "I was impressed by the fact that Mr. Bookman had adhered to the MRA's four principles. Although he had suffered from a stroke during the war and had difficulty walking, he was full of spirit and looked younger than his age of 78. I am interested in MRA's development in Japan and I made a motion to my cabinet to decorate Mr. Bookman." Toyoda Jo notes that Ichiro's religious beliefs and beliefs in idealistic movements were a source of his spiritual strength. This spiritual strength is one of the attributes that set Ichiro apart from other *obotchan* (silver-spoon boy) leaders, such as Prince Konoe.[77]

The Japan–Soviet Peace Treaty Negotiations

In March 1956, Ichiro took up his most important, and his last, foreign policy initiative in earnest: to conclude a peace treaty with the Soviet Union. The Soviet Union was not a signatory to the San Francisco Peace

Treaty and, as a corollary, Japan had not ended its state of war with the Soviet Union. Ichiro believed that, after making peace with the United States and its allies, the next cardinal foreign policy was to normalize relations with the Soviet Union (the United States had maintained diplomatic relations with the Soviet Union during the Cold War). Ichiro listed the rationales for restoring relations with the Soviet Union: (1) to end the state of war with the Soviet Union; (2) for Japan to become a member of the United Nations (the Soviet Union was vetoing Japan's admission to the UN); (3) to repatriate 560,000 Japanese internees detained in Siberia since 1945; and (4) to restore the territories taken by the Soviet Union. The so-called Japanese northern territories comprise Etorofu, Kunashiri, Habomai, and Shikotan Islands.[78]

It was a politically risky agenda because the United States did not support it. The Eisenhower administration objected to Ichiro's request to use New York City as a site for the negotiations. Secretary of State Dulles declined to see Foreign Minister Shigemitsu for consultation on this matter. The first round of negotiations began in London in January 1955, led by Matsumoto Shunichi (a HR member and former ambassador to England). However, the dispute over the "northern territories" stalled the negotiations. At home, the Liberal Party (before the conservative merger) obstructed the negotiations. The MOFA insisted that the negotiations were illegal because Japan did not have diplomatic relations with the Soviet Union. Knowing the MOFA's objection, a Soviet delegation at the initial contact visited Ichiro's house through the back door. Convinced that he was doing the right thing, Ichiro told them that they should come openly through the main entrance.[79]

Ichiro believed that the Japanese, or the Americans for that matter, could not misinterpret the rationale for his initiative because he was outspokenly anticommunist. His move could not possibly be misconstrued as communizing Japan. Nevertheless, Ichiro's inner circle was isolated. This diplomatic initiative was embroiled in the power struggle within the LDP, and Yoshida's protégés, Ikeda and Sato, vehemently attacked the initiative. They denounced Kono as "red" when he went to the Kremlin in May 1956 and negotiated with Nikita Khrushchev. Kono fiercely demanded Japan's interests to the extent that he suffered anemia and passed out during the intense talks with Khrushchev. Yet, Kono was criticized as a traitor who gave up the islands for the sake of fishing rights. Even Shigemitsu, Ichiro's foreign minister and plenipotentiary for the final talks in Moscow in July 1956, did not cooperate with Ichiro. Ito Takashi writes, "Shigemitsu, who had up to then maintained a rigid antitreaty stand and demanded the return of all four disputed islands, did an incredible about-face in Moscow. He agreed to the treaty in exchange for only two islands and asked for a go-ahead from his government." Stunned by Shigemitsu's sudden change, Ichiro recalled him in August 1956. The MOFA was sabotaging the negotiations, backed by the Eisenhower administration, and Shigemitsu was caught between Ichiro and the MOFA. Ichiro writes, "Mr. Shigemitsu was acting strange."[80]

Given the impasse, Ichiro went to Moscow himself in October 1956 despite his poor physical condition. He was 73 years old and people feared that he might die from a long journey. Ichiro knew that this would be his last mission. The business circles were also cool to Ichiro's initiative. Donald Hellmann, in his in-depth study of the negotiation process, writes that the specific bond linking the business world with the conservative party was missing in this decision-making. Hellmann attributes the business impotence to "the unusual absence of close ties between the prime minister and the dominant elements of the Japanese business world[.]" Kataoka also notes that the financial circles abandoned the *tojinha* (party politicians' group) and favored Yoshida. In turn, Ichiro received minimal cooperation from the Left. The Left understood Ichiro's initiative correctly, knew that it would not benefit their cause, and they only gave token support.[81]

Faced with obstruction by the Right and indifference by the Left, Ichiro had to negotiate with tough Soviet politicians such as Khrushchev and Jacob Malik in the Kremlin, without any support. Hellmann writes that given the lack of domestic and international support, "Japan could not but play a passive role" vis-à-vis the Soviet Union . . . "Hatoyama eventually succeeded in forcing a decision, but only at the cost of his political life." Kataoka argues that the U.S. administration did not like Ichiro's initiative and abandoned Ichiro: Dulles, who used Ichiro to oust Yoshida from power, this time used Yoshida to oust Ichiro.[82]

Signing of the Japan–Soviet Joint Declaration

Despite his intense negotiations, Ichiro failed to conclude a peace treaty with the Soviets due to the deadlock on the territorial issue. In lieu of a peace treaty, the two countries signed a joint declaration to restore their relations in October 1956. It was still a significant diplomatic breakthrough for Japan. The Soviets agreed to return the internees, to endorse Japan's admission to the UN, and to "hand over" Habomai and Shikotan upon the conclusion of a peace treaty. However, they disagreed on how to solve the return of Kunashiri and Etorofu. Japan demanded that they continue to negotiate the territorial issue along with the negotiations for a peace treaty. Conversely, the Soviets insisted that the territorial issue should be excluded from future negotiations for a peace treaty and that they would return Habomai and Shikotan only upon "the enforcement" (rather than signing) of a peace treaty and the U.S. return of Okinawa and Ogasawara islands to Japan.[83]

In the end, Japan conceded to the Soviet demand to remove the territorial issue from the issues that they would continue to negotiate. By so doing, the Soviet tried de facto to deny the existence of the territorial issue with Japan. The only legal recourse left for Japan to claim that the territorial issue is still unresolved is the so-called Matsumoto letter, in which the Soviets acknowledged that unresolved issues included the territorial issue. In essence, Ichiro chose to save the lives of 560,000 internees in Siberia (as well as normalizing relations with the Soviet Union and Japan's admission to the UN) over Kunashiri and Etorofu.[84]

Ichiro writes, some argued that Japan should not resume relations with the Soviet Union before it returned Etorofu and Kunashiri. However, he considered this argument inhuman, neglecting the plight of the internees in Siberia. Ichiro also wanted Etorofu and Kunashiri back; however, he reasoned that people's lives are limited but territories will remain. With this premise, Ichiro undertook the daunting task without U.S. consent. Had Ichiro not negotiated with the Soviets, it is doubtful that the ailing POWs in Siberia would have been able to return home alive. Takashima Masuo, former administrative vice minister of foreign affairs and Japan's Supreme Court justice, were among these POWs. Proving the severity of the conditions, he for long suffered from the aftereffects of the frostbite that he had during his detention. Had Japan not resumed diplomatic relations with the Soviet Union in 1956, when would Japan have been admitted to the UN? Ichiro dared to choose a politically unpopular path for the sake of Japan's national interest and of the people.[85]

In the extremely adverse conditions, Ichiro negotiated as forcefully as anyone could have and secured the maximum concessions from the Soviet Union. No progress has been made regarding the return of the islands to this day. Even Mikhail Gorbachev and Boris Yeltsin did not return them. Japan and Soviet/Russia are yet to conclude a peace treaty. Writer Saki Ryuzo states that he became Ichiro's fan when he (high school student) heard Ichiro's campaign speech that he would take the *inishiachibu* (initiative, a new word borrowed from English) and kept his word in the Japan–Soviet negotiations. Sake deplores that since then, Japanese policy-makers have not taken any initiative toward Soviet/Russia.[86]

Ichiro writes that after the signing ceremony for the joint declaration, the Soviets held a huge reception in the Kremlin, with 1,500 foreign dignitaries. When the band played *Kimigayo* (the Japanese de facto national anthem, see chapter 8), he could not help crying. He wondered if the Kremlin had ever played *Kimigayo* before such a huge crowd, even when Japan was considered equal to Russia/Soviet Union in the past. Upon his return to Japan, Ichiro was greeted with enthusiasm by the crowd. People occupied sidewalks from Haneda airport to his house in Otowa and waved at his entourage with *Hinomaru* (Japanese flags, see chapter 8). He felt that had he given in to the Soviets earlier, as Shigemitsu had suggested, the people would not have been as happy.[87]

As a result of the Japan–Soviet Joint Declaration, Japan's admission to the UN was unanimously approved at its General Assembly in December 1956. Japan, the former enemy of the Allied Powers, was accepted by the international community. Shigemitsu was appointed to be Japan's chief representative to the UN and gave Japan's maiden speech at the General Assembly, stating that Japan would be a bridge between the East and the West. Having assumed his final diplomatic role, Shigemitsu died in January 1957. Unlike Shidehara, Yoshida, and Ashida, this diplomat-turned-politician did not fulfill his ambition of becoming prime minister.[88]

Kaoru accompanied Ichiro to Moscow; a harsh long voyage. Ichiro expresses his gratitude toward his wife in his memoirs and attributes to her dedication his miraculous recovery from his stroke to the extent that he was able to function as prime minister just a few years after the stroke. Japanese husbands rarely acknowledge their wive's dedication because it is taken for granted. However, Ichiro candidly did so, referring to the British prime ministers, such as Neville Chamberlain and Winston Churchill, who acknowledged their wives' dedication to their political careers. Ichiro recalls when they visited New York City on the way back from Moscow, Kaoru received a citation from Barnard College (Teachers' College) of Columbia University. She made an ad-lib speech saying "I have been given awards many times as a prime minister's wife, but this is the first time I have been given an award for myself. I am flattered. I will donate this citation to my alma mater." Ichiro wrote "I was very proud of her."[89]

Ichiro was no different from many established Japanese men when it came to relationships with women, and even had an illegitimate child. Little is written about this as it was not customary to write about such affairs in biographies. Kaoru condoned Ichiro's affairs and used to say that she had seven children: her six children and Ichiro. Among them, Ichiro was the most troublesome.[90]

Retirement

Unlike Yoshida, Ichiro did not hang on to power. Although Yoshida claimed that he reluctantly became proxy prime minister, he grew preoccupied with power and was forced to resign. Ono, who served both Ichiro and Yoshida, writes that Yoshida failed to choose the right time for his retirement: had Yoshida resigned just after the conclusion of the San Francisco Peace Treaty, he would be remembered as a great statesman comparable to the Meiji leaders. By contrast, Ichiro recognized a pitfall that once one has attained power, it is difficult to give it up. Ichiro told Kono that knowing the right time to retire was an even more difficult thing for a politician than attaining power, and asked him to be candid about when to resign. Ichiro voluntarily resigned after signing the Japan–Soviet Joint Declaration.[91]

Ichiro writes that he had already made up his mind to retire when he decided to go to Moscow. As soon as he returned from Moscow, he began preparing for his resignation from the premier's position. As he had succeeded in normalizing relations with the Soviet Union, he had nothing to regret. His heart was filled with satisfaction and his mind was as clear as *meikyo shisui* (a clear mirror and still water). Ichiro retired from the premier's post in December 1956 and the third Hatoyama cabinet resigned *en masse*. Unlike Yoshida, Ichiro did not become a don afterward. Ichiro made a clean departure from his position of power. Toyoda writes that being idealistic and clean (uncorrupted), Ichiro was a rare politician. Toyoda notes that after the Hatoyama cabinet, the LDP's involvement with the business circles deepened and scandals ensued. Ichiro won the HR elections for the last time in May 1958, his fifteenth consecutive win. Afterwards, other than participating in the fraternity youth activities, he spent a quiet life of rehabilitation, tending his rose garden until his death in March 1959. He was 76 years old.[92]

An Overall Assessment of Ichiro's Political Leadership

In the overall assessment of Ichiro's leadership ability, his personal attributes—gentleness, honesty, idealism, and outspokenness—constitute positive and negative qualities for Ichiro's leadership. Many analysts agree that Ichiro had a certain aspect of naïveté but that he matured through hardships and turned himself into a political leader. Ichiro first joined the *Seiyukai*, which encompassed the Liberals. From this party, Ichiro set out on his political career, defended democracy and parliamentarism in the dark age of militarism, and was suppressed as a liberalist. In the postwar period, Ichiro created the Japan Liberal Party, largely comprising *Seiyukai* members. The party was labeled conservative vis-à-vis the JCP that was legalized by the SCAP. Regardless of being labeled as a liberalist or as conservative, Ichiro subscribed to the same creed and fought fascism, both of the Right and Left.

From a historical perspective, Ichiro inherited Itagaki's Liberal Party by creating the Japan Liberal Party. Ichiro also inherited Okuma's Progressive Party by creating the Japan Democratic Party. The LDP, created by the merger of the two parties, embodies the integration of the two mainstream democratic parties that originated in the early Meiji era. Ichiro led all three: the Japan Liberal Party (thesis); the Japan Democratic Party (antithesis in terms of rivalry among the conservatives); and the LDP (synthesis). In the post–San Francisco Peace Treaty era, Ichiro tried to restore real sovereignty for Japan by revising the constitution and formulating Japan's own foreign policy. Half a century later, time has finally caught up with Ichiro as his grandson Yukio proposed constitutional revisions (see chapter 8).

The Strong Will to Carry Out Long-Term Vision

Ichiro not only had a long-term vision but also a strong will to bring his vision into reality. Ono writes that unlike the other *obotchan* (silver-spoon boy) politicians, Ichiro was strong-willed and tenacious. Ichiro stood firm against the military regime during the prewar period in defense of a democratic parliament when most of his colleagues in the parliament kept quiet. Knowing that the odds were against him, Ichiro dared to challenge the legislation of the Konoe and Tojo cabinets. It was a courageous act, demonstrating Ichiro's strong will to act on his political convictions. Ono also notes that in spite of poor health in 1956, Ichiro's tenacity enabled him to go all the way to Moscow and negotiate with the tough Soviets.[93]

Kono writes that Ichiro was not the puppet of Miki and Kono, as some saw him. Constitutional revisions and normalizing relations with the Soviet Union were Ichiro's own ideas. Ichiro told Miki and Kono that the two agenda items were his ultimate missions and asked them to help him carry them out. Miki was not in favor of these initiatives, but Ichiro persisted. In the end, Miki agreed. Being moved by Ichiro's strong convictions, Kono took charge of the unwanted task of normalizing relations with the Soviet Union and worked for it to exhaustion. Otherwise, Kono, a staunch anticommunist, would not have gone to Moscow, enduring accusations of being a "red" by his conservative rivals. Kono writes, Ichiro's passion for his convictions and his tenacity toward overcoming obstruction at home and abroad, as exemplified in the Japan–Soviet negotiations, are "attributes of true political leadership."[94]

Kono adds, Ichiro did not undertake policy agenda for the sake of obtaining popularity or prolonging his power. On the contrary, constitutional revisions and normalizing relations with the Soviet Union were most unpopular agenda. Ichiro dared to undertake these tasks, despite the objections from the United States, because he truly believed that they were in Japan's long-term national interest. Kono writes, Ichiro taught him that the essence of genuine political leadership is the determination to carry out national policy based on a long-term vision for the sake of the nation's future, rather than policy based on short term and private interests.[95]

The Use of Confidantes

Ichiro was aware of his gentle and naive nature and compensated for his weaknesses by using strong confidantes, such as Miki and Kono. Although Ichiro and Miki's relationship began as political opponents, they developed mutual respect for each other and became indispensable allies during the war era. If Miki was chief of staff for Ichiro's postwar political career, Kono was deputy chief of staff. While Yoshida shrewdly deceived Ichiro, Ono, Ogata, Shigemitsu, and Ashida, Miki and Kono were not deceived. Miki and Kono took care of unpleasant aspects of politics, money, and personnel decisions, for Ichiro. Without their loyalty and political skills, Ichiro could not have become prime minister.

"Pedestal Carrier" and "Pedestal Rider"
Miki pledged allegiance to Ichiro despite the fact that Miki was in many ways a more mature and tougher politician, who could confront Yoshida. Miki also had a long-term vision. Immediately after he succeeded in the conservative merger, he advocated rejuvenation of party politicians, by setting the retirement age at 60 years. It was an un-self-preserving initiative and became his legacy. Miki remained loyal to Ichiro for several reasons. They shared the same political convictions. They shared a good rapport; their different personalities—soft Ichiro and tough Miki—gravitated toward each other. Miki also owed his career to Ichiro's brother-in-law Suzuki. Toyoda therefore argues that Miki's deep sense of indebtedness to Ichiro's family, as well as his vision and ingenious political tactics, accounted for Ichiro's success. Toyoda

however adds that without Ichiro's caliber as a political leader, Miki's efforts would have been useless. In this sense, the Hatoyama cabinet was a co-production of Ichiro and Miki.[96]

The most critical qualities that set Ichiro apart from Miki were Ichiro's charismatic attributes and his thoroughbred origin. These attributes gave Ichiro the caliber of a leader. He was born into a reputable political family and was groomed to be a political leader. Ichiro's purebred background gave him legitimacy as a leader. Ichiro's elite background as well as his clean and honest image fit well to speak of high ideals, whereas Miki, with his less reputable background and a fierce image, did not fit well to speak of such ideals. Toyoda notes that although Miki was a year younger than Ichiro, he looked much older and stern. Miki recognized his disadvantages and used to say that Ichiro was born to be a "general of generals," while he was a mere "general of soldiers." Tomimori refers to a saying that it takes two types of people in politics: *katsugu hito* (people who carry the pedestal) and *katugareru hito* (people who ride on the pedestal). Miki was the former and Ichiro was the latter.[97]

In summary, Toyoda writes that Ichiro inherited Kazuo's attributes for political leadership, expanded them, and perfected them. The major difference between the two is that Ichiro was not as enthusiastic about studying as Kazuo, whose scholarly attributes were passed down to Hideo. Toyoda also states that like Kazuo, Ichiro did not have the maneuvering skills of grand-scale shrewd leaders, such as Hara Takashi and Ito Hirobumi. However, Ichiro had the charismatic quality to become a "pedestal rider," had an expansive array of loyal supporters, and reached the pinnacle of power.[98]

The Interactions Between Personal Attributes and the Environment

Finally, interactions between personal attributes and environment should be examined for the case of Ichiro's political career. The environment had an enormous impact on his political career by presenting the constraints to which he had to apply his attributes. However, Ichiro often defied the environment and his personal attributes affected his career gravely. For instance, on the surface, it appears that the rise of militarism was beyond Ichiro's control and he was subjected to the military's oppression. Yet, Ichiro could have avoided oppression had he remained silent. Ichiro could not do so because of his political convictions and outspokenness. In a similar vein, it appears that Ichiro's purge was unavoidable given the omnipotence of the SCAP that tried to eradicate any remnants of prewar Japan. Yet, he could have escaped this seemingly fatal event, had he exercised prudence and remained low-key. The two cases indicate that had he applied his attributes scrupulously, Ichiro could have overridden the environmental confines.

Conversely, Ichiro could not overcome the environmental constraints for the case of constitutional revisions. It was simply a premature political agenda for his time—the constitution remains intact to this day. Ichiro also could not overcome the environmental constraints and failed to conclude a peace treaty with the Soviet Union, although he succeeded in normalizing relations with that country. The obstacles were insurmountable. Japan and Soviet/Russia are yet to conclude a peace treaty to this day. In retrospect, Ichiro attempted to achieve Japan's long-term national interest in each instance, well ahead of his time; he challenged the constraints of the political structure against odds, and was punished by the authority that ruled Japan at each time: the military regime, the SCAP, and the U.S. government.

In summary, the environment presented formidable obstacles to achieving his political agenda; however, in some of the cases, Ichiro could have overcome the structural constraints by careful application of his attributes. In this sense, his attributes (and the lack thereof) as much as the environment determined the course of events. In the end, Ichiro endured adverse environments, such as the rise of the military and U.S. occupation, and rose to the occasion. Tomimori writes that like a phoenix, Ichiro had an indomitable spirit, survived many downturns, and revived each time. Ichiro proved to be a "pedestal rider."[99]

CHAPTER 6

THE THIRD GENERATION: IICHIRO, THE MOF, AND THE MOFA

With the conservative merger of November 1955, factional feuds within the LDP replaced inter-party rivalries among conservative parties. Ishibashi Tanzan succeeded Ichiro as premier in December 1956, after an intense fight between Ishibashi and Kishi Nobusuke. Then, with the death of Ishibashi, Kishi became premier in February 1957. Kishi resigned in June 1960, embroiled in the revision of the U.S.–Japan Security Treaty, and Yoshida's protégés, Ikeda Hayato and Sato Eisaku, took power. During the reign of the "Yoshida school," Japan drove itself to economic recovery and growth in high gear. In the era of high-speed economy, Ichiro's son, Iichiro, scaled the bureaucratic pyramid of the MOF, Japan's economic miracle-maker, together with the Ministry of International Trade and Industry (MITI).

The Prewar Period

Iichiro was born in November 1918. Ichiro and Kaoru had five daughters and a son. Iichiro proved himself academically as the only son of the renowned elite family and graduated from the Faculty of Law at Tokyo Imperial University in 1941. Iichiro maintained straight *yu* (As) throughout his years at the university. Although his mother did not give Iichiro lessons at half past three in the morning, as Haruko had done, she stayed up until two o'clock in the morning reading books while Iichiro was studying. It was Kaoru who bought a villa in Karuizawa so that Iichiro could study in a cooler environment in the summer. Ichiro acknowledges Kaoru's dedication to their son writing, "my wife did not go to bed until after my son came out from his study around two o'clock in the morning. I think that her attitude had a good influence on my son, as my mother's did on me." Iichiro himself wrote in the Reader's Digest in January 1950, "my mother was always waiting for me until two o'clock in the morning, to hear what I did during the day. She used to say 'If I could be instrumental for you to develop a will to work hard, that is the best gift I could give you.' "[1]

However, Iichiro refused his father's request to succeed to his seat in the HR. Despite his mother's solicitation, he refused to become a lawyer or a politician. Iichiro detested politics. As he grew up, Iichiro had observed the negative aspects of politics through his father's career. When his younger son Kunio decided to become a politician, Iichiro opposed it. Iichiro said to Kunio, "if you want to be a politician, you must be a bad person." Kunio asked, "Then, my grandfather must have been a very bad person (because he was prime minister)." Iichiro replied "Didn't you know that?" Therefore, against his parents' wishes, Iichiro became a public servant and entered the MOF in 1941. He married Ishibashi Yasuko (1922–), the eldest daughter of Ishibashi Shojiro, founder of Bridgestone Tire Company, in 1942. With the outbreak of the Pacific War, Iichiro enlisted in the Navy and was sent to the war front in the South Pacific, such as the Palau Islands and the Truk Islands. The warship he was supposed to be aboard was sunk. The MOF considered him dead and had sent a wreath to the Otowa palace. However, he unexpectedly came home on December 31, 1945, four and a half months after Japan had surrendered. He was extremely thin and looked like a beggar. Ichiro writes in his diary, "Iichiro suddenly came home at night. Everybody cried. We could not help but crying, looking at his poor appearance."[2]

Postwar Career

Iichiro returned to the MOF and worked at its Budget Bureau, arguably the most powerful bureau in the Japanese bureaucracy, for six years. He also worked at the Trade Promotion Bureau of the MITI in 1951, then went back to the MOF's Budget Bureau. He climbed straight up the pyramid of the MOF. Iichiro became the deputy director general of the Budget Bureau in 1963, director general in 1965, then the administrative vice minister of finance in June 1971 at the age of 52. The position of administrative vice minister is the highest rank in the civil service (the minister's position is held by politicians) and yet that of finance is considered the most powerful. Those who were jealous of Iichiro said that he had obtained the position because of his father's fame. However, political analyst Ito Hirotoshi notes that one cannot assume the top position in the MOF because of one's father's fame. The bureaucracy is meritocratic and Iichiro had the capacity to reach the top position. The budget officer's job is extremely demanding and requires meticulousness, persistence, and stamina. An individual budget officer is in charge of more than a few ministries' budgets simultaneously, and works 20 hours a day at the time of the budget appropriations (they have cots in the ministry and sleep there). Iichiro did all this. A former MOF official who worked with Iichiro states, "Mr. Hatoyama was a competent budget officer and the name Hatoyama had nothing to do with his actual performance. He was not a strong administrator who would lead the ministry with a forcible personality, but was a fine administrator who let his subordinates do their work freely."[3]

In fact, notwithstanding his gentle personality, Iichiro's budget assessment was so rigorous that it was said, "*pempengusa mo haenai*" ("even a persistent weed cannot grow [where he had assessed]"). Even Prime Minister Tanaka Kakuei (1972–1974), who excelled in controlling bureaucrats, said, "I cannot win over Hatoyama." Rigorous budget officers are referred to as *waru* (villain) in the political circles. Iichiro represented such *waru*. Iichiro devoted himself to the MOF's work to the extent that he did not see his children for a month at the time of the budget appropriations. Iichiro's service at the MOF coincided with the period of Japan's high-speed economic growth, in which business, bureaucracy, and politics collaborated. Iichiro was a leading warrior for Japan's economic growth: the making of Japan's economic miracle.[4]

Overall, it is reasonable to state that Iichiro succeeded on merit at the MOF, and that it is difficult to ascertain to what extent the name, wealth, and connections of the Hatoyama family played a role in his bureaucratic career; at least they did not hurt. In contrast, these factors undeniably played a decisive role in advancing his political career.

The Run for the HC

After serving in the MOF for three decades, Iichiro retired from the ministry in June 1974 and ran for the House of Councilors (HC) at the age of 55. Prime Minister Tanaka highly evaluated Iichiro's competence and encouraged him to run for the Diet. Iichiro's son, Kunio, was working at Prime Minister Tanaka's office as a private secretary. Iichiro declined but in the end, he was obliged to run. Iichiro not only detested politics, but also generally distrusted politicians. As a MOF official, Iichiro had seen enough of politicians' soliciting concerning budget appropriations. Even if he was a competent bureaucrat and tried to resist politicians' unreasonable demands, he may have been forced to make budgets not of his liking on many occasions. He used to say to his aides, "the worst problem with politicians is that they are preoccupied with their local constituents, the next elections, and political contributions. They do not have time to think about the national interest and study national policy." Therefore, Iichiro chose the HC, the nominal upper house of the Diet, similar to the House of Lords in the British Parliament. The HC also has fewer elections. The HC's term is six years as opposed to the HR's four years (the latter would have additional elections when dissolved). Further, instead of the "local districts," he ran from the HC's "national district" that does not represent local interests.[5]

Iichiro made an unusually candid confession in a newspaper magazine interview during the campaign. He said, "I detest politics. I get goose bumps when I think of elections. I do not like elections and campaign speeches. One cannot do this unless he likes it. I did not want to run. I was hoping that someone else would run because the election in the national district is hard (it encompasses the entire nation). I was obliged to run only because so few people wanted to run." His candidness was even more surprising because he made this confession during his first campaign. The only clear policy platforms Iichiro articulated in the campaign was to maintain conservative rule in the HC (leftist opposition parties were catching up with the LDP in the upper house) and to carry out the *yen*'s redenomination; to make the current 100 *yen* into a new 1 *yen*. Iichiro argued that the *yen*'s redenomination was critical in order to stimulate the Japanese economy and felt that the sooner the better. Tanaka had encouraged Iichiro saying that if he really wanted to enforce the redenomination, he should become a politician. Iichiro continued to advocate the redenomination; however, it never gained enough political momentum to become a reality.[6]

Iichiro was soft-spoken and disliked being exposed to the mass media and to the public. This is a major drawback for a politician; however, he had a strong promoter, his mother. Kaoru had made Iichiro take *yokyoku* (Japanese classical poem chanting) lessons. Kaoru held a rose viewing party for the mass media at the Otowa palace in May 1974, 15 years after Ichiro's death. The party's real purpose was to introduce Iichiro as a candidate for the HC. The guests were surprised to see Iichiro make a speech at the party. Kaoru also energetically participated in his campaign at the age of 85. In addition, Iichiro had the nationwide organizational support of the *Yuai Seinen Renmei* (Fraternity Youth League), a new name (in 1973) of the *Yuai Seinen Doshikai* (Fraternity Youth Society) that Ichiro had founded in 1953. Kaoru succeeded its presidency at Ichiro's death in 1959. She held the position for 15 years but gave it to Iichiro in 1974. The *Yuai Seinen Seiji Renmei* (Fraternity Youth Political League), the league's political branch that was founded in 1973, immediately decided to support its new president's campaign nationwide. Further, his wife Yasuko financially supported Iichiro's campaign with her fortune from the Bridgestone Tire Company. Due to his name recognition, as well as his organizational and financial supports, Iichiro won with the fourth highest score out of 50 seats contested for the "national district" of the HC. It was an extraordinary achievement for a latecomer in politics.[7]

One of the major reasons why Iichiro ran for the HC, despite his disdain for politics, was to realize Kaoru's wish to see her son become a politician while she was alive. Although Iichiro had proven himself as the highest official at the MOF, he was obliged to prove himself as a politician because of his family's expectations. As Ichiro's only son, Iichiro was expected to follow in the footsteps of his father and grand-father. Before his death, Ichiro had again asked Iichiro to succeed to his seat in the HR, however, Iichiro had refused. Although he rejected his parents' wishes and chose the career of a bureaucrat, he succumbed to the family's expectations and entered politics after retirement. Especially his mother's expectations and pressure grew enormous after Ichiro's death. The pressure for self-actualization, as a prime minister's son, had been always at the back of Iichiro's mind. When Iichiro won the first HC election, he said to his aide, "it took time (for me to become a Diet member), but my father (in the heavens) would be pleased."[8]

An Exceptional Appointment to be Foreign Minister

Iichiro belonged to the Nakasone faction of the LDP, a minority group vis-à-vis the mainstream Tanaka faction. Nakasone Yasuhiro was the successor of the Hatoyama faction, via Kono Ichiro. Iichiro made his political début as director of the LDP's Accounting Bureau in the Miki cabinet (1974–1976). Prime Minister Miki Takeo, known as "Mr. Clean," appointed Iichiro to that position in order to straighten up the party's finances in the aftermath of the scandals concerning Prime Minister Tanaka's money politics. Then, Prime Minister Fukuda Takeo (1976–1978) appointed Iichiro to be foreign minister in December 1976. It was unprecedented for a newcomer to assume such an important ministerial position, where seniority (number of terms) in the Diet, that of the HR in particular, usually determines ministerial positions. For the case of the HC members, the earliest time when they could assume a ministerial post was at the second term, no matter how competent they were.[9]

Prime Minister Fukuda, a former MOF official himself, had known Iichiro since the latter joined the MOF in 1941 and had closely observed this rising star's career progress. Upon entering politics, Fukuda had collaborated with Iichiro, an elite MOF official. For instance, when Fukuda became finance minister for the first time, Iichiro was the Budget Bureau's deputy director general. Then, when Fukuda became finance minister for the second time, Iichiro was its director general. As Iichiro had entered politics himself, Fukuda planned to make Iichiro governor of Tokyo, after giving him experience in the positions of foreign minister and MITI minister. Therefore, because of Fukuda's strong confidence in Iichiro's competence, Iichiro was exceptionally appointed as foreign minister in his first term in the HC. Iichiro went to his father's graveyard to report the news. Then, he jokingly said to his family, "I am not a prime minister, but a minister is a minister." Iichiro was relieved of the heavy expectations and pressure that he had endured.[10]

Tenure as Foreign Minister

Iichiro became foreign minister at a time when Japan encountered extremely difficult foreign policy issues. The year 1977 was a year of big changes in the world. The American administration changed from a Republican to a Democratic president. Hua Kuofeng assumed power in China in the aftermath of the Great Proletarian Cultural Revolution. The international laws of the sea drastically changed, most notably with the introduction of the "200-mile economic zones." According to Hirano Minoru, a reporter of the Kyodo News Service (the largest news service agency in Japan), the MOFA failed to cope with these dramatic changes, and, in the end, Japan was forced to make concessions with both the Soviet Union and the United States. For instance, Japan missed its timing to seize on the coming of 200-mile economic zones, and was obliged to negotiate with the Soviet Union, which had already legislated the 200-mile economic zones in its national laws. Then, the United States confronted Japan regarding its trade deficits with Japan. Japan dealt with the issue in a makeshift fashion as usual, and the U.S. government retaliated by another sharp appreciation of the *yen*. It hit the highest record (to that day) of ¥253 to the dollar in October 1977. The *yen*'s exchange rate had been fixed at ¥360 to the dollar until 1971 during the Nixon administration; however, the administration changed the international monetary system to the "float system" and appreciated the *yen*'s value to counter U.S. trade deficits with Japan. It was dubbed "Nixon shock." Yet another sharp appreciation of the *yen* in 1977 severely damaged Japan's export. Hirano writes that the year 1977 ended as "a year of frustration for Japan's diplomacy."[11]

Hirano attributes the fundamental reason for these diplomatic failures to the "reactive" nature of the Japanese foreign policy for the past 30 years (it was later noted by Kent E. Calder and became a major subject for the study of Japanese foreign policy). Hirano states that the MOFA does not have a strong domestic *jiban* (local electoral base or constituency) because it does not represent any specific domestic interest and was therefore weak vis-à-vis foreign governments' pressure. In contrast, economic agencies, such as the MITI and the Economic Planning Agency (EPA), have strong domestic *jiban* and can therefore put the protection of domestic interests first. Caught between the interests of domestic industry and foreign pressure, the MOFA had resorted to delaying and obscuring tactics in order to distract foreign pressure. Even though the MOFA officials were aware that such makeshift tactics would not work at a time of drastic changes, they once again relied on these methods.[12]

Iichiro became foreign minister at a time when the MOFA had to deal with powerful domestic economic agencies backed by strong interest groups. Hirano writes that having no experience in foreign policy and being soft-spoken, Iichiro failed to coordinate various domestic interests and arrive at a consistent foreign policy for Japan. Iichiro's nonaggressive personality lowered the morale of the MOFA and Japan succumbed to foreign pressures. Hirano writes that during Iichiro's 11 months' tenure as foreign minister, the press club at the MOFA was filled with nothing but frustration and anxiety: the most frustrating year since he joined the MOFA press club in 1969. The frustration on the part of the MOFA officials spread to the reporters at the press club and, in turn, the reporters vented their frustration on Iichiro. However, Hirano notes that nobody actually had ill feelings toward Iichiro, even if they were at the height of frustration and exhaustion. Instead, reporters tried to cheer up this gentle foreign minister. This was solely because of his likable personality and *jintoku* (virtuous nature).[13]

Iichiro was referred to as a "shy blue-blood." He was gentle, kind, modest, and reserved. His personality did not lend itself to being a strong leader. The Japanese people generally associate the image of a dove with the Hatoyama family as *hato* means dove or pigeon and *yama* means mountain. Nobody fits the dove image better than Iichiro among the Hatoyama politicians. He jokingly stated at the inauguration, "Mr. Fukuda (prime minister) is the first foreign minister and

I am the second foreign minister." When he was asked about politically sensitive issues, such as the Sino-Japanese and the Japan–Korea issues, he stated that they were matters for the prime minister, not the foreign minister. These statements reflect his modest personality as well as a "problem avoidance" mentality—the bureaucratic way of dealing with issues. Iichiro was essentially an elite bureaucrat.[14]

However, it would be unfair to attribute Iichiro's weak leadership in the MOFA solely to his personal attributes. The bureaucratic inertia in general, and the MOFA's reactive policy-making style, in particular, constituted structural impediments to exercising strong leadership. In addition, the institutional power of the bureaucracy vis-à-vis the LDP factional politics made it difficult for any minister (political appointee) to exercise strong leadership in the ministry. With the intensification of the factional politics within the LDP, ministerial posts were given to each faction according to the balance of power among factions, with little regard for the expertise required for each post. Consequently, each minister had to rely on the expertise of the ministry's high officials. Being a former bureaucrat himself, Iichiro knew this better than anybody else. Iichiro, a former MOF official, was made to administer the MOFA. Only in 2001 did Tanaka Makiko, Prime Minister Tanaka's daughter, challenge the monolithic MOFA, as foreign minister of the Koizumi cabinet. She tried to reform the ministry in earnest; however, caught between the LDP factional rivalries and the bureaucratic resistance, she was dismissed in January 2002.[15]

Ito also writes that during the dominance of the LDP factional politics, the Japanese did not require a new type of politician like Iichiro who is clean (uncorrupted), honest, and thoroughbred. In comparison, although his elder son Yukio has many of Iichiro's weak attributes as a politician, he has been more successful as a political leader because the political environment (the breakdown of the "1955 system") called for a new type of political leader (see chapter 8).[16]

Post–Foreign Minister Career

Iichiro resigned the foreign minister's position when Fukuda reshuffled his cabinet in November 1977. Fukuda then tried to make Iichiro governor of Tokyo when the incumbent Governor Minobe Ryokichi (son of Tatsukichi) announced that he would not seek the fourth term in 1979. Iichiro was popular and came at the top in the primary election by the LDP's Tokyo-*to* metropolitan league. However, former Prime Minister Tanaka (still influential) chose the lesser-known Suzuki

Shunichi, who had more experience in administration, as the LDP's official candidate for the final election by the citizens. Fukuda's plan failed. Yet, Iichiro was nonchalant about it. After Iichiro was passed over for governor, his political career was inconspicuous. He neither assumed any other ministerial posts nor assumed important party positions. Although his faction leader Nakasone became prime minister and held the position for an unusually long period (November 1982–November1987), Iichiro did not actively participate in party politics.[17]

Iichiro developed cancer and was hospitalized in 1986. He was treated early and his life was saved; however, he was referred to as a *waka inkyo* (young retiree) in the Diet. This author interviewed Iichiro in October 1986 concerning Japan–Soviet relations. Iichiro was polite and calmly stated his views on Japanese foreign policy toward the Soviet Union. He appeared to be a modest and reserved gentleman. Being gentle and polite, he appeared to be atypical politician. Overall, this author's personal impressions of Iichiro concurred with the assessments of the other observers mentioned here. Before the interview, she saw a (more conservative) HC member of the LDP, whom she had interviewed a few days earlier, in an elevator of the HC hall. He greeted her with a big smile; however, when she told him that she was going to see Iichiro, his countenance suddenly changed and showed his displeasure. This attitude of Iichiro's colleague in the LDP showed the depth of his isolation.[18]

Iichiro won the HC elections for three consecutive terms (July 1974, June 1980, July 1986). After serving three terms, he retired from politics in 1992. Iichiro died in December 1993 at the age of 75. Toyoda Jo writes that although Iichiro did not become prime minister, he must have died content in the fact that he had become foreign minister (the position his grandfather had missed). Kaoru also must have died content with the thought that she could tell good news to Haruko in the heavens.[19]

An Overall Assessment of Iichiro's Political Leadership

Although Iichiro was a crème de la crème of the bureaucracy, he was not a first-rate politician. It is primarily because Iichiro had no desire for power nor ambition to exercise power. In contrast, several of his seniors at the MOF with similar attributes and competence successfully transformed themselves into political leaders. They include Ikeda (prime minister, 1960–1964), Sato (prime minister, 1964–1972), and Fukuda (prime minister, 1976–1978). The fundamental difference between Iichiro and others was his lack of political ambition. Iichiro, the second heir of the Hatoyama dynasty, had already earned fame and esteem in society.[20]

A Comparison with Prime Minister Tanaka Kakuei

A comparison of Iichiro with Prime Minister Tanaka is useful. Both were born in the same year and died in the same year at the age of 75. Both became Diet members, both had fame and wealth, and both lived in a luxurious estate in Bunkyo-*ku*, Tokyo. However, the two politicians could not be more different in terms of their ambition for power and money. While Iichiro had no desire for power and money, Tanaka augmented his political clout by strengthening the collusion of power of the "Iron Triangle" among politics, bureaucracy, and industry, and obtained ultimate political power. While Iichiro simply inherited the Otowa palace, a 1,400 *tsubo* (1.14 acre) property, from Ichiro, Tanaka built his Mejiro palace by himself. Tanaka's acquisition of property coincided with his acquisition of power; as he acquired power, he bought property as if it were the symbol of his power, and his estate eventually expanded to the size of 2,600 *tsubo* (2.12 acres).[21]

The amount of taxable assets when their offspring inherited their assets was ¥15.2 billion ($128 million) for Iichiro and ¥11.9 billion ($100 million) for Tanaka. Thus, the assets of the Hatoyama dynasty's third generation surpassed that of *Imataiko* ("contemporary Regent"); Tanaka was likened to *Taiko* (Regent) Toyotomi Hideyoshi who had risen from rags to riches and became a political leader in the late sixteenth century. Iichiro's ¥15.2 billion assets included ¥5 billion ($42 million) for the Otowa palace, ¥2.6 billion ($22 million) for the estate in Karuizawa, ¥6 billion ($50 million) worth of Bridgestone Tire stock, and ¥1.5 billion ($13 million) in bank accounts. Iichiro's three children together were levied the inheritance tax of ¥5 billion ($42 million) in total. Yet, they were able to pay it in full by selling the stocks they had inherited at that time, and managed not to sell the Otowa palace or their estate in Karuizawa. In contrast, Tanaka's offspring could not pay their inheritance tax of ¥7.6 billion (64 million) without selling the Mejiro palace. Ito Hirotoshi writes that this shows the difference between a genuine dynasty and a *nouveau riche*.[22]

Personal Attributes

Iichiro's former secretary recalls, "Mr. Hatoyama was a modest person and did not promote himself. He stayed behind the scenes and let others get the praise for what he himself had done. I often felt frustrated, because I saw many politicians who were only good at self-promotion without real competence, whereas Mr. Hatoyama had real competence."

Another former secretary states, "Mr. Hatoyama did everything he had to do as foreign minister. The MOFA officials appreciated him because he knew how to get the budget. Yet, his overall evaluation was low because the expectations were too high (the publicity about him as the star of the Fukuda cabinet) despite the extremely difficult international political environment. It was also because of the lack of self-promotion on his part. He was not a type of person to say, 'I did this myself.' "[23]

Iichiro primarily takes after Kazuo's modest and principled nature. A long-time acquaintance of the Hatoyama family commented, "Iichiro is personable and polite, and yet he is principled and stubborn. He is not chauvinistic but energetic and persuasive. Although he appears weak, he is actually strong. Since he has no desire for power or money, it is hard to appease him. He is the scion of a dynasty, both in a positive and a negative sense." Iichiro could have exercised stronger political leadership if he had wanted, as Kazuo did despite his modest personality. The critical difference is that Iichiro did not have the desire to do so. Iichiro ran for the HC only because of Prime Minister Tanaka's forceful request and the family's pressure. A veteran political analyst also states that had Iichiro really wanted to become Tokyo governor and campaigned more actively, he might have done so. Although Iichiro became a politician, as necessitated by his surroundings, he did not enjoy being a politician and did not behave like one. He was never comfortable walking on the red carpet of the Diet.[24]

Iichiro was also down-to-earth, honest, and open, which is another personal attribute passed down from Kazuo. In addition, his position of having nothing to lose gave him the luxury of being true to himself. A former local assemblyman of Taito-*ku*, Tokyo, recalled the time when he used to drink with Iichiro at Iichiro's favorite restaurant T in Asakusa, downtown Tokyo. Iichiro liked *sake* and he became merry when he was drunk. He treated everybody equally and was popular among the *geisha*. The assemblyman stated that most of the politicians were drinking at fashionable and exorbitantly expensive restaurants in Akasaka in the center of Tokyo, engaging in the so-called *machiai seiji* (saloon politics). The LDP and opposition party leaders, who were at odds with each other at the Diet during the day, were engaged in secret deal-making at night. So were the rivaling factional leaders within the LDP. In contrast, Iichiro was drinking at his favorite restaurant downtown with his favorite friends. His behavior was not that of those who sought promotion within the LDP. Yet, Iichiro was nonchalant about it.[25]

Despite his reserved nature, Iichiro was not exceptional as a man with power and wealth when it comes to relationships with women. What was unusual about Iichiro was that he was open about his affairs.

For instance, while he was working at the MOF, a *geisha* in Akasaka, with whom he had a close relationship, committed suicide. Iichiro paid her funeral expenses and even made a memorial speech at her public memorial service. It was unprecedented for a government high-ranking official to do such things. Later, Iichiro was involved with a hostess of a restaurant in Asakusa. The Taito-*ku* assemblyman recalled, "Mr. Hatoyama went to restaurant T so often that it was said that if you want to see Mr. Hatoyama at night, you had better go to restaurant T. That was his hideout."[26]

Yasuko condoned Iichiro's relationship with the mistress of restaurant T. Iichiro continued this relationship even after the affair was disclosed by gossip magazines while he was foreign minister. He was also found vacationing with her in Izu, a spa resort, when his mother died in August 1982. On that occasion, it did cause a stir within his family. However, he still continued this relationship and served as an executive of a company that owned the restaurant T from 1985 until his death in 1993. An acquaintance of the Hatoyama family recalled "Iichiro was utterly open about his affairs and his wife accepted it. His father was a playboy and even had an illegitimate child. The Hatoyama's wealth, and the time in which Ichiro and Iichiro lived, allowed them to behave like this. If Yukio and Kunio did the same thing now, it would cause a national scandal."[27]

The Political Environment

Iichiro had great opportunities to promote his political career. He was under the tutelage of powerful political leaders. Prime Minister Tanaka was instrumental in launching his political career, while Prime Minister Fukuda pushed him all the way up to foreign minister. In contrast to Kazuo, Iichiro became foreign minister easily. Nevertheless, his political career did not flourish due to the environment and the lack of ambition on his part. Iichiro entered politics too late. Ito notes that Iichiro's lack of political ambition partly reflects the fact that he was already "burned out" as an MOF official. His former secretary also stated, "Mr. Hatoyama had both capability and vitality as a political leader. Had he entered politics earlier, he could have succeeded as a political leader, as well."[28]

The Interactions Between Personal Attributes and the Environment

In the overall assessment, Ito argues that Iichiro lacked three essential requirements for strong leadership—political ambition, an appropriate political environment, and luck. As in the cases of Kazuo and Ichiro, both personal attributes and environmental factors played a part in determining Iichiro's political career. However, it seems that his personal attributes, specifically the lack of political ambitions, played a more important role than the political environment. Had Iichiro had a stronger desire for power and political ambitions, he could have exercised more effective leadership. Other MOF officials, with comparable attributes and competence, did become prime ministers in similar political settings.[29]

In summary, Iichiro's resume—a graduate of Tokyo Imperial University, MOF Budget Bureau director general, administrative vice minister of finance, HC member, foreign minister—is quite impressive. Nevertheless, he did not have the strong personal impact in politics that one might expect from such an outstanding vitae. Ito writes that Iichiro placed himself within a stable institution and did not try to start something new. Kazuo challenged the *hambatsu* oligarchy for the sake of establishing a democratic parliament. Ichiro defied militarism during the prewar and wartime periods. He then created three political parties and challenged Yoshida's "one-man" and secret politics. In contrast, Iichiro aligned himself in safe "orders": first in the monolithic bureaucracy and then in the ruling LDP.[30]

In hindsight, it was unfortunate that Ichiro had only one son, who detested politics. Had Ichiro more sons, there would have been a third-generation career politician in the Hatoyama family. His five daughters did not become politicians. It was not a time for a woman to be expected to become a politician in Japan. The Hatoyama Dynasty's political legacy has been passed down to its fourth generation: Kunio and Yukio. As for the 1,400-*tsubo* Otowa palace, Yasuko moved out of the house at Iichiro's death. She undertook a major restoration of the house and opened it to the public, as the *Hatoyama kaikan* (hall) in 1996. It exhibits memorabilia of the family members, including numerous decorations and certificates of merit, Ichiro's death mask, and Kaoru's *kimono* wedding gown.[31]

CHAPTER 7
THE FOURTH GENERATION: KUNIO AND YUKIO

This chapter first examines the political careers of the fourth generation of the Hatoyama Dynasty, Kunio and Yukio, together. Although the brothers had separate careers in the beginning, they created the DPJ together in September 1996; it is difficult to follow one's career without mentioning the other's. This chapter then highlights Kunio's decision to leave the DPJ to run in the Tokyo gubernatorial election in April 1999 and its aftermath, illuminating the brothers' sibling rivalry in light of intra-party politics and against the backdrop of national politics. This chapter concludes with an assessment of Kunio's political leadership, since he began his political career before Yukio, and leaves an assessment of Yukio's to chapter 8. Their political leadership is still in the making and it is impossible to make an overall assessment. Therefore, this book examines their political leadership only thus far, and leaves the final assessment as a future task.

The Early Childhood of Yukio and Kunio

Iichiro had a daughter and two sons. The eldest was Kazuko. She was named after Kazuo (its female form). She graduated from the Sacred Heart Women's University with the highest score in her class and thereby fulfilled the expectation of the lineage of the elite dynasty. She married Inoue Tamon, a scholar and the second son of Inoue Kaoru, president of the Daiichi Kangyo Bank. Yukio, born in February 1947 and Kunio, born in September 1948, are the undisputed "blue-bloods" of Japanese politics and are likened to the Kennedy brothers (and now perhaps also to the Bush brothers) in American politics. Between the two brothers, Kunio takes after their grandfather Ichiro, while Yukio takes after their father Iichiro. Although Yukio is the elder son and was expected to carry on the family's tradition, he had no desire to become a politician. Inheriting Kazuo's scholarly attributes in general and Ichiro's academic excellence in math and science in particular, Yukio initially pursued an academic career in engineering. Yukio stated that when he was a child, he did not wish to enter the world of politics because his grandfather was rarely at home. He decided to study engineering because he felt that engineers could build the future of the world.[1]

The brothers are a good parallel to the second generation brothers, Ichiro and Hideo. Like Hideo, Yukio was a quiet boy while Kunio was wild, like Ichiro. Kunio's grandmother Kaoru used to say, "Kunio is just like his grandfather, being gentle, kind, and yet impatient." Kunio himself stated that he was wild and did not like studying while his brother was quiet and liked studying. Yet, Kunio adds, his grades were always better than Yukio's. An episode illustrates their difference. Kunio likes to collect butterflies to the extent that it has become his lifetime passion. He raises butterflies at home and wrote a book titled *Cho o kau hibi* (Days of raising butterflies). In contrast, Yukio said "I used to catch butterflies with my brother, but I began to feel sorry for killing them and stopped collecting them." Yukio's gentle nature is suited more for a scholar than for a politician. One of his high school classmates recalls that Yukio stayed alone and did not play with his classmates; he was so quiet that nobody noticed his presence in class. Therefore, all his former classmates were astonished to hear of Yukio's decision in 1986 to run for the HR and opposed his decision.[2]

Although Kunio was the younger brother, he considered himself the heir to the Hatoyama Dynasty and decided to follow in the footsteps of their grandfather. Kunio had already set his goal of becoming prime minister as far back as when he was an elementary schoolboy. In his third grade composition class, Kunio wrote, "I want to become a politician and prime minister." His mother recalled what Kunio did during the 1955 HR elections in which Ichiro had run as the first LDP prime minister. Kunio wrote the candidates' names in *kanji* (Chinese characters used in Japanese) on a piece of paper in order to mark their votes. Kunio listened to the radio news and anxiously counted the votes as results were announced. That he did so at an age when children seldom know how to write persons' names in *kanji* is all the more indicative of his interest and intent. Kunio vividly recalls the time when Ichiro came back from Moscow in 1956 after signing the Japan–Soviet Joint Declaration. The people's enthusiastic cheers that Ichiro received for the diplomatic breakthrough impressed his grandson and made him realize the greatness of being prime minister.[3]

Kunio probably had the strongest desire for power in the family. As his father did not follow in his grandfather's footsteps, Kunio wanted to fill the void in the dynasty's political lineage. In Kunio's case, becoming a political leader had in itself become an end. Kunio strove to prove himself as such. His academic excellence is proven by the fact that he maintained the highest scores for all the subjects at the prestigious high school attached to Tokyo Teachers University (at present the Tsukuba University) and he was referred to as the brightest student that appears only once in every five years. Kunio was also at the top, out of 630 students, in the selection exam to move up from the general program to the major program at Tokyo University. He graduated from the Faculty of Law at the university, with the highest standing.[4]

Kunio Runs for the HR

Kunio said in an interview that since he was a stubborn and selfish child, his father perceived a danger in him becoming a politician only because he longed to become one. Iichiro wanted Kunio to experience the hardships of life first, rather than going straight to politics. Iichiro specifically wanted him to study harder (he was preoccupied with collecting butterflies and playing golf), become a lawyer, and then to enter politics if he still wanted to. However, against his father's wishes, upon graduating from the university, Kunio became a private secretary of Prime Minister Tanaka in July 1972, and then ran in the HR elections. It was the reverse of Iichiro who had refused to enter politics, against his parents' wishes.[5]

Tanaka told Kunio that the key to winning elections is to know one's constituents thoroughly: to pay 30,000 individual household visits and make 20,000 street corner speeches. Tanaka also advised Kunio to run as soon as he became eligible. In keeping with Tanaka's advice, Kunio ran in the HR general elections in December 1976 from Tokyo District 8 (the current Tokyo District 2), comprising three wards in downtown Tokyo: Taito-*ku*, Bunkyo-*ku*, and Chuo-*ku*. Many of his constituents are middle- and small-sized business owners and merchants. The district was originally the constituency of Kunio's great grandfather and then of his grandfather. Since Iichiro refused to become a politician, with the death of Ichiro in 1959, Yamada Hisatsugu, former administrative vice minister of foreign affairs and the Hatoyama family's long-time confidante, succeeded to the district. The family's *koenkai* (politician's support groups) in the district were disbanded. At that time, the Hatoyama family and Yamada made an agreement that Yamada would return the district to the family should a family member decide to run in the future. However, when Kunio decided to run in 1976, Yamada had already won three terms and did not honor the promise.[6]

The competition was severe for Kunio. Tokyo District 8 had three seats for the HR. Until the 1994 revision, the HR election law adopted a medium-size election district system where more than one seat could be assigned to each district (Ichiro failed to revise the law to introduce a small-size district system in 1956). Kunio had to contend with Yamada, as well as with two other incumbents in the district: Kaneko Mitsuhiro, JCP general secretary, and Fukaya Takashi of the LDP. Iichiro and others advised Kunio not to run, because should the LDP have three candidates, the votes for the party would be split and all three might lose. It turned out that Kunio could not obtain official endorsement of the LDP because he was a novice. Nevertheless, Kunio kept to his mentor's advice and continued individual household visits in his constituency.[7]

Kunio Wins the HR General Elections at the Top

In this predicament, Kunio turned to the New Liberal Club (NLC). It was a splinter of the LDP, led by Kono Yohei, the second son of Kono Ichiro. Five junior members of the LDP created this breakaway party just before the HR elections in order to jump on the anti-Tanaka bandwagon in the wake of the Lockheed bribery scandal. In the end, Kunio ran as an independent, with the recommendation of the NLC. To everyone's surprise, he collected the *fudohyo* ("floating votes" or swing votes) of the undecided voters and won with the highest total in the district. Thus, continuing the family legacy, Kunio started his political career at the age of 28, with the ultimate goal of becoming prime minister.[8]

Kunio owed much of his first election victory to his wife Emily. Kunio's engagement in February 1973 to Takami Emily, a 17-year-old Australian-Japanese "TV talent" (commercial girl) caused a sensation. The public had expected that Kunio would marry a daughter of a distinguished family. This author recalls that when their engagement became public, her school teacher asked in class, "Why must a scion of the Hatoyama dynasty marry a cover girl? Is she from a renowned family?" Kunio answered the question. He candidly stated in a press interview, "I chose her 70 per cent for love and 30 per cent for her capacity to help my campaigns." Emily was a eleventh grader at the American School in Japan (ASIJ). Ito Hirotoshi points out her poor knowledge of politics by quoting her press interview. Emily said, "I rather like the JCP . . . Factions? I do not know much about these things." Emily made this statement when Kunio was a secretary of Prime Minister Tanaka, the

LDP's largest faction leader. It did not matter to Kunio. Emily was young, pretty, and popular. People flocked to shake hands with Emily more than with Kunio. A person close to the Hatoyama family commented that Kunio owed his first election victory to the popularity of Emily as well as to riding on the opportune "New Liberal Club wind" (anti-LDP bandwagon). Kunio also had the support of the Fraternity Youth League, to which he succeeded after his father's death in 1994.[9]

Kunio Joins the LDP's Tanaka Faction

Within less than two years, Kunio joined the LDP's Tanaka faction. He lost in the next HR elections in October 1979, as the mass media attacked his opportunistic switch. Splitting the vote with Kunio, Yamada lost as well. However, with Yamada's subsequent decision to retire, Yamada's supporters "returned" to the Hatoyama family and Kunio won in the following elections in June 1980. Iichiro was also reelected to the HC in the "double elections" in which both the HR and the HC elections were held simultaneously. With the exception of the one loss in 1979, Kunio consecutively won the HR elections seven times and has been a HR member for more than 22 years, until he resigned from the lower house in February 1999.[10]

Kunio Appointed Education Minister

Kunio began as an education *zoku* (tribe or group) *giin* (Diet member) within the LDP. LDP Diet members are trained to become specialists in specific interests and function as brokers between the private and the public sectors. They are called, for example, agriculture *zoku giin* or national defense *zoku giin*. These *zoku giin*, along with the bureaucracy and industry, constitute the so-called Iron-Triangle for the collusion of power. Nowhere was the *zoku giin* more prevalent than in the Tanaka faction. It was referred to as a "department store of the *zoku giin*." Kunio became an education *zoku giin* because his grandfather had been minister of education and the Hatoyama Dynasty had a number of distinguished educators and scholars in its direct lineage, as well as among its in-laws (Kikuchi Dairoku and Minobe Tatsukichi, see figure 1.1). Kunio climbed the elite ladder for the education *zoku giin* from political vice minister of education in 1984 to the LDP's education bureau director, and to the HR's education committee chair in June 1989. Then, Kunio was appointed minister of education in the first Miyazawa cabinet in November 1991, at the unusually young age of 43.[11]

As minister of education, Kunio displayed strong leadership skills. Facing down the ministry's bureaucracy, high school officials, and the private educational sector, Kunio forced through a change sought by parents and students on the commercially conducted admission tests that were used to judge students seeking to enter private high schools. It was somewhat similar to the controversy and opposition to the use of the Scholastic Aptitude Test (SAT) in college admissions in the United States. Specifically, Kunio abolished the use of "deviation values" from the tests as decisive admission criteria. While using this data was convenient for school officials, strict reliance on deviation values made the admissions a severe competition of statistical numbers. Kunio admonished his opponents to "think from the standpoint of the students." His decision lifted an enormous burden from the applicants' shoulders, given Japan's notorious "admission exam hell" in the higher educational system. Kunio proved himself an heir of the "educational dynasty."[12]

Kunio also opposed the introduction of the "consumption tax" (equivalent to a sales tax in the United States) during the Nakasone cabinet (1982–1987). The LDP proposed the bill in order to secure national revenue to compensate for the reduced income tax from the higher-bracket income taxpayers. However, Kunio needed to protect the interests of his constituents who are largely small-sized business owners and merchants. Kunio's objection to the bill was an outright act of defiance against the LDP, and he was almost expelled from the party for his objection. Kunio stated, "given the history of rebelliousness of this family, it was not a big deal for me to rebel on the consumption tax." Despite the strong opposition of the general public, the bill to impose a 3 percent consumption tax passed the Diet in 1987 during the Takeshita cabinet (1987–1989).[13]

Yukio Enters Politics

Meanwhile, Yukio entered politics in 1986. After graduating from Tokyo University, Yukio went to Stanford University and earned a Ph.D. in engineering. While at Stanford, Yukio met Hashimoto Miyuki. Miyuki is a former *Takarajennue* (chorus girl of the well-known Takarazuka theater company in Hyogo-*ken*, near Kobe) under the stage name of Waka Miyuki. Her stage career did not flourish. She then married the brother-in-law of the owner of *Chocho*, a famous Japanese restaurant in San Francisco, where Yukio met her. She divorced her husband and married Yukio. She was four years older than Yukio. Iichiro opposed their marriage and did not attend the wedding ceremony. Returning home, Yukio first joined the faculty of Tokyo Institute of Technology (TIT, the Japanese equivalent of the Massachusetts Institute of Technology) and later he joined the Senshu University. Yukio then sought to run for the HC, as his father had; however, Iichiro strongly opposed the idea. In July 1986, Yukio first contested an election for the HR, running from Hokkaido District 4 (the current Hokkaido District 9), in the large northernmost island.[14]

The need for self-actualization was an important motivational factor that eventually led Yukio to politics. Although his need for self-actualization had already been somewhat satisfied when he started his academic career at the prestigious TIT, there was still an unfulfilled void in him. When asked why he had finally decided to enter politics himself, Yukio replied that the display of American patriotism he saw during that country's bicentennial celebration (while he was studying at Stanford) touched him and made him realize that he should serve his own country. Yukio stated, "I grew up in Japan when patriotism was misconstrued as militarism and was rejected. The observation of American patriotism made me think about the dignity of the nation and the individual." Therefore, he added, had he not gone to the United States, he would not have pursued a political career. Whatever the immediate cause that triggered his desire to enter politics, the "Hatyoama dynasty's political blood" deep down in Yukio's makeup had finally awoken. After all, he grew up observing his grandfather become prime minister, his father become foreign minister, and his younger brother successfully launching his political career.[15]

In fact, Yukio in his adolescence had entertained an idea that he might become a politician someday. When he was preparing for a college entrance exam, he told Kunio, "you become a politician first but I might follow you. Then, we will help each other." As Iichiro's elder son, Yukio felt the same pressure that his father had felt. Ito notes that there is an unwritten code in the Hatoyama family that any family's son is not considered a person unless he is a politician. His mother dreamed of her husband becoming prime minister. After Iichiro's death, her expectations for her sons grew stronger. Therefore, the idea that he had to become a politician was always in the back of Yukio's mind. Political writer Itagaki Eiken thinks that in hindsight, Yukio's move from TIT (a national university) to Senshu University (a private university) became a prelude to a career change. Yukio moved to this private university in order to help his father and brother in their campaigns; national university employees were not allowed to participate in political activities. Itagaki states that this move suggested that Yukio had decided to learn about politics firsthand through campaigning for his father and brother, for an eventual run for himself. In order to carry on the family's legacy, Yukio gave up his successful academic career and entered politics at the age of 39.[16]

Yukio could not run from a district in Tokyo because Kunio had already succeeded to Ichiro's district. Then, Saegusa Saburo, a HR member and a former deputy governor of Hokkaido gave Yukio his district. Transferring a district from one person to another was not uncommon. Saegusa was a liaison between the MOF and Hokkaido (being remotely located, the region received sizable government subsidies for development) and knew Iichiro well. The connection between the Hatoyama family and the district actually goes back to Kazuo. Kazuo acquired farm land in Kuriyama-*cho* in 1894 during the Meiji government's Hokkaido frontier campaign with his partners and became an absentee landlord. His partners soon abandoned the land and sold it to Kazuo. The land was called *aza* Hatoyama, named after the landlord, and grew to have 46 tenant households in 1926. Kazuo enjoyed farming and his family spent every summer in the farm (there is a family picture with young Ichiro and Hideo). Ichiro then relinquished the land to the tenants prior to the enforcement of the Farm Land Release Law that began in 1946. Ichiro befriended a HR member from the district, Nanjo Tokuo. Nanjo passed down his district to his successor. It was Saegusa.[17]

Thus, his great grandfather's ownership of the land in Hokkaido, his grandfather's personal ties with a politician in the district, and his father's ties with this politician's successor gave Yukio a district to run for the HR. Although Yukio himself had nothing to do with the district, the Hatoyama family's connection with the area became a "divine wind" for starting Yukio's political career. Yukio renamed a shrine in the property, called Koyo Shrine, as Hatoyama Shrine and offered a prayer there during his campaign. The center of the district is the port city of Muroran, with a population of 110,000, where the steel industry had flourished but died down. Seven major companies in Muroran, including the giant New Japan Steel, which are said to in effect run the politics and economy of Muroran, supported Yukio. The constituents in the district, touched by Saegusa's selfless decision to give his district to his friend's son and also by Yukio's courage to run in a faraway district, supported Yukio. His fresh image, coming from a completely different background from the traditional LDP politicians, appealed to the younger generations in the district so that they spontaneously organized a group to support him. Yukio won with the second highest total in the district.[18]

Yukio made his political début ten years after Kunio. Iichiro (HC) and Kunio (HR) also won in the "double HR and HC elections" in July 1986.

It was a glorious moment for the Hatoyama dynasty. Yukio joined the Takeshita faction (splinter of the Tanaka faction) of the LDP, to which Kunio had belonged. Since then, Yukio has consecutively won the elections from Hokkaido District 4. Nevertheless, the "distance" between Yukio and his constituents did not shrink. Although during the campaign Yukio said that his family would live in Muroran city and that his son would go to school there, they did not leave Tokyo. Yukio himself seldom visited the luxurious house in Muroran. Even his *koenkai* (support groups) officials and local politicians had few chances to talk to him in person. They could see him only on television.[19]

Mother's Indulgence and Influence

Mother's power is also evident in the fourth generation of the Hatoyama dynasty. While Kunio and Yukio inherited political fame from their paternal lineage, they inherited fortune from their mother. As with Kunio, Yasuko's influence on Yukio was enormous. There was at least an implicit expectation on her part that Yukio would succeed to the legacy of the Hatoyama dynasty. Her wealth added to her motherly influence on Yukio after he entered politics. Yukio released an accounting of his assets to the public for the first time in 1991 when he was appointed political deputy director general of the Hokkaido Development Agency. His total assets of approximately ¥8 billion ($67.2 million) were the highest among the then 512 HR members, and significantly greater than the holdings of the next person in line. His assets increased in 1993 to ¥11.6 billion ($97.4 million), owing to the inheritance from his father, who died that year. Out of the ¥11.6 billion, ¥7 billion was in Bridgestone tire stock and ¥2.16 billion was in bank accounts, gained by the sale of Bridgestone Tire stock inherited previously through a living will. Yukio's assets had depreciated to ¥2.3 billion ($19.6 million) by 1997, because of the collapse of the so-called bubble economy; however Yukio still ranked second among the then 500 HR members, while Kunio was third with ¥1.9 billion ($16.3 million).[20]

According to an acquaintance of the Hatoyama family, Yasuko was a gentle and caring mother and had provided unlimited support for her two sons' campaigns both financially and spiritually. As she did for Iichiro's elections, Yasuko went everywhere for her sons' campaigns with an energy unimaginable considering her thin figure. Yasuko was not a so-called education mom (who is keen on children's education and drives them to study) because Yukio and Kunio did well academically without being forced to study. However, she was indulgent with her sons. She bought a luxurious apartment for Kunio when he got married and later bought him a 200-*tsubo* (0.16 acre) residential property in Honkomagome, Bunkyo-*ku*, Tokyo (while an ordinary citizen could barely afford to buy a 20-*tsubo* property in downtown Tokyo). The new house cost ¥0.5 billion ($4.3 million), whereas his constituents (mostly merchants) are trying hard to save a penny. Yasuko also bought Yukio a 200-*tsubo* property in Denenchofu, Ota-*ku*, Tokyo and a three-story office building in Muroran, Hokkaido, when Yukio decided to run for the HR from a Hokkaido district.[21]

Yukio's Dependence on Miyuki

Yukio is also dependent on his wife Miyuki. He publicly admits it and unabashedly told the press, "I am enlivened by her energy." His former high school classmate noticed that Yukio changed after the marriage, and thinks that Miyuki made Yukio more confident by assuring him that he could do well as a politician. Being a former chorus girl, Miyuki is not shy and rather enjoys being exposed to the public, and energetically supported Yukio's campaign. Yukio designed his own method of political campaigning, based on what he called "logical management," by analyzing the constituents and creating a target list of the constituents in his district. However, his campaign manager told him that such a scientific method would not work in Japan, and that the best campaign strategy was to meet as many constituents as possible on a one to one basis. Yukio was obliged to resort to the traditional campaign method, and walked with Miyuki for two years and three months throughout the district before his first run.[22]

Later, shortly after the 1996 HR general elections, the mass media disclosed that Yukio had a mistress for ten years in Muroran, Hokkaido. However, Miyuki said that she was also to blame for leaving him alone, and preempted the escalation of the scandal. Yukio was saved by Miyuki's tolerance, and they are known as one of the best couples in the political circle. Miyuki has become a food critic and appears on TV and in magazines. She also published a cooking book, entitled *Hatoyama-ke no omotenashi* (Hatoyama family's home entertainment) in 1999 and has become something of a Japanese Martha Stewart.[23]

Yukio Leaves the LDP

While Yukio was serving his first term in the HR in September 1988, he joined Takemura Masayoshi in organizing the "Study Group on Utopian

Politics," composed of ten first-term HR members from the LDP. Although Takemura was a novice to national politics, he was a seasoned politician in local politics and had been Yokaichi city mayor and Shiga-*ken* governor. Takemura created this group to discuss much needed reforms of the LDP when the Recruit bribery scandal shook not only the LDP but also the entire governing circles. Hosokawa Morihiro, a former Kumamoto-*ken* governor and LDP Diet member (whose maternal grand-father is Konoe Fumimaro), left the LDP and created a breakaway party, the *Nihon Shinto* (the Japan New Party, JNP), in May 1992. The JNP fared well in the July 1992 HC general elections enough to force the Miyazawa cabinet to call for the HR general elections in July 1993. Other reform-minded LDP leaders, such as Ozawa Ichiro and Hata Tsutomu, left the LDP on the eve of the HR general elections and created their breakaway party, the *Shinseito* (the Renewal Party), in June 1993. Takemura and Yukio also left the LDP that month and created the *Shinto Sakigake* (the New Party *Sakigake* [Pioneers], NPS). Takemura became president and Yukio became *daihyo kanji* (secretary general, the number two position). Because of the massive defections, the LDP lost in the elections and Hosokawa formed the first anti-LDP coalition cabinet in August 1993. The cabinet consisted of seven political parties and a political group, including the JSP. This anti-LDP political reformation ended the "1955 system," the 38-year monopoly of power by the LDP, established during Ichiro's premiership. It was a landmark for postwar politics.[24]

Takemura was appointed chief cabinet secretary of the Hosokawa coalition cabinet and Yukio was appointed deputy chief cabinet secre-tary. However, the cabinet collapsed in April 1994 due to Hosokawa's abrupt resignation involving alleged illegal campaign contributions. Ito writes that Hosokawa was another weak and irresponsible aristocratic leader, like his grandfather. Hata succeeded Hosokawa and formed another anti-LDP coalition cabinet, this time excluding the JSP and the NPS. Being a minority cabinet, the Hata cabinet lasted only 59 days. In June 1994, in order to regain power, the LDP co-opted Murayama Tomiichi, president of the Social Democratic Party of Japan (SDPJ, the renamed JSP), and formed an unprecedented coalition cabinet of the LDP, the SDPJ, and the NPS. The coalition was an anomaly because the LDP and JSP had been archenemies for decades. Takemura acted as a catalyst for the formation of the Murayama cabinet and thereby obtained the position of finance minister. It marked the defeat of the anti-LDP political reformation. Since then the LDP has consecutively formed either coalition cabinets or cabinets of its own, rendering the 1993 reformation short-lived.[25]

Kunio Leaves the LDP

Kunio also joined the anti-LDP bandwagon and left the LDP. However, he did not join any political party at first. Kunio became minister of labor in the short-lived Hata coalition cabinet. Then, Kunio joined Ozawa when he created another party *Shinshinto* (the New Frontier Party, NFP) in December 1994. Kunio became the party's public relations planning committee chair. Although his political career seemed to be faring well, Kunio considered running in the Tokyo gubernatorial election in March 1995. It was a chaotic time for national politics. Two anti-LDP coalition cabinets (that of Hosokawa and Hata), collapsed in under a year. Then, an unprecedented Murayama coalition cabinet emerged. In this unpredictable situation, Kunio considered his first Tokyo run. Iichiro's aborted gubernatorial run in 1979 might have been in the back of Kunio's mind. Having served four terms (1979–1995), Governor Suzuki Shunichi decided not to run for the fifth term. Kunio had the NFP's endorsement and was considered the prospective winner. In the end, he decided not to run stating, "I belong in the Diet." A strong factor behind Kunio's decision was the opposition of his mother. Yasuko told her son that the Hatoyama family's lineage did not lie in local politics and that he should remain on the national political stage, rather than take such a detour.[26]

Yukio's Candidacy for Hokkaido Governor

As Kunio considered his run for Tokyo governor, Yukio considered his run for Hokkaido governor at the same time. The incumbent Yokomichi Takahiro, who had served three terms (1983–1995), decided not to run for a fourth term. Yokomichi had been a HR member from 1969 to 1983 and was referred to as the "JSP's prince." Yokomichi was popular among the Hokkaidoites. The LDP and business circles could not defeat him. The LDP considered Yukio the best candidate to regain its power in post-Yokomichi Hokkaido. It was during the Murayama coalition cabinet of the LDP, the SDPJ, and the NPS. The LDP's Hokkaido branch, as well as Hokkaido's big business groups, solicited Yukio to run. Yukio felt that if he could help Hokkaido's economy recover, he would be willing. He had been disappointed with Takemura's opportunistic moves and wanted to leave the NPS (details given later). Yukio might have also been attracted to the position because it is directly elected by the electorate (as are American governors). A governor could exercise strong leadership, as Governor Hashimoto Daijiro of Kochi-*ken* (younger brother of Hashimoto Ryutaro, prime minister 1996–1998) had demonstrated. With the endorsement of the LDP and the NPS, Yukio decided to run. However, Yukio's *koenkai* (support groups), his mother, and Prime Minister Murayama opposed his decision. Yukio retracted it. In hindsight, had Yukio run, he would probably have won, and thereby the DPJ would not have been created (at least not in 1996). As for Yokomichi, instead of returning to his fold, he joined the DPJ at its inception.[27]

The Hatoyama Brothers Create the DPJ

Opposition parties denounced the Murayama coalition cabinet and the subsequent Hashimoto coalition cabinet as *yago* (an illegitimate marriage), as they comprised mutually irreconcilable parties: the LDP and the SDPJ. Yukio decided to create his own party based on a denial of such an unprincipled union. Kunio was not as enthusiastic as Yukio, but their mother persuaded Kunio to help his elder brother. The Hatoyama family made substantial financial contributions to the new party. The brothers' mother was said to have contributed ¥5 billion (about $42 million) for the party's creation, while the brothers together gave another ¥1.5 billion (about $12.6 million). Because of the family's legacy and enormous investments, the mass media referred to the party as the *Hatoyama Shinto* (Hatoyama New Party) and Yukio was expected to become its president.[28]

Yukio announced a plan to create a new party in April 1996; however, it took several months to actually form the DPJ. During this period, Ito writes, Yukio disclosed every process of the party creation, and the clumsy and immature negotiation process became public knowledge. For instance, Yukio first invited Funada Hajime, an influential member of the NFP, but the two could not come to terms on the makeup of the new party. Funada specifically opposed the wholesale participation of the SDPJ and the NPS, because these two parties encompassed former socialists. After Funada dropped out, Yukio invited Kan Naoto, a member of the NPS.[29]

The "Package Participation of the SDPJ and the NPS"

The so-called package participation of the SDPJ and the NPS became the focal point of the party formation. Yukio (the NPS) was inclined to accept the wholesale participation of the two parties, whereas Kunio (the NFP) strongly opposed the idea. When Yokomichi, the "JSP's prince," suggested the idea to Kunio, Kunio was upset and nearly poured beer on Yokomichi's face. Kunio expressed stronger opposition than anyone else among the DPJ's founding members. Kunio criticized Yukio by saying, "my elder brother was inclined to accept the package participation of the SDPJ and the NPS for the sake of having a large membership for the new party and also for the sake of persuading Kan to join the party." Kunio also opposed the participation of the leaders of the two parties, Murayama and Takemura.[30]

Political analyst Kobayashi Kichiya writes that it is speculated that Ozawa, NFP president, was acting behind the scenes for Kunio's opposition. According to a press reporter, Ozawa contemplated forming a coalition cabinet with the DPJ after the HR general elections in October 1996. The participation of Murayama and Takemura in the DPJ would make the distance greater between the NFP and the DPJ and thereby would remove a possibility of forming an NFP–DPJ coalition cabinet. It is therefore speculated that Ozawa made a deal with Kunio. In this deal, Kunio agreed to insist that he would not join the DPJ unless other founding party members refused the participation of Murayama and Takemura, as well as the package participation of the SDPJ and the NPS. In return, Ozawa gave Kunio 20,000 votes in the election in his Tokyo District 2. Kunio figured that the DPJ's founding members would give in to his demand because the Hatoyama brothers were the core of the party. In the end, Yukio gave in to Kunio's demand. The party excluded Murayama and Takemura and did not accept the wholesale participation of the two parties, although it had allowed massive participation from the two parties.[31]

Kunio criticizes Yukio for allowing the massive participation of the former socialists. Kunio confessed that he and Yukio had very different ideas of the party from the onset and that he was not deeply involved in the initial stage of the party creation. Kunio actually decided not to join the party when he realized that Yukio had been collaborating with Kan and Yokomichi and wanted to include leftists. In fact, Kunio wrote to his mother about his decision. He changed his mind only because Yasuko asked him to help Yukio and the brothers had already put too much effort and investment into its creation. Kunio hoped that the party might change toward the direction he wanted as time passed. Therefore, he decided to join the party in the end.[32]

The Hatoyama Brothers' Naïveté: The "Takemura Exclusion"

The Hatoyama brothers made the process of the so-called Takemura exclusion transparent. The founding members of the DPJ did not want Takemura to join the party because he was thought to be machiavellian. Takemura left the LDP, became president of the NPS, became chief cabinet secretary of the Hosokawa coalition cabinet, and then became finance minister of the Murayama coalition cabinet. Because of his opportunistic moves between the anti-LDP and pro-LDP coalition cabinets, Takemura was dubbed a "Balkan politician" (who moves among small parties). However, Yukio was Takemura's follower from the LDP years. The DPJ's founding members did not want the clean image of the prospective party president to be tarnished by rejecting his senior and allegedly made Kunio the culprit of the Takemura exclusion. In an effort to remove this notoriety, Kunio later stated at a political rally in October 1996, "I could not tarnish my brother because he was expected to become party president. It has been said that I was the culprit in the Takemura exclusion, but the truth was that we worked out a division of labor." Meanwhile, Takemura, a seasoned politician, used this situation to his advantage and appealed to the public by saying "I am the one who was excluded." Ito writes, the general public, who were ignorant of what was going on in politics, felt that the Hatoyama brothers were mean-spirited and sympathized with Takemura. Those who were informed on politics thought that making this process open displayed the brothers' naïveté as *obotchan* (silver-spoon boy) politicians.[33]

Kobayashi notes that Yukio's stance to make the process transparent defied conventional wisdom. The creation of a new party should not be announced until the groundwork is laid and all the strategies are made. Then, the party can project a fresh image, attract the electorate, and can win elections. The NLC (in 1976) and the JNP (in 1993) were able to gain many votes because they contested HR general elections while each still portrayed a fresh image to the electorate. In contrast, the DPJ's fresh image had been tainted by the revelation of its immature formation process before the HR elections. Ito also thinks that Yukio made the announcement of the party creation prematurely and that disclosing every detail before things were finalized had incurred misunderstanding on the part of the electorate. The longer the formation took, the weaker the DPJ's fresh image. Ito writes that by the time of the actual forma-tion, people had already grown tired of the party and the mass media had already chewed up Yukio and swallowed him.[34]

The transparent process also exposed the brothers' dependence on their mother. In press interviews, Yukio and Kunio often referred to their mother by saying, "my mother said so and so" and "my mother is opposed to this and that," although they were in their late forties at that time. A relative of the family said that the brothers were under their mother's thumb and that it was she who convinced Yukio to create a new party with Kunio. Yukio admitted that he was motivated by his mother's encouragement. He stated, "my mother told me that she was disappointed in the NFP that was picketing in front of the HR budget committee conference room. She told me that 'you and Kunio resign the Diet and create a new party.' She must have been ashamed of me and Kunio being Diet members without doing anything to change politics." Yukio also said that "my generation was not given the kind of special education that my great-grandmother had given to my grandfather (the early morning lessons). However, it is true that men of the Hatoyama family are all *amaembo* (indulged by their mothers and wives). Hatoyama women are mentally stronger than their men. In this sense, the Hatoyama blood is being passed down."[35]

Eto Jun, a conservative critic, expressed his concern with the immature way the Hatoyama brothers created the DPJ and deplored the brothers' lack of political leadership in contrast to their grandfather's. He poignantly described them as *futari de ichinin mae* (two persons worth one person's stature), meaning that only the two brothers put together matched the caliber of Ichiro. Eto might have read the article (May 1951) commenting that only Ichiro and Yoshida together made a politician of the same stature as Hara Takashi, and made the analogy for the Hatoyama brothers. Eto further states that it could be a sign of the decline of the Hatoyama dynasty.[36]

The Actual Creation of the DPJ

Kunio and Yukio, joined by 48 other Diet members (44 HR members and 4 HC members), created the *Nihon Minshuto* (the Democratic Party of Japan, DPJ) in September 1996, the day after Prime Minister Hashimoto dissolved the HR. The 50 Diet members gathered at the Hitotsubashi Hall of the Japan Education Building to announce the formation of the party and pledged to win the forthcoming general elections in October. A number of leaders of major labor unions that had supported the SDPJ also attended the meeting. That the party creation was declared at the Japan Education Building—the fortress of the Japan Teachers Union, a backbone of the JSP—was indicative of the party's nature and future.[37]

The 50 original members hoped to create a new party that embraced realistic liberal ideals. According to political writer Itagaki Eiken, they wanted to make the DPJ a political party for the citizens: a goal that the JSP had failed to fulfill. The DPJ chose unconventional slogans such as "citizens' leadership" and "fraternity," that would appeal to a Japanese electorate disappointed in the collusion of power in the "Iron Triangle."

The DPJ's platforms called for "establishing a responsible social democratic liberalism," "removing power from the bureaucracy," and "constructing a mature, independent, and coexistent citizen-centered society." As Yukio described it, the party was trying to "blow a whirlwind" into Japanese politics. Yukio was 49 years old and Kunio was 48 years old.[38]

Yukio is Outmaneuvered by Kan

Notwithstanding the expectation that Yukio become its first president, Yukio was outmaneuvered by Kan and was obliged to share the presidency with Kan. Kan was a member of a JSP's splinter, *Shakai Minshu Rengo* (the Social Democratic Federation, SDF), until it was absorbed in the NPS in 1994. He then served as the minister of public health and welfare of the first Hashimoto coalition cabinet of the LDP, the SDPJ, and the NPS in 1996. Kan's popularity surged when he exercised strong leadership in dealing with the *yakugai eizu* (medically caused AIDS) scandal. It involved the sales and transfusions of untreated blood products that infected unwitting recipients with the AIDS-causing virus. Kan fought the secrecy and procrastination of the bureaucracy and accused ministry officials of wrongdoing. Kan had executed what the DPJ had set out to do: to achieve "citizens' leadership" and "to remove power from the bureaucracy." Following this, Kan responded to Yukio's call to join the DPJ.[39]

Kan was by far a more tactically astute politician than Yukio. With Yukio's insistence that Kan join the DPJ, Kan tantalized Yukio and succeeded in making Yukio accept the massive participation of SDPJ and NPS members, despite Kunio's strong objections. Kan also objected to excluding Takemura, but in vain. Although Kan paid lip service to Yukio in an interview by saying that he regarded his role as that of Yukio's *nyobo* (wife), Kan's popularity obliged Yukio to give him a top position in the party. As a compromise, the DPJ adopted an unusual copresident system. Thus, Yukio, the founder and financier of the DPJ, ended up sharing the presidency with Kan, while Kunio became one of two vice presidents. Although Kunio had a 10-year longer and a more distinguished political career than Yukio, Kunio was obliged by seniority and the associated cultural norms to play a supporting role to his elder brother in the DPJ. Also, being newer and more liberal, Yukio's fresh image fit the DPJ better than that of Kunio, who had been immersed in the LDP politics for 20 years.[40]

Kunio's Growing Dissatisfaction with the DPJ

Kunio was ill at ease with the DPJ from the onset because of the massive participation of the SDPJ and the NPS. Kunio stated in an interview that the party turned out to be exactly as Kunio had feared. Kunio argues that the way the party was created was wrong to begin with. People gathered from different parts of the spectrum of ideology and then tried to create the party's platforms. Not surprisingly, they could not agree on any major issues. Because of this divisive nature, the DPJ resorted to rhetoric that only appealed in the mass media but lacked reality. Kunio admits that there are great politicians in the DPJ who have long-term vision, such as Iwakuni Tetsundo (former Izumo mayor). However, because of the dominance of the former SDPJ members in the party, they cannot realize their ideas insofar as they remain in the party. Kunio also notes that the DPJ's supporters are limited to labor unions, big cities, civil movement groups, and environmental protection groups. For a party to become a ruling party, it should obtain support from a wider strata of society.[41]

Kunio adds that he was personally hurt when he was actively involved in the formation of the Constitutional Research Council at the Diet in 1999. Kunio was pro–constitutional revision, whereas the DPJ's majority remained anti-revision. Former SDPJ members within the DPJ strongly opposed Kunio's involvement in the council, and some of them were even hysterical and angry with him. Although Kunio was a vice president of the party, labor unions scolded him. Kunio felt that the DPJ was no different from the SDPJ. Kunio argued that if these socialists wanted to defend the constitution, they should have stayed in the SDPJ with its president Doi Takako. Although he did not agree with Doi ideologically, he respected her because she had stayed in the SDPJ (despite the party's decline) and had consistently defended the constitution. In contrast, these former SDPJ members had abandoned the party, "infiltrated" the DPJ, and yet still vehemently defended the constitution. Because of their dominance in the DPJ, Kunio states, the atmosphere in the party was such that if a member supported constitutional revisions, he was considered insane. Kunio notes, "only my brother changed the atmosphere when he proposed constitutional revisions after he became the party president (see chapter 8)."[42]

In summary, Kunio missed an opportunity to create a liberal conservative party to his liking because of the leftists' power in the DPJ. Another reason for his growing dissatisfaction with the DPJ is more personal but is important. Despite his lifelong political ambition and the earlier start he had on his political career, Kunio was obliged to defer to Yukio in the DPJ. As long as Yukio remained in the DPJ, Kunio's chance of becoming its leader was small. In a parliamentary-cabinet system, the president of the largest party in the HR normally becomes prime minister when that party forms a cabinet on its own, while the head of an influential party, the largest or otherwise, has a chance of becoming prime minister in a coalition cabinet. Given the strong presence of his elder brother in the DPJ, the opportunities for Kunio to achieve his ambition to exercise national-level political leadership would continue to fade as long as he remained in the party.

An episode from the early 1980s illustrates how little known Yukio had been in political circles. Yukio attended an annual new year's party for Kunio's *koenkai* (support group) at the Hotel New Otani. At one point, Yukio was standing next to Kunio when Kunio's influential supporter approached. This supporter did not recognize Yukio. Even when he saw Yukio's name tag, he did not realize that Yukio was a member of the same Hatoyama family, although it is an extremely rare surname. He said to Yukio, "Is your name Hatoyama? I like your name." Being embarrassed, Kunio said "This is *my* elder brother." Nevertheless, Kunio had to stay in the shadow of Yukio when they created the DPJ only because he was a year and seven months younger.[43]

In another episode from December 1998, Kunio made his displeasure apparent at Iichiro's fifth annual memorial service. Former Prime Minister Nakasone paid lip service to Yukio describing him as "a man of the caliber to become prime minister." Kunio sarcastically responded, "I am the younger brother who apparently is not the thoroughbred in this family." Kunio no longer wished to remain in the shadow of his elder brother and wanted to establish his political eminence somewhere else. Consequently, Kunio decided to leave the DPJ and the HR and run in the Tokyo gubernatorial election in April 1999.[44]

The diminished opportunity for Kunio to fulfill his ambitions at the national level, caused by his elder brother's entry into politics, was the major reason for Kunio's decision to run for Tokyo governor. However, in addition to the sibling rivalry, the DPJ's structural problems, which restricted Kunio's opportunities in national politics, as well as the general state of Japanese politics, also account for his decision.

The Structural Problems of the DPJ

Notwithstanding the fresh image portrayed by the two young leaders, the DPJ did not "blow a whirlwind" into politics as its leadership had expected. The party won only 52 seats (out of 500 seats) in the October 1996 HR elections. It had hoped to take anywhere from 70 to as many as 100 seats, but instead had managed to add only six seats to the 46 that the party had held at its inception in September. The election could only be seen as a defeat for the DPJ. It made the party the third largest party in the lower house, far behind the LDP, which won 239 seats, and the NFP, which won 142. Ito points out that the DPJ's moderate gain in its maiden HR elections can be construed as the verdict on the Hatoyama dynasty by the electorate, which had sensed the weakness and indulgence of the fourth generation of the famed dynasty.[45]

The party's composition also accounts for the failure. The DPJ consists of individuals from formerly irreconcilable parties. The 50 original members included 29 former SDPJ members (58 percent), 14 NPS members (28 percent), 5 Citizens' League members (10 percent), 1 NFP member (2 percent), and 1 independent (2 percent). The DPJ leadership had expected more NFP participation but it turned out that Kunio was the only person who came from that party. This makeup shows that the DPJ was essentially a *yoriai jotai* (a hodgepodge household), as often referred to by the mass media, comprised mainly of splinter elements from what were diametrically opposing parties (see figure 1.4).[46]

The HR general elections of October 1996 did not change the fundamental makeup of the DPJ. Among the 52 party members who won seats, there were 25 former SDPJ members (48.0 percent), 14 NPS members (26.9 percent), 2 Citizens' League members (3.8 percent), 2 NFP members (3.8 percent), and 9 independents (17.3 percent). This composition fragmented the party structure and made its policy ambivalent. Lingering influence from former socialists was seen as preventing the DPJ from putting together clear and realistic policy alternatives to those of the LDP. Kunio, who had objected to the package participation of the SDPJ and the NPS, described the party as having unfortunately become a "(political) asylum" for people from the SDPJ. Such internal divisiveness was an intrinsic structural defect of the DPJ. Then, on the occasion of its first anniversary in September 1997, the party changed its leadership structure and eliminated the copresident system. Kan was elected as its sole president and Yukio as secretary general, demoting him to the number two position. Although Kunio retained his vice president post, Kan's assumption of power as the sole head of the DPJ signaled the decline of the Hatoyama brothers' prestige in the party.[47]

The DPJ's Expansion and Fragmentation

The DPJ's expansion in April 1998 further fragmented the party and demoted the brothers' ranks. The sudden breakup of the NFP in

December 1997 moved the DPJ to be the second largest party and, therefore, the largest opposition party. Then, in that month, three other new opposition parties, formed out of the remains of the NFP—the *Minseito* (the Good Government Party, GGP), *Shinto Yuai* (the New Party Fraternity, NPF), and *Minshu Kaikaku Rengo* (the Democratic Reform Federation, DRF)—joined the DPJ (see figure 1.4). The merger increased the DPJ's HR delegation to 92 members, or 18.4 percent of the 500 seats.[48]

The expanded DPJ elected Kan as president. It elected Hata (prime minister in 1994, left the NFP in December 1996, started his own *Taiyoto* [the Sun Party], and joined the DPJ at this time) as secretary general. Yukio became deputy secretary general and Kunio was made one of four vice presidents. Kunio dropped to a position that might be regarded as number four in the party at best. Even Yukio was obliged to give his number two slot to Hata because he was a senior politician and prime minister, though only for 59 days. Kan was reelected to the party presidency in January 1999 at the party national congress, despite the exposure of his extramarital affairs. Yukio and Kunio maintained their positions. Thus, the DPJ's expansion accelerated the decline in the Hatoyama brothers' prestige within the party. This factor also served to put a damper on any hopes Kunio might have had of leading the party and advancing toward his career goals.[49]

The HC Elections and Its Aftermath

The general elections for the HC were held in July 1998. The elections took place when the support rate for the incumbent Hashimoto coalition cabinet had hit the record low of 31.1 percent in the April 1998 *Yomiuri Shimbun* (the largest daily newspaper) poll. Worse, only 29.3 percent of the respondents supported the LDP. The LDP lost in the elections; however, the DPJ could not claim a victory either. At stake were 126 seats of the total 252 seats in the upper house. The LDP lost 16 seats, reducing its total to 44 of the 126 being contested; the DPJ gained 9 seats, increasing its total to 27, and the JCP also gained 9 seats to give it 15. As a result, the LDP's total HC delegation fell to 103 seats (40.9 percent), out of 252, while the DPJ's rose to 47 (18.7 percent) and the JCP's to 23 (9.1 percent). The LDP lost control of the upper house.[50]

The elections were considered by most observers to have been a referendum on the financial reforms the Hashimoto cabinet had initiated. The elections could be seen as having given the DPJ the momentum it needed to increase its power base in the Diet. However, rather than representing an endorsement of the DPJ, the result was really a rejection of the LDP. That both the DPJ and the JCP gained only 9 seats each indicates that either the electorate did not have a definite alternative to the LDP in mind, or that neither of those parties was considered viable. While the LDP may have lost its credibility to run the government, the DPJ was far from having gained such credibility.[51]

With the resignation of Prime Minister Hashimoto, Obuchi Keizo succeeded to the LDP-led cabinet in July 1998. To make matters worse for the DPJ, the defeat compelled the LDP to form yet another surprising coalition in January 1999, this time with the Liberal Party (the LP), a new party created by Ozawa 12 months previously due to the NFP's breakup. The LDP had an absolute majority with 266 seats in the HR in January 1999, as more than a dozen LDP members who had left the party during the 1993 political reformation returned to the fold. In comparison, the DPJ had 94 seats and the Liberal Party had 38 seats in the HR at that time. Despite this lead, the LDP leadership felt vulnerable after the party's defeat in the HC elections, and sought a tie with the Liberal Party. The LDP–Liberal Party coalition was all the more surprising given that Ozawa had become a political enemy of the LDP after his 1993 defection and has been involved in the creation of three new parties. The Obuchi coalition cabinet weakened the DPJ's position in the Diet. Moreover, despite having a delegation smaller than the DPJ's, the New *Komeito*'s (the Clean Government Party, CGP) status as a middle-of-the-road party gave it more clout in the parliamentary battles. The dwindling position of the DPJ boded ill for Kunio's ambitions.[52]

The DPJ's Declining Popularity

The DPJ has never gained its desired level of support from the electorate. According to *Yomiuri Shimbun* opinion polls, the support rate for the DPJ after its inception was 8.4 percent, in October 1996. Since then, its support has decreased, touching 2.5 percent in July 1997. The rate slightly recovered to 3.3 percent in September 1997 at the party's first anniversary, and rose to 4.8 percent in March 1998 in anticipation of its expansion the following month. Thus, the original DPJ has never regained the popularity it had at its formation. These support rates have never exceeded the original party's representation in the HR, 10.4 percent, or 52 out of 500 seats (see table 7.1). Expansion hardly contributed to the DPJ's popularity. According to the subsequent *Yomiuri* poll, support for the DPJ stayed at 4.6 percent in April and rose to

Table 7.1 *Yomiuri* polls on party support rates: the original DPJ (10/96–3/98) (%)

	10/96	2/97	3/97	6/97	7/97	9/97	3/98
DPJ	8.4	3.6	4.1	4.2	2.5	3.3	4.8
LDP	—	33.1	33.0	35.2	35.4	37.5	29.7
None	—	48.4	48.6	45.9	47.6	—	54.3

Sources: "*Minshuto kyo ketto isshunen*" (Today is the DPJ's first anniversary), *Yomiuri Shimbun*, September 28, 1997 and "*Shijiritsu teimei ni shokku*" (Shocked by the low support rates), *Yomiuri Shimbun*, April 22, 1998.

Table 7.2 *Yomiuri* polls on party support rates: the expanded DPJ (4/98–3/99) (%)

	4/98	5/98	6/98	7/98	8/98	9/98	10/98	11/98	12/98	1/99	2/99	3/99
DPJ	4.6	6.5	5.5	11.9	21.4	15.3	13.7	11.2	9.8	9.1	8.0	8.5
LDP	29.3	30.4	28.7	20.7	—	—	25.7	27.1	25.3	30.4	25.1	28.3
None	54.4	49.9	51.5	46.2	—	—	44.4	47.9	49.7	45.9	52.0	49.4

Sources: "*Honshi zenkoku seron chosa*" (*Yomiuri* national opinion polls), *Yomiuri Shimbun*, January 27, 1999, "*Honshi zenkoku seron chosa*" (*Yomiuri* national opinion polls), *Yomiuri Shimbun*, March 25, 1999, and "*Minshuto wa doko e*" (Where is the DPJ going?), *Yomiuri Shimbun*, April 24, 1999.

6.5 percent in May 1998. The rate peaked at 21.4 percent that August as a result of the previous month's HC elections, but has since gradually declined to 6.3 percent in July 1999. With the exception of August 1998, these numbers were much lower than the size of the party's representation in the HR; 18.8 percent, or 94 out of 500 seats (see table 7.2).[53]

As these poll results show, the DPJ failed to capture the hearts of the majority of the electorate. It suffered from internal divisiveness and was unable to devise clear policy platforms. Comprised as it was of politically irreconcilable elements, the DPJ's internal contradictions doomed it to failure. Such defects contributed to Kunio's decision to leave the DPJ. However, in addition to the failings of the DPJ, there were more fundamental problems in politics that accounted for Kunio's decision. In fact, the DPJ's failure could be seen as a symptom of the deeper shortcomings that have plagued the political system since 1993.

National Politics and Systemic Weaknesses

More than 20 political parties were formed since the 1993 political reformation. Yet, as with the DPJ, these new organizations have been unable to present an effective challenge to the LDP. The primary problem has been that most were splinters of the LDP, and were led by former LDP leaders, such as Ozawa. To the electorate, these parties seemed to be little different from the LDP. Neither the Hosokawa coalition cabinet nor the Hata coalition cabinet had much impact beyond the fact of their existence and did little to set themselves apart. The subsequent splintering of the new parties into yet smaller ones alienated voters even further. The electorates grew tired of the mushrooming of new parties. Ito writes, by the time the DPJ was formed, new parties had come to be nothing but objects of distrust by independents who have a strong political awareness. Therefore, the DPJ has been unable to obtain their votes. Disillusioned by the new parties, some of the electorate has turned back to the LDP, expecting the party's new generation to carry out sweeping reforms of economic and political systems. Worse, some of the LDP defectors themselves returned to the fold.[54]

Japan's political climate since 1993 has given the country's opposition parties a great opportunity to create a second pole from which to compete with the LDP. The series of attempts to do so, however, have thus far failed, as the experience of the Hosokawa and Hata coalition cabinets bears out. This was another reason for Kunio to leave the HR.

The Position of the LDP

Kunio still had another option to remain at the national scene. It was to return to the LDP (as some of his colleagues had done) in the hope of rising to the top there. In January 1999 (when Kunio decided to run for Tokyo governor), the LDP had an absolute majority in the HR. However, a *Yomiuri* poll conducted in January 1999 showed that only 35.4 percent of the respondents said they supported the Obuchi coalition cabinet. Its support rates had hovered around 24 percent through late 1998 before rising in January 1999, while the nonsupport rates had ranged from 60 to 63 percent. The cabinet's increased popularity was attributable primarily to the forming of the coalition with the Liberal Party in that month and was not due to some newfound appreciation of the LDP. Forming the coalition appeared to have given the Obuchi cabinet a more stable image. As many as 58 percent of the respondents to the same poll said that they did not evaluate favorably the performance of the Obuchi cabinet since its July 1998 inception, against only 38 percent who did.[55]

Moreover, despite the increase in the Obuchi cabinet's popularity, the support rate for the LDP remained lower. Answering another January 1999 *Yomiuri* poll, only 30.4 percent of the respondents said they supported the LDP, yet it was a 5.1 percent increase from the previous month. The number decreased by 5.3 to 25.1 percent in the next month. In contrast, the numbers who did not support any party shifted from 49.7 percent (December 1998), to 45.9 percent (January 1999), to 52 percent (February 1999), exceeding a majority. Another poll conducted by a private think tank in November 1998 showed that as many as 72 percent of adult respondents felt, "they could not believe in political parties any more" (multiple choices). Consequently, the mass media ridiculed the state of political parties by saying that Japan's largest political party was the *museito* (no political party). These results reveal an alarming apathy among voters. Kunio made a decision to run in the Tokyo gubernatorial election during this period.[56]

Between August 1993 and February 1999 (when Kunio announced his decision), eight new cabinets were formed in Japan, two by anti-LDP coalitions and six led by the LDP. The anti-LDP coalition cabinets of Hosokawa and then Hata were short-lived and accomplished little. Of those cabinets with LDP involvement, the Murayama and the first Hashimoto cabinets suffered from being ungainly coalitions composed of irreconcilable elements, while the next two Hashimoto cabinets failed to implement any substantial reforms. The first Obuchi cabinet did not look promising at the outset, with former prime minister Nakasone going so far as to nickname Obuchi as the *shinku shusho* ("vacuum prime minister") and one foreign analyst likening the premier to "cold pizza"; his second cabinet owed the increase in its opinion poll approval rate to its alliance with the Liberal Party.[57]

The disappointment with these cabinets has left the electorate all the more disillusioned, and its interest in politics has slackened to an unprecedented level. The majority do not feel like supporting any party. With respect to Kunio's dilemma, this apathy put him in a no-win situation: he could no longer remain in the DPJ yet neither could he go back to the LDP. Thus, the deep apathy of the voter, which has accompanied the loss of the ruling LDP's credibility, as well as the perceived lack thereof among the new political parties, constituted the final reason for Kunio's decision to leave national politics.

In summary, the diminished opportunities for Kunio to fulfill his ambition at the national level, because of the chaos in national politics in general and the failure of the DPJ in particular, interwoven with the threads of sibling rivalry caused by his elder brother's entry into politics, contributed to Kunio's decision to leave the HR and run in the Tokyo gubernatorial election. It was a critical move for Kunio. It meant giving up a more than 22-year career in the HR, the power house of Japanese politics, and abandoning the district seat that had been passed down to him from his great grandfather. Kunio's eldest son, Taro, would have been the logical candidate if Kunio were to have sought to emulate his forebears and push for a dynastic succession in Tokyo District 2. However, Taro was 24 years old at that time and thus one year short of the HR's minimum eligibility. There was also a rumor that his wife, Emily, might run for the seat to keep it in the family. The decision, moreover, meant that Kunio had given up his lifelong goal of becoming prime minister.[58]

Kunio's 1999 Tokyo Gubernatorial Candidacy

Notwithstanding the enormous cost of abandoning his lifelong dream, Kunio announced his candidacy in the Tokyo gubernatorial election in February 1999. Responding to a reporter's question on whether he might return to national politics after establishing a reputation as governor of Tokyo, Kunio unequivocally denied such a possibility by replying "I am sacrificing my career in national politics for the election." His mother strongly opposed Kunio's candidacy again. In an interview, Yasuko said that she did not want to see the name of Hatoyama disappear from Tokyo District 2. Kunio nonetheless did not listen to his mother this time. Kunio was inspired by the example of incumbent Governor Aoshima Yukio, a popular comedian and former HC member. He had run as an independent in 1995 and won by capturing the swing votes. It was Aoshima's surprising decision not to seek a second term in 1999 that induced Kunio to enter the race. It had been predicted that Aoshima would win easily; his last minute decision not to run thus opened the door to great opportunities for prospective contenders in the race.[59]

Kunio's chances of winning the election at first seemed better in 1999 than in 1995. When he announced his candidacy, with the slogan of "coexistence between urban vitality and nature," which was in tune with contemporary sentiments, there were few strong contender. As an independent, he expected to obtain a large share of the swing votes as Aoshima did in 1995. Kunio could also count on unofficial support from the DPJ and the CGP. The Hatoyama family had maintained close ties with the latter ever since Ichiro had forged a friendship with Ikeda Daisaku, the founder of the *Sokagakkai* religious sect that constituted the CGP's backbone. There was, however, widespread criticism about Kunio's candidacy. First, despite his pledge not to go back to national politics, people speculated that he intended to use his service as governor as a stepping stone for a return to national politics. People also questioned his status as an independent. In a newspaper interview, one Tokyoite was quoted as saying that it was not right for a DPJ's founding member to run as an independent; another stated that it was wrong for Kunio to switch to being an independent in order to catch the swing votes and yet still count on unofficial support from the DPJ.[60]

Then, Ishihara Shintaro, influential former HR member of the LDP, announced his candidacy, as an independent, at the last minute in March 1999 with the slogan "Tokyo that can say 'No.' " Ishihara, a 66-year-old award-winning and best-selling novelist, was a formidable contender and was a more experienced and outspoken politician than Kunio. Ishihara had been elected once to the HC and eight times to the HR, had served as transportation minister and Environment Agency director general, and had made public his own ambition to become prime minister. He continued writing books all the while, including *"No" to ieru Nihon* (Japan That Can Say "No"). But in 1995, Ishihara had suddenly resigned from the HR due to his own disillusionment with politics. Therefore, his decision to return to politics in 1999 was unexpected. In announcing his candidacy in March, Ishihara said that while a lone Diet member did not have the power to affect the entire the nation, the governor of Tokyo, directly elected and backed by its citizens, could make a difference in national politics.[61]

The Tokyo Gubernatorial Election

The Tokyo gubernatorial election, along with other local elections, took place in April 1999. It was a landslide victory for Ishihara with 1,664,558 votes (30.5 percent of the total vote), whereas Kunio came in second with 851,130 votes (15.6 percent). The voter turnout was 57.87 percent, 7.2 percent higher than in the previous election. It was the second victory in a row for an independent candidate contesting for the post of Tokyo governor, again illustrating the inability of the established political parties to attract the disillusioned electorate. In retrospect, had Ishihara not run, Kunio would almost surely have won. However, Kunio was no match for Ishihara. In addition, Ishihara had a strong personal stake in the Tokyo gubernatorial election. He ran in the election in 1975 and lost to the incumbent Minobe Ryokichi, although he obtained an impressive 2,330,000 votes. The votes were split between two strong contenders in 1975 (Minobe on the liberal and Ishihara on the conservative side), whereas votes were spread among six major contenders in 1999. It was Ishihara's only loss in public elections. Therefore, this time Ishihara did not make an announcement of his candidacy until all the other candidates had made theirs, to see if he really had a chance to win. In contrast, Kunio was pressed to make his announcement early to avoid portraying the indecisive image demonstrated in his previous election bid in 1995.[62]

The supplementary HR elections were held simultaneously with the local elections in April. Nakayama Yoshikatsu, who had the DPJ's official endorsement, won the vacant seat in Tokyo District 2, created by Kunio's resignation. Thus, the DPJ at least managed to hold on to the seat that had been that of the Hatoyama Dynasty for so long. As for the dynasty's brothers, their luster has dimmed since the founding of the DPJ in 1996—due to the rise of Kan within the party, the party's expansion, and the party's failure to emerge as a strong opposition.[63]

Kunio Plans to Return to National Politics

In his concession speech, Kunio expressed a strong desire to return to national politics by saying, "I will continue my political activities and hope to revive like a phoenix." As early as May 1999, DPJ Secretary General Hata personally invited Kunio to rejoin the party as vice president (allowing him to come back with the standing he had at his departure) and work with Yukio. However, Kunio was more interested in creating a new party of his own that would focus on environmental issues and welfare problems. There also emerged in July 1999 a possibility for Kunio to rejoin the LDP, when Prime Minister Obuchi personally invited him to come back, a move that Kunio's mother strongly encouraged. There is a Japanese saying, *yoraba taiju no kage* (a big tree provides larger shade): the LDP–Liberal Party coalition cabinet's rising popularity, contrasted with the DPJ's decline, made a return to the big tree an attractive prospect for Kunio. At the end of July 1999, however, Kunio decided not to go back to the LDP as he was still interested in creating his own party. The mass media reported, "the pigeon would not return to his old nest" (a pun as the *hato* part of his surname means "pigeon" in Japanese).[64]

Kunio later justified his running for governor of Tokyo by stating that he had been suffering in the DPJ, he became *yakeppachi* (reckless), and committed *uchijini* (political suicide). He also stated that he had felt he could go back to national politics in a state of *tabula rasa* (blank slate) had he resigned the HR and left the DPJ. Theoretically, he had several options after the defeat in the gubernatorial election, including rejoining the DPJ, rejoining the LDP, and creating a new party of his own. However, he confessed that rejoining the DPJ was out of the question.[65]

The Escalating Sibling Rivalry

Meanwhile, the DPJ kept courting Kunio; however, Kunio insisted that he would not rejoin the party unless the party leadership removed all the former socialist elements. Then, an unexpected turn of events emerged for Yukio. The DPJ members tried to establish a post-Kan leadership in the midst of the growing dissatisfaction with his leadership in May 1999. Kan has been criticized as being dictatorial and opportunistic, and the party members had turned back to Yukio. Yukio was elected party president in September 1999 on its third anniversary. With Yukio's ascension to power in the DPJ, Kunio proposed to Yukio to break up the party and eliminate former socialists. However, Yukio strongly opposed his idea and, as a result, their relationship deteriorated.[66]

According to Kunio, Yukio was so frustrated with Kunio's insistence to break up the party that he told the press that Kunio was doing so because he was jealous. In an off-the-record press interview in October 1999, Yukio allegedly said that Kunio had not rejoined the DPJ because he was jealous of Yukio and Kunio's wife Emily was jealous of Yukio's wife Miyuki. The press leaked Yukio's remarks. Kunio was upset and countered that he had not rejoined the DPJ because of the presence of former socialists, not because of jealousy. Yukio publicly apologized to Kunio for his remarks and also offered to apologize to Kunio in person; however, Kunio refused to see him. Kunio instead began a public campaign to attack Yukio, by saying that his personality had changed since he had become the party president. Kunio even tried to make DPJ's junior members leave the party. It became a gossip topic in weekly magazines. Their sibling feud escalated to the extent that they did not visit their father's grave site together at the sixth memorial in December 1999. Kunio visited the cemetery one hour after Yukio and their mother in order to avoid seeing Yukio.[67]

Yukio stayed calm and said to the reporters at the memorial that it was his fault that the press missed seeing the brothers together at the cemetery. However, Kunio continued to refuse to see Yukio. While Yukio's remarks might have been inappropriate, Kunio responded rather emotionally and continued to attack Yukio. Kunio stated, "I am not Christ. I will never forgive my brother. I will never see him. I will get revenge on him." There has been no sign of reconciliation, leaving their mother distressed.[68]

More LDP-Led Coalition Cabinets

In October 1999, Prime Minister Obuchi co-opted the CGP and formed his second reshuffled cabinet, comprised of the LDP, the Liberal Party, and the CGP. Then, in April 2000, Ozawa left the coalition, being frustrated with the alliance with the neutral CGP. Immediately after the Obuchi–Ozawa meeting, Obuchi suffered a stroke and died. Ozawa's move also resulted in the Liberal Party's split into Ozawa's faction and an anti-Ozawa faction. The latter created the Conservative Party, led by Ogi Chikage, a former actress from Takarazuka theater. Mori Yoshiro formed a coalition cabinet of the LDP, the CGP, and the Conservative Party, in April 2000.[69]

Kunio Returns to the LDP and the HR

Having tantalized the LDP and the DPJ, Kunio finally returned to his "old nest" in May 2000, just before the HR general elections in June, and ran for the HR. Kunio after all followed the axiom; protection by a large tree. Nonaka Hiromu, then LDP secretary general and an old-guard in the Hashimoto faction, the largest faction within the LDP, persuaded Yukio to rejoin the party. For this, Kunio was criticized as a "traitor" bought by Nonaka. Kunio himself stated, "I cannot deny that I acted like a chameleon and people justifiably called me such." However, Kunio justifies his move by saying, "Prime Minister Obuchi called me in October 1999, when I was hurt by my brother's jealous remarks, and asked me to give advice on the welfare policy for the elderly (Kunio had written a book on 'group homes' for the elderly). Later, Mr. Obuchi asked me to return to the LDP and help reform the party. Former Prime Minister Hashimoto also asked me to return and I was scheduled to meet Obuchi on April 3. However, he suffered a stroke after his meeting with Ozawa on April 1 and died the following morning. Due to his sudden death, I decided to run for the HR from the LDP and rejoined the party in May."[70]

Kunio had no desire to return to the DPJ, the dwindling opposition party, dominated by the former socialists and poorly run by his brother. During the campaign, Kunio went so far as to characterize the DPJ as an illegitimate marriage of irreconcilable groups: the former socialists, who still relied on their ties with the old-fashioned labor unions, and liberal conservatives, like himself, who challenged the old guards in the LDP. Kunio also referred to the DPJ as a *gottani* (hodgepodge casserole), where *daikon* (giant radish) and *hampen* (fish cake) are cooked together with strawberries and cakes in a pot. The electorate will not eat such casserole. He even argued that the JCP was better than the DPJ and that the party was doomed.[71]

Kunio also denounced as whimsical Yukio's statement in Hokkaido that the people could not expect economic recovery if they kept depending on public projects. Yukio said this despite the fact that his district had been hit by massive volcanic eruptions. Although Yukio's statement was in line with the DPJ's policy to oppose the LDP's excessive public projects, it was ill-received by local residents who depended on tourism. Yukio nearly lost his seat for this. Kunio states, "My brother tried to bring public projects to his district when he belonged to the LDP. Yet, this time, he flatly rejected the idea. This is an example of my brother's 'ingenious ability to change his stance.' Because of this ability, he was able to become president of such a hodgepodge party. My brother acted like a 'chameleon,' changing his opinions freely in order to appeal to the mass media and the people." [72]

Kunio seems to be oblivious to the fact that he himself had acted like a chameleon. However, Kunio even attacked Yukio as being ungrateful to former prime minister Takeshita Noboru. Kunio states, "My brother could not have become a politician without Mr. Takeshita (who helped Yukio to win his first election). Yet, my brother said during this campaign that Japan would improve if we defeated Mr. Takeshita (who was still influential as a kingmaker of his successors such as Hashimoto and Obuchi). When my brother was in the LDP, he followed Takeshita's advice and made every effort to bring public projects to his district. In turn, when he left the LDP, he argued that public spending was the source of all evil and that Takeshita was a villain. We should not let such an ungrateful person be engaged in politics."[73]

Kunio Runs in the PR District

Having abandoned his local district (Tokyo District 2, now a single-member district), Kunio ran for the HR from the Tokyo Block, one of 11 proportional representation (PR) districts, in June 2000. The revised HR election law (1994) specified 300 single-member districts and 13 PR districts (which the law termed "blocks") with 200 seats, totaling 500 seats. However, after the first HR elections held under the revised law in October 1996, the law was amended to reduce the number of seats in the PR districts to 180 seats in 11 blocks, making the total 480 seats. The PR districts employ the so-called *kosoku meibosei* (binding list system), in which each party creates a list that ranks its candidates for each district. The Tokyo Block had 17 seats. Kunio was listed second on the LDP candidate list for the Tokyo Block. The LDP obtained 19.49 percent of the total votes in the block, which gave the LDP four seats, out of 17. Being ranked second, Kunio won. It was Kunio's eighth victory in HR elections. In comparison, the DPJ obtained

29.02 percent and won six seats in the block. Meanwhile, Nakayama of the DPJ was reelected in Tokyo District 2, over the LDP's Fukaya, Kunio's long-time rival during the age of medium-size districts.[74]

Political Animal: *"Detari Haittari"*

Kunio frequently switched parties depending on the political climate of the time. Riding on the anti-LDP bandwagon, Kunio in his first election ran as an independent with the recommendation of the NLC, despite the fact that he had been under the tutelage of Prime Minister Tanaka; joined the LDP (the Tanaka faction); left the LDP in the wake of the anti-LDP political reformation and became an independent; then joined the NFP; left the NFP to create the DPJ with Yukio; left the DPJ, ran in the Tokyo gubernatorial election as an independent and lost; considered forming his own party but rejoined the LDP; and ran for the HR in a PR district and won.

Kunio justified his switches by stating, "[regardless of party affiliation], I had consistently advocated liberal conservatism (pro-reforms). Switching parties for the sake of one's beliefs is better than staying in a party for the sake of retaining one's position. I had been consistently critical of the DPJ even when I was a member of the party." Kunio also states, "I am sorry for my supporters and my colleagues in the DPJ; however, I had repented for my mistake and would try to redeem my mistake in my future political activities."[75]

Kobayashi argues that Kunio's series of moves was based on his political calculations for the sake of winning elections. Kobayashi notes that Kunio had developed keen political instincts because for decades he had fought severe elections with powerful contenders in the former Tokyo District 8, such as Fukaya and Kaneko. Given that Kunio's constituents were largely merchants and small-size business owners, he had become a defender of *shomin* (common people) in order to win in his district. Therefore, Kunio took bold actions to oppose the consumption tax against the party discipline. Later, as a DPJ member, Kunio again opposed the LDP move to increase the consumption tax from 3 to 5 percent during the 1996 HR elections. In response, Fukaya, his LDP rival in the district, was also obliged to oppose the consumption tax raise. In the 1996 HR elections, Kunio defeated Fukaya in the new single-member Tokyo District 2.[76]

Kobayashi seems to assess Kunio's frequent switches as a positive indication of political instincts; however, Kunio did so at the cost of jeopardizing his integrity. For this, Kunio was criticized as *detari haittari* (leaving and entering), the ridicule originally made to his grandfather. It might be a necessary attribute for a politician to quickly perceive a change in the political wind and to make a move accordingly; however, the excessive switches can be construed as opportunistic and unprincipled. Kunio's run in the Tokyo gubernatorial election was a prime example. He made a critical decision to run in the race, at the cost of abandoning his seat in the HR that was passed down from his great-grandfather. He chose the seemingly more promising road of becoming governor of Tokyo and establishing a name for himself in local politics. He lost and, reneging his pledge not to return to national politics, rejoined the LDP and ran for the HR. He ran in the PR district with virtual guarantee of winning, instead of his old single-member district, which is much more competitive.[77]

In summary, Kunio's moves are consistent with the dilemmas politicians faced in the post-1993 political reformation; however, Kunio's case was extreme. Kunio had sought opportunities like a weathervane based on the shifting winds of the political climate. Kunio was essentially a "political animal" who determined his moves by political instinct, rather than principles. For Kunio, winning the elections has become an end in itself. Despite the victorious comeback in 2000, it remains to be seen whether Kunio will continue to win. He won this time because he was listed second among the LDP candidates in the PR block: 19.49 percent of the Tokyo Block's voters cast their votes for the LDP, not for Kunio. Had Kunio been listed fifth, he would have lost, and there is no guarantee that he will be listed second next time. It also remains to be seen if next time Kunio will try to run from Tokyo District 2 (his old district), in recourse to the Hatoyama name.

The June 2000 HR General Elections

As for the overall results of the June 2000 HR general elections out of 480 seats, the LDP lost 38 seats and ended up with 233 seats (48.5 percent), while the DPJ gained 32 seats to end up with 127 seats (26.5 percent). The Mori cabinet managed to secure its majority standing in the HR only by a coalition with the CGP (which lost 11 seats to end up with 31 seats) and the Conservative Party (which also lost 11 seats to end up with 7 seats), totaling 271 seats. The result appeared to be a DPJ victory vis-à-vis the LDP; however, Kunio denied such an appraisal and argued that the election proved that the DPJ could not ever become a ruling party. Kunio argued that the DPJ could not obtain a majority in the HR even with the best of opportunities. The LDP was in adverse conditions: the sudden death of Prime Minister Obuchi [it could be a favorable condition for the LDP, because some voters gave the party "sympathy votes" for the late prime minister. In fact, his young daughter Yuko ran in his place and easily won despite the fact that she had virtually no experience in politics]; criticism against the way the party leadership chose Prime Minister Mori (closed-door and secret); and Mori's own ill-conceived statements, including his remarks about the emperor being the "God of the Nation."[78]

Kunio warns that the DPJ should be not overjoyed with the gain. Kunio contends that the DPJ merely picked up the electorate's rebellious votes against the LDP. The electorate did not vote for the DPJ for the sake of making the party the ruling party. A precedent was the JSP's gain in the February 1990 HR elections. Kunio states that although the JSP obtained 136 seats (out of 512 seats then), few, including those who had voted for the party, thought that the JSP could be the ruling party. This is true for the DPJ at present. Nobody thinks that the party could really be a ruling party. Kunio argues that the DPJ will remain in "perpetual opposition" as the JSP had been. Kunio asserts, "this is the peak of the DPJ."[79]

The July 2001 HC General Elections

In fact, some of the electorate had returned to the LDP in the HC general elections in July 2001. At stake were 121 seats of the total 247 seats in the upper house (the number of the HC seats will be reduced from the original 252 to 242 by the next elections in 2004. This time, 121 seats were contested, making the total number 247 in this transition period). The LDP gained four seats to have 65 seats out of the 121 seats, whereas the DPJ also gained four seats to have 26 seats. As a result, the LDP's total HC delegation rose to 111 seats (44.9 percent), out of 247, while the DPJ's increased to 59 (23.9 percent). The new LDP-led coalition cabinet, headed by Koizumi Junichiro since April 2001, managed to secure its majority standing in the HC only by a coalition with the CGP (unchanged with 23 seats) and the Conservative Party (two-seat loss to have 5 seats).[80]

The LDP's gain this time (compared to the massive loss in the HC elections three years ago) owed much to the new Prime Minister Koizumi, who had succeeded the unpopular Prime Minister Mori. Koizumi is a maverick. He opposed the LDP's faction politics and left the Mori faction (former Fukuda-Abe line) alone and formed an unprecedented cabinet that included five women, such as Justice Minister Moriyama Mayumi and Foreign Minister Tanaka Makiko. However, the LDP's modest gain despite the unusual popularity of Prime Minister Koizumi indicates the depth of apathy on the part of the

electorate. Those who voted for the LDP this time did so only in anticipation of Koizumi's leadership in carrying out reforms. They could turn
away from the LDP again, as they did in the previous HC and HR elections, should Koizumi fail in his promised reforms.

Kunio Appointed to Chair the HR Steering Committee

In January 2002 Kunio was appointed to chair the HR steering committee, succeeding Suzuki Muneo, an influential member of the LDP's
Hashimoto faction. Suzuki was embroiled in a feud with Foreign Minister
Tanaka concerning the MOFA reforms and resigned the post. Kunio had
belonged to the Takeshita faction (the predecessor of the Hashimoto
faction) before his defection; however, he became an independent (no
factional affiliation) within the LDP after he came back. It was unprecedented that an independent HR member was given such an important
post. In fact, LDP Secretary General Yamazaki Taku had requested to
Nonaka, then secretary general of the Hashimoto faction, that he choose
Suzuki's successor from the Hashimoto faction. However, Nonaka chose
Kunio. Although Kunio is nominally an independent, he is still close to
Nonaka and is referred to as a "hidden member" of the Hashimoto
faction. Nonaka calculated that by giving the post to Kunio, the
Hashimoto faction could distract criticism against the faction concerning
the controversy involving Suzuki, and yet could maintain a certain influ-
ence on the Koizumi cabinet by running the HR via Kunio.[81]

In June 2002, the HR's vote on a resolution to recommend that Suzuki
resign from the HR stumbled due to the voting method. The LDP
wanted an anonymous voting method, whereas the DPJ insisted that the
vote be done with the voters' names on it. The procedural issue was
further delayed by the discovery that the HR steering committee chair
(Kunio) was drinking with another committee member from one of the
ruling parties in the chair's office at the HR. The committee in the end
decided to use a "standing-up vote" as a compromise, and the resolution
was passed that month with all the parties in favor, including the LDP.
The resolution has no binding effect. This episode seems to show the low
morale of the ruling parties in general and that of Kunio in particular.[82]

An Assessment of the Political Leadership of Kunio

In assessing Kunio's political leadership so far, Kunio can be seen as
being more conservative than Yukio. While Yukio created the NPS, a
liberal breakaway party of the LDP, with Takemura, Kunio joined the

NFP, a more conservative breakaway party, led by Ozawa. Although Kunio created the DPJ with Yukio, he was ill at ease with the party from its inception. In hindsight, it was inevitable for Kunio to leave the DPJ, which was "nothing but a political asylum of former socialists" in Kunio's eyes, and return to the LDP. Running for governor was a stepping stone for Kunio to return to the LDP.

Overall, Kunio appears to have more charismatic qualities than Yukio. According to Ito, Kunio can speak passionately about his politics and make jokes in his speech, whereas Yukio's speech is too abstract and hard to understand. Kunio is down-to-earth and more likable, whereas Yukio is serious and uninteresting. Ito writes that dealing with constituents in downtown Tokyo and being immersed in LDP politics for more than two decades, Kunio's appearance had dramatically changed. Ito even goes so far as to state that few politicians have changed in appearance as much as Kunio: Kunio was a tall, slim, and handsome young man when he began campaigning in 1976, but he has put on weight and assumed the image of an impudent politician. In the words of Ito, Kunio has assumed the aura of a professional politician, while Yukio still looks like an amateur politician.[83]

Kobayashi contrasts the characteristics of the brothers as Kunio being a feisty, selfish, sharp, and stubborn realist, while Yukio is a gentle, kind, naïve, serious, and shy idealist. Kobayashi adds that what they have in common is that both have nothing to fear or lose. Because they were brought up in a generous and liberal environment, they can speak and act idealistically with impunity. This is both their strength and their weakness. Kobayashi also points out that although Kunio might have more charismatic attributes and leadership skills than Yukio, there is room to improve himself, such as controlling his short-temperedness. Nakasone also commented that Kunio had the potential to grow to be a competent leader as he further accumulates experiences in politics. He should, however, learn to control his emotions and also develop a long-term strategy for the nation.[84]

Despite a couple of misfortunes, such as his unsuccessful involvement in the DPJ and his loss in the Tokyo gubernatorial election, Kunio overall had a very fortunate political career so far. His good fortune is largely due to the fact that he is a scion of the Hatoyama Dynasty. Kunio became education minister at a very young age. Kunio was also labor minister of the Hata coalition cabinet. Kunio was once again welcomed by the LDP leadership after the defection and won a seat in the HR. Without the family's political legacy, it is doubtful that Kunio would have been able to make such an easy comeback to national politics.

The Political Environment

Kunio's political career has been affected by the drastic structural changes in politics. He was trained in the "1955 system" of the LDP's dominance and had a promising career in the stable structure. However, the "1955 system" collapsed in 1993 and the time no longer required career politicians who functioned as brokers between the business and bureaucracy. Kunio had to pursue his career in an uncharted environment. Kunio stated in August 2000 that he had left the LDP because the party had been resisting any political reforms and he wanted to establish a two-party system that subscribed to liberal conservatism. In Kunio's opinion, there had been three opportunities for establishing a two-party system. The first opportunity was the Hosokawa coalition cabinet in 1993. Kunio asked Hosokawa to maintain the cabinet for four years: Kunio thought that the LDP, in the opposition, would break up in four years assuming the Hosokawa cabinet remained in existence. The cabinet could ally with those liberal conservatives who would leave the LDP and, therefore, it would not have to ally with socialists. There would then come a chance to establish a two-party system, run by two major liberal conservative parties. However, Hosokawa abandoned his cabinet in less than eight months, and the opportunity that Kunio had in mind was gone.[85]

According to Kunio, the second chance was the post-Murayama coalition cabinet. The cabinet emerged after the collapse of the Hata coalition cabinet. Since Ozawa excluded the SDPJ and the NPS from the Hata cabinet, they allied with the LDP, overthrew the Hata cabinet, and formed the anomalous Murayama coalition cabinet. Kunio thought that the LDP might break up as a result of the illegitimate coalition. It presented another opportunity to create a two-party system. Contrary to Kunio's expectations, some of the LDP defectors returned to its fold, making the party the absolute majority party again.[86]

The third opportunity to create a two-party system came with the creation of the DPJ. What Kunio had in mind was to create a neoconservative party made up of the rightist members of the NFP, such as Funada Hajime and Sonoda Hiroyuki. The party would be small in size, but it would have great potential to become the second pole: its members would share the same ideology of liberal conservatism and the party could formulate coherent policy. Therefore, Kunio opposed the package inclusion of SDPJ and NPS members. Nevertheless, the DPJ ended up being a political asylum for former JSP members who were supported by labor unions. It was not what Kunio wanted for the DPJ.

Kunio states, "I told my brother that the DPJ should keep a certain distance from labor unions. In retrospect, I should have told him then that I did not want any element of the left at all. My brother was more pragmatic and told me that 'we could get support from labor unions (if we let former JSP members in).' " Kunio deplored the participation of socialists that had deprived him of the third opportunity to create a two-party system.[87]

The Interactions Between Personal Attributes and the Environment

Kunio had personal attributes more suited to a political leader than Yukio. However, Kunio was impatient and moved too opportunistically, and consequently, lost the solid standing he had held in the LDP, the DPJ, and elsewhere. Will another opportunity arise for Kunio in the near future? Kunio believes that breaking up the DPJ would present such an opportunity. Kunio hopes to break up the DPJ and create a new liberal conservative party to his liking; a small party with only the Right faction of the DPJ. In this regard, Kunio considers the constitutional revision a litmus test for the DPJ's breakup. The issue will illuminate the difference between the Left and Right factions of the party. Then a chance will come to break up the party and create a new party with the DPJ's Right faction. Kunio believes that it is his mission to prepare a political environment for creating such a new party.[88]

Then will Kunio leave the LDP again? His wish for creating a new party indicates that Kunio is using the LDP as a temporary harbor. Kunio's new party would be too small to become the second pole alone. It will have to ally with other parties, such as the Liberal Party, or with reform-minded members of the LDP. However, the series of such attempts by LDP defectors have thus far failed, and the electorates grew tired of new parties. Then, will Kunio stay with the LDP and try to become its leader? There is a precedent to his disadvantage. Kono Yohei defected from the LDP and created the NLC in 1976; however, he disbanded the party ten years later and returned to the LDP. Although Kono became an influential member of the party and served as foreign minister and party president, he has not become prime minister. In fact, Kono is the only LDP past president who has not become prime minister. In addition to being a small faction leader, being a defector once might account for the exception. From this precedent, Kunio might have a hard time redeeming his past in the party. Or times have changed, and the past record of defection would not matter as much to the desperate LDP leadership, who made Kunio chair of the HR steering committee.[89]

In conclusion, Kunio is faced with a difficult situation. It is partly of his own making and is also due to the unstable political environment. It remains to be seen whether the electorates will support this young scion of a famed political dynasty, whether he will exercise strong leadership in the LDP, or in a new party, and achieve his ultimate goal of becoming prime minister. In turn, what leadership has Yukio exercised in the DPJ? What policy has the DPJ formulated since its inception and how did it challenge the LDP? The next chapter examines the DPJ's policy and Yukio's leadership in the party.

CHAPTER 8
THE DPJ'S POLICY AND YUKIO'S LEADERSHIP

This chapter first examines policy-making of the DPJ through five case studies and then assesses Yukio's political leadership in the party, by comparing it with that of Kan Naoto, another DPJ leader, where appropriate. This chapter analyzes the legislation concerning the national flag and anthem in-depth, because this shows the party's divisive nature most vividly. It also studies Yukio's proposal for constitutional revision in-depth, because this marked the critical departure of Yukio's stance from a traditional liberalism to a more realistic "neoliberalism."

The DPJ's Three Patterns of Behavior

The case studies of the DPJ's policy-making show that the party exhibited three typical patterns of behavior in its policy-making process. The first pattern is one of divergence, a move away from the positions of the ruling LDP. This pattern of behavior derived from the DPJ's *raison d'être* to become a moderate liberal party that can challenge the LDP. Specifically, the predominance of members of the former JSP and its splinters within the party led the DPJ to take a divergent course. In addition, the DPJ could not ignore the influence of the labor unions, which supported the party. These reasons mandated that the DPJ diverge from the LDP. The DPJ tried to attract voters by presenting distinct policy alternatives that would spark reforms in the political, economic, and financial systems. This pattern of behavior stood for principles and shows the DPJ as being a "policy seeker."[1]

The second pattern is a move toward convergence with the position of the LDP. This pattern of behavior derived from the premise that the DPJ must be part of the ruling side in order to exercise power. Some of the party leaders were also concerned that voters might turn away from the party if it strictly subscribed to its liberal positions. Therefore, the DPJ was inclined to compromise with the positions of the ruling party, at the expense of its fundamental beliefs and platforms. This pattern of behavior represented political pragmatism and showed the DPJ as being an "office seeker."[2]

The third pattern was one of ambivalence, in which the DPJ oscillated between convergence with and divergence from the LDP. This pattern suggests that the DPJ was unable to determine which direction the party should choose, either the policy-seeker's direction or the office-seeker's direction. The party swung between the two, neither able to define a basic policy nor to devise coherent policy options.

Case One: "Wholesome Opposition" vs. "Constructive Opposition"

The controversy over the party's basic policy stance symbolically illustrates the three patterns of behavior. The DPJ was split over whether the party should become *kenzen yato* ("wholesome opposition party") or *kensetsuteki yato* ("constructive opposition party"). The former position stood by the *raison d'être* of the DPJ, as a genuine opposition party to challenge the LDP. In contrast, the latter preferred the party to cooperate with the Hashimoto coalition cabinet in the legislative process, even willing to form a coalition with the cabinet. Yukio adhered to the "wholesome opposition," whereas Kan chose the "constructive opposition." While the party had originally agreed on "wholesome opposition" at its inception, the voice for "constructive opposition" grew as Kan's power soared vis-à-vis Yukio's. The two camps intensely debated on the issue, as the party leadership was expected to demonstrate a clear policy stance at its first party congress in March 1997. Yukio insisted on "wholesome opposition," arguing that the unprincipled coalition of the SDPJ and the NPS with the LDP (in the Murayama and the first Hashimoto cabinets) ruined these parties and that the DPJ should keep its ideals high and not compromise with the LDP. In contrast, Kan argued that it was easier for the DPJ to criticize the Hashimoto cabinet and that the party should instead join the cabinet and challenge the LDP from within it.[3]

It is surprising that Kan became a strong advocate for convergence. Yukio and Kan had many aspects in common. First, the two leaders had unique backgrounds as politicians. They were young politicians by the standard norm of Japanese politics, where seniority is critical, with Yukio being 49 and Kan 50 at the time of the DPJ's creation. They belonged to *dankai no sedai* (postwar baby-boom generation), that mobilized a massive opposition to the revision of the U.S.–Japan

Security Treaty in 1960, and shared many liberal ideas. Another unique aspect of the two leaders is that both hold science degrees. Yukio studied engineering at Tokyo University and Stanford University, while Kan was a science major at the Tokyo Institute of Technology. Their backgrounds sharply contrasted with those of the great majority of politicians who held law degrees. Both Yukio and Kan left the NSP to create the DPJ. With these unique young leaders, the DPJ tried to bring a whirlwind to politics.[4]

In comparison, Kan was much more liberal than Yukio. If Yukio was a Japanese Kennedy, Kan was a Japanese Jerry Brown. Kan in 1974 served as secretary general in the election campaign for Ichikawa Fusae, a legendary feminist and civic leader (see chapter 4). Kan ran in the HR general elections for the first time in 1976, and after losing three times in elections for public office, won in the 1980 HR general elections with the highest number of votes in his Tokyo district. Kan had by then joined the Social Democratic Federation (SDF) that was absorbed in the NPS in 1994. He then served as the minister of public health and welfare of the first Hashimoto coalition cabinet in 1996. His experience in the cabinet (dealing with the HIV scandal) made him realize that the party must be on the ruling side to have an impact on policies. This experience, along with his personal desire to become prime minister, accounted for his preference for "constructive opposition."[5]

In early March 1997, Yukio and Kan reached an agreement that the party would pursue "constructive opposition." However, the leftist members of the party strongly opposed Yukio's concession to Kan. In response to the leftists' grumbling, Kan then conceded to "wholesome opposition" in mid-March. By late March, however, Kan managed to persuade the leftist group to seek "constructive opposition" "for the time being." In this agreement, the DPJ would cooperate with the Hashimoto coalition cabinet, by providing policy proposals to the latter, but it would not join the latter as it was. The agreement also stated that the DPJ would promote a partial "policy coalition" with other parties, including the ruling parties, as necessary. Thus, "constructive opposition" won the debate.[6]

It took more than half a year after the party's foundation to decide its basic policy stance. Although the DPJ eventually decided to move closer to the ruling side, the swing between the two policy stances in the series of debates demonstrates its incoherence. Although the addition of the qualifier "for the time being" might have been a necessary compromise on the part of Kan to obtain a consensus from the leftist group, it indicates the party's ambivalence. As a result, the mass media dubbed the party a *yuto* (neither ruling nor opposition party), an orthographic play on words: the syllable *yu* comes between *ya*, as in *yato* (opposition party), and *yo*, as in *yoto* (ruling party), in the Japanese alphabet. This pun aptly illustrates the DPJ's ambivalent nature.[7]

In short, the DPJ's eventual decision to seek a pragmatic "constructive opposition" shows the second pattern of behavior, of convergence to the LDP. However, the facts that the decision came after prolonged vacillation between two positions and that the party added a phrase of a temporary nature indicate the third pattern of behavior of ambivalence. Although the two leaders had liberal backgrounds in common, they grew to support different policy lines. Paradoxically, Kan became a force for convergence despite his leftist background, whereas Yukio became a force for divergence in spite of his LDP starting point. The two leaders' difference on the basic party stance made the party position more ambivalent.

Case Two: National Security Policy

Yukio and Kan also differed on national security policy. The party platform stipulates that the U.S.–Japan Security Treaty is the basis for Japan's national security. However, it also provides that the party's position on this treaty is the so-called *jochu naki Ampo*, literally meaning "the U.S.–Japan Security Treaty without permanent stationing of U.S. forces." Although the party accepted the U.S.–Japan Security Treaty, it argued that permanent stationing of U.S. forces in Japan was no longer necessary and therefore it would seek a gradual withdrawal of U.S. forces. This stance reflects the influence of the former SDPJ members within the party. They still had reservations about the treaty, even after the SDPJ itself accepted the treaty when the LDP co-opted its president Murayama Tomiichi and made him prime minister in 1994. The DPJ's platform also stipulates that Japan would seek *jishu* (self-reliant) security policy by establishing regional stability through forging strong trust with Asian countries and setting up diverse regional security systems at the ASEAN (Association of Southeast Asian Nations) Regional Forum (ARF). The party ultimately would like to establish a "universal security system" through the creation of international police forces at the UN.[8]

Yukio supported the party's official position of "the U.S.–Japan Security Treaty without permanent stationing of U.S. Forces," whereas Kan tried to remove this provision from the party's "basic outlines for diplomacy and security policy" to be published in September 1997. Kan tried to remove the phrase because its meaning had been criticized as ambiguous. Kan was concerned that the United States might misconstrue the provision to mean that the party was requesting the immediate and complete withdrawal of U.S. forces. Kan initially managed to remove this provision from the "basic outlines." Its revised version only requested the withdrawal of the U.S. Marines in Okinawa and accepted the stationing of the U.S. Navy's Seventh Fleet and the U.S. Air Force "for the time being." Nevertheless, former SDPJ members, such as Yokomichi Takahiro (one of the party vice presidents), still strongly opposed the removal of the provision. Yokomichi was concerned that the removal would be interpreted as a major change in the party's security policy. Yokomichi insisted that the basic security policy should remain unchanged and that the party should adhere to the provision that it had established at its inception. In turn, Kan was concerned that revival of the provision would provoke a possible negative response from the U.S. government.[9]

In the end, Kan conceded to reviving the provision; however, he managed to get a compromise from the leftist members to use a more positive expression for the English translation of the term. As a result, the term *jochu naki Ampo* is translated as "U.S.–Japan Security Treaty with conditional stationing," instead of the literal translation, "U.S.–Japan Security Treaty without permanent stationing." By using a more positive translation, Kan tried to clarify the party's basic policy: it accepts the treaty on the condition that both the United States and Japan should consult with each other on the forms and terms of the stationing of U.S. Troops according to changes in the situation. However, the compromise left the impression that the party used a double standard in explaining the term for domestic and overseas consumption. Thus, although the party retained the provision in its basic outlines for diplomacy and security policy, it failed to convey a clear message to the electorate.[10]

In summary, the party's final decision to retain its original provision indicates divergence from the LDP. Yet, that the decision took more than one year, after swinging back and forth between two positions, attests to the third pattern of ambivalence. The DPJ's national security policy is its Achilles heel, and many political analysts, including Kobayashi Kichiya, argue that the party does not have a realistic prescription to decrease Japan's military dependence on the United States. Instead, the DPJ leadership, as well as its members, have remained divided on the issue. The Hatoyama brothers disagreed on the bill concerning the new guidelines for the U.S.–Japan Security Treaty in May 1999 (the two governments had signed the new guidelines in September 1997). Yukio opposed the bill because he believed that the bill would endanger Japan as it would involve the nation in collective security engagements. In contrast, Kunio was in favor of the bill, believing that it would be vital for Japan's national security. Yukio later changed his stance on national security policy, and made a surprising proposal for constitutional revisions.[11]

Case Three: Revision of the Special Measures Law Concerning Land Use by U.S. Forces

In April 1997, the DPJ decided to vote for revision of the law concerning special measures on land expropriation by the U.S. forces. The original law had allowed compulsory land use by U.S. military facilities in Okinawa since the reversion of Okinawa to Japan in 1972. The leases for some land used by the U.S. forces were about to expire on May 14, 1997. The Hashimoto coalition cabinet submitted a bill to revise the special measures law to allow the continued use of the land without the permission of the landowners. According to an opinion poll conducted in March 1997 by the *Yomiuri Shimbun*, 47 percent of the DPJ members in the Diet were opposed to the bill, whereas 32 percent were in favor. In comparison, 58 percent of the entire Diet membership (regardless of party affiliation) supported the bill (out of 58 percent, 26 percent expressed "conditional support"), while 23 percent were against it.[12]

Despite opposition from the party members, the DPJ decided to support the bill. Kan felt that the party's opposition would only be counterproductive because the bill was already expected to pass due to an agreement between the LDP and the NFP. Kan thought that the party's overt opposition in this situation would give an impression of a "rebellions opposition party," and that it would cause friction with the LDP in the future. Kan also thought that opposition to the bill would create a potential policy inconsistency and illegality if the DPJ ever came to power (and the party opposed such measures). Kan's logic seems unconvincing. There are precedents for parties changing their positions once they come to power, but none for changing their stance before they take power. Socialist Murayama abandoned his party's traditional policy by accepting the SDFs and the U.S.–Japan Security Treaty when he became prime minister. U.S. President Bill Clinton changed his policy stance toward China when he took office in 1993, untying the human rights issue from the most favored nation (MFN) status issue. Neither Murayama nor Clinton changed their stance before taking power. Opposition parties would lose their *raison d'être* should they compromise their policy stance for the sake of maintaining coherence among the successive cabinets.[13]

Yukio was initially against the bill; however, he decided to follow the party line of supporting the bill. By contrast, the SDPJ voted against the bill although it was part of the Hashimoto coalition cabinet. Yukio criticized the SDPJ as an "un-constructive ruling party," as opposed to the DPJ being a "constructive opposition party." The bill passed by an overwhelming majority, including opposition parties such as the NFP and the DPJ.[14]

In summary, the DPJ's decision to vote for the bill displays the second pattern of behavior, convergence to the ruling side. Yet, the decision was inconsistent because the majority of the party members (47 percent), including Yukio, were initially opposed to the bill. It was also contradictory because the bill would enable the continued stationing of U.S. forces in Okinawa, whereas the party sought the withdrawal of U.S. forces from Okinawa in its national security policy (Case Two). Further, that the party voted for the bill primarily out of a concern for its image (to avoid being seen as a rebel), points to a lack of firm principles. All of these contradictions and mixed priorities signify the ambivalent nature of the party, demonstrating the third pattern of behavior.

Case Four: The Medical Insurance Bill

Subsequently, in May 1997, the DPJ decided to vote against the bill concerning medical insurance systems submitted by the Hashimoto coalition cabinet. The party bound all its members to oppose the bill by invoking *togi kosoku* (party discipline). It is common practice for political parties to apply party discipline for important bills in order to enforce organizational solidarity. The party opposed the bill primarily because labor unions, the party's primary supporters, were concerned that it would increase the cost of medical insurance. The party leadership was also concerned with its credibility as an opposition party. Having just voted for the previous bill (Case Three), Yukio was concerned that if the party voted for yet another bill initiated by the cabinet, it would give the impression to the electorate that the DPJ had decided on full cooperation with the cabinet. Therefore, Yukio felt that the party should oppose the bill and that continued negotiation with the LDP would be counterproductive.[15]

In contrast, Kan initially had tried to work out a consensus with the Hashimoto cabinet to modify the bill to make it more agreeable to the DPJ members. They had strongly requested provisions for preferential treatment of infants and reduction of family burden in paying medical expenses. However, the cabinet did not include these provisions in a modified bill, and many DPJ members strongly resented it. As a result, Kan gave up on working out a compromise bill and invoked party discipline to bind all its members to oppose the bill.[16]

In summary, the DPJ's decision to oppose the bill supports the first pattern of behavior, divergence from the ruling cabinet. Nevertheless, Kan had tried to support the bill through an amendment. Also, the motivation for divergence was shaky because the decision was partly based on a shallow political strategy that the party had better vote against this bill since it had voted in favor of the previous bill. This concern for its image rather than for policy preferences also reveals the party's ambivalence and thereby shows the third pattern of behavior.

In the overall analysis, the four cases examined here present different yet similar patterns. Cases One and Three support the second pattern of behavior, a move toward convergence with the ruling cabinet, whereas Cases Two and Four endorse the first pattern of behavior, a move toward divergence from the ruling side. More important, however, all cases show the third pattern of behavior. There was a pattern in the party's behavior to oscillate between convergence and divergence before arriving at a policy alternative.

The ambivalence of the DPJ's policy-making, derived from the leadership split as well as the divisions among its members, has deepened with the party's expansion in April 1998. Nowhere was the divisiveness more apparent than in the legislation for the national flag and anthem in 1999. It is useful to examine the issue closely as it epitomizes the party's ambivalent nature.

Case Five: Legislation for the National Flag and Anthem

The Obuchi coalition cabinet of the LDP and the Liberal Party submitted the bill concerning the national flag and anthem to the HR in June 1999 and swiftly passed it that August. The bill designates a flag called *Hinomaru* (literally meaning "round sun") as the national flag, and a song *Kimigayo* ("his majestic reign") as the national anthem, and establishes their specifications. This legislation symbolized the Obuchi cabinet's effort to "totally liquidate unsettled postwar issues" that were considered "taboos" due to their association with Japan's past militarism. The bill was controversial because *Hinomaru* and *Kimigayo* were symbols of Imperial Japan from the Meiji era until the end of World War II. An editorial in the conservative *Yomiuri Shimbun* hailed the bill's passage as a departure from the "postwar democracy" under which Japan was swayed by leftists who regarded anything to do with nationhood as undemocratic and even reactionary. In contrast, the *Asahi Shimbun* (a daily of liberal standing) and the *Chunichi Shimbun* (a daily of neutral standing), criticized the bill's passage as an LDP victory, which promoted its conservative agenda of intensifying the "color of nationhood."[17]

The Origin of *Hinomaru* and *Kimigayo*

According to the HR's cabinet research bureau, *Hinomaru* first appeared in the literature in the late *Heian* period (twelfth century) when the *Tale of Heike* cited warriors carrying military fans with a *Hinomaru* picture. During the Tokugawa Shogunate (seventeenth to nineteenth centuries), ships hoisted the *Hinomaru* to distinguish them from foreign ships. Then, in 1870, the Meiji government issued a decree concerning rules for commercial vessels, stipulating that Japanese vessels should fly the *Hinomaru* and detailing specifications. Since then, *Hinomaru* has been considered the de facto national flag.[18]

Kimigayo is more controversial because its text specifically praises the imperial reign and wishes it eternal prosperity. The text reads:

Kimi ga yo wa	His majestic reign
chiyo ni yachiyo ni	for thousands of years
sazareishi no iwao to narite	pebbles grow into rocks
koke no musu made	until covered with moss

The original text of *Kimigayo* appears in *Kokin Wakashu* (the first anthology of Japanese poems compiled by imperial command in 905). The author of the original poem is unknown, and its first phrase reads *waga kimi wa* (my lord), instead of *kimi ga yo wa* (his majestic reign), with the rest being the same as the current text. The first phrase was changed to the current form during the *Kamakura* period (late twelfth to fourteenth centuries). Since then, *Kimigayo* has been recited by the commoners on ceremonial occasions, but there was no official musical score until 1880. When the Meiji government adopted *Kimigayo* as a song to hail the emperor at ceremonies, Hayashi Hiromori, a musician in the Imperial Household Agency, transcribed a Western score for *Kimigayo* with the help of European music teachers. It was played for the first time in November 1880 on the emperor's birthday. Then, in 1893, the MOE incorporated the song into the public school curriculum and required that it be sung at public school ceremonies.[19]

With Japan's defeat in World War II and the enforcement of the new constitution, the status of the emperor changed from "ruler of Japan" to "symbol of the state and of the unity of the people" (Article 1). When the bill establishing *Kimigayo* was submitted in 1999, opposition parties argued that *Kimigayo* was unconstitutional. The LDP countered that there were many possible interpretations of *Kimigayo*'s text. Thus, the exact meanings of the words *kimi* and *kimigayo* became the focal point of deliberations in the lower house. The word *kimi* means "lord" or "emperor," while *kimigayo* means "*kimi*'s reign." Given the new status of the emperor, however, Chief Cabinet Secretary Nonaka Hiromu stated in June 1999 that the government interpreted the word *kimi* as "emperor as the symbol of Japan," and thus it was appropriate to interpret the *Kimigayo*'s text as wishing long prosperity and peace to "Japan" that embraces the emperor as its symbol. Prime Minister Obuchi also said in June 1999 that the word *kimigayo* meant "Japan" that embraced the emperor as the symbol of the state and of the unity of the people, based on the will of the people.[20]

Opposition parties disputed the government's interpretation. The DPJ's Ito Hidenari criticized the government interpretation of the word *kimi* as lacking historical depth and breadth. Shii Kazuo, general secretary of the JCP, said that there was no way the phrase *kimigayo* could be interpreted as "Japan," and that insofar as the text wished for an eternal imperial reign, it was inappropriate for a democratic nation.[21]

Another problem with the bill was that although the bill designates *Hinomaru* and *Kimigayo* as the national flag and anthem, it has no provisions to make their actual observance—raising *Hinomaru* and singing *Kimigayo*—obligatory. The cabinet deliberately did not specify when and how *Hinomaru* and *Kimigayo* were to be used, or make their observance mandatory, because the LDP's past efforts to legislate them since the 1960s had failed.

Postwar Controversies

With the occupation of Japan, the SCAP banned hoisting *Hinomaru* and singing *Kimigayo* in 1945. When Japan regained its sovereignty in 1952, the government resumed the use of *Hinomaru* and *Kimigayo*, although the latter was played without the words at official ceremonies. As early as 1958, the MOE issued the *gakushu shido yoryo* (teacher's manual), stating that it was desirable to hoist the national flag (it did not say *Hinomaru*, as if it were already established as such) and to sing *Kimigayo* at public schools. The term *shido* (literally meaning "guidance") is actually a euphemism for directive, with the connotation of mandatory compliance. In 1961, the government created subcommittees on the national flag and on the national anthem; however, they failed to recommend legislation of the national flag and anthem, due to the leftist parties' opposition. In 1974, Prime Minister Tanaka expressed his intention to legislate the national flag and anthem but never succeeded.[22]

Then, in 1989, the MOE issued a new teacher's manual that strengthened its guidance on the observance of *Hinomaru* and *Kimigayo* at public school ceremonies. The Japan Teachers' Union (JTU), backed by the JCP and the JSP, opposed such guidance and refused to observe it. The JTU argued that there was no legal basis for public schools to teach *Hinomaru* and *Kimigayo* as the national flag and anthem. Consequently, there were many incidents of nonobservance and acts of defiance at school ceremonies, and school principals were caught in between the MOE and the JTU. When the LDP co-opted SDPJ President Murayama into a coalition cabinet in 1994, Murayama accepted *Hinomaru* and *Kimigayo*. The SDPJ followed suit at its party congress that year and the JTU removed opposition to *Hinomaru* and *Kimigayo* from its agenda in 1995. Then, in February 1999, JCP Chairman Fuwa Tetsuzo came out in favor of the idea of legislating the national flag and anthem, while adhering to his opposition to *Hinomaru* and *Kimigayo* per se. However, Prime Minister Obuchi stated then that he considered *Hinomaru* and *Kimigayo* as established as the national flag and anthem and that he was not planning to legislate them.[23]

In March 1999, a high school principal in Hiroshima prefecture became embroiled in a dispute over the singing of *Kimigayo* at a graduation ceremony and committed suicide. This incident gave a new impetus to the legislation within the LDP. Immediately after the incident, Chief Cabinet Secretary Nonaka stated the necessity for the legislation, and Prime Minister Obuchi instructed the cabinet to take the necessary steps. Just three months later, in June 1999, the cabinet submitted the bill to the Diet. In response, the SDPJ retracted its earlier acceptance of *Hinomaru* and *Kimigayo*, and the JTU decided to oppose the bill.[24]

Public Opinion Polls

According to the poll conducted by the *Yomiuri Shimbun* in March 1999, shortly after the principal's suicide, 60.7 percent of the 1,954 respondents thought that both *Hinomaru* and *Kimigayo* were established as the national flag and anthem, and 64.2 percent felt that both hoisting

Hinomaru and singing *Kimigayo* were desirable at public school ceremonies. Also, 68.1 percent supported the idea of legislating *Hinomaru*
and *Kimigayo* as the national flag and anthem (43.0 percent definite
support and 25.1 percent moderate support), whereas 25.7 percent were
opposed (11.5 percent definitely opposed and 14.2 percent moderately
opposed). Another poll conducted by the independent Japan Research
Council on Public Opinion Polls in July 1999, after submission of the
bill, yielded similar results. Out of 1,928 respondents, 68.3 percent
thought that both *Hinomaru* and *Kimigayo* were suitable for the
national flag and anthem. Also, 71.3 percent said they supported the bill
(44.9 percent definite support and 26.4 percent moderate support),
whereas 25.1 percent opposed it (9.8 percent were definitely opposed
and 15.3 percent moderately opposed it).[25]

Judging from the results of the two polls, it appears that the majority of the Japanese accept *Hinomaru* and *Kimigayo* as the national flag
and anthem. However, *Hinomaru* commands much larger support,
while *Kimigayo* receives much less support, due to its direct association
with the emperor. In terms of age brackets, the younger generations
have more negative views on *Hinomaru* and *Kimigayo* than the older
generations, who have an attachment to both.[26]

The Debate in the Diet

Conservative parties, such as the LDP and the Liberal Party, supported
the bill. LDP Secretary General Mori Yoshiro stated in June 1999 that
Hinomaru and *Kimigayo* were accepted by the vast majority of the
people, and that few would oppose the legislation. Liberal Party
President Ozawa Ichiro stated that most of the people considered
Hinomaru and *Kimigayo* to be the national flag and anthem, and that
the Diet could not possibly decide otherwise. The CGP was more
cautious. Although President Kanzaki Takenori said that he considered
Hinomaru and *Kimigayo* to be established as the national flag and
anthem, he deemed the legislation merely a possibility. In contrast,
Secretary General Fuyushiba Tetsuzo said that the imposition of
Hinomaru and *Kimigayo* violated the constitutional right of freedom of
conscience. In the end, the CGP decided to support the bill. The CGP
held the deciding vote in the Diet, where the LDP, even with its coalition with the Liberal Party, lacked a majority in the HC. Therefore, the
LDP leadership invited the CGP to enter into a new coalition and the
latter supported the bill in return (the three-party coalition was formed
in October).[27]

While the high school principal's suicide was a catalyst, this *quid pro quo* with the CGP was a decisive requirement for the submission of the bill. Chief Cabinet Secretary Nonaka, of the old guard in the LDP, engineered it. As of February 1999, Prime Minister Obuchi was not planning to submit a bill any time soon. Even after the principal's suicide, Obuchi merely stated that he would like to legislate it during the year 2000. In contrast, Nonaka, known for a more straight approach, seized the opportunity when the CGP showed interest in joining the coalition and arranged the swift submission of the bill. Nonaka allegedly said that he wanted to have the legislation before November 1999, the tenth anniversary of Emperor Akihito's coronation.[28]

In turn, leftist parties such as the SDPJ and the JCP remained unequivocally opposed. SDPJ Secretary General Fuchigami Sadao stated that it was necessary to keep in mind the fact that *Hinomaru* and *Kimigayo* were imposed on Asian peoples as symbols of Japanese wars of aggression. JCP Chairman Fuwa said that it was necessary to create a new national flag and anthem that were suitable to the present Japan, while party General Secretary Shii stated that it was wrong to initiate the legislation without having discussions with the general public.[29]

The DPJ was the only party that could not come up with a consensus on the bill. The party merely decided that it would discuss the issue with a view to supporting the bill, and that it would do its best to form a consensus. In the end, the party decided to make the vote "free," instead of invoking party discipline. Secretary General Hata Tsutomu justified the voting format by saying that this bill concerned individual belief, and the party would not bind the freedom of thought of its members. In addition, given the stronger objections to *Kimigayo* than to *Hinomaru* among the party members as well as the general public, the party decided to submit an amendment to the government-sponsored bill, only designating *Hinomaru* as the national flag but omitting *Kimigayo*.[30]

President Kan expressed his approval of the government bill, stating that the party recognized *Hinomaru* and *Kimigayo* as being already established as the national flag and anthem, and that if there was a consensus among the people on the bill, the party would follow it. In contrast, Yukio, then deputy secretary general, stated that he personally had nothing against *Hinomaru* and *Kimigayo* but he was opposed to the bill. He was concerned that the legislation would accelerate leftists' mobilization efforts against *Hinomaru* and *Kimigayo* and deepen the predicaments of school principals. Nevertheless, when the party's policy research council recommended supporting the bill, Yukio leaned toward voting for the bill for the sake of building the party consensus, and he was even willing to make the vote a party discipline matter.[31]

The Diet Votes

The HR passed the bill in the plenary session in July 1999, with an overwhelming majority of 403 in favor, 86 against, no abstentions, and 10 absent. Of those who voted, 82.4 percent supported the bill. The vote was striking in that there was no revolt against the party discipline (with the exception of the DPJ). All members of the LDP, the CGP·Reform Club, and the Liberal Party who were present for the session voted in favor of the bill, whereas all members of the SDPJ and the JCP who were present voted against the bill. The only party in which the votes were split among its members was the DPJ; with 45 in favor, 46 against, and 1 absent (see table 8.1). The DPJ-sponsored amendment bill was rejected. Contrary to the sheer cohesiveness of the other five parties, the DPJ was evenly split. In addition, the DPJ's leadership was split. Notwithstanding his earlier statement in favor of the bill, Kan voted against the bill, whereas Yukio voted for the bill despite his earlier opposition to it. Hata also voted for the bill. Thus, the bill again exposed the *yoriai jotai* (hodgepodge household) nature of the DPJ and the lack of coherence among its leaders.[32]

The votes in the HC's plenary session in August 1999 displayed the same pattern as in the HR. Out of 251, 166 voted in favor and 71 against, with 5 abstaining and 9 absent. Of those who voted, 68.5 percent were in favor. While there was absolute cohesion in the other 5 parties, the DPJ was again split with 20 in favor and 31 opposed, with 5 abstaining. Kan stated that the party's split vote correctly reflected

Table 8.1   HR's votes on the national flag and anthem bill

	In favor	Opposed	Abstain	Absent	Total
LDP	260	0	0	0	260
DPJ	45	46	0	1	92
CGP·Reform Club	52	0	0	0	52
LP	38	0	0	1	39
JCP	0	26	0	0	26
SDPJ	0	14	0	0	14
Others	8	0	0	8	16
Total	403	86	0	10	499

Source: "*Kokki-kokka hoan, Shuin o tsuka*" (The HR passed the national flag and anthem bill), *Yomiuri Shimbun*, July 23, 1999.

THE DPJ'S POLICY AND YUKIO / 211

the wide range of opinions among the people on this issue and that it would not jeopardize the party's solidarity. The DPJ-sponsored amendment bill was again rejected (see table 8.2).[33]

The new law went into effect on August 13, 1999, immediately after the passage in the HC. Only two days later, *Kimigayo*, now the official national anthem, was sung for the first time at the fifty-fourth Memorial Day of the end of World War II. At past Memorial Day ceremonies, *Kimigayo* was played during the ingress and egress of the emperor and the empress, but it was not sung. This time too the emperor and empress did not sing, however LDP politicians sang most enthusiastically. Takahashi Tetsuya, professor of philosophy at Tokyo University, states, "the fact that the emperor and empress did not sing reaffirmed that *Kimigayo* is a song of the subjects hailing their rulers: If *Kimigayo* meant "Japan," as the Obuchi cabinet claimed, the emperor and empress should have sung as well."[34]

In summary, the legislation demonstrated the lack of leadership both on the ruling side and the opposition side. The LDP won passage of the bill by an unprincipled coalition. The party formed a coalition with the Liberal Party, run by its "traitor" and Nonaka's archenemy Ozawa, only because it was defeated in the HC general elections in July 1998. Nonaka used to call Ozawa a devil and yet he courted Ozawa to form a coalition. It was a prime example of a marriage of convenience. The coalition with the CGP was also a marriage of convenience as the LDP had little in common with that party in their platforms. This later obliged Ozawa to leave the coalition. These coalitions, both attributed to Nonaka's making, did not represent what the electorates had chosen.[35]

Table 8.2 HC's votes on the national flag and anthem bill

	In favor	Opposed	Abstain	Absent	Total
LDP	101	0	0	0	101
DPJ·Green Wind Club	20	31	5	0	56
CGP·Reform Club	24	0	0	0	24
LP	12	0	0	0	12
JCP	0	23	0	0	23
SDPJ	0	13	0	0	13
Others	9	4	0	0	22
Total	166	71	5	9	251

Source: "*Kokki-kokka-ho seiritsu*" (The national flag and anthem law established), *Yomiuri Shimbun*, August 10, 1999.

In turn, the Liberal Party and the CGP abandoned their own principles, lured by becoming part of the cabinet. Worse, several younger CGP Diet members allegedly met Nonaka and received ¥2 million (about $18,600) per person during the Diet session. Referring to this scandal, Yukio accused the CGP of changing its position on the bill during the session. Meanwhile, the SDPJ's retraction of its earlier acceptance of *Hinomaru* and *Kimigayo* and its vote against the bill cast doubts on the party's credibility. The only party that maintained a coherent position on this issue was the JCP. As for the DPJ, the party demonstrated its own inconsistency and indecisiveness, thereby supporting the third pattern of behavior.[36]

As part of his effort to overcome the party's impasse, experienced in this legislation, Yukio proposed to revise the constitution in October 1999.

Yukio's Proposal for Constitutional Revision

Article 9 of Japan's constitution has been arguably the most controversial issue in postwar Japanese politics. This two-paragraph-long, so-called peace clause reads:

[1] Aspiring sincerely to an international peace based on justice and order, the Japanese people forever renounce war as a sovereign right of the nation and the threat or use of force as means of settling international disputes.

[2] In order to accomplish the aim of the preceding paragraph, land, sea, and air forces, as well as other war potential, will never be maintained. The right of belligerency of the state will not be recognized.

Nevertheless, within less than a decade after the document was enacted, Japan possessed the SDFs on the land, at sea, and in the air. This situation is obviously contradictory. However, the Yoshida cabinet interpreted the SDFs as being constitutional and kept the article intact. Those on the left vehemently opposed the interpretation. Ichiro tried to solve the contradiction by revising the article, but in vain. As a result, Japan left such a quintessential issue as its right to self-defense ambiguous. Article 9 had posed a constant obstacle to the U.S.–Japan alliance, limiting Japan's involvement in the maintenance of regional security in East Asia. The article had also been a bottleneck for Japan's participation in international peace activities, such as United Nations peacekeeping operations (UNPKOs). Even after Japan's involvement in the Persian

Gulf War was criticized as being "too little, too late," Japan shied away from actively committing itself to UNPKOs. Meanwhile, Germany (former West Germany), which also had constitutional constraints on its use of armed forces, revised its Basic Laws (constitution) more than 40 times since 1947 in order to participate in the North Atlantic Treaty Organization's (NATO) military operations and UNPKOs. In contrast, Japan's Article 9 has survived and remained intact.[37]

Only in 1999 did the political atmosphere change enough to challenge the "sanctity" of Article 9. Prime Minister Obuchi established the Constitutional Research Council at the Diet in 1999, as part of the LDP's efforts to "totally liquidate unsettled postwar issues" before the turn of the century. It was against this background that Yukio published his proposal for revising the constitution.

Yukio's Proposal: Neoliberalism

Yukio argues that traditional liberalism in Japan, characterized by a stubborn pro-constitutionalism and anti-U.S. sentiments, is outdated. Following his grandfather, Yukio contends that it is a sophism to say that Japan does not maintain any armed forces (paragraph 2 of Article 9) but that it can maintain armed forces for self-defense (the government interpretation of the article). Yukio argues that the SDFs are nothing but armed forces and it is time to recognize this fact. He proposes to revise Article 9 as follows: [1] Japan shall maintain land, sea, and air forces, as well as other war potential. [2] Japan shall neither use these forces for acts of aggression nor shall Japan employ conscription. Yukio contends that stipulating Japan's possession of armed forces will remove the ambiguity of Article 9 and will end the futile and protracted debate regarding the constitutionality of the SDFs. Yukio adds, however, that there is one condition that must be met if this revision is to work. Taking note of the fact that Asian countries would have misgivings about such revisions insofar as Japan ignores its past acts of aggression (as conservatives do), Yukio calls on Japan to acknowledge these acts unequivocally and conduct a comprehensive review. Doing so would eliminate any lingering problems with Asian countries.[38]

Second, Yukio argues that Japan should decrease its dependence on the United States for meeting its national security needs. In its place, he believes that Japan should establish *jishu* (self-reliant) defense capability and create an environment in which this could be made possible. Concerning the U.S.–Japan Security Treaty, Yukio argues that

Table 8.3 Comparisons on the revision of Article 9

	Revision of paragraph 1	Revision of paragraph 2	Add a new clause on the right to collective self-defense
Liberal (JCP and SDPJ)	No	No	No
Neoliberal (Yukio)	Yes	Yes	No → Yes (Oct. 1999) → (Oct. 2000)
Neoconservative (Ozawa)	No	No (adds paragraph 3)	No (assumes this right in paragraph 3)
Conservative (Nakasone)	No (either way)	Yes	Yes

Sources: Yukio, "*Jieitai o guntai to mitomeyo,*" ([The Constitution] should acknowledge the SDFs as armed forces), *Bungei Shunju*, October 1999, p. 263; Ozawa, "*Nihonkoku kempo kaisei shian,*" (A draft proposal for revisions of the Japanese constitution), *Bungei Shunju*, September 1999, p. 98; Nakasone, "*Waga kaikenron,*" (My discourse on constitutional revisions), *Shokun*, April 2000, pp. 55–56; and *Chunichi Shimbun*, October 17, 2000.

permanent stationing of foreign troops in a sovereign country is unnatural and that Japan should not remain a protectorate of the United States. Yukio was also reluctant to assert Japan's right to collective self-defense at the time of the publication of the article. The official interpretation of Article 9, made by the cabinet's Legal Bureau in 1973, is that Japan possesses the rights to both individual and collective self-defense but cannot exercise the latter. Yukio agreed, believing that exercising the right to collective self-defense would be dangerous: Japan would be involved in wars that it does not want through the U.S.–Japan Security Treaty. However, in October 2000, Yukio changed his stance on this matter. In a TV interview, he said that Japan's right to collective self-defense should be stipulated in the constitution, though stressing that such a right should be exercised in an extremely restrained fashion. Thereby, Yuiko realized the logic that Japan has to accept exercise of that right if it wants to stand on its own feet as an equal alliance partner of the United States.[39]

Because Yukio broke away from the traditional liberalism, his views are dubbed "neoliberalism." It is useful to present two proposals by prominent constitutional revisionists in order to provide a frame of reference with which to assess Yukio's proposal. The first is that of Nakasone Yasuhiro and the second is that of Ozawa Ichiro (see table 8.3).

Nakasone's Proposal: Orthodox Conservatism

Former prime minister Nakasone (1982–1987) represents orthodox conservatism on this issue. Nakasone is a successor to Ichiro's faction in the LDP and he has been the most outspoken and longest-standing advocates for constitutional revisions. He even composed a song for constitutional revision (*kempo kaisei no uta*) in 1956 and sang it in the street when the constitution was considered holy writ. Responding to Yukio's article, Nakasone published his latest proposal in April 2000. Nakasone states that he was opposed to Prime Minister Yoshida, who opted for a policy of *ikkoku heiwa-shugi* (pacifism in a single nation). Instead, Nakasone, along with his mentor Ichiro, argued that Japan should take charge of its national defense once its sovereignty was restored and assume international responsibilities upon admission to the United Nations. However, Yoshida, a "shrewd machiavellian" in the words of Nakasone, defended the constitution because the people supported it. Nakasone adds that he himself could not take up constitutional revisions during his time in office owing to the strong public support for the constitution. In his latest proposal, Nakasone asserts Japan's right to collective self-defense in the constitution. He argues that this right exists to protect the right to individual self-defense and that an alliance relationship presupposes the exercise of this right. Accordingly, Nakasone proposed to revise paragraph 2 of Article 9 (relinquishment of armed forces) in order to stipulate Japan's right to self-defense and add a third paragraph on its right to collective self-defense. However, he left paragraph 1 (renunciation of war) intact.[40]

Ozawa's Proposal: Neoconservatism

By comparison, Ozawa represents "neoconservatism." Ozawa argues that Japan's defense policy should be based on strengthening the U.S.–Japan Security Treaty in recourse to the right to collective self-defense. He contends that the rights to self-defense, either individual or collective, are natural rights of the nation and therefore no laws can deny such rights. He interprets the spirit of Article 9 to exercise these rights in a restrained manner; Japan should not exercise such rights unless under direct military attack. Ozawa also argues that Japan should become an "ordinary nation" that can assume responsibility as a member of the international community such as participating in UNPKOs. With this premise, Ozawa proposed revisions of Article 9 in September 1999. However, instead of making any change to the article's existing two paragraphs, Ozawa adds a third paragraph to the article: [3] The preceding second paragraph does not prevent Japan from exercising its right to self-defense and from maintaining armed forces to exercise that right. Ozawa also proposed the addition of a new article to follow Article 9 that would articulate Japan's commitment to international peace, including the creation of standing UN forces.[41]

A Comparative Assessment: Yukio vs. Nakasone vs. Ozawa

There was a critical difference between Yukio's original proposal and Nakasone's regarding the right to collective self-defense. However, Yukio's modified proposal of 2000 accepts assertion of the right, though in an extremely limited fashion. Nakasone, too, puts specific restrictions on exercise of collective self-defense. In this sense, there seems to be no substantive difference between the two proposals. In fact, Nakasone praises Yukio for the leap he made from the traditional liberal stance and states that Yukio *is* Ichiro's grandson. Both, he says, are taking Ichiro's position on revising the constitution in order to create Japan's own charter. Nakasone also supports Yukio's idea to shorten the time for debate in the Diet's Constitutional Research Council from five to two years. It is interesting that Nakasone, in the old guard of the conservative LDP, and Yukio, a young leader of the liberal DPJ, have come to hold very similar ideas about the revision of Article 9 (see table 8.3).[42]

A major difference between the two is that Nakasone thinks that paragraph 1 (renunciation of war) can be kept intact so long as paragraph 2 (relinquishment of armed forces) is rewritten while Yukio would rewrite Article 9 altogether. It is astounding that Yukio's proposal is even bolder than that of the pioneer of constitutional revision. In contrast, despite his assertion for Japan's right to collective self-defense, Ozawa retained the original two paragraphs intact. Yukio states that Ozawa's proposal fell into the same sophism as the current interpretation of Article 9 and failed to end the postwar debate on the constitutionality of the SDFs. Instead, Yukio asserted ending the inaccurate interpretation of the article once for all. In summary, Yukio's proposal is the boldest among the three.[43]

New Signs in Favor of Revision

There remains political opposition to constitutional revisions even within the LDP. The party has yet to come up with a consensus on the issue. This is because the party is a large one that encompasses a wide spectrum of ideologies, ranging from such pro-revisionists as Nakasone to such anti-revisionists as former prime minister Miyazawa who considers the current interpretation of Article 9 acceptable. However, there are some new signs in favor of constitutional revisions. The CGP, part of the coalition cabinet, dropped its long-held anti-revision position in November 2000. It might overshadow the reluctance of moderates within the LDP.[44]

As for the DPJ, it still suffers from the leftists' opposition to constitutional revisions. However, the power of the party's left-wing has dwindled. As a result of the June 2000 HR general elections, the percentage of former SDPJ members in the DPJ decreased from 28 to 21 percent. In turn, the number of individuals who do not belong to any intra-party groups (primarily based on their previous party affiliations) has increased from 28 to 45 percent. Further, a number of candidates from the younger generations that are less influenced by the leftist ideology were elected. Those who won HR elections no more than three times constitute as many as 72 percent of the total 127 DPJ delegation in the HR—those who won for the first time constitute 34 percent alone. These dramatic changes to the party's makeup will greatly affect its policy. The party's possible support of revision was given a boost in September 2000 when Secretary General Kan announced that he was ready to support constitutional revision. It was astounding that Kan abandoned his long-held anti-revision stance.[45]

On the Left, both the JCP and the SDPJ still adhere to the constitution. However, they are too weak to protect it, with 20 and 19 seats respectively in the HR. Moreover, the SDPJ acknowledged the SDFs as constitutional in 1994 when its president, Murayama, became prime minister. Then in October 2000, the JCP decided to accept the use of the SDFs only for emergencies. Although the party has yet to accept the SDFs as constitutional, this decision is regarded as a step toward doing so. Now that the leftist parties are accepting the constitutionality of the SDFs, they should have less reason to oppose revision of Article 9 (see table 8.4).[46]

Finally, the public supports constitutional revision. According to an opinion poll conducted by the *Yomiuri Shimbun* in March 2000, as many as 60 percent of respondents supported the idea of constitutional revision (essentially revision of Article 9); a 7 percent increase over the previous year and up from the 50 percent or so that had held true in *Yomiuri* polls since 1993. Major reasons for supporting the revision included "to enable Japan to actively participate in UNPKOs" and "the political interpretation and practice of Article 9 caused ambiguity and confusion." Only 27 percent of the respondents were opposed to

Table 8.4 Political parties' positions on Article 9

House of Representatives (HR) as of June 26, 2000

A constitutional revision requires **320 votes** (two-thirds) out of total 480 at the HR.

LDP*	233	Conservative	Pro-revision
CP*	7	Conservative	Pro-revision
LP	22	Conservative	Pro-revision
CGP*	31	Centrist	Dropped anti-revision position in 11/00
DPJ	127	Liberal	Split between pro-revision and anti-revision
SDPJ	19	Left	Anti-revision
JCP	20	Left	Anti-revision
Others	21		

House of Councilors (HC) as of June 26, 2000

A constitutional revision requires **168 votes** (two-thirds) out of total 252 at the HC.

LDP*	106
CP*	6
LP	5
CGP*	23
DPJ	55
SDPJ	12
JCP	23
Others	22

* These three parties form a coalition cabinet.

Source: "*Kokkai no shin-seiryoku*" (New balance of power at the Diet), *Yomiuri Shimbun*, June 26, 2000.

revision, down 4 percent from the previous year. In addition, 72.5 percent thought that a new revised constitution should clearly stipulate Japan's right to self-defense, while only 17.6 percent were opposed. The polls also showed that the younger generations were more supportive of revision than the older generations.[47]

Yukio's position as a liberal leader means his proposal lacks the negative baggage that many see as being associated with such proposals from conservative leaders. It appears that with the proposal having come from such an individual, the general public has finally overcome its blind belief in the constitution and pacifism. That a young liberal leader broke a half century–old taboo and made a bolder proposal for revision of Article 9 than the most outspoken conservative leaders has been a development of great significance. Yukio's proposal rekindled enthusiasm for revision among conservative leaders, such as Nakasone. Yukio challenged this formidable political legacy. It shows his earnest effort to reinvent the DPJ as a realistic and responsible party.[48]

In summary, a liberal leader's proposal for revision of Article 9 seems to suggest that the article has outlived its original rationale—to demilitarize and contain Japan. Japan stands at a critical turning point in its constitutional history. It remains to be seen whether the leftist members of the DPJ will change their long-held position on Article 9, as Yukio and Kan did. As Kunio argued, constitutional revision is the litmus test for the DPJ.

An Assessment of Yukio's Political Leadership

Yukio's Idealism and Fraternalism

In assessing Yukio's political leadership so far, one of the most distinctive features of Yukio is his idealism. Yukio belongs to the baby-boom generation that grew up in the liberal political culture of postwar Japan. Yukio was also nurtured in the ivory towers of academia. More important, the philosophical foundation for Yukio's idealism is rooted in the legacy of liberalism of the Hatoyama family. Kazuo dedicated himself to the creation of a liberal and democratic civil society during the Meiji era. Ichiro succeeded to Kazuo's mission, fought militarism, and was stigmatized as a "liberalist." Yukio founded the DPJ, after Ichiro's Japan Democratic Party, with idealistic slogans such as "fraternity" and "citizen leadership." Yukio tried to revive Ichiro's fraternalism in earnest. Since Kunio had already succeeded their father and become president of the Fraternity Youth League in 1994, Yukio became its permanent advisor. The league's three principles are "mutual respect, mutual understanding, and mutual help." Its logo is "Y & I," standing for You and I, a pun on *yuai* (fraternity). As Coudenhove conceptualized, the group believes that fraternity is the mediator of equality and freedom: the former balances the latter two, which tend to go to extremes and can conflict with each other.[49]

Yukio also joined the Moral Rearmament (MRA), a world peace organization, in which Ichiro was involved (but not Iichiro and Kunio). Fujita Yukihisa, an executive board member of the MRA's Japanese branch, contacted Yukio in October 1995 when he read a newspaper article reporting that Yukio was promoting liberalism by reviving Ichiro's idealism. Yukio responded positively. The Hatoyama family's Fraternity Youth League had lost its edge with time and Yukio wanted to learn from the MRA. Yukio and Fujita became close friends and Fujita joined the DPJ at its inception. Yukio attended an MRA international symposium in Switzerland in August 1996 and gave a speech in English. Yukio acknowledged MRA's contribution to world peace and pledged that he would revive the Hatoyama family's ties with the organization. Noting that Japanese children hardly learn an accurate history of Japan's acts of aggression during World War II, Yukio stated that the Japanese should sincerely apologize for its past acts of aggression to Asian people and work out a true reconciliation with them. It was Yukio's debut in international politics.[50]

Yukio tried to infuse the core values of democracy—egalitarianism, liberalism, and fraternity—into society. While he was originally an LDP member, he soon joined the "Study Group on Utopian Politics" within the party, left the party, and founded the NPS and the DPJ. Yukio in June 1996 called for a "revolution for fraternity" in a magazine article. Yukio wrote that politicians had lost their self-respect: instead of winning elections for the sake of policies, they use policies for the sake of winning elections. They become Diet members for the sake of becoming ministers, not for the sake of legislating national policies. As a result, the LDP's hierarchy has become more rigid than that of the bureaucracy. Now, politicians must restore their own self-respect. They should give up their Diet seats if they cannot legislate better national policies. Only a political party made up of those who have such a resolve can change Japan. Yukio wrote, "politics is love and love is based on self-respect . . . This is what I call 'revolution for fraternity.' "[51]

In the article, Yukio first identifies fraternity with liberalism. Yukio argues that a liberal society should be based on independent individuals with the spirit of fraternity. He also argues that a true democracy should be based on a horizontal network of independent individuals, rather than on a hierarchical organization, as in the existing parties. Yukio then identifies liberalism as coexistence. He calls for coexistence with nature, coexistence with foreigners (such as by giving suffrage to resident aliens), and coexistence between the North and the South in the world. These ideas constitute the essence of Yukio's revolution for fraternity. Yukio's vision of civil society presumes highly educated mature citizens, and it is questionable whether the Japanese citizens have reached that level.[52]

Yukio: A New Breed of Politician

Political analysts have mixed views of Yukio's political leadership. Former *Jiji Tsushin* reporter Igarashi Fumihiko thinks that Yukio is an ideal person to lead the nation. One of the unique aspects of Yukio's political leadership is that he is not driven by a desire for power. Igarashi writes that Yukio has no personal interest in power and that he is free of the so-called minister syndrome (a preoccupation with becoming state ministers) that most politicians have. Yukio turned down a chance to become the NPS president, although he practically owned the party (he contributed half of the expenses for forming the party). Even when Takemura later offered his presidency to Yukio in January 1996, he declined. Igarashi also notes that Yukio did not create the DPJ for the sake of power. Although everybody expected Yukio to become president, Yukio simply said that Kan should be president. In contrast, Igarashi argues, Kan had a strong desire for power. Kan was reluctant to leave the welfare minister's post (of the first Hashimoto coalition cabinet) when Yukio asked him to join the DPJ. Kan did not resign the ministerial post even after he had finally left the NPS (that was part of the Hashimoto cabinet) and joined the DPJ. In turn, neither Prime Minister Hashimoto nor the LDP leadership asked Kan to resign the post when he moved to the DPJ. Igarashi states that this episode shows not only Kan's greed but also the "indulgent relationship" that has long existed between the LDP and opposition parties.[53]

The way Yukio responded to the result of the 1996 HR elections also shows his indifference to power. Yukio was not as disappointed as other party officials with the fact that the DPJ had managed to increase its delegation in the HR only by 6 seats to 52. Although the party failed to "blow a whirlwind" through politics as it had hoped, Yukio appeared to be content with the result, stating that the result was fairly good for a new party less than a month old and that the party had managed to blow a breeze. Igarashi argues that Yukio is a completely new type of politician who cannot be measured by the traditional gauges of politicians. Igarashi also states that Yukio represents the younger generation that grew up in postwar Japan. This generation grew up without having the hang-ups of the older generations, which had gone through World War II. This generation does not have the same racial biases and is thus willing to help people in the world. Yukio has all these positive aspects of the postwar generation.[54]

Itagaki Eiken writes that Yukio possesses the qualifications of a powerful leader: ambition, commitment, leadership attributes, and a political sense. Although he was a latecomer to politics, Yukio grew rapidly since he was elected for the first time in 1986. Yukio generally takes after Iichiro's quiet and reserved nature; however, unlike his self-effacing father, Yukio can speak about his ideals eloquently. Kobayashi also notes that Yukio did not stand out at the LDP but he grew rapidly when he became the NPS secretary general and learned to express himself clearly. However, Kobayashi points out that Yukio's words sounded utopian and even alien to those who were accustomed to the machiavellian world of politics. Yukio induced an outburst of laughter among the press corps when he announced that the DPJ would be based on the spirit of fraternity, love, and trust. Former prime minister Nakasone commented that "politics is not as sweet as fraternity, which is like soft ice cream that will melt under the sun." Yukio's other conservative opponents criticized him as having "only ideals but no policy." Despite the derision and criticism, Yukio was unabashedly serious about his beliefs and countered that "one cannot be a politician without ideals."[55]

Yukio's language was too abstract and logic-ridden for the general public to understand. Yukio argued that politicians should engage in more logical discussions, proposed to apply science and the laws of logic to politics, and even coined a word; "to science (used as a verb) politics." Kobayashi notes that Yukio's bold statements and behavior were beyond the conventional measure for politicians. Yukio even appeared not to be hurt by criticisms. Consequently, he is called "*shin kankaku* (new sense) type" and is referred to as an E.T. (Extraterrestrial) or a spaceman. In response to the comment that Yukio should transform himself from an E.T. to an earthly person in order to become a stronger political leader, Yukio countered that politicians should have global and space-wide vision for the future. Kobayashi adds that in order to realize one's ideals and vision, a politician should deal with the ugly machiavellian schemes of his political enemies. However, like his grandfather, Yukio is not good at it. Ichiro was always straightforward and was not good at scheming; however, he had competent confidantes, such as Miki and Kono, who acted as his *kuroko* (behind-the-scenes players). In contrast, Yukio does not surround himself with confidantes. Kobayashi states that it is Yukio's drawback.[56]

According to Ito Hirotoshi, Yukio is able to speak of high ideals without impunity because of his family's legacy of idealism and liberalism. Yukio can afford to be honest and clean (morally and financially) because of his wealth. As in the case of his father, it is difficult to appease Yukio because he is neither hungry for money nor for power. Yukio can afford to adhere to principles because he has nothing to fear or lose. He has the luxury of being true to himself because he is the Hatoyama scion.[57]

Honesty, Modesty, and Openness

Challenging the LDP's practice of secret deal-making, Yukio proclaimed honesty as his political motto. Yukio ranked first as "the most desirable prime minister in the twenty-first century" in January 1996 in a survey conducted among political journalists by a major monthly magazine

Bungei Shunju. Those who chose Yukio evaluated him as "clean and honest," "sincere," and "has strong ideals and will not trade them." Yukio has often told the press that "I would like to be honest" and "I would like to be natural." Honesty, gentleness, and openness are the traits that run in the Hatoyama family. While they are positive attributes for a person, they are not necessarily assets for a politician. Kazuo was a man of integrity, detested political manipulation, and did not exploit the opportunities presented before him. Ichiro was open to the extent that he had the reputation of not being able to keep a secret. As for Iichiro, his honesty was startling when he expressed his dislike of politics during his first campaign. Yukio seems to have inherited all these attributes of his forebears in a distilled form. Yukio often uses humble expressions such as "Let me do this" or "I would be obliged if you would let me do this." Ito notes that after the mass media was disillusioned with the DPJ, they even criticized Yukio's humble way of talking (that they used to like) as a sign of his weak leadership.[58]

Another aspect of Yukio's weak leadership might be his indecisiveness. Yukio showed indecisiveness on a couple of occasions. As seen above, Yukio was swayed by Kan regarding the choice between "wholesome opposition" and "constructive opposition" at the DPJ's inception. Yukio also abandoned his personal stance for the sake of party solidarity and voted for the special measures law concerning land use in Okinawa. Yukio was against the legislation of the national flag and anthem but ended up voting in favor. In all, instead of consolidating the two opposing forces within the DPJ, Yukio was swayed by both. While the absence of desire for money and power has enabled Yukio to be a clean politician, the lack of decisiveness has made him a rather weak leader.

Overall, Yukio seems to lack charisma. Just like his father, Yukio appears not to have the aura of a leader with forceful vitality and persuasiveness. By comparison, being more aggressive, Kan and Kunio seem to have more charismatic qualities. Coupled with his gentle and quiet nature, Yukio's honesty and humility have not made him a strong leader. Ito argues that the Hatoyama tradition is that of "pedestal riders," and this family legacy made Yukio one as well. Yet, Yukio could not fulfill the expectations the general public held for the dynasty's heir. Former prime minister Nakasone also noted that Yukio's caliber as a political leader was smaller than his grandfather. Ito argues that Yukio's popularity was essentially created by the mass media out of their expectations. His honesty and sincerity appealed to the political journalists who were accustomed to dishonest and arrogant politicians. However, the mass media were disappointed with Yukio's naïveté, displayed during the process of the party creation, and mercilessly devoured Yukio before the party's maiden HR elections.[59]

Yukio's Descent in Power

Yukio failed to exploit the great opportunities presented to him. First, due to Kan's entry into the DPJ, Yukio missed the opportunity to become the first sole president. Ironically, it was Yukio who had insisted on the participation of Kan in the party. Ito states that Yukio's misfortune was that the legitimate pedestal rider (Yukio) failed to make Kan a pedestal carrier. Opinion polls indicate Kan's popularity over Yukio. According to a *Yomiuri* poll concerning "who is the most desirable as prime minister" in September 1996, Kan came second as the most desirable prime minister (13.7 percent), after the incumbent Prime Minister Hashimoto (29.1 percent). Their standings were reversed with 18.3 percent for Kan and 10.1 percent for Hashimoto in May 1997. In January 1999, Kan had still maintained the first standing with 17.0 percent. He was followed by Ozawa and Kajiyama Seiroku (tied at 8.0 percent), Doi Takako (7.1 percent), Koizumi Junichiro (7.0 percent), incumbent Prime Minister Obuchi (6.6 percent), Kato Koichi (4.0 percent), and Tanaka Makiko (2.8 percent). Yukio ranked ninth, with 1.5 percent, barely making the top ten list.[60]

Yukio lost his copresidency to Kan at the party's first anniversary. The party's expansion further demoted Yukio to the number three post of deputy secretary general, whereas Kan kept the presidency. Yukio's decrease in power is attributable to his modesty and naïveté, whereas Kan's increase in power owes much to his pragmatism and shrewd political skills. Yet, Yukio did not bear a grudge and supported Kan's presidency wholeheartedly. For Yukio, the position itself was not important. Like Kazuo, Yukio was not the type of person who sought power for the sake of power. Like Iichiro, Yukio was nonchalant about the position. Only after party members had grown tired of Kan, did they return to its original founder and elect Yukio president at the party's third anniversary.

Neoliberalism

Realizing some of his weaknesses, Yukio reinvented himself by fusing Ichiro's postwar conservatism with his own generation's liberalism. A fusion of conservatism with liberalism, hence "neoliberalism." Yukio even called his new political philosophy *hoshu honryu* (mainstream conservative). It appears incomprehensible for a liberal party's leader to describe his creed as such; however, it represents his genuine effort to make liberalism viable. It is possible to detect Yukio's neoliberalism as early as 1995 when the Diet hotly debated the so-called non-war reso-lution (pledging no war) at the fiftieth anniversary of the end of World War II. Those on the Left insisted on the use of the term "non-war" in the resolution, whereas conservatives opposed it because this phrase would deny the SDFs. To the astonishment of the attendants, Yukio expressed his opposition to the use of the term at a meeting organized by a pro-JSP labor union. One of the JSP members commented that Yukio might be a new type of a politician who would express his views without hesitation.[61]

Yukio's proposal for constitutional revisions is a prime example of his neoliberalism. Yukio contends that his neoliberalism is based on *jishushugi* (self-reliance) and aims to reduce Japan's dependence on U.S. protection. However, he does not seem to have a concrete idea of how to realize such self-reliant defense policy, and merely reiterates the abstract DPJ platforms of establishing regional stability in East Asia. Yukio's stance for self-reliance sounds fine in words; however, it seems naïve to advocate such policy without having clear policy alternatives. This might be a limitation of his neoliberalism. From a larger perspective, Ichiro's grandson revived his political agenda five decades later, and the agenda completed its full circle. It took a half century for the public to break the constitutional taboo and catch up with Ichiro. Yukio's proposal for revision of Article 9 should not be misconstrued as a move toward Japan's remilitarization. On the contrary, by acknowledging the SDFs as legitimate armed forces, Yukio tried to end the fallacy in the present interpretation of Article 9 and preempt unrestrained use of the SDFs overseas through a disingenuous interpretation of the article. Even so, Yukio's leftist colleagues in the DPJ criticized his proposal as a dangerous move.[62]

The Political Environment

Yukio is confronted with serious constraints to making the DPJ an alternative party to the LDP. The intrinsic divisiveness of the DPJ presents a formidable obstacle. Former JSP members, such as Yokomichi, are basically incompatible with Yukio. In hindsight, as Kunio argued, had Yukio been able to muster forces of neoliberals, excluding socialists, the DPJ would have been more successful, or at least more consistent. In this regard, Kobayashi criticizes the socialists, who had been members of the moribund SDPJ and the NSP, for join-ing the DPJ. Kobayashi states that they decided to join the DPJ even before Yukio announced the party's basic ideals and platforms. They did not care what the party would stand for. They decided to join the DPJ only to survive in the Diet. Kobayashi argues that they abandoned their ideals and principles and acted as if there were *nobushi* (samurai without masters) who worked for any lord insofar as he provided them with lodging and food. Consequently, Kobayashi writes, the DPJ ended up becoming an political asylum for these desperate Diet members who had lost hopes of remaining in their previous fold.[63]

Insofar as the DPJ harbored former JSP members, it remained a "perpetual opposition," as in the case of the JSP. The DPJ was doomed from the outset. Paradoxically, the Hatoyama brothers themselves epitomized the contradictory party structure, with Yukio coming from the NPS, and Kunio from the NFP. Yukio himself stated in March 1996 that the litmus test for the success of the new party was whether he and Kunio could agree on policy platforms. In this sense, the party had failed.[64]

In a larger context, the sense of apathy that prevailed among the electorate, who were disillusioned with politics and did not feel like supporting any party, also posed a serious impediment for any new party to emerge as a second pole to challenge the LDP. Japanese politics is in a state of great uncertainty, in which no party holds a majority in both the HR and the HC. While it is a great opportunity for ambitious politicians to rise to the occasion and bring changes sought by the electorate, the depth of uncertainty seems insurmountable for Yukio or any other politician. Since the 1993 political reformation, the Hosokawa and Hata coalition cabinets failed to bring the changes they had promised, and no other anti-LDP politicians have as yet risen to the occasion. As for the LDP's latest prime minister, Koizumi, he has so far failed to carry out the reforms he had promised.

In summary, despite the lack of some leadership attributes on his part and the structural obstacles, both at the level of national politics and of the DPJ, Yukio was very fortunate overall. Yukio was given a district in Hokkaido, due to the family connections, and began a fortuitous political career ("golden parachute"). Yukio was assisted by the family's fame and fortune and created his own political party, which became the second largest party. Although Yukio inherited a rather apolitical personality from his father, he successfully transformed himself from a scholar to a political leader within a decade. It is due to his good fortune of being in an opportune political environment, in addition to his greater ambition and commitment to changing Japan. Had the LDP's monopoly of power continued, where seniority (number of terms in the

HR) determines positions in the party and cabinet, Yukio would not have surpassed Kunio, who has ten year's seniority in the LDP, and become a party president. Ito writes that Yukio had the good fortune to be a politician when the electorate wanted a new breed of political leader—a clean, fresh thoroughbred with the tradition of idealism and liberalism. Yukio satisfied the electorate's expectations because they believed that the Hatoyama family members were legitimate and proper. Yukio was chosen as a pedestal rider because of the family legacy.[65]

The Interactions Between Personal Attributes and the Environment

Yukio's case demonstrates that personal attributes and the political environment interact closely in exercising political leadership. His attributes, characterized by abstract idealism and political naïveté, combined with the fundamental structural problems of the DPJ, have prevented Yukio from making the DPJ an alternative party to the LDP. Although Yukio tried to overcome his weaknesses by reinventing himself as a neoliberal, he seems not to be completely at ease with being a politician. The comparison of Yukio with Kunio seems to suggest the importance of personal attributes over the political environment in determining political leadership. Yukio and Kunio are only one year and seven months apart in age and grew up in an almost identical environment. Nevertheless, they pursued different careers and subscribed to different ideologies. Even after they created the DPJ together, they continued to disagree and fell apart. The comparison of Yukio with Kan also indicates the importance of personal attributes over the political environment. The two politicians were in exactly the same situation and environment and had the same opportunities at the inception of the DPJ. Yet, Kan exercised stronger leadership in the DPJ than Yukio. This owes to the differences in their personal attributes and leadership skills. While Yukio might have a great concern for public good and long-term vision, he does not have the skills to be a shrewd politician.

In conclusion, the structural constraints—both of politics in general and within the DPJ in particular—present a formidable obstacle to Yukio's leadership; just as important is Yukio's lack of leadership skills. Yukio was reelected to the DPJ presidency in September 2000, and again in September 2002 after a runoff election against Kan. After the presidential election in 2002, however, criticisms of Yukio's leadership surged. First, his rivals alleged that it was favoritism on the part of Yukio to give the secretary general position (the number two position) to senior conservative member Nakano Kansei, who had dropped his candidacy for the presidential position at the last minute in favor of Yukio. They demanded resignations of Yukio and Nakano. Then, they held Yukio responsible for the losses in the supplementary elections for the Diet (both HR and HC) in October 2002. Out of seven seats contested, the DPJ won only in Yamagata District 4 where a vacancy was created due to the resignation of the LDP leader Kato Koichi. Yukio, out of desperation, contemplated forming a new party, along with the Liberal Party and the SDPJ, in the midst of a rumor of the dissolution of the HR and the resultant HR elections possibly in spring 2003. He did so without first building a consensus on the idea among party members. Anti-Yukio members seized the opportunity and forced Yukio to resign in December 2002. A new presidential election was held that month, between Kan and the party's deputy secretary general, Okada Katsuya. Kan won the election to serve the party presidency for a third term. In the aftermath of Yukio's resignation, several party members left the party and some formed a new party along with the Conservative Party; however Yukio had stayed in the party. It remains to be seen whether Yukio can rise to future occasions and emerge as a stronger opposition leader to challenge the LDP.[66]

CHAPTER 9
CONCLUSION

In the genealogy of the Hatoyama Dynasty, Kazuo, the first generation, passed down two distinct career attributes to the family: that of a politician and that of a scholar. Kazuo was a prominent academic, educator, lawyer, and politician. Kazuo's graduation from Yale Law School at the top of his class in 1880 suffices to illustrate his exceptional academic excellence and diligence. The closest American counterpart of Kazuo in terms of academic origin, integrity, and liberalism would be Woodrow Wilson. Kazuo's two career attributes were split between his two sons. Ichiro inherited Kazuo's political attributes whereas Hideo inherited Kazuo's scholarly attributes. Following his parents' expectations, Ichiro pursued a political career and achieved political power. In contrast, Hideo became a law professor. Only later in his life did Hideo become a HR member.

Iichiro, the third generation, did not inherit Ichiro's political attributes. Iichiro was not a politician by nature and became a bureaucrat. Nevertheless, Iichiro vindicated the family's reputation by reaching the pinnacle of the bureaucratic pyramid and, after retirement, becoming a HC member and foreign minister. In turn, Yukio, the elder brother of the fourth generation, was a scholar by nature but changed his career to a politician. In contrast, Kunio, the younger brother, takes after Ichiro and has pursued a political career from his youth. The fourth generation brothers make a good parallel to the first generation brothers: politician Ichiro and scholar Hideo.

In summary, Ichiro (second generation) and Kunio (fourth generation) predominantly displayed Kazuo's political attributes, whereas Hideo (second generation) and Yukio (fourth generation) displayed Kazuo's scholarly traits. Thus, the family has maintained two career tracks: that of an education dynasty and that of a political dynasty.

The Hatoyama Dynasty's Leadership Attributes

Among many political leadership attributes, its idealism and liberalism distinguish the Hatoyama political dynasty from others. Such fundamental values were passed down from Kazuo, to Ichiro, to Yukio (and to Kunio to a lesser extent). Throughout the generations, the dynasty's politicians have aspired to establish a democratic civil society in Japan. Yukio's DPJ is an embodiment of their ideals. Rebelliousness, another political legacy of the Hatoyama family, is the other side of the idealist coin. Kazuo challenged the *hambatsu* oligarchy during the Meiji period. Ichiro rebelled against the military regime during the prewar and wartime periods. In the postwar period, Ichiro defied the U.S. government and restored diplomatic relations with the Soviet Union. In turn, Iichiro demonstrated his rebelliousness by becoming a bureaucrat. Both Yukio and Kunio challenged the LDP and created the DPJ.[1]

In addition, such traits as gentleness, honesty, modesty, and naïveté are distinctive attributes that run in the Hatoyama family. Kazuo had all of these attributes. Ichiro inherited most of these traits from Kazuo. Specifically, Ichiro was too candid to be a shrewd politician. In turn, Iichiro's excessive modesty did not lend itself to being a political leader. These qualities were then passed down to Yukio and were distilled in him. By contrast, Kunio is more aggressive and tougher than Yukio; however, he moved too frequently and fell into a bind. In all, Ito Hirotoshi states that nurtured in the well-tended greenhouse of fame and wealth, the Hatoyama politicians have fostered idealistic views of the world, lacking the toughness of the "weed." Good or bad, these qualities are the legacy of the Hatoyama dynasty.[2]

In an overall assessment of the Hatoyama Dynasty's political leadership, Kazuo established the Hatoyama political dynasty, whereas Ichiro was both a beneficiary of, and a contributor to, the family's political legacy. By contrast, the third and the fourth generations were mainly beneficiaries. Iichiro became foreign minister easily in spite of being a latecomer to politics. Kunio became education minister at a very young age. Yukio became copresident of the DPJ, with only a ten-year tenure at the HR. The clan's political prosperity was heightened by, and culminated in, Ichiro. After that peak, it declined with Iichiro. The family's political legacy then revived with Kunio and recovered with Yukio's ascendance to the DPJ's presidency. However, with Yukio's weak leadership in the DPJ and Kunio's dishonorable return to the LDP, the dynasty's luster appears to have dimmed with the fourth generation.

The Role of the Hatoyama Women

The role of the Hatoyama clan's women in advancing their husbands' political careers and their son's educations in preparation for their political careers should not be ignored. Haruko started this tradition through her extraordinary determination to make her sons political leaders. Kaoru and Yasuko observed Haruko's tenets and provided the best education for their sons and geared them toward politics. Their dedication played a key role in retaining the political lineage in the family. Moreover, Haruko and Kaoru were pioneering educators of Japanese women in their own right. In this privileged environment, the Hatoyama boys excelled academically and all six—up to the fourth generation—went to Tokyo University. That was the norm for the Hatoyama men. The Hatoyama women provided their sons with a protected environment and reared somewhat naïve elite boys.[3]

The Fallen Political Parties

Japanese politics is in a state of great uncertainty. It has been stalemated since the 1993 political reformation failed. In a 1996 article, Kobayashi Kichiya finds fault with most political parties. The LDP is corrupted and unprincipled to the extent that it formed a coalition cabinet with its archenemy, the SDPJ. Ozawa's NFP has finished its *raison d'être* of making the LDP an opposition party (in 1993) and therefore should dissolve. The DPJ is immature in every respect, its platforms are unclear, and it has failed to attract electorates from the outset. In turn, the SDPJ is moribund. The SDPJ was co-opted by the LDP for the sake of power and has abandoned its original principles of socialism. Kobayashi likens the party to a wrecked ship and says that many crew members moved from this sinking ship to *Minshuto-maru* (the DPJ ship). Even its vice captain, Secretary General Sato Kanju, abandoned the old ship and moved to the new ship. Kobayashi writes that the SDPJ's days are numbered. Kobayashi argues that political reforms should begin with reform of the politician's consciousness, not of the election system. Yukio issued the same caveat in 1996.[4]

Itagaki Eiken writes of the DPJ that the party's formation was a historic moment in Japanese politics. It was 51 years after Ichiro created the Japan Liberal Party; 42 years since the formation of the Japan Democratic Party; and 41 years since the conservative merger. The birth of the DPJ signified the revival of the Hatoyama political legacy. The DPJ has grown from the original 46 HR members (September 1996), to 92 members as a result of the expansion (April 1998), and to

126 members, after the June 2000 HR general elections. However, the DPJ has yet to fulfill its ultimate mandate. As of July 2001, after the HC general elections, the LDP had 238 seats (49.6 percent) and the DPJ had 126 seats (26.3 percent) in the HR (480 seats), while the LDP had 111 seats (44.9 percent) and the DPJ had 59 seats (23.9 percent) in the HC (247 seats). The DPJ has remained a little larger than half of the LDP in the Diet. If Yukio has half the caliber of Ichiro, the DPJ has half the caliber of the LDP. Yet, as Kunio argued, it might the peak of the DPJ.[5]

In summary, most political parties have abandoned their principles. This includes the Buddhism-based Clean Government Party that formed a coalition with the LDP in 1999. The only party that has adhered to its original ideals is the JCP. It is therefore not surprising that the electorate has little support for any party. The opinion polls show that the *museito* ("no political party") is still the most popular sentiment of the electorate. According to the *Asahi Shimbun*'s poll in October 2001, while the popularity of the Koizumi cabinet remained high at 71 percent (1 percent decrease from the previous month), the support rate for the LDP remained much lower at 39 percent (2 percent decrease). In comparison, only 6 percent of the respondents said that they supported the DPJ (2 percent decrease), whereas 44 percent answered that they did not support any party (3 percent increase).[6]

The support rates for the cabinet and political parties have substantially deteriorated since then. According to a poll by the *Jiji Tsushinsha* (a large news service agency) in June 2002, the support rate for the Koizumi cabinet decreased to 34 percent (3.6 percent decrease from the previous month), whereas the nonsupport rate increased to 45.2 percent (2.4 percent increase). The support rates for political parties were as follows: the LDP for 20.6 percent (0.1 percent decrease); the DPJ for 4.5 percent (1.6 percent decrease); the Clean Government Party for 3.2 percent (0.8 percent decrease); the JCP for 2.9 percent (0.5 percent increase); the SDPJ for 2 percent (0.4 percent increase); the Liberal Party for 1.1 percent (0.4 percent decrease); and the Conservative Party for 0.1 percent (the same). In contrast, 63 percent answered that they did not support any party (1.1 percent increase). This result is alarming.[7]

The Hereditary Diet Members

The problem with "inbreeding" might partly account for the deadlock in politics. Currently, as many as 29 percent of HR members inherited their seats from their fathers or grandfathers. Nowhere is the dominance of hereditary Diet members more evident than in the LDP. The

Koizumi cabinet is the epitome of political inbreeding. Prime Minister Koizumi is a third generation HR member. His grandfather Koizumi Matajiro was minister of the postal and telecommunication service of the Hamaguchi cabinet in 1929. He was the first minister from the commoner class and was referred to as a "tattoo minister" (his family's job was that of steeple jack, which was traditionally associated with mafia-type organizations). Prime Minister Koizumi's father Junya, Matajiro's son-in-law, was director general of the Defense Agency in the third Ikeda cabinet and in the first Sato cabinet. In turn, Fukuda Yasuo, the Koizumi cabinet's chief cabinet secretary, is former prime minister Fukuda Takeo's son, while Abe Shinzo, its deputy chief cabinet secretary, is a son of former foreign minister Abe Shintaro, and a grandson of former prime minister Kishi Nobusuke. Tanaka Makiko, the Koizumi cabinet's first foreign minister, is former prime minister Tanaka Kakuei's daughter. Ishihara Nobuteru, the cabinet's minister of administrative and regulatory reforms, is Tokyo Governor Ishihara Shintaro's son. In addition, LDP's Policy Affairs Research Council (PARC) President Aso Taro is former prime minister Yoshida Shigeru's grandson. Nakasone Hirofumi, a HC member, is former prime minister Nakasone Yasuhiro's son, and is expected to switch to the HR to succeed his father. The list goes on. Among this long list of hereditary Diet members, the Hatoyama family stands out, in that no other Japanese family has produced Diet members in its direct lineage in four successive generations. In this sense, the Hatoyama family is the pioneer in hereditary Diet members.[8]

While the phenomenon of political dynasties has appeared in American government, from the Adams, the Roosevelt, the Kennedy, to the Bush families, it is more extreme in Japan. Their instant name recognition and automatic transfer of election districts from their forebears give hereditary candidates for the Diet an enormous advantage over nonhereditary candidates. Former prime minister Obuchi's daughter Yuko's run and easy victory in the 2000 HR elections is a prime example. The increasing number of hereditary Diet members is alarming, causing grave side-effects for Japan's representative democracy, making the system elitist, unresponsive, and ultimately incompetent. Their prevalence ossifies the political system and accelerates political decay.

Japanese Political Leaders

Japan needs a strong political leader. Kobayashi argues that "coordinator-leaders" or "accommodator-leaders" can no longer guide Japan during political turmoil. Japan needs a leader who has original ideas and the ability to translate these ideas into actual policies and implement them. Ozawa, currently Liberal Party president, argues that Japan needs a leader who has a will to power; one who can establish and use his own power base in order to exercise strong leadership. Ozawa argues that after the "1955 system" was established, strong leadership was not even sought and the prime minister's power was restrained. In fear of the concentration of power, the LDP avoided singular leadership and made decisions by consensus. As a result, nobody took responsibility for policy-making. Ozawa contends that it is time to break this deadlock and establish stronger leadership in the post of prime minister.[9]

Polls on Japanese Leaders in the Twenty-First Century

Opinion polls have indicated that the general public desire a strong leader. According to opinion polls taken by the *Chunichi Shimbun* in August and November 2000, Ishihara Shintaro and Tanaka Makiko shared the top rank, whereas incumbent Prime Minister Mori Yoshiro obtained a low support rate. As for the DPJ leaders, Kan still had a higher support rate than Yukio (see table 9.1). Those politicians who gained high support rates are known to be assertive and have strong personalities. Ishihara became governor of Tokyo where he can exercise strong leadership. Tanaka has broken away from the mainstream LDP factional politics and became an independent despite the huge

Table 9.1 Polls on Japanese leaders in the twenty-first century

	August 2000 (%)	*November 2000 (%)*	
1 Ishihara Shintaro	25.6	12.6	(2)
2 Tanaka Makiko	25.3	26.7	(1)
3 Kan Naoto	5.3	8.5	(3)
4 Hashimoto Ryutaro	4.7	3.6	(8)
5 Doi Takako	4.5	4.9	(7)
6 Ozawa Ichiro	3.5	6.3	(4)
7 Koizumi Junichiro	3.0	5.1	(6)
8 Mori Yoshiro	2.5	0.7	(11)
9 Kato Koichi	2.4	5.7	(5)
10 Hatoyama Yukio	2.2	1.3	(10)
		Fuwa Testuzo 1.5	(9)

Sources: "*Nijuisseiki Nihon no rida?*" (Who should be the Japanese leader in the twenty-first century?), *Chunichi Shimbun*, August 6, 2000 and "*Mori naikaku shijiritsu seron chosa kekka*" (Results of the poll on Mori cabinet support rates), *Chunichi Shimbun*, November 2, 2000.

disadvantages. She was instrumental in forming the Koizumi cabinet and became the first female foreign minister in April 2001, only to be dismissed in January 2002. Prime Minister Koizumi was also a maverick, leaving the Mori faction and forming the cabinet that included an unprecedented five female cabinet members; however, failing in his promised reforms.[10]

Conclusions

In conclusion, the Hatoyama Dynasty has been the "exemplar" of modern Japanese politics for 150 years. This book is the outcome of this author's efforts to understand the Hatoyama Dynasty's political legacy, in search for a new light in Japanese politics. Kazuo's diligence, integrity, and dedication to establishing a civil society in the Meiji era are remarkable. Ichiro's courage to defy the military and tenacity to adhere to his beliefs are impressive. Haruko's determination to make their sons political leaders and Kaoru's devotion to her husband and son are exceptional. The first two generations maximized their potential. By comparison, the grand scale of the first two generations is lost in the current generation and its contemporaries. It remains to be seen whether Yukio can turn the DPJ into a more credible opposition party; and whether Kunio can prove himself as a leader in the LDP, or start his own party. It also remains to be seen whether the fifth generation will carry the torch. The fifth generation of the Hatoyama Dynasty are all in their twenties and it is premature to predict whether there will be a fifth generation of the Hatoyama political dynasty. With a deep sense of political apathy prevailing among the younger generations, young scions of the Hatoyama Dynasty might be indifferent to their political legacy. Yukio himself stated that it was his mission to change the status quo, in which fourth-generation politicians like him, let alone the second-generation politicians, are engaged in politics. Then, as Eto predicted, the dynasty's fourth generation might signal its demise.[11]

APPENDIX

SCAPIN 919, "Removal and Exclusion of Diet Member"

May 3, 1946

a. As Chief Secretary of the Tanaka Cabinet from 1927 to 1929, he necessarily shares responsibility for the formulation and promulgation without Diet approval of amendments to the so-called Peace Preservation Law which made that law the government's chief legal instrument for the suppression of freedom of speech and freedom of assembly, and made possible the denunciation, terrorization, seizure, and imprisonment of tens of thousands of adherents to minority doctrines advocating political, economic, and social reform, thereby preventing the development of effective opposition to the Japanese militaristic regime.

b. As Minister of Education from December 1931 to March 1934, he was responsible for stifling freedom of speech in the schools by means of mass dismissals and arrests of teachers suspected of "leftist" leanings or "dangerous thoughts." The dismissal in May 1933 of Professor Takigawa from the faculty of Kyoto University on Hatoyama's personal order is a flagrant illustration of his contempt for the liberal tradition of academic freedom and gave momentum to the spiritual mobilization of Japan, which under the aegis of the military and economic cliques, led the nation eventually into war.

c. Not only did Hatoyama participate in thus weaving the pattern of ruthless suppression of freedom of speech, freedom of assembly, and freedom of thought, hut he also participated in the forced dissolution of farmer-labor bodies. In addition, his indorsement of totalitarianism, specifically in its application to the regimentation and control of labor, is a matter of record. His recommendation that "it would be well" to transplant Hitlerite anti-labor devices to Japan reveals his innate antipathy to the democratic principle of the right of labor freely to organize and to bargain collectively through representatives of its own choice. It is a familiar technique of the totalitarian dictatorship, wherever situated, whatever be its formal name, and however be it distinguished, first to weaken and then to suppress the freedom of individuals to organize for mutual benefit. Whatever lip service Hatoyama may have rendered to the cause of parliamentarianism, his sponsorship of the doctrine of regimentation of labor identifies him as a tool of the ultra-nationalistic basis as a pre-requisite to its wars of aggression.

   d. By words and deeds he has consistently supported Japan's acts of aggression. In July 1937 he traveled to America and Western Europe as personal emissary of the then Prime Minister Konoe to justify Japan's expansionist program. While abroad he negotiated economic arrangements for supporting the war against China and the subsequent exploitation of that country after subjugation. With duplicity, Hatoyama told the British Prime Minister in 1937 that "China cannot survive unless controlled by Japan," and that the primary motive behind Japan's intervention in China involved the "happiness of the Chinese people."

   e. Hatoyama has posed as an anti-militarist. But in a formal address mailed to his constituents during the 1942 election in which he set forth his political credo, Hatoyama referred to the attack on Pearl Harbor as "fortunately . . . a great victory," stated as a fact that the true cause of the Manchuria and China "incidents" was the anti-Japanese sentiment (in China) instigated by England and America, ridiculed those who in 1928 and 1929 had criticized the Tanaka cabinet, boasted that that cabinet had "liquidated the (previous) weak-kneed diplomacy toward England and America," and gloated that "today the world policy drafted by the Tanaka Cabinet is steadily being realized." This identification of himself with the notorious Tanaka policy of world conquest, whether genuine or merely opportunistic, in and of itself brands Hatoyama as one of those who deceived and misled the people of Japan into militaristic misadventure.

Political Reorientation of Japan, September 1945 to September 1948 (PRJ), Vol. II, pp. 494–495, in Hans H. Baerwald, *The Purge of Japanese Leaders Under the Occupation*, University of California Publications in Political Science, Vol. VIII, Berkeley, Calif.: University of California Press, 1959, pp. 22–23.

NOTES

Chapter 1   Introduction

1. Sato Tomoyasu, *Keibatsu* (clans by marriage), Tokyo: Tachikaze Shobo, 1994, p. 260.
2. Ibid., p. 257.
3. Donald C. Hellmann, *Japanese Foreign Policy and Domestic Politics: The Peace Agreement with the Soviet Union*, Berkeley, Calif.: University of California Press, 1969.
4. John W. Dower, *Empire and Aftermath: Yoshida Shigeru and the Japanese Experience, 1878–1954*, Cambridge, Mass.: Council on East Asian Studies, Harvard University, 1979; Chalmers Johnson, *Japan: Who Governs: The Rise of the Developmental State*, New York: W. W. Norton, 1995; and Herbert P. Bix, *Hirohito and the Making of Modern Japan*, New York: HarperCollins, 2000.
5. Tetsuya Kataoka, *The Price of a Constitution: The Origin of Japan's Postwar Politics*, New York: Crane Russak, 1991, p. 133.
6. Dower, op. cit., p. 275.
7. Kataoka, op. cit., p. 103 and Kataoka Tetsuya, *Nippon eikyu senryo* (permanent occupation of Japan), Tokyo: Kodansha, 1999, p. 251.
8. Ibid. (1999), p. 352 and (1991), p. 9. Gerald L. Curtis examines Ichiro's bill in *The Logic of Japanese Politics: Leaders, Institutions, and the Limits of Change*, New York: Columbia University Press, 1999.
9. "*Shuin no seshu giin*" (hereditary Diet members in the HR), *Chunichi Shimbun*, June 25, 2000 and "*Sanin no seshu giin*" (hereditary Diet members in the HC), *Chunichi Shimbun*, July 29, 2001.
10. Robert Elgie, *Political Leadership in Liberal Democracies*, New York: St. Martin's Press, 1995, pp. 2 and 23; James MacGregor Burns, *Leadership*, New York: Harper & Row, 1978, p. 126; Robert Tucker, *Politics as Leadership*, Columbia, Miss.: University of Missouri Press, 1981, p. 11; and Harold D. Lasswell, "Political Systems, Styles and Personalities," in Elgie, p. 316. For a detailed discussion of the definition, see Elgie, pp. 2–4.
11. Ibid. (Elgie), p. 5 and (Tucker), p. 14. Carlyle, quoted in Tucker.
12. Lasswell, op. cit., pp. 316–347.
13. Elgie, op. cit., p. 6 and Robert Tucker, *Political Culture and Leadership in Soviet Russia: From Lenin to Gorbachev*, New York: W. W. Norton, 1987, p. vii.

14. Tucker, op. cit. (1981), pp. 2–7.
15. Ibid., p. 14.
16. C. A. Gibbs, "The Principles and Traits of Leadership," in C. A. Gibbs, ed., *Leadership: Selected Readings, Harmondsworth*, U.K.: Penguin Books, 1969, p. 205.
17. Ibid., pp. 207–208 and 211–212; and R. M Stogdill, "Personal Factors Associated with Leadership: A Survey of the Literature," in ibid, p. 127.
18. Ibid.
19. Burns, op. cit., p. 19.
20. Ibid., p. 63.
21. Elgie, op. cit., pp. 7–8 and 23–24.
22. Tucker, op. cit. (1981), pp. 14 and 31.
23. Mehran Tamadonfar, *The Islamic Polity and Political Leadership*, Boulder, Colo.: Westview Press, 1989, p. 2.
24. Abraham H. Maslow, *Motivation and Personality*, New York: Harper Brothers, 1954 and Ike Nobutaka, *Japanese Politics: An Introductory Survey*, New York: Knopf, 1957, pp. 10–36.
25. John K. Galbraith, *The Anatomy of Power*, Boston, Mass.: Houghton Mifflin, 1983, pp. 38–71.
26. Burns, op. cit., p. 112.

Chapter 2   The First Generation: Kazuo and the Meiji Government

1. John K. Fairbank, Edwin O. Reischauer, and Albert M. Craig, *East Asia: Tradition and Transformation*, Boston, Mass.: Houghton Mifflin, revised ed., 1989, pp. 486–500. For the historical background of this chapter, see also Robert A. Scalapino, *Democracy and the Party Movement in Prewar Japan*, Berkeley, Calif.: University of California Press, 1953 and Andrew Fraser, R. H. P. Mason, and Philip Mitchell, *Japan's Early Parliaments, 1890–1905: Structure, Issues and Trends*, New York: Routledge, 1995.
2. Hatoyama Ichiro, *Watashi no jijoden* (Autobiography), Tokyo: Kaizosha, 1951, pp. 19 and 30–31.
3. Ibid., pp. 31–32 and Toyoda Jo, *Hatoyama Ichiro: Eisai no kakei* (Hatoyama Ichiro: An elite's genealogy), Tokyo: Kodansha, 1989, pp. 31–34.
4. Ibid. (Toyoda) and Ike Nobutaka, *Japanese Politics: An Introductory Survey*, New York: Knopf, 1957, pp. 16–36.
5. Ibid. (Toyoda), pp. 16–36.
6. Hatoyama, op. cit., pp. 34–35.
7. Ibid., pp. 36–37.
8. Ibid., pp. 37–38 and 52, and Toyoda, op. cit., pp. 40–41.
9. Ibid. (Hatoyama), pp. 52–54.
10. Toyoda, op. cit., p. 117.
11. Ibid., p. 42 and Hatoyama, op. cit., p. 55.
12. Ibid. (Hatoyama), pp. 55–58.
13. Ibid., pp. 58–60.
14. Ibid., pp. 69–70 and 103, and Ito Hirotoshi, *Hatoyama ichizoku* (Hatoyama dynasty), Tokyo: Pipurusha, 1996, pp. 78–81.

15. Ibid. (Hatoyama), pp. 70–71 and 80.
16. Ibid., p. 103 and Toyoda, op. cit., pp. 60–62.
17. Fairbank et al., op. cit., pp. 501–507.
18. Ibid., pp. 508 and 536–539, and Mark Borthwick, *Pacific Century: The Emergence of Modern Pacific Asia*, Boulder, Colo.: Westview, 1992, p. 135.
19. Ibid. (Fairbank et al.), and Hatoyama, op. cit., pp. 60–62.
20. Ibid. (Hatoyama), pp. 103–104.
21. Ibid., pp. 62–63. Kato's given name is occasionally referred to as "Komei"; however, the correct pronunciation is "Takaaki."
22. Ibid., pp. 63–64.
23. Hatoyama Haruko (Haruko), *Jijoden* (Autobiography), Tokyo: Ozorasha, *fukkoku-ban* (reproduction, the original version was published in 1929), 1990, pp. 15–58. At the initial *haihan chiken*, in July 1871, there were 3 *fu* (Tokyo, Osaka, and Kyoto) and 302 *ken*, including "Matsumoto-*ken*." They were restructured into 3 *fu* and 72 *ken* by the year end and Matsumoto-*ken* became "Chikuma-*ken*." It was incorporated into the present Nagano-*ken*, with Matsumoto city as its capital, in 1888.
24. Ibid., pp. 19–42.
25. Ibid., pp. 42–54.
26. Ibid., pp. 54–66.
27. Ibid., pp. 66–67.
28. Ibid., pp. 68–87 and Hatoyama, op. cit., pp. 71–76.
29. Ibid. (Hatoyama), pp. 76–84.
30. Haruko, op. cit., pp. 151–153 and 241–248.
31. Hatoyama, op. cit., pp. 79–80 and 84–85.
32. Ibid., pp. 103–106.
33. Ibid., pp. 106–111.
34. Haruko, op. cit., pp. 159–163.
35. Ito, op. cit., pp. 85–86.
36. Toyoda, op. cit., p. 61.
37. Ibid. and Haruko, op. cit., pp. 158–167.
38. Ibid. (Haruko).
39. Ibid., pp. 241–242.
40. Toyoda, op. cit., pp. 65–66.
41. Ito, op. cit., pp. 84–86.
42. Hatoyama, op. cit., pp. 180–184 and Scalapino, op. cit., pp. 153–154.
43. Haruko, op. cit., pp. 189–195 and Toyoda, op. cit., pp. 79–80. Haruko writes that Kazuo lost his first HR election by less than "fifteen" votes, while Toyoda writes that he was "four" votes shy.
44. Ibid. (Haruko), pp. 189–195.
45. Ibid., pp. 152–153 and 189–195; and Tawara Kotaro, *Nihon no seijika: Oya to ko no shozo* (Japanese politicians: Portraits of parents and offspring), Tokyo: Chuokoronsha, 1997, p. 86.
46. Toyoda, op. cit., pp. 84–85 and Hatoyama, op. cit., pp. 180–189.
47. Haruko, op. cit., pp. 159 and 247–248.
48. Toyoda, op. cit., pp. 84–89; Fairbank et al., op. cit., pp. 538–549; Fraser et al., op. cit., p. 244.

49. Ibid. (Toyoda), pp. 90–91 and Ito, op. cit., pp. 86–87.
50. Fairbank et al., op. cit., p. 549 and Hatoyama, op. cit., pp. 182–183.
51. Ibid. (Hatoyama), pp. 189–190 and Toyoda, op. cit., pp. 91–92. Ozaki actually did not propose a republic in the speech; however, the *hambatsu* newspapers alleged that he was a republican, which caused an uproar and led to his resignation (Isa Hideo, *Ozaki Yukio-den* [Biography of Ozaki Yukio], Tokyo: Kankokai, 1951, pp. 597–604).
52. Ibid. (Hatoyama), pp. 189–190, 210–211, and 239.
53. Haruko, op. cit., pp. 161–163 and 240–241.
54. Ibid., pp. 158–167 and Hatoyama, op. cit., pp. 186–187.
55. Ibid. (Hatoyama), pp. 182–184. Hoshi then joined Ito in forming the *Seiyukai* in 1900. Because of these actions, Hoshi is known as a machiavellian.
56. Fairbank et al., op. cit., pp. 549–551 and Toyoda, op. cit., pp. 92–94.
57. Ibid. (Fairbank et al.), pp. 549–551 and (Toyoda), pp. 92–94.
58. Haruko, op. cit., pp. 152–153 and 241–248.
59. Ibid., pp. 225–232.
60. Ibid., pp. 241–242 and Fairbank et al., op. cit., pp. 687–689. The latter cites the duration of the second Saionji cabinet as being from August 1911 to December 1911; however, it was from August 1911 to December 1912.
61. Ibid. (Haruko), pp. 152–153 and 240–243.
62. Ibid, pp. 152–153 and 240–243.
63. Hatoyama, op. cit., pp. 248–250.
64. Haruko, op. cit., pp. 243–249 and Toyoda, op. cit., pp. 118 and 196–198.
65. Ibid. (Haruko), pp. 245–246.
66. Ito, op. cit., p. 69; Toyoda, op. cit., pp. 103–106; and Hatoyama, op. cit., pp. 255–257. Hara's given name is occasionally referred to as "Kei"; however, the correct pronunciation is "Takashi."
67. Ibid. (Toyoda), pp. 90–91 and (Hatoyama), pp. 220–221.
68. Ibid. (Toyoda and Hatoyama) and Haruko, op. cit., pp. 158–167.
69. Ibid. (Toyoda), pp. 224–238.
70. Hatoyama, op. cit., pp. 17–21 and 269–271.
71. Fairbank et al., op. cit., pp. 688–689 and Fraser et al., op. cit., pp. 2–3.
72. Haruko, op. cit., pp. 248–249.
73. Ibid., pp. 166–167 and Hatoyama, op. cit., pp. 20–21 and 139–143.
74. Quoted in Toyoda, op. cit., pp. 115–116.
75. Ibid., pp. 111–114; Ito, op. cit., pp. 89–90; and Haruko, op. cit., pp. 152–153 and 195–197.
76. Ibid. (Toyoda), pp. 65–66 and 117.
77. Ibid., p. 118.
78. Ibid., pp. 118 and 196–198.
79. Ibid., p. 100.
80. Hatoyama, op. cit., pp. 222–226 and 239–241.

Chapter 3   The Second Generation: Ichiro and Prewar Politics

1. Masuda Hiroshi, *Seijika tsuiho* (Purge of politicians), Tokyo: Chuokoron Shinsha, 2001, p. 23; Tetsuya Kataoka, *The Price of A Constitution: The*

NOTES / 243

Origin of Japan's Postwar Politics, New York: Crane Russak, 1991, p. 133; and
Matsumoto Seichio, *Shikan: Saishoron* (Historical view: Discourse on prime
ministers), Tokyo: Bungei Shunjusha, 1980, p. 256. For background of this
chapter, see John K. Fairbank, Edwin O. Reischauer, and Albert M. Craig, *East
Asia: Tradition and Transformation*, Boston, Mass.: Houghton Mifflin, revised
ed., 1989 and Robert A. Scalapino, *Democracy and the Party Movement in
Prewar Japan*, Berkeley, Calif.: University of California Press, 1953.

2. Hatoyama Ichiro, *Watashi no jijoden* (Autobiography), Tokyo: Kaizosha,
1951, pp. 23–24.

3. Hatoyama Ichiro, *Hatoyama Ichiro, Hatoyama Ichiro kaikoroku* (Memoirs of
Hatoyama Ichiro), Tokyo: Bungei Shunjusha, 1957, pp. 66–67.

4. Ibid., pp. 67–73 and Hatoyama, op. cit. (1951), pp. 170–173.

5. Ibid. (1951), pp. 117–126, 178–179, and 196–205.

6. Ibid., pp. 170–173; Hatoyama, op. cit. (1957), pp. 67–69; and
"*Matsurigotoko: Boseiyui no fukei*" (On politics: Scenes of maternal dominance), *Yomiuri Shimbun*, May 11, 1999.

7. Ibid. (1957), p. 71 and Hatoyama Haruko, *Jijoden* (Autobiography),
Tokyo: Ozorasha, 1990, pp. 207–219.

8. Hatoyama, op. cit. (1951), pp. 26–27 and 210–213, and Matsumoto, op.
cit., p. 265.

9. Ibid. (Hatoyama), pp. 321–323 and Hatoyama Ichiro (Kawate Shoichiro,
ed.), Wakaki chi no kiyoku moete (Young blood, burning purely), Tokyo:
Kodansha, 1996, entirety. The latter are biographies of Ichiro and Kaoru,
and includes Ichiro's numerous love letters to Kaoru that she had kept.

10. Hatoyama, op. cit. (1957), pp. 154–155; and Ito Hirotoshi, Hatoyama
ichizoku (Hatoyama Dynasty), Tokyo: Pipurusha, 1996, pp. 229–233; and
Mikikai, ed., *Miki Bukichi* (Biography of Miki Bukichi), Tokyo: Mikikai,
1958, p. 1.

11. Ibid. (Hatoyama), p. 29 and Hatoyama, op. cit. (1951), pp. 257–259.

12. Toyoda Jo, *Hatoyama Ichiro: Eisai no kakei* (Hatoyama Ichiro: An elite's
genealogy), Tokyo: Kodansha, 1989, pp. 222–226.

13. Ibid., pp. 183–184; Mikikai, op. cit., pp. 174–187; and *Ono Bamboku,
Ono Bamkoku kaikoroku* (Memoirs of Ono Bamboku), Tokyo: Kobundo,
1962, pp. 59–60.

14. Ibid. (Toyoda), pp. 181–182.

15. Ibid. and Mikikai, op. cit., pp. 36–47 and 152–155.

16. Ibid. (Mikikai), pp. 73–86 and 192–193.

17. Toyoda, op. cit., pp. 184–185 and Ono, op. cit., pp. 62–63.

18. Ibid. (Ono), pp. 59–62.

19. Hatoyama, op. cit. (1951), pp. 17–20 and 267–271; and Miyazaki
Yoshimasa, *Hatoyama Ichiro* (Hatoyama Ichiro), Tokyo: Jiji Tsushinsha,
1985, pp. 45–50.

20. Mikikai, op. cit., pp. 155–164 and Fairbank et al., op. cit., pp. 697–698.
The latter cites the second movement as having happened in 1923 but it
happened in 1924.

21. Hatoyama, op. cit. (1951), pp. 300–304; Toyoda, op. cit., pp. 238 and
241–242; and Suzuki Kisaburo Denki Hensankai, ed., *Suzuki Kisaburo*

(Biography of Suzuki Kisaburo), Tokyo: Suzuki Kisaburo Denki Hensankai, 1955, pp. 367–373. Suzuki's biography identifies Kazuo as Kazuko's father, but it only describes Kazuko's mother as a "clever and exemplary lady" without identifying her by name. It also states, "Kazuko married Suzuki at the age of 18 in April 1894 . . . Kazuko dedicated her life entirely to Suzuki and their children and died in April 1929 at the age of 53" (pp. 367–373). Thus, it figures that Kazuko was born sometime between April 1875 and April 1876. Haruko's autobiography, of which half is a biography of Kazuo, does not mention Kazuko at all. Kazuo's first marriage presumably ended when he succeeded to the Hatoyama family at his father's death while he was in the United States.

22. Ibid. (Toyoda), pp. 242–244.
23. Hatoyama, op. cit. (1951), pp. 278–279.
24. Mikikai, op. cit., pp. 164–173.
25. Hatoyama, op. cit. (1951), pp. 290–294 and Toyoda, op. cit., pp. 244–247.
26. Ibid. (Hatoyama), pp. 281–283 and 297–299, and (Toyoda), pp. 247–254.
27. Ibid. (Hatoyama), pp. 283–285 and 300–304; (Toyoda), pp. 252–256; and Hatoyama, op. cit. (1957), pp. 156–157.
28. Ibid. (Hatoyama, 1951), pp. 290–294 and (Toyoda), pp. 256–258.
29. Ibid. (Toyoda), pp. 258–259; and Hatoyama, op. cit. (1957), pp. 38–39.
30. Ibid. (Toyoda), pp. 260–263 and 280–281, and Hatoyama, op. cit. (1951), pp. 298–299.
31. Ibid. (Toyoda), pp. 259–261 and Hatoyama, op. cit. (1957), pp. 221–223.
32. Ibid. (Hatoyama).
33. Toyoda, op. cit., pp. 160–161 and 284–286.
34. Ibid., pp. 264–265 and 270–271, and Fairbank et al., op. cit., pp. 710–713.
35. Hatoyama, op. cit. (1951), pp. 305–310 and Hatoyama Ichiro, "*Jiyushugisha no techo*" (A note of a liberalist), *Chuokoron*, January 1936, pp. 129–139.
36. Ibid. (1951), pp. 26–27 and 305–309.
37. Hatoyama Ichiro, "*Gikai seiji o mamoru*" (To defend parliamentary politics), *Kaizo*, December 1936, pp. 267–274.
38. Hatoyama, op. cit. (1951), pp. 305–309.
39. Ibid., pp. 313–315; and Hatoyama, op. cit. (1957), pp. 12–13.
40. Ibid. (1951), pp. 324–336.
41. Ibid., pp. 328–329; and Kono Ichiro, *Imadakara hanaso* (Now I can talk), Tokyo: Shunyodo, 1958, pp. 127–135.
42. Ibid. (Hatoyama), pp. 321–323; and Toyoda, op. cit., pp. 293–300.
43. Ibid. (Toyoda), pp. 310, 316–317, and 321.
44. Mikikai, op. cit., pp. 238–239.
45. Ibid., pp. 239–240 and Hatoyama, op. cit. (1951), pp. 316–317.
46. Ibid. (Hatoyama), pp. 318–319; Hatoyama, op. cit. (1957), pp. 15–16; and Ono, op. cit., pp. 50–51.
47. Ibid. (1951), pp. 349–351; (1957), pp. 16–20; and Hatoyama Ichiro, *Hatoyama Ichiro·Kaoru nikki* (Diary of Hatoyama Ichiro and Kaoru), Tokyo: Chuokoron Shinsha, Vol. 1, 1999.
48. Mikikai, op. cit., pp. 244–247.

49. Ibid., pp. 248–250; and Hatoyama, op. cit. (1957), pp. 15–20.
50. Ibid. and Toyoda, op. cit., pp. 333–334.
51. Ibid. (Hatoyama), pp. 32–34 and Hatoyama, op. cit. (1951), pp. 356–357.
52. Ibid. (1951), pp. 358–361. Furusawa Koichi wrote postscripts for Hatoyama's autobiography.
53. Kimura Tsuyoshi, *Kudenhofu Mitsuko-den* (Biography of Coudenhove Mitsuko), Tokyo: Kajima Shuppankai, 1971, pp. 389–396 and Count Richard Nicholas Coudenhove-Kalergi, *The Totalitarian State Against Man*, translation by Sir Andrew McFadyean, Glarus, Switzerland, Paneuropa Editions Ltd., 1938, pp. 6–13. His mother Mitsuko had never come back to Japan since she departed in 1896. For the Coudenhove family, also refer to his autobiography, *Bi no kuni: Nihon eno kikyo* (The Country of beauty: Homecoming to Japan), translation by Kajima Morinosuke, Tokyo: Kajima Kenkyujo Shuppan, 1968; and Yoshida Naoya, *Cho no maiso: Kudenhofu Mitsuko-den* (Burial of a butterfly: Biography of Coudenhove Mitsuko), Tokyo: Iwanami Shoten, 1997.
54. Ibid. (Coudenhove), pp. 15, 18, 90, 160, and 186; and Kimura, pp. 340–359 and 386–388. Coudenhove's wife was a renowned stage actress. The American movie "Casablanca" is loosely based on his life.
55. Ibid. (Kimura), pp. 340–359 and 386–388.
56. Hatoyama, op. cit. (1951), pp. 326–327.
57. Ibid. Hideo, quoted in Toyoda, op. cit., pp. 115–116.
58. Ibid. (Toyoda), pp. 264–276.
59. Ibid., pp. 334–335 and Fairbank et al., op. cit., pp. 712–721.
60. Hatoyama, op. cit. (1957), pp. 20–22.

Chapter 4   The U.S. Occupation and Ichiro's Purge

1. Masumi Junnosuke, *Postwar Politics in Japan, 1945–1955*, Berkeley, Calif.: Institute of East Asian Studies, University of California, 1985, pp. 37–45. For the background of this chapter, also refer John W. Dower, *Embracing Defeat: Japan in the Wake of World War II*, New York: W. W. Norton, 1999. Prince Higashikuni was one of the 14 *miya-ke*, immediate relatives of the imperial family. The postwar reforms reduced the number of the *miya-ke* to four families.
2. Charles L. Kades and Milton J. Esman, interview with Alex Gibney, *Reinventing Japan, The Pacific Century*, No. 5, Annenberg/CPB project, 1992; and Mark Gayn, *Japan Diary*, New York, N.Y.: William Sloane, 1948, pp. 33–43. For details of the SCAP policy, refer to Charles A. Willoughby and John Chamberlain, *MacArthur 1941–1951*, New York: McGraw-Hill, 1954, and Harry Emerson Wildes, *Typhoon in Tokyo: The Occupation and Its Aftermath*, New York: Macmillan, 1954.
3. Esman, Kades, and Nakasone Yasuhiro, interview with Gibney, ibid.
4. Ibid. (Kades) and Matsumoto Seichio, *Shikan: Saishoron* (Historical view: Discourse on prime ministers), Tokyo: Bungei Shunjusha, 1980, pp. 251–252.
5. Esman and Richard Poole, interview with Gibney, ibid. and Dower, op. cit., pp. 360–390.

6. Hatoyama Ichiro, *Watashi no jijoden* (1951), Tokyo: Kaizosha, 1951, pp. 328–329; and Hatoyama Ichiro, *Hatoyama Ichiro kaikoroku* (Memoirs of Hatoyama Ichiro), Tokyo: Bungei Shunjusha, 1957, pp. 23–28.

7. Ibid. (1957), pp. 35–36 and 128; and Kodama's autobiography, quoted in Ito Hirotoshi, *Hatoyama ichizoku* (Hatoyama Dynasty), Tokyo: Pipurusha, 1996, pp. 23–131 and 179–180.

8. Ibid. (Hatoyama), pp. 33–36 and Mikikai, ed., *Miki Bukichi* (Biography of Miki Bukichi), Tokyo: Mikikai, 1958, pp. 257–269.

9. Ibid. (Mikikai), pp. 258 and 270–271.

10. Hatoyama, op. cit. (1957), pp. 41–43.

11. Ibid., pp. 36–38 and Hatoyama Ichiro, *Hatoyama Ichiro·Kaoru nikki* (Diary of Hatoyama Ichiro and Kaoru), Tokyo: Chuokoron Shinsha, Vol. 1, 1999, p. 412. SWNCC stands for State-War-Navy Coordinating Committee.

12. Hans H. Baerwald, *The Purge of Japanese Leaders Under the Occupation*, University of California Publications in Political Science, Vol. VIII, Berkeley, Calif.: University of California Press, 1959, pp. 16–21.

13. Ibid. and Matsumoto, op. cit., p. 258.

14. Wildes, op. cit., p. 58; and Hatoyama, op. cit. (1999), p. 414.

15. *Mikikai*, op. cit., pp. 271–273; and Masuda Hiroshi, *Seijika tsuiho* (Purge of politicians), Tokyo: Chuokoron Shinsha, 2001, pp. 278–303.

16. Ibid. (Mikikai), pp. 273–274 and 292–293; and Hatoyama, op. cit. (1957), pp. 27–28. The statistics slightly differ on the election result by sources.

17. Ibid. (Hatoyama), pp. 46–47; Masuda, op. cit., pp. 48 and 60–61; and Wildes, op. cit., pp. 58–60.

18. Ibid. (Hatoyama).

19. Hatoyama, op. cit. (1999), p. 440. Minobe was married to Hideo's wife's sister, Tami. He was erroneously labeled as a liberalist for his *Tenno kikansetsu* (Discourse on the Emperor as the government organ) and expelled from the HP in 1935. Ichiro asked Minobe to join his cabinet as minister at-large; however, Minobe declined. Minobe opposed the GHQ's order to revise the imperial constitution as he deemed it a world-class constitution, whereas Ichiro felt that the revision was unavoidable insofar as the GHQ strongly wanted it. Minobe told Ichiro that he would not join Ichiro's cabinet if it planned to revise the constitution (Hatoyama, 1957, p. 48).

20. Hatoyama, op. cit. (1957), pp. 48–49.

21. Mikikai, op. cit., pp. 294–295.

22. SCAPIN 919, Section a. and b.; and Wildes, op. cit., p. 61.

23. SCAPIN 919, Section c. and d.; and Baerwald, op. cit., p. 23.

24. SCAPIN 919, Section e.

25. Hatoyama, op. cit. (1957), pp. 49–51.

26. Ibid., pp. 38–39 and Gayn, op. cit., p. 466.

27. Ibid. (Hatoyama), pp. 38–43.

28. Masuda, op. cit., p. 32; and Yoshida Shigeru, *The Yoshida Memoirs: The Story of Japan in Crisis*. London: Heinemann, 1961, pp. 131–132.

29. Masumi, op. cit., pp. 100–104 and Toyoda Jo, *Hatoyama Ichiro: Eisai no kakei* (Hatoyama Ichiro: An elite's genealogy), Tokyo: Kodansha, 1989, pp. 248–249. Hoshijima quoted in Masumi.

30. Hatoyama, op. cit. (1951), pp. 331–332 and (1957), p. 46.
31. Mikikai, op. cit., pp. 277–281.
32. Hatoyama, op. cit. (1957), pp. 38–39 and 45–46. Mitsuchi was cited as "Mizuchi" in some English literature; however, the correct name is "Mitsuchi."
33. Mikikai, op. cit., pp. 277–279 and Masuda, op. cit., pp. 38–42.
34. Hans H. Baerwald, "Postwar Japan—A Reminiscence," JPRI Occasional Paper, No. 27, July 2002, pp. 3–4 and Dower, op. cit., p. 262.
35. Hatoyama, op. cit. (1957), pp. 44–45 and (1999), p. 435. Hatoyama records the date as "April 4" in his diary, while his memoirs (p. 44) and Gayn's diary (p. 161) record it as "April 6."
36. Gayn, op. cit., pp. 161–164.
37. Ibid. and Wildes, op. cit. p. 60.
38. Ibid. (Gayn), pp. 184 and 200. The date should be May 4.
39. Ibid., pp. 16, 134, 162, and 474. Underlining by author.
40. Ibid., pp. 186–187.
41. Ibid., pp. 478–479 and 485.
42. Hatoyama, op. cit. (1951), pp. 333–335. Masumi notes that the book is "said to have been ghostwritten by Yamaura" (op. cit., p. 101). Dower refers to the book and seems to take it at face value in *Empire and Aftermath: Yoshida Shigeru and the Japanese Experience, 1878–1954*, Cambridge, Mass.: Council on East Asian Studies, Harvard University, 1979, pp. 250–251.
43. Ibid. (Hatoyama) and Yamaura Kanichi, "*Hatoyama tsuiho no shukunsha*" ([M]VP of Hatoyama's purge), *Bungei Shunju*, September 1950, pp. 113–115.
44. Ibid. (Yamaura).
45. Ibid. See SCAPIN 919, Section e.
46. Ibid. and Hatoyama, op. cit. (1951), pp. 334–335.
47. Baerwald, op. cit., pp. 5–11 and 21.
48. Ibid., p. 23.
49. Ibid., pp. 21, 24 and 99–106.
50. Wildes, op. cit., p. 58.
51. Ibid., pp. 59–60.
52. Hanai Hitoshi, *Sengo Nihon o kizuita saishotachi: From Yoshida Shigeru to Tanaka Kakuei* (Prime ministers that built postwar Japan: From Yoshida Shigeru to Tanaka Kakuei), Tokyo: Nesuko, 1996, pp. 59–77.
53. Kojima Noboru, *Kowa joyaku: Sengo Nichibei kankei no kiten* ([San Francisco] Peace Treaty: The origins of postwar U.S.–Japan relations), Tokyo: Chuokoronsha, Vol. 1, 1997, pp. 387–391. This author wrote to Kojima to obtain information; however, he had been hospitalized and died in 2001.
54. Masuda, op. cit., pp. 38–58.
55. Ibid. and Hatoyama, op. cit. (1957), p. 39.
56. Ibid. (Masuda).
57. Ibid., pp. 29–42 and 58–61. Narahashi, quoted (p. 33). Napier, interview with Masuda (p. 41).

58. Ibid., pp. 58–61.
59. Ibid., pp. 60–61; Matsumoto, op. cit., pp. 256–257; and Wildes, pp. 55–60.
60. Toyoda, op. cit., pp. 248–249 and 354.
61. Mikikai, op. cit., pp. 304–305 and Masuda, op. cit., pp. 69–70.
62. Ibid. (Masuda).
63. Ibid., p. 25 and Wildes, op. cit., p. 61.
64. Toyoda, op. cit., p. 355 and Hatoyama, op. cit. (1957), p. 11.

Chapter 5   Ichiro and Postwar Politics

1. Masuda Hiroshi, *Seijika tsuiho* (Purge of politicians), Tokyo: Chuokoron Shinsha, 2001, p. 61. For early postwar politics, refer to Masumi Junnosuke, *Postwar Politics in Japan, 1945–1955*, Berkeley, Calif.: Institute of East Asian Studies, University of California, 1985 and John W. Dower, *Empire and Aftermath: Yoshida Shigeru and the Japanese Experience, 1878–1954*, Cambridge, Mass.: Council on East Asian Studies, Harvard University, 1979.
2. Hatoyama Ichiro, *Hatoyama Ichiro kaikoroku* (Memoirs of Hatoyama Ichiro), Tokyo: Bungei Shunjusha, 1957, pp. 53–55; Yoshida Shigeru, *The Yoshida Memoirs: The Story of Japan in Crisis*, London: Heinemann, 1961, pp. 13–30; and Dower, op. cit., pp. 14–32.
3. Ibid. (Yoshida), pp. 13–30 and (Dower), pp. 14–32.
4. Ibid. (Dower), pp. 227–272; Mark Gayn, *Japan Diary*, New York, N.Y.: William Sloane, 1948, pp. 162, 200, and 466; and Kataoka Tetsuya, *Nippon eikyu senryo* (Permanent occupation of Japan), Tokyo: Kodansha, 1999, pp. 135–168.
5. Hatoyama, op. cit., pp. 55–56.
6. Yoshida, op. cit., pp. 72–75.
7. Kono Ichiro, *Imadakara hanaso* (Now I can talk), Tokyo: Shunyodo, 1958, pp. 148–150 and Matsumoto Seichio, *Shikan: Saishoron* (Historical view: Discourse on prime ministers), Tokyo: Bungei Shunjusha, 1980, pp. 253–254.
8. Dower, op. cit., pp. 305–318. For details of the Yoshida cabinets, see Dower and Yoshida, op. cit.
9. Ibid., pp. 305–318.
10. Ibid., pp. 305–318 and Masumi, op. cit., pp. 177–182. Tomabechi's name was cited as "Yoshizo" in some English literature; however, the correct name is "Gizo" as in Yoshida, op. cit., p. 255.
11. Kataoka, op. cit., pp. 148–168; and Tetsuya Kataoka, *The Price of a Constitution: The Origin of Japan's Postwar Politics*, New York: Crane Russak, 1991, pp. 62–65.
12. Ibid. (Kataoka, 1999), pp. 167–168; Matsumoto, op. cit., pp. 250–252; and George F. Kennan, *Memoirs 1925–1950*, Boston, Mass.: Little, Brown, 1967, pp. 376–396.
13. Chalmers Johnson, *Conspiracy at Matsukawa*, Berkeley, Calif.: University of California Press, 1972, p. 17.

14. Kennan, op. cit., pp. 376–382.
15. Ibid., pp. 376–390.
16. Ibid., pp. 388–389.
17. Ibid., pp. 391–396.
18. Hatoyama Ichiro, *Hatoyama Ichiro·Kaoru nikki* (Diary of Hatoyama Ichiro and Kaoru), Vol. 1, Tokyo: Chuokoron Shinsha, 1999, p. 646; and Yoshida, op. cit., pp. 164–165.
19. Richard Poole and Milton J. Esman, Interview with Alex Gibney, "Reinventing Japan," *The Pacific Century*, No. 5, Annenberg/CPB project, 1992; Kataoka, op. cit. (1991), pp. 65–69; and Kataoka, op. cit. (1999), pp. 167–168, 210–211, and 252.
20. Ibid. (Kataoka, 1991), pp. 65–69 and (1999), pp. 167–168, 210–211, and 252.
21. Hatoyama, op. cit. (1957), pp. 61–66 and 79–82.
22. Ibid., pp. 77–78 and 82–84.
23. Baerwald, op. cit. (1959), pp. 72–73. The Democratic Liberal Party was formed in March 1948.
24. Gayn, op. cit., pp. 472–475.
25. Ibid. and Matsumoto, op. cit., p. 473.
26. Dower, op. cit., pp. 378–400 and 436–449.
27. Ibid., pp. 1, 305, and 315–316.
28. Hatoyama, op. cit. (1957), pp. 85–89; and Hatoyama op. cit. (1999), p. 757.
29. Ibid. (1957), pp. 264–265; Kataoka, op. cit. (1991), pp. 92–93; and Kataoka, op. cit. (1999), pp. 207–210.
30. Ibid. (Hatoyama), pp. 93–96; and Yoshida, op. cit., p. 164.
31. Hatoyama, op. cit. (1999), pp. 778–779; and Mikikai, ed., *Miki Bukichi* (Biography of Miki Bukichi), Tokyo: Mikikai, 1958, pp. 336–337.
32. Ibid. (Hatoyama), pp. 779–780; and Hatoyama, op. cit. (1957), pp. 96–97.
33. Ibid. (1999), p. 780, (1957), pp. 98–101; and *"Hatoyama Ichiro·Kaoru nikki kanko"* (Publication of diary of Hatoyama Ichiro and Kaoru), *Yomiuri Shimbun*, April 2, 1999. A recent case in which a Japanese leader suffered a stroke due to political rivalry is Prime Minister Obuchi Keizo in April 2000. After a talk with Ozawa Ichiro, Obuchi suffered a stroke and died (see chapter 7).
34. Ibid. (1957), pp. 101 and 103–104.
35. Ibid., pp. 114–116 and Yoshida, op. cit., p. 93.
36. Mikikai, op. cit., pp. 343–350 and Ono Bamboku, *Ono Bamboku kaikoroku* (Memoirs of Ono Bamboku), Tokyo: Kobundo, 1962, pp. 69–70 and 141–142.
37. Ibid. (Ono), pp. 81 and 141–142, and Hatoyama, op. cit. (1957), pp. 114–116.
38. Ibid. (Hatoyama), pp. 116–117.
39. Ono, op. cit., pp. 65–67–352 and Masumi, op. cit., p. 284.
40. Ibid. (Masumi), p. 287 and Hatoyama, op. cit. (1957), pp. 116–118.
41. Ibid. (Masumi), p. 292; (Hatoyama), pp. 118–122; and Mikikai, op. cit., pp. 364–369.

42. Ibid. (Masumi), p. 293; and Kono, op. cit., pp. 209–210.
43. Hatoyama, op. cit. (1957), pp. 126–127 and Mikikai, op. cit., pp. 370–377.
44. Ibid. (Hatoyama), pp. 127–131; and (Mikikai), pp. 378–380.
45. Ibid. (Hatoyama), pp. 127–131; (Mikikai), pp. 380–386; and Tomimori Eiji, "*Sugao no saisho: Hatoyama Ichiro*" (Real face of the prime minister: Hatoyama Ichiro), *Asahi Chronicle Weekly 20th Century*, 1999, pp. 32–33.
46. Yamada Eizo, *Seiden Sato Eisaku* (Orthodox biography of Sato Eisaku), Tokyo: Shinchosha, 1988, quoted in Tawara Kotaro, *Nihon no seijika: Oya to ko no shozo* (Japanese politicians: Portraits of parents and offspring), Tokyo: Chuokoronsha, 1997, pp. 77–78.
47. Hatoyama, op. cit. (1957), p. 131; Mikikai, op. cit., pp. 385–386; and Ike Nobutaka, *Japanese Politics: An Introductory Survey*, New York: Knopf, 1957, pp. 166–167.
48. Ibid. (Mikikai), pp. 386–387; and Kono, op. cit., pp. 183–185.
49. Ibid. and Miyazaki Yoshimasa, *Hatoyama Ichiro* (Hatoyama Ichiro), Tokyo: Jiji Tsushinsha, 1985, pp. 197–198.
50. Dower, op. cit., p. 465; and Ono, op. cit., pp. 81–91.
51. Ibid. (Ono) pp. 65–66; Mikikai, op. cit., pp. 408–412; and Hatoyama, op. cit. (1957), pp. 136–140.
52. Dower, op. cit., pp. 490–492; and Mikikai, op. cit., pp. 413–418.
53. Ibid. (Mikikai), pp. 418–419; and Hatoyama, op. cit. (1957), pp. 140–142.
54. Ibid. (Mikikai) pp. 418–419; and (Hatoyama) pp. 140–142.
55. Ibid. (Hatoyama), pp. 143–145; and (Mikikai), pp. 419–420.
56. Ibid. (Hatoyama), pp. 146–149.
57. Ike, op. cit., p. 160.
58. Hatoyama, op. cit. (1957), pp. 152–156.
59. Ibid., pp. 143–145 and 191; and Mikikai, op. cit., pp. 425–428.
60. Ibid. (Hatoyama), pp. 165–167.
61. Mikikai, op. cit., pp. 426–428; and Kono, op. cit., pp. 185–187.
62. Ibid. (Mikikai), pp. 426–428.
63. Hatoyama, op. cit. (1957), pp. 168–172.
64. Ono, op. cit., pp. 111–117.
65. Mikikai, op. cit., pp. 429–430; and Kono, op. cit., pp. 112–113.
66. Hatoyama, op. cit. (1957), pp. 162–165; Mikikai, op. cit., pp. 436–447; and Ono, op. cit., p. 121.
67. Ibid. (Mikikai), pp. 436–447.
68. Hatoyama, op. cit. (1957), pp. 181–183.
69. Ibid., pp. 120–121 and 191–192.
70. Ibid., pp. 34–35 and 191–192.
71. Ibid., pp. 116–117.
72. Ibid., pp. 158–161; and Kono, op. cit., pp. 95–107.
73. Dower, op. cit., pp. 447–448; Kataoka, op. cit. (1991), pp. 138–140 and 152; and Kataoka, op. cit. (1999), pp. 326–329.
74. Hatoyama, op. cit. (1957), pp. 187–189; Miyazaki, op. cit., pp. 227–229; and Gerald L. Curtis, *The Logic of Japanese Politics: Leaders, Institutions, and*

the Limits of Change, New York: Columbia University Press, 1999, pp. 146–148. The bill was introduced in spring 1956 after the creation of the LDP in November 1955.

75. Ibid. (Hatoyama), pp. 189–191; and Ito Hirotoshi, *Hatoyama ichizoku* (Hatoyama Dynasty), Tokyo: Pipurusha, 1996, pp. 163–166.

76. Ibid. (Ito), pp. 160–163. *The Mainichi Shimbun*, March 26, 1955, quoted in Ito.

77. Hatoyama, op. cit. (1957), p. 189; and Toyoda Jo, *Hatoyama Ichiro: Eisai no kakei* (Hatoyama Ichiro: An elite's genealogy), Tokyo: Kodansha, 1989, pp. 553–554.

78. Ibid. (Hatoyama), pp. 174–177 and 193–203.

79. Ibid., pp. 174–177 and 193–203. For details of the negotiation, refer to Donald C. Hellmann, *Japanese Foreign Policy and Domestic Politics: The Peace Agreement with the Soviet Union*, Berkeley, Calif.: University of California Press, 1969 and Matsumoto Shunichi, *Mosukuwa ni kakeru niji: Nisso kokko kaifuku hiwa* (The rainbow over Moscow: Secret story of the restoration of the Japan–Soviet relations), Tokyo: *Asahi Shimbunsha*, 1960.

80. Ibid., pp. 174–177 and 193–203; Kono, op. cit., pp. 47–56; and Ito Takashi, "Shigemitsu Mamoru and the 1955 System," in Tetsuya Kataoka, ed., *Creating Single-Party Democracy: Japan's Postwar Political System*, Stanford, Calif.: Hoover Institution Press, 1992, pp. 115–116.

81. Hellmann, op. cit., pp. 119–120, 122–133, and 151; and Kataoka, op. cit. (1999), pp. 357–358.

82. Ibid. (Hellmann), p. 154 and (Kataoka), pp. 322–339.

83. Hatoyama, op. cit. (1957), pp. 195–207.

84. Ibid., pp. 195–207.

85. Ibid., pp. 195–207, and Interview with Takashima, Mayumi Itoh, November 1986.

86. Mayumi Itoh, "Views of Soviet Politics and New Thinking," in Gilbert Rozman, *Japan's Response to the Gorbachev Era, 1985–1991: A Rising Superpower Views a Declining One*, Princeton, N.J.: Princeton University Press, 1992, pp. 224–242 and Saki Ryuzo, *"inishiachibu"* (Initiative), *Chunichi Shimbun*, September 13, 2000.

87. Hatoyama, op. cit., pp. 207–209 and 220–221.

88. Ito Takashi, op. cit., p. 116.

89. Hatoyama, op. cit. (1957), pp. 105 and 109.

90. Ito Hirotoshi, op. cit., pp. 180–182.

91. Ono, op. cit., p. 81 and Kono, op. cit., pp. 189–190.

92. Hatoyama, op. cit., pp. 220–221 and Toyoda, op. cit., pp. 553–555.

93. Ono, op. cit., p. 63.

94. Kono, op. cit., pp. 209–210.

95. Ibid., pp. 5–7.

96. Mikikai, op. cit., pp. 498–454; and Toyoda, op. cit., pp. 553–554.

97. Ibid. (Mikikai), p. 493 (Toyoda), pp. 553–554; and Tomimori, op. cit., pp. 32–33.

98. Ibid. (Toyoda), p. 118.

99. Tomimori, op. cit., pp. 32–33.

Chapter 6   The Third Generation: Iichiro, the MOF, and the MOFA

1. Hatoyama Ichiro, *Hatoyama Ichiro kaikoroku* (Memoirs of Hatoyama Ichiro), Tokyo: Bungei Shunjusha, 1957, p. 70. Ito Hirotoshi, *Hatoyama ichizoku* (Hatoyama Dynasty), Tokyo: Pipurusha, 1996, pp. 172 and 233. Iichiro's article in Reader's Digest is quoted in Hatoyama. For background of this chapter, see Masumi Junnosuke, *Contemporary Politics in Japan* (translation), Berkeley, Calif.: University of California Press, 1995 and Chalmers Johnson, *MITI and the Japanese Economic Miracle: The Growth of Industrial Policy, 1925–1975*. Stanford, Calif.: Stanford University Press, 1982.
2. Ibid. (Ito), pp. 44–46 and 172–184; and Hatoyama Ichiro, *Hatoyama Ichiro·Kaoru nikki* (Diary of Hatoyama Ichiro and Kaoru), Tokyo: Chuokoron Shinsha, Vol. 1, 1999, p. 419.
3. Ibid. (Ito), pp. 174–178.
4. Ibid., pp. 174–178 and Chalmers Johnson, "Japanese 'Capitalism' Revisited," JPRI Occasional Paper, No. 22, August 2001, p. 7.
5. Ibid. (Ito), pp. 174 and 187, and Toyoda Jo, *Hatoyama Ichiro: Eisai no kakei* (Hatoyama Ichiro: An elite's genealogy), Tokyo: Kodansha, 1989, pp. 552–553.
6. Ibid. (Ito), pp. 184–186 and 189–190.
7. Ibid., pp. 188–189; and Toyoda, op. cit., pp. 552–553.
8. Ibid., pp. 189, 224, and 233; and Miyazaki Yoshimasa, *Hatoyama Ichiro* (Hatoyama Ichiro), Tokyo: Jiji Tsushinsha, 1985, p. 249.
9. Ibid. (Ito), pp. 190–191.
10. Ibid., pp. 189–190.
11. Hirano Minoru, *Gaiko kisha nikki: Hatoyama gaiko no ichinen* (Diary of a diplomatic reporter: One year of Hatoyama diplomacy), Tokyo: Gyosei Tsushinsha, 1980, pp. 1–2.
12. Ibid., pp. 1–2 and Kent E. Calder, "Japanese Foreign Economic Policy Formation: Explaining the Reactive State," *World Politics*, Vol. 40, No. 4 (July 1988), pp. 517–541. Also see Dennis T. Yasutomo, *The New Multilateralism in Japan's Foreign Policy*, New York: St. Martin's Press, 1995.
13. Ibid. (Hirano), pp. 1–3.
14. Ito, op. cit., pp. 191–194.
15. Hayasaka Shigezo, "*Koizumi hitori shibai no makuaki: Ohimesama o oroshita Koizumi ichiza no butai wa itsumade motsuka*" (Koizumi solo play opens: How long will the Koizumi troupe that fired the princess last?), *Voice*, April 2002, pp. 82–89.
16. Ito, op. cit., pp. 193–194.
17. Ibid., pp. 191–193.
18. Ibid., p. 193 and Mayumi Itoh, "Japanese Perceptions of the Soviet Union: Japanese Foreign Policy Elites' Perceptions of the Soviet Union and Japanese Foreign Policy Toward the Soviet Union" (dissertation), 1988. Interview with author, October 1986.
19. Toyoda, op. cit., p. 553.
20. Ito, op. cit., p. 171.
21. Ibid., pp. 47–51.

22. Ibid., pp. 47–51. The exchange rate was calculated at ¥119.05 to the dollar.
23. Ibid., quoted in pp. 183 and 193.
24. Ibid., quoted in pp. 171 and 191.
25. Ibid., pp. 180–183.
26. Ibid., pp. 180–183.
27. Ibid., pp. 180–183.
28. Ibid., p. 175.
29. Ibid., p. 193.
30. Ibid., pp. 174–175.
31. Ibid., pp. 41–47.

Chapter 7   The Fourth Generation: Kunio and Yukio

1. Toyoda Jo, *Hatoyama Ichiro: Eisai no kakei* (Hatoyama Ichiro: An elite's genealogy), Tokyo: Kodansha, 1989, p. 552; and Ito Hirotoshi, *Hatoyama ichizoku* (Hatoyama Dynasty), Tokyo: Pipurusha, 1996, pp. 254–258. For background of this chapter, refer to Gerald L. Curtis, *The Logic of Japanese Politics: Leaders, Institutions, and the Limits of Change*, New York: Columbia University Press, 1999 and Ronald J. Hrebenar, *Japan's New Party System*, Boulder, Colo.: Westview, 2000.
2. Ibid. (Ito), pp. 171 and 254–257.
3. Ibid., pp. 256–258.
4. Ibid., p. 258; Toyoda, op. cit., p. 552; and Kobayashi Kichiya, *Nijuisseiki rida koho no shingan* (Assessment of potential leaders in the twenty-first century), Tokyo: Yomiuri Shimbunsha, 1996, p. 108.
5. Ibid. (Kobayashi), p. 108.
6. Ito, op. cit., pp. 210–214; and Sato Tomoyasu, *Keibatsu* (Clans by marriage), Tokyo: Tachikaze Shobo, 1994, p. 257.
7. Ibid. (Ito), pp. 210–214.
8. Ibid., pp. 210–214; Curtis, op. cit., pp. 66–67; and Hrebenar, op. cit., pp. 6, 38, and 160. The NLC fared well initially but was disbanded in 1986.
9. Ibid. (Ito), pp. 212 and 244–245.
10. Ibid., pp. 214 and 217.
11. Ibid., pp. 260–261; and Sato, op. cit., pp. 260 and 263.
12. Ibid. (Ito), pp. 260–261 and (Sato), pp. 260 and 263.
13. Kobayashi, op. cit., pp. 102–103.
14. Ito, op. cit., pp. 198–199 and 239–241; and Itagaki Eiken, *Hatoyama Yukio de Nihon wa do kawaru: Honto ni kokumin no tame no seiji o jitsugen dekirunoka* (How can Hatoyama Yukio change Japan: Can he really realize politics for the people?), Tokyo: Keizaikai, 1996, pp. 86–87.
15. Ibid. (Ito), pp. 198–199 and 239–241 and (Itagaki), pp. 87–106.
16. Ibid. (Ito), p. 242 and (Itagaki), pp. 87 and 98.
17. Ibid. (Itagaki), pp. 87–91; Hatoyama Ichiro, *Wakaki chi no kiyoku moete* (Young blood, burning purely), Tokyo: Kodansha, 1996, pp. 50–51; and Tawara Kotaro, *Nihon no seijika: Oya to ko no shozo* (Japanese politicians: Portraits of parents and offspring), Tokyo: Chuokoronsha, 1997, pp. 79–80.

18. Ibid. (Itagaki), pp. 90–96 and Ito, op. cit., pp. 198–200.
19. Ibid. (Ito), pp. 200–202.
20. Ibid., pp. 179–180 and 265–267. Figures are calculated at an April 1999 exchange rate of US$1 = ¥119.
21. Ibid., pp. 178–179.
22. Ibid., pp. 239–243 and Itagaki, op. cit., pp. 93–96.
23. Ibid. (Ito), 239–243.
24. Ibid., pp. 18–27 and 263–264.
25. Ibid., pp. 18–27 and 263–264.
26. Ibid., pp. 217–218 and 264.
27. Ibid., pp. 207–210.
28. Ibid., pp. 30–33, 236, and 267; "Two Brothers in Search of a Party," *The Economist*, Vol. 340, No. 7981 (August 31, 1996), pp. 22–33. The exchange rates were calculated at US$1 = ¥119.05 as of April 20, 1999 when the contribution was made.
29. Ibid. (Ito), pp. 30–33.
30. Ibid. (Kobayashi), p. 107 and Hatoyama Kunio, "*Ani Yukio yo, ogoru nakare*" (My brother Yukio, do not be proud), *Bungei Shunju*, August 2000, pp. 125–126.
31. Ibid. (Kobayashi), pp. 102–103.
32. Kunio, op. cit., pp. 125–126.
33. Ito, op. cit., pp. 24–36. Kunio, quoted (p. 35).
34. Ibid., pp. 22–23 and Kobayashi, op. cit., pp. 102–107.
35. Ibid. (Ito), pp. 35–38; Itagaki, op. cit., pp. 134–136; and "*Matsurigotoko: Seijika haha o kataru*" (Thinking about politics: Politicians talk about their mothers), *Yomiuri Shimbun*, May 11, 1999.
36. Ibid. (Ito), p. 254 (Eto quoted). Eto had opposed the SCAP's censorship during its occupation of Japan. He has been an influential conservative critic and shocked the Japanese by committing suicide in July 1999, following his wife's death.
37. Itagaki, op. cit., pp. 3–19.
38. Ibid., pp. 3–19 and Warashina Mitsuharu, *Minshu riberaru no seiken koso: Nijuisseiki no tobira o hiraku Minshuto* (Democratic liberal ideas on government: The DPJ opens the door of the twenty-first century), Tokyo: Nihon Hyoronsha, 1997, pp. 177–182.
39. Ito, op. cit., pp. 30–33.
40. Ibid., pp. 30–33. The DPJ uses the word *daihyo* (representative) for its leader's position, instead of *toshu* (party president), in its efforts to be egalitarian; however, this book translates the position as "president" to be in consonance with the American norm.
41. Kunio, op. cit., pp. 126–130.
42. Ibid., pp. 126–130.
43. Ito, op. cit., p. 262.
44. "*Tochiji wa suteppu?*" (Tokyo governor is a step?), *Chunichi Shimbun*, February 8, 1999.
45. "*Shuinsen tosensha*" (Winners of the HR elections), *Yomiuri Shimbun*, October 21, 1996 and Ito, op. cit., pp. 15–18 and 38.

46. *"Minshuto ketto"* (The creation of the DPJ), *Chunichi Shimbun*, September 28, 1996.

47. Kunio, op. cit., pp. 126–130 and *"Asu ketto isshunen"* (Tomorrow is the party's first anniversary), *Chunichi Shimbun*, September 27, 1997.

48. *"Shin Minshuto ketto"* (The creation of the new DPJ), *Yomiuri Shimbun*, April 7, 1998.

49. *"Shin Minshuto shin yakuin no yokogao"* (Profiles of the new DPJ's officials), *Yomiuri Shimbun*, April 7, 1998 and *"Minshuto Kan daihyo o saisen"* (The DPJ reelects President Kan), *Yomiuri Shimbun*, January 19, 1999.

50. *"Shijiritsu teimei ni shokku"* (Shocked by the low support rates), *Yomiuri Shimbun*, April 22, 1998 and *"Saninsen kekka"* (Results of the HC elections), *Yomiuri Shimbun*, July 15, 1998.

51. Ibid. (July 15, 1998).

52. *"Jiji renritsu naikaku hossoku"* (LDP–LP coalition cabinet starts), *Yomiuri Shimbun*, January 4, 1999.

53. *"Minshuto kyo ketto isshunen"* (Today is the DPJ's first anniversary), *Yomiuri Shimbun*, September 28, 1997 and *"Minshuto wa doko e"* (Where is the DPJ going?), *Yomiuri Shimbun*, April 24, 1999.

54. *"Umarete wa kie . . . : Seito neminguko"* (Born and disappear: Thinking about naming of political parties), *Chunichi Shimbun*, January 26, 1998 and Ito, op. cit., p. 18.

55. *"Honshi zenkoku seron chosa"* (*Yomiuri* national opinion polls), *Yomiuri Shimbun*, January 27, 1999.

56. Ibid. and *"Shinjirarenaku nattamono wa"* (Things that you can no longer believe), *Yomiuri Shimbun*, January 25, 1999.

57. *"Obuchi-san shidoryoku ni gimonfu"* (Mr. Obuchi's leadership questioned), *Yomiuri Shimbun*, February 5, 1999.

58. *"Tochiji wa suteppu?"* (Tokyo governor is a step?), *Chunichi Shimbun*, February 8, 1999.

59. *"Kyoshu sadamaranu Hatoyama Kunio-shi"* (Indecisive Mr. Hatoyama Kunio), *Yomiuri Shimbun*, February 4, 1999 and *"Hatoyama Kunio-san: 'Aokukusai yume' ou purinsu"* (Mr. Hatoyama Kunio: The prince who pursues "an adolescent dream"), *Yomiuri Shimbun*, March 19, 1999.

60. *"Tochiji wa suteppu?"* (Tokyo governor is a step?), *Chunichi Shimbun*, February 8, 1999.

61. *"Tochijisen: Ishihara Shintaro-san"* (Tokyo gubernatorial race: Mr. Ishihara Shintaro), *Yomiuri Shimbun*, March 17, 1999.

62. *"Tochiji ni Ishihara-shi"* (Tokyo Governor Elect is Mr. Ishihara), *Yomiuri Shimbun*, April 12, 1999 and *"Ishihara-shi jishin tappuri"* (Mr. Ishihara is very confident), *Chunichi Shimbun*, March 11, 1999.

63. *"Shuin hoketsu senkyo kekka"* (Results of the HR supplementary elections), *Yomiuri Shimbun*, April 12, 1999.

64. *"Yuryoku gokoho haisha no ben"* (Concession speeches by the five contenders), *Yomiuri Shimbun*, April 12, 1999 and *"Hatoyama-shi furusu ni kaerazu"* (Mr. Hatoyama [Kunio] will not return to his old nest), *Yomiuri Shimbun*, July 31, 1999.

65. Kunio, op. cit., pp. 124–130.

66. Ibid., pp. 124–130 and *"Takamaru Hatoyama-shi taiboron"* (Increasing expectations for Mr. Hatoyama [Yukio]), *Yomiuri Shimbun*, May 23, 1999.
67. Ibid. (Kunio), pp. 124–130; Kobayashi Kichiya, *Ichiryu no rida, niryu no bosu* (First-rate leaders and second-rate bosses), Tokyo: *Futabasha*, 2000, pp. 174–175; and *"Hatoyama kyodai saketa gassho"* (The Hatoyama brothers offer prayers separately), *Yomiuri Shimbun*, December 18, 1999.
68. Ibid. (Kobayashi), pp. 174–175 and (*Yomiuri Shimbun*) and Hatoyama Kunio, *"Ikari no 'zetsuen sengen': Hatoyama Kunio gekihaku"* (Angry "ultimatum": Hatoyama Kunio's fiery confession), *Shukan Gendai*, December 18, 1999, pp. 56–57. Kunio seemed to have reconciled with Yukio in December 2002 when Yukio resigned presidency of the DPJ (see chapter 8).
69. *"Ozawa-shi, renritsu ridatsu"* (Mr. Ozawa leaves coalition), *Yomiuri Shimbun*, April 2, 1999 and *"Mori shin-naikaku hossoku"* (Mori new cabinet formed), *Yomiuri Shimbun*, April 6, 2000.
70. Kunio, op. cit. (*Bungei Shunju*), pp. 125–130, and Hatoyama Kunio and Yamai Kazunori, *Gurupu homu nyumon* (Introduction to group home), Tokyo: Riyonsha, 1999.
71. Ibid., (*Bungei Shunju*), pp. 125–130.
72. Hatoyama Kunio, *"Hatoyama-ke yondai no 'suparuta to honin': Ani 'Hatoyama Yukio' o kataru"* ("Sparta and *laissez faire*" of the four generations of the Hatoyama family: Talking about elder brother "Hatoyama Yukio"), *Shincho 45*, July 2000, pp. 72–76.
73. Ibid., pp. 72–76.
74. Kunio, op. cit. (*Bungei Shunju*), pp. 124–130; Curtis, op. cit., pp. 161–162; and *"Shuinsen kaihyo kekka"* (Results for the HR election votes), *Asahi Shimbun*, June 26, 2000.
75. Ibid. (Kunio), pp. 129–130.
76. Kobayashi, op. cit. (1996), pp. 105–106.
77. Ito, op. cit., pp. 218–219 and 264–265.
78. *"Shuinsen kaihyo kekka"* (Results for the HR election votes), *Asahi Shimbun*, June 26, 2000 and Kunio, op. cit. (*Bungei Shunju*), pp. 124–130.
79. Ibid. (Kunio), pp. 124–130.
80. *"Saninsen kaihyo kekka"* (Results for the HC election votes), *Asahi Shimbun*, July 31, 2001.
81. *"Nonaka-shi ga Hatoyama-shi suisen"* (Mr. Nonaka recommends Mr. Hatoyama), *Chunichi Shimbun*, January 31, 2002.
82. *"Suzuki-shi, Shuin jishoku kankoku ketsugi"* (A resolution to recommend that Mr. Suzuki resign from the HR), *Asahi Shimbun*, June 20, 2002.
83. Ito, op. cit., pp. 171–172, and 211.
84. Kobayashi, op. cit. (1996), pp. 105–107 and Kobayashi, op. cit. (2000), p. 179. Nakasone quoted in 1996.
85. Ito, op. cit., pp. 260–263; and Kunio, op. cit. (*Bungei Shunju*), pp. 125–130.
86. Ibid. (Kunio), pp. 125–130.
87. Ibid., pp. 125–130.
88. Ibid., pp. 125–130.
89. For Kono's political career, see Curtis, op. cit., pp. 66–67; and Hrebenar, pp. 6, 38, and 160.

Chapter 8   The DPJ's Policy and Yukio's Leadership

1. Pierre Salmon, "Unpopular Politics and the Theory of Representative Democracy," in Albert Breton, Gianluigi Galeotti, Pierre Salmon, and Ronald Wintrobe, eds., *Preferences and Democracy* (Boston, Mass.: Kluwer Academic Publishers, 1993), pp. 20–23.
2. Ibid., pp. 20–23.
3. *"Minshuto no kihon seisaku"* (The DPJ's basic policy), *Chunichi Shimbun*, September 23, 1996 and *"Minshu wa kenzen yato tsuranuku"* (The DPJ will adhere to wholesome opposition), *Yomiuri Shimbun*, March 9, 1997.
4. Hatoyama Yukio and Kan Naoto, *Minekiron* (Discourse on civil interest), Tokyo: PHP Kenkyujo, 1997, pp. 43–54 and 167–178 and Ito Hirotoshi, *Hatoyama ichizoku* (Hatoyama dynasty), Tokyo: Pipurusha, 1996, pp. 30–33.
5. Ibid. (Ito), pp. 30–33.
6. *"Minshuto ga hatsu no totaikai"* (The DPJ convenes its first party congress), *Yomiuri Shimbun*, March 23, 1997.
7. *"Minshu 'kenzen yato' nao ryudoteki"* (The DPJ's "wholesome opposition" still fluid), *Yomiuri Shimbun*, March 11, 1997.
8. Igarashi Fumihiko, *Kore ga Minshuto da!: Jiritsu to kyosei no shimin chushin-gata shakai e* (This is the DPJ! Toward a citizen-centered society based on self-reliance and coexistence), Tokyo: Taiyo Kikaku Shuppan, 1996, pp. 168–171; and Warashina Mitsuharu, *Minshu riberaru no seiken koso: Nijuisseiki no tobira o hiraku Minshuto* (Democratic liberal ideas on government: The DPJ opens the door of the twenty-first century), Tokyo: Nihon Hyoronsha, 1997, pp. 177–190.
9. *"'Churyu naki ampo' morikomanu hoshin"* ("The U.S.–Japan Security Treaty without stationing" will not be provided), *Yomiuri Shimbun*, August 6, 1997.
10. *"Yureru Minshu no Ampo seisaku"* (Swaying DPJ's security policy), *Yomiuri Shimbun*, September 4, 1997.
11. Kobayashi Kichiya, *Nijuisseiki rida koho no shingan* (Assessment of potential leaders in the twenty-first century), Tokyo, *Yomiuri Shimbunsha*, 1996, pp. 113–114 and Hatoyama Kunio, *"Ani Yukio yo, ogoru nakare"* (My brother Yukio, do not be proud), *Bungei Shunju*, August 2000, p. 130.
12. *"Tokusoho kaisei, 58% sansei"* (58% in favor of the revision of the special measures law), *Yomiuri Shimbun*, March 24, 1997.
13. *"Tokusoho kaisei, Minshuto sansei e"* (The DPJ decided to vote for the revision of the special measures law), *Yomiuri Shimbun*, April 8, 1997.
14. *"Shamin no taio ni gimon"* (A question on the SDPJ's response), *Yomiuri Shimbun*, April 2, 1997.
15. *"Meiso no Minshuto"* (Straying DPJ), *Yomiuri Shimbun*, May 9, 1997.
16. Ibid.
17. *"Kokki · kokka ni kejime ga tsuita"* (The national flag and anthem issue saw a solution), *Yomiuri Shimbun*, August 10, 1999; *"Kokki·kokka hoan, Kokkai tsuka"* (The national flag and anthem bill passes the Diet), *Asahi Shimbun*, August 10, 1999; *"Kokki · kokka hoseika"* (The legislation of the national flag and anthem), *Chunichi Shimbun*, August 10, 1999.

18. Ibid. (*Chunichi Shimbun*).
19. Ibid. and " '*Kimigayo' gengakufu o hakken*" ("*Kimigayo*"'s original score found), *Chunichi Shimbun*, August 17, 1999. Translation of the text by the author.
20. " '*Kimigayo' shusho ga shinkenkai*" (Prime minister issued a new interpretation of "*Kimigayo*"), *Yomiuri Shimbun*, June 30, 1999.
21. Ibid.
22. *Chunichi Shimbun*, op. cit. (August 10, 1999).
23. Ibid.
24. "*Kokki · kokka hoan, 29 nichi shingi iri*" (Deliberations on the national flag and anthem bill begins on the 29th), *Yomiuri Shimbun*, June 25, 1999.
25. "*Honsha zenkoku seron chosa*" (*Yomiuri* national polls), *Yomiuri Shimbun*, April 9, 1999 and "*Kokki · kokka seron chosa*" (Polls on the national flag and anthem), *Chunichi Shimbun*, August 3, 1999.
26. Ibid. (*Yomiuri Shimbun* and *Chunichi Shimbun*).
27. *Yomiuri Shimbun*, June 25, 1999, op. cit.
28. "*Nonaka-shi, tsugi no te wa*" (What is Mr. Nonaka's next strategy?), *Yomiuri Shimbun*, July 6, 1999 and Matsumoto Kenichi, "*Sennenki ni omou*" (A thought on the millennium), *Chunichi Shimbun*, August 15, 1999.
29. *Yomiuri Shimbun*, June 25, 1999, op. cit.
30. "*Kokki · kokka de yureta Minshu*" (The DPJ swayed by the national flag and anthem bill), *Yomiuri Shimbun*, July 17, 1999.
31. Ibid. and "*Minshu daihyo Kokki · kokka hoseika yonin*" (DPJ president approves the legislation of the national flag and anthem), *Yomiuri Shimbun*, June 26, 1999.
32. "*Kokki · kokka hoan, Shuin o tsuka*" (The HR passed the national flag and anthem bill), *Yomiuri Shimbun*, July 23, 1999 and "*Minshu 'yoriai jotai' rotei*" (The DPJ exposed the "hodge podge household"), *Yomiuri Shimbun*, July 23, 1999.
33. "*Kokki · kokkaho seiritsu*" (The national flag and anthem law established), *Yomiuri Shimbun*, August 10, 1999.
34. "*Kimigayo hatsu no 'kokka seisho'*" (*Kimigayo* first "sung as the national anthem"), *Yomiuri Shimbun*, August 17, 1999 and "*Gojuyonen me no 'Kimigayo'*" ("*Kimigayo*" at the fifty-fourth [memorial]), *Chunichi Shimbun*, October 4, 1999.
35. "*Kensho: Shinrenritsu eno sujimichi*" (Assessment: logic of the new coalition), *Yomiuri Shimbun*, October 6, 1999 and "*Mini fuzai no seiken anteisaku*" (The strategy to stabilize power in the absence of public support), *Chunichi Shimbun*, October 7, 1999.
36. "*Hatoyama-shi hatsugen, Komei hanpatsu*" (CGP objects to Mr. Hatoyama's statement), *Yomiuri Shimbun*, October 9, 1999. The exchange rate was calculated at US\$1 = ¥107.56 as of October 9, 1999.
37. "*Kempo o kangaeru: NichiDoku soi*" (Thinking about the constitution: Comparisons between Japan and Germany), *Yomiuri Shimbun*, May 2, 2000. For Japan's participation in UNPKOs, see Mayumi Itoh, *Globalization of Japan: Japanese Sakoku Mentality and U.S. Efforts to Open Japan*, New York: St. Martin's Press, 1998.

38. Hatoyama Yukio, "*Jieitai o guntai to mitomeyo*" ([The constitution] should acknowledge the SDFs as armed forces), *Bungei Shunju*, October 1999, pp. 262–273.

39. Ibid., pp. 264–267; "*Hatoyama, 'Kaiken koso jimin bunretsu eno kusabi to naru!'*" (Hatoyama argues that "his plans for constitutional revisions will be a wedge to break up the LDP"), *Shukan Posuto*, January 28, 2000, pp. 30–35; and "*Hatoyama-shi no 'shudanteki jieiken' hatsugen*" (Mr. Hatoyama's statement on the "right to collective self-defense"), *Chunichi Shimbun*, October 17, 2000.

40. Nakasone Yasuhiro, "*Waga kaikenron*" (My discourse on constitutional revisions), *Shokun*, April 2000, pp. 55–63 and Nakasone Yasuhiro, "*Kaiken junen de dekiru*" (The constitution can be revised in ten years), *Chunichi Shimbun*, August 8, 2001.

41. Ozawa Ichiro, *Nihon kaizo keikaku* (Blueprint for a new Japan), Tokyo: Kodansha, 1993, pp. 102–114 and Ozawa Ichiro, "*Nihonkoku kempo kaisei shian*" (A draft proposal for revisions of the Japanese constitution), *Bungei Shunju*, September 1999, pp. 94–100.

42. Nakasone, op. cit., pp. 58–59 and 63.

43. Yukio, op. cit., p. 263.

44. "*Komei 'yoto shiko' senmei ni*" (The CGP further converges with the "ruling [LDP]"), *Chunichi Shimbun*, November 4, 2000.

45. Morikawa Yoshihiko, "*Minshuto yo 'Jimin taishitsu kire'*" (The DPJ should break 'LDP nature'), *AERA*, Vol. 660, September 4, 2000, pp. 21–22; and Kan Naoto, Interview with Tawara Soichiro, *Sunday Project*, *TV Asahi*, a major Japanese broadcasting network, September 10, 2000.

46. "*Jieitai yonin: 'utenraku eno ippo'*" ([JCP] accepts the SDF: "The first step toward falling for the right"), *Chunichi Shimbun*, October 18, 2000.

47. "*Zenkoku seron chosa: Kempo ni kansuru ishiki*" (National opinion polls on the constitution), *Yomiuri Shimbun*, April 15, 2000.

48. "*Sekinin seito' e dappi mezasu*" ([Yukio] aims for changing the DPJ into a "responsible party"), *Chunichi Shimbun*, November 7, 2000.

49. Igarashi, op. cit., pp. 61–64.

50. Itagaki Eiken, *Hatoyama Yukio de Nihon wa do kawaru: Honto ni kokumin no tame no seiji o jitsugen dekirunoka* (How can Hatoyama Yukio change Japan: Can he really realize politics for the people?), Tokyo: Keizaikai, 1996, pp. 103–105.

51. Hatoyama Yukio, "*Waga riberaru: Yuai kakumei*" (My liberalism: Revolution for fraternity), *Ronza*, June 1996, pp. 42–51.

52. Ibid., pp. 42–51.

53. Igarashi, op. cit., pp. 80 and 93–94.

54. Ibid.

55. Itagaki, op. cit., p. 100 and Kobayashi, op. cit. (1996), pp. 106–107 (Nakasone quoted).

56. Ibid. (Kobayashi), pp. 112–113 and Kobayashi Kichiya, *Ichiryu no rida, niryu no bosu* (First-rate leaders and second-rate bosses), Tokyo: Futabasha, 2000, pp. 184–193.

57. Ito, op. cit., p. 171.

58. Ibid., pp. 19–23 and 274.
59. Ibid. (Nakasone quoted).
60. Ibid., p. 33; *"Kan · Hatoyama no seiji"* (Politics of Kan and Hatoyama), *Yomiuri Shimbun*, October 15, 1997 and *"Obuchi-san shidoryoku ni gimonfu"* (Mr. Obuchi's leadership questioned), *Yomiuri Shimbun*, February 5, 1999.
61. Kobayashi, op. cit. (1996), pp. 106–107.
62. Hatoyama Yukio, *"Hatoyama Yukio wa tsukaeruka"* (Can Hatoyama Yukio be useful?), *Ronza*, March 2001, pp. 44–45 and Kobayashi, op. cit. (2000), pp. 188–189.
63. Kobayashi, op. cit. (1996), pp. 102–108.
64. Itagaki, op. cit., pp. 134–136 (Yukio quoted).
65. Ito, op. cit., pp. 30, 259, and 265.
66. *"Hatoyama Minshu daihyo jinin"* (DPJ President Hatoyama resigns), *Chunichi Shimbun*, December 2, 2002 and *"Minshu daihyo ni Kan-shi senshutsu"* (Kan was elected as DPJ president), *Yomiuri Shimbun*, December 11, 2002.

Chapter 9   Conclusion

1. Ito Hirotoshi, *Hatoyama ichizoku* (Hatoyama Dynasty), Tokyo: Pipurusha, 1996, pp. 3–5 and Kobayashi Kichiya, *Ichiryu no rida, niryu no bosu* (First-rate leaders and second-rate bosses), Tokyo: Futabasha, 2000, pp. 177–179.
2. Ibid. (Ito), pp. 223–224.
3. Ibid., pp. 223–224.
4. Kobayashi Kichiya, *Nijuisseiki rida koho no shingan* (Assessment of potential leaders in the twenty-first century), Tokyo: Yomiuri Shimbunsha, 1996, pp. 166–177, 181–183, and 190–193.
5. Itagaki Eiken, *Hatoyama Yukio de Nihon wa do kawaru: Honto ni kokumin no tame no seiji o jitsugen dekirunoka* (How can Hatoyama Yukio change Japan: Can he really realize politics for the people?), Tokyo: Keizaikai, 1996, p. 16 and *"Kokkai no shin seiryoku bunya"* (Diet's new balance of power), *Asahi Shimbun*, July 31, 2001.
6. *"Jugatsu no honsha seron chosa"* ([*Asahi Shimbun*'s] Opinion poll of October [2001]), *Asahi Shimbun*, October 16, 2001.
7. *"Jiji Tsushinsha rokkugatsu seron chosa"* (Jiji Tsushinsha's June opinion poll), *Chunichi Shimbun*, June 16, 2002.
8. Koizumi Masaya, *"Ani' Koizumi Junichiro no sugao"* ("My elder brother" Koizumi Junichiro's real face), *Shincho 45*, June 2001, pp. 42–47; and Anzai Kota, *"'Sori' o unda Koizumi-ke sandai"* (Three generations of the Koizumi family that produced "prime minister"), *Shincho 45*, June 2001, pp. 48–53.
9. Kobayashi, op. cit. (1996), pp. 15–16; and Ozawa Ichiro, *Nihon kaizo keikaku* (Blueprint for a new Japan), Tokyo: Kodansha, 1993, pp. 26–32.
10. *"Nijuisseiki Nihon no rida?"* (Who should be the Japanese leader in the twenty-first century?), *Chunichi Shimbun*, August 6, 2000 and *"Mori naikaku shijiritsu seron chosa kekka"* (Results of the poll on Mori cabinet support rates), *Chunichi Shimbun*, November 2, 2000.
11. Yukio, quoted in Ito, op. cit., p. 248.

BIBLIOGRAPHY

Bibliographical information is given under the following headings in alphabetical order:
  I. Theory on political leadership (A. Books and B. Book chapters).
  II. The Works on the Hatoyama Dynasty and the DPJ (A. Books in English, B. Books in Japanese, C. Articles and book chapters in English, and D. Articles in Japanese).
  III. The works on Japanese politics (A. Books in English, B. Books in Japanese, and C. Articles in English).
  IV. Magazines and newspapers.

I. Theory on Political Leadership

A. Books

Blondel, Jean. *World Leaders.* London: Sage Publications, 1980.
———. *Political Leadership: Towards a General Analysis.* London: Sage Publications, 1987.
Breton, Albert, Galeotti, Gianluigi, Salmon, Pierre, and Wintrobe, Ronald, eds., *Preferences and Democracy.* Boston, Mass.: Kluwer Academic Publishers, 1993.
Burns, James MacGregor. *Leadership.* New York: Harper & Row, 1978.
Edinger, Lewis, J., ed. *Political Leadership in Industrialized Societies: Studies in Comparative Analysis.* New York: John Wiley & Sons, 1967.
Elgie, Robert. *Political Leadership in Liberal Democracies.* New York: St. Martin's Press, 1995.
Galbraith, John Kenneth. *The Anatomy of Power.* Boston, Mass.: Houghton Mifflin, 1983.
Gardner, John. *On Leadership.* New York: The Free Press, 1990.
Gibbs, C. A., ed. *Leadership: Selected Readings.* Harmondsworth, England: Penguin Books, 1969.
Kellerman, Barbara, ed. *Political Leadership: A Source Book.* Pittsburgh, Pa.: University of Pittsburgh Press, 1984.
Magstadt, Thomas M. and Schotten, Peter M. *Understanding Politics: Ideas Institutions, and Issues.* 4th ed., New York: St. Martin's Press, 1996.
Maslow, Abraham H. *Motivation and Personality.* New York: Harper Brothers, 1954.

Mughan, Anthony and Patterson, Samuel C., eds., *Political Leadership in Democratic Societies*. Chicago: Nelson-Hall, 1992.

Paige, Glenn D. *The Scientific Study of Political Leadership*. New York: The Free Press, 1977.

Sheffer, Gabriel, ed. *Innovative Leadership in International Politics*. Albany: State University of New York Press, 1993.

Stern, Geoffrey. *Leaders and Leadership*. Oxford: LSE and the BBC, 1993.

Tamadonfar, Mehran. *The Islamic Polity and Political Leadership*. Boulder, Colo.: Westview Press, 1989.

Tucker, Robert. *Politics as Leadership*. Columbia, Miss.: University of Missouri Press, 1981.

——. *Political Culture and Leadership in Soviet Russia: From Lenin to Gorbachev*. New York: W. W. Norton, 1987.

B. Book Chapters

Gibbs, C. A. "The Principles and Traits of Leadership." In Gibbs, ed., *Leadership: Selected Readings*. Harmondsworth, England: Penguin Books, 1969, pp. 205–222.

Lasswell, Harold D. "Political Systems, Styles and Personalities." In Robert Elgie, *Political Leadership in Liberal Democracies*. New York: St. Martin's Press, 1995, pp. 316–347.

Salmon, Pierre. "Unpopular Politics and the Theory of Representative Democracy." In Albert Breton, Gianluigi Galeotti, Pierre Salmon, and Ronald Wintrobe, eds., *Preferences and Democracy*. Boston, Mass.: Kluwer Academic Publishers, 1993, pp. 13–39.

Stogdill, R. M. "Personal Factors Associated with Leadership: A Survey of the Literature." In Gibbs, ed., *Leadership: Selected Readings*. Harmondsworth, England: Penguin Books, 1969, pp. 91–133.

II. The Works on the Hatoyama Dynasty and the DPJ

A. Books in English

Baerwald, Hans H. *The Purge of Japanese Leaders Under the Occupation*. University of California Publications in Political Science, Vol. VIII, Berkeley, Calif.: University of California Press, 1959.

Coudenhove-Kalergi, Richard Nicholas. *The Totalitarian State Against Man*. Translation by Sir Andrew McFadyean, Glarus, Switzerland, Paneuropa Editions Ltd., 1938.

Dower, John W. *Empire and Aftermath: Yoshida Shigeru and the Japanese Experience, 1878–1954*. Cambridge, Mass.: Council on East Asian Studies, Harvard University, 1979.

——. *Japan in War and Peace: Selected Essays*. New York: New Press, 1993.

——. *Embracing Defeat: Japan in the Wake of World War II*. New York: W. W. Norton, 1999.

Gayn, Mark. *Japan Diary*. New York: William Sloane, 1948.

Hellmann, Donald C. *Japanese Foreign Policy and Domestic Politics: The Peace Agreement with the Soviet Union.* Berkeley, Calif.: University of California Press, 1969.

Ike, Nobutaka, *Japanese Politics: An Introductory Survey.* New York: Knopf, 1957.

Kataoka, Testuya. *The Price of a Constitution: The Origin of Japan's Postwar Politics.* New York: Crane Russak, 1991.

Masumi Junnosuke. *Postwar Politics in Japan, 1945–1955.* Berkeley, Calif.: Institute of East Asian Studies, University of California, 1985.

Sebald, William. *With MacArthur in Japan.* New York: Norton, 1965.

Wildes, Harry Emerson. *Typhoon in Tokyo: The Occupation and Its Aftermath.* New York: Macmillan, 1954.

Willoughby, Charles A. and Chamberlain, John. *MacArthur 1941–1951.* New York: McGraw-Hill, 1954.

Yoshida, Shigeru. *The Yoshida Memoirs: The Story of Japan in Crisis* (translation). London: Heinemann, 1961.

B. Books in Japanese

Coudenhove-Kalergi, Richard Nicholas. *Jiyu to Jinsei* (Liberty and Life). Translation by Hatoyama Ichiro, Tokyo: Kangensha, 1953.

———. *Bi no kuni: Nihon eno kikyo* (The country of beauty: Homecoming to Japan). Translation by Kajima Morinosuke, Tokyo: Kajima Kenkyujo Shuppan, 1968.

Gayn, Mark. *Nippon Nikki* (Japan Diary). Translation by Imoto Takeo, Tokyo: Chikuma Shobo, 1963.

Hanai Hitoshi. *Sengo Nihon o kizuita saishotachi: From Yoshida Shigeru to Tanaka Kakuei* (Prime ministers that built postwar Japan: From Yoshida Shigeru to Tanaka Kakuei). Tokyo: *Nesuko,* 1996.

Hatoyama Haruko. *Hatoyama no issho* (A life of Hatoyama [Kazuo]). Tokyo: *Jikashuppan* (self-publication), 1929.

———. *Jijoden* (Autobiography). Tokyo: Ozorasha, *fukkoku-ban* (reproduction), 1990.

Hatoyama Ichiro. *Gaiyu nikki sekai no kao* (Journal of trip abroad: Face of the world), Tokyo: Chuokoronsha, 1938.

———. *Watashi no jijoden* (Autobiography). Tokyo: Kaizosha, 1951.

———. *Aru daigishi no seikatsu to iken* (Life and opinions of a HR member). Tokyo: Tokyo Shuppan, 1952.

———. *Watashi no shinjo* (My beliefs). Tokyo: Tokyo Bunko, 1952.

———. *Hatoyama Ichiro kaikoroku* (Memoirs of Hatoyama Ichiro), Tokyo: Bungei Shunjusha, 1957.

———. *Wakaki chi no kiyoku moete* (Young blood, burning purely). Kawate Shoichiro, ed., Tokyo: Kodansha, 1996.

———. *Hatoyama Ichiro·Kaoru nikki* (Diary of Hatoyama Ichiro and Kaoru). Ito Takashi and Suetake Yoshiya, eds., Tokyo: Chuokoron Shinsha, Vol. 1, 1999.

——— et al. *Shinseikatsu ni kansuru juni no iken* (Twelve opinions concerning new life). Tokyo: Nihon Kyubunsha, 1955.

Hatoyama Kunio and Yamai Kazunori. *Gurupu homu nyumon* (Introduction to group home). Tokyo: Riyonsha, 1999.

Hatoyama Yukio and Kan Naoto. *Minekiron* (Discourse on civil interest). Tokyo: PHP Kenkyujo, 1997.

Hirano Minoru. *Gaiko kisha nikki: Hatoyama gaiko no ichinen* (Diary of a diplomatic reporter: One year of the Hatoyama diplomacy). Tokyo: Gyosei Tsushinsha, 1980.

Igarashi Fumihiko. *Kore ga Minshuto da!: Jiritsu to kyosei no shimin chushin-gata shakai e* (This is the DPJ! Toward a citizen-centered society based on self-reliance and coexistence). Tokyo: Taiyo Kikaku Shuppan, 1996.

Isa Hideo. *Ozaki Yukio-den* (Biography of Ozaki Yukio). Tokyo: Kankokai, 1951.

Itagaki Eiken. *Hatoyama Yukio de Nihon wa do kawaru: Honto ni kokumin no tame no seiji o jitsugen dekirunoka* (How can Hatoyama Yukio change Japan: Can he really realize politics for the people?). Tokyo: Keizaikai, 1996.

Ito Hirotoshi. *Hatoyama ichizoku* (Hatoyama dynasty). Tokyo: Pipurusha, 1996.

Kataoka Tetsuya. *Nippon eikyu senryo* (Permanent occupation of Japan). Tokyo: Kodansha, 1999.

Kimura Tsuyoshi. *Kudenhofu Mitsuko-den* (Biography of Coudenhove Mitsuko). Tokyo: Kajima Shuppankai, 1971.

Kobayashi Kichiya. *Nijuisseiki rida koho no shingan* (Assessment of potential leaders in the twenty-first century). Tokyo: Yomiuri Shimbunsha, 1996.

———. *Ichiryu no rida, niryu no bosu* (First-rate leaders and second-rate bosses). Tokyo: Futabasha, 2000.

Kojima Noboru. *Kowa joyaku: Sengo Nichibei kankei no kiten* (The [San Francisco] Peace Treaty: The origin of postwar U.S.–Japan relations). Tokyo: Chuokoronsha, Vol. 1, 1997.

Kono Ichiro. *Imadakara hanaso* (Now I can talk). Tokyo: Shunyodo, 1958.

Masuda Hiroshi. *Seijika tsuiho* (Purge of politicians). Tokyo: Chuokoron Shinsha, 2001.

Matsumoto Seichio. *Shikan: Saishoron* (Historical view: Discourse on prime ministers). Tokyo: Bungei Shunjusha, 1980.

Matsumoto Shunichi. *Mosukuwa ni kakeru niji: Nisso kokko kaifuku hiwa* (Rainbow across Moscow: Secret story of the resumption of Japan–Soviet diplomatic relations). Tokyo: Asahi Shimbunsha, 1960.

Mikikai, ed. *Miki Bukichi* (Biography of Miki Bukichi). Tokyo: Mikikai, 1958.

Miyazaki Yoshimasa. *Hatoyama Ichiro* (Hatoyama Ichiro). Tokyo: Jiji Tsushinsha, 1985.

Ono Bamboku. *Ono Bamboku kaikoroku* (Memoirs of Ono Bamboku). Tokyo: Kobundo, 1962.

Sato Tomoyasu. *Keibatsu* (Clans by marriage). Tokyo: Tachikaze Shobo, 1994.

Suzuki Kisaburo Denki Hensankai, ed. *Suzuki Kisaburo* (Biography of Suzuki Kisaburo). Tokyo: Suzuki Kisaburo Denki Hensankai, 1955.

Tawara Kotaro. *Nihon no seijika: Oya to ko no shozo* (Japanese politicians: Portraits of parents and offspring). Tokyo: Chuokoronsha, 1997.

Toyoda Jo. *Hatoyama Ichiro: Eisai no kakei* (Ichiro Hatoyama: The genealogy of the elite). Tokyo: Kodansha, 1989.

Yamada Eizo. *Seiden Sato Eisaku* (Orthodox biography of Sato Eisaku). Tokyo: Shinchosha, 1988.

Yoshida Naoya. *Cho no maiso: Kudenhofu Mitsuko-den* (Burial of a butterfly: Biography of Coudenhove Mitsuko), Tokyo: Iwanami Shoten, 1997.

Warashina Mitsuharu. *Minshu riberaru no seiken koso: Nijuisseiki no tobira o hiraku Minshuto* (Democratic liberal ideas on government: The DPJ opens the door of the twenty-first century). Tokyo: Nihon Hyoronsha, 1997.

C. Articles and Book Chapters in English

Hans H. Baerwald. "Postwar Japan—A Reminiscence." Japan Policy Research Institute (JPRI) Occasional Paper, No. 27 (July 2002), pp. 1–7.

Ito, Takashi. "Shigemitsu Mamoru and the 1955 System." In Tetsuya Kataoka ed., *Creating Single-Party Democracy: Japan's Postwar Political System.* Stanford, Calif.: Hoover Institution Press, 1992, pp. 110–118.

Itoh, Mayumi. "Views of Soviet Politics and New Thinking." In Gilbert Rozman, ed., *Japan's Response to the Gorbachev Era, 1985–1991: A Rising Superpower Views a Declining One.* Princeton, N.J.: Princeton University Press, 1992, pp. 224–242.

D. Articles in Japanese

Hatoyama Ichiro. *"Jiyushugisha no techo"* (A note of a liberalist). *Chuokoron* (January 1936), pp. 129–139.

——. *"Gikai seiji o mamoru"* (To defend parliamentary politics). *Kaizo* (December 1936), pp. 267–274.

Hatoyama Kunio. *"Ikari no 'zetsuen sengen': Hatoyama Kunio gekihaku"* (Angry ultimatum: Hatoyama Kunio's fiery talk). *Shukan Gendai* (December 18, 1999), pp. 56–57.

——. *"Ani yo, hitori de gyudonya e ike!"* ("Brother, go to a fast-food restaurant alone"). *Shukan Asahi* (January 21, 2000), pp. 33–34.

——. *"Hatoyama-ke yondai no 'suparuta to honin': ani 'Hatoyama Yukio' o kataru"* ("Sparta and *laissez faire*" of the four generations of the Hatoyama family: Talking about elder brother "Hatoyama Yukio"). *Shincho 45* (July 2000), pp. 72–76.

——. *"Ani Yukio yo, ogorunakare"* (My brother Yukio, do not be proud). *Bungei Shunju* (August 2000), pp. 124–130.

Hatoyama Yukio. *"Waga riberaru yuai kakumei"* (My liberal fraternity revolution). *Ronza* (June 1996), pp. 42–51.

——. *"Jieitai o guntai to mitomeyo"* ([The constitution] should acknowledge the SDFs as armed forces). *Bungei Shunju* (October 1999), pp. 262–273.

——. *"Hatoyama Yukio wa tsukaeruka"* (Can Hatoyama Yukio be useful?). *Ronza* (March 2001), pp. 44–59.

—— and Shinohara Fumiya. *"Shinshinto no wadachi wa fumanai"* ([DPJ] will not repeat the same mistake of the NFP). *Voice* (March 2000), pp. 204–213.

Kishi Nobuhito. *"Kore ga Minshuto 'Nihon-ban yangu repoto' da"* (This is DPJ's "Japanese young report"). *Chuokoron* (July 2000), pp. 100–107.

Nakasone Yasuhiro. *"Waga kaikenron"* (My discourse on constitutional revisions). *Shokun* (April 2000), pp. 54–63.

Ozawa Ichiro. *"Nihonkoku kempo kaisei shian"* (A draft proposal for revisions of the Japanese constitution). *Bungei Shunju* (September 1999), pp. 94–100.

Tomimori Eiji. "*Sugao no saisho: Hatoyama Ichiro*" (Real face of the Prime Minister: Hatoyama Ichiro). *Asahi Chronicle Weekly 20th Century* (1999), pp. 32–33.
Yamaura Kanichi. "*Hatoyama tsuiho no shukunsha*" ([M]VP of Hatoyama's purge). *Bungei Shunju* (September 1950), pp. 112–117.

III. The Works on the Japanese Politics

A. Books in English
Akaha, Tsuneo and Langdon, Frank L., eds. *Japan in the Posthegemonic World.* Boulder, Colo.: Rienner, 1993.
Baerwald, Hans H. *Party Politics in Japan.* Boston: Allen & Urwin, 1986.
Bix, Herbert P. *Hirohito and the Making of Modern Japan.* New York: HarperCollins, 2000.
Borthwick, Mark. *Pacific Century: The Emergence of Modern Pacific Asia,* Boulder, Colo.: Westview, 1992.
Calder, Kent, E. *Crisis and Compensation: Public and Political Stability in Japan.* Princeton, N.J.: Princeton University Press, 1988.
———. *Strategic Capitalism: Private Business and Public Purpose in Japan's Industrial Finance.* Princeton, N.J.: Princeton University Press, 1993.
———. *Pacific Defense: Arms, Energy, and America's Future in Asia.* New York: William Morrow and Co., 1996.
Campbell, John Creighton. *How Policies Change: The Japanese Government and the Aging Society.* Princeton, N.J.: Princeton University Press, 1990.
Curtis, Gerald L. *The Japanese Way of Politics.* New York: Columbia University Press, 1988.
———. *The Logic of Japanese Politics: Leaders, Institutions, and the Limits of Change,* New York: Columbia University Press, 1999.
Davis, Glenn and Roberts, John G. *An Occupation Without Troops: Wall Street's Half-Century Domination of Japanese Politics.* Tokyo: Yenbooks, 1996.
Fairbank, John K., Reischauer, Edwin O., and Craig, Albert M. *East Asia: Tradition and Transformation,* Boston, Mass.: Houghton Mifflin, revised ed., 1989.
Flanagan, Scott C. *The Japanese Voter.* New Haven: Yale University Press, 1991.
Fraser, Andrew, Mason, R. H. P., and Mitchell, Philip. *Japan's Early Parliaments, 1890–1905: Structure, Issues and Trends.* New York: Routledge, 1995.
Fukui, Haruhiro. *Party in Power: The Japanese Liberal Democrats and Policy Making.* Berkeley: University of California Press, 1970.
Green, Michael J. *Japan's Reluctant Realism: Foreign Policy Challenges in an Era of Uncertain Power,* New York: Palgrave Press, 2001.
Grimes, William W. *Unmaking the Japanese Miracle: Macroeconomic Politics, 1985–2000.* Ithaca, N.Y.: Cornell University Press, 2001.
Hane, Mikiso. *Eastern Phoenix: Japan Since 1945.* Boulder, Colo.: Westview Press, 1996.
Herzog, Peter J. *Japan's Pseudo-Democracy.* New York: New York University Press, 1993.
Hrebenar, Ronald J. *The Japanese Party System: From One-Party Rule to Coalition Government.* Boulder, Colo.: Westview Press, 1986.

———. *Japan's New Party System*. Boulder, Colo.: Westview Press, 2000.

Hunter, Janet. *The Emergence of Modern Japan: An Introductory History Since 1853*. New York: Longman, 1989.

Ike, Nobutaka. *Japanese Politics: An Introductory Survey*. New York: Knopf, 1957.

Inoguchi, Takashi. *Global Change: A Japanese Perspective*. New York: Palgrave Press, 2001.

Itoh, Mayumi. *Globalization of Japan: Japanese Sakoku Mentality and U.S. Efforts to Open Japan*. New York: St. Martin's Press, 1998.

Jain, Purnendra and Inoguchi Takashi, eds. *Japanese Politics Today: Beyond Karaoke Democracy?* New York: St. Martin's Press, 1997.

Johnson, Chalmers A. *An Instance of Treason: Ozaki Hotsumi and the Sorge Spy Ring*, Stanford, Calif.: Stanford University Press, 1964.

———. *Conspiracy at Matsukawa*. Berkeley, Calif.: University of California Press, 1972.

———. *MITI and the Japanese Economic Miracle: The Growth of Industrial Policy, 1925–1975*. Stanford, Calif.: Stanford University Press, 1982.

———. *Japan: Who Governs: The Rise of the Developmental State*. New York: W. W. Norton, 1995.

Kataoka, Testuya, ed. *Creating Single-Party Democracy: Japan's Postwar Political System*. Stanford, Calif.: Hoover Institution Press, 1992.

Kato, Junko. *The Problem of Bureaucratic Rationality*. Princeton, N.J.: Princeton University Press, 1994.

Kennan, George F. *Memoirs 1925–1950*. Boston, Mass.: Little, Brown, 1967.

Lincoln, Edward, J. *Japan's Unequal Trade*. Washington, D.C.: Brookings Institution Press, 1990.

———. *Troubled Times: U.S.–Japan Trade Relations in the 1990s*. Washington, D.C.: Brookings Institution Press, 1999.

———. *Arthritic Japan: The Slow Pace of Economic Reform*. Washington, D.C.: Brookings Institution Press, 2001.

Masumi, Junnosuke. *Contemporary Politics in Japan* (translation). Berkeley, Calif.: University of California Press, 1995.

Mochizuki, Mike M., ed. *Toward a True Alliance: Restructuring U.S.–Japan Relations*. Washington, D.C.: Brookings Institution Press, 1997.

Muramatsu, Michio. *Local Power in the Japanese State*. Berkeley, Calif.: University of California Press, 1997.

Nakano, Minoru. *The Policy-Making Process in Contemporary Japan*. New York: St. Martin's Press, 1997.

Otake, Hideo. *Power Shuffles and Policy Processes: Coalition Government in Japan in the 1990s*. New York: Japan Center for International Exchange, 2000.

Pempel, T. J. *Patterns of Japanese Policymaking: Experiences from Higher Education*. Boulder, Colo.: Westview Press, 1978.

———. *Policy and Politics in Japan: Creative Conservatism*. Philadelphia, Pa.: Temple University Press, 1980.

———, ed. *Uncommon Democracies: The One-Party Dominant Regimes*. Ithaca, N.Y.: Cornell University Press, 1990.

Pyle, Kenneth B. *The Japanese Question: Power and Purpose in a New Era*. Lanham, Md.: AEI Press, 1992.

Reed, Steven R. *Making Common Sense of Japan.* Pittsburgh, Pa.: University of Pittsburgh Press, 1993.

Reischauer, Edwin O. *The Japanese Today: Change and Continuity.* Cambridge, Mass.: Harvard University Press, 1988.

Richardson, Bradley M. and Flanagan, Scott C. *Politics in Japan.* Boston: Little, Brown, 1984.

Rozman, Gilbert. *Japan's Response to the Gorbachev Era, 1985–1991: A Rising Super-power Views a Declining One.* Princeton, N.J.: Princeton University Press, 1992.

———, ed. *Japan and Russia: The Tortuous Path to Normalization, 1949–1999.* New York: St. Martin's Press, 2000.

Samuels, Richard J. *"Rich Nation Strong Army": National Security and the Technological Transformation of Japan.* Ithaca, N.Y.: Cornell University Press, 1994.

Scalapino, Robert A. *Democracy and the Party Movement in Prewar Japan.* Berkeley, Calif.: University of California Press, 1953.

Schwartz, Frank J. *Advice and Consent: The Politics of Consultation in Japan.* Cambridge, U.K.: Cambridge University Press, 1998.

Thayer, Nathaniel, B. *How the Conservatives Rule Japan.* Princeton, N.J.: Princeton University Press, 1969.

Vogel, Ezra F. *Japan As Number One: Lessons for America.* Cambridge, Mass.: Harvard University Press, 1979.

Vogel, Steven K. *Free Markets, More Rules: Regulatory Reform in Advanced Industrial Countries.* Ithaca, N.Y.: Cornell University Press, 1996.

Yasutomo, Dennis T. *The New Multilateralism in Japan's Foreign Policy.* New York: St. Martin's Press, 1995.

Zagoria, Donald S., ed. *Soviet Policy in East Asia.* New Haven: Yale University Press, 1982.

B. Books in Japanese

Inoue Mitsusada, Kasahara Kazuo, and Kodama Kota. *Nihonshi* (Japanese history). Tokyo: Yamakawa Shuppansha, 1972.

Maeo Toru and Masuda Toshio. *Mezameyo Nihon* (Wake up Japan). Tokyo: Sanra Shuppan, 2000.

Ishikawa Masumi, *Sengo seijishi* (Postwar political history). Tokyo: Iwanami Shoten, 1995.

Nakasone Yasuhiro. *Nijuisseiki Nihon no kokka senryaku* (Japan's national strat-egy for the twenty-first century). Tokyo: PHP Kenkujo, 2000.

Ozawa Ichiro. *Nihon kaizo keikaku* (Blueprint for a new Japan). Tokyo: Kodansha, 1993.

C. Articles in English

Calder, Kent E. "Japanese Foreign Economic Policy Formation: Explaining the Reactive State." *World Politics,* Vol. 40, No. 4 (July 1988), pp. 517–541.

Johnson, Chalmers A. "Japanese 'Capitalism' Revisited." JPRI Occasional Paper No. 22 (August 2001), pp. 1–9.

Hosokawa, Morihiro. "Are U.S. Troops in Japan Needed?" *Foreign Affairs*, July–August 1998, pp. 2–5.

IV. Magazines and Newspapers

AERA
Asahi Shimbun
Bungei Shunju
Chunichi Shimbun
Chuokoron
The Economist
Kaizo
Ronza
Shincho 45
Shokun
Shukan Asahi
Shukan Gendai
Shukan Posuto
Voice
Yomiuri Shimbun

INDEX

General Headquarters (GHQ, SCAP), 75–77, 79–102, 109, 112, 124

genro (elder statesmen), 44, 54, 59, 61, 114

Genyosha, 31, 64

"Gerrymander," 132

Gibbs, C. A., 11–14

Gladstone, William E., 50, 121

Gorbachev, Mikhail, 134

Government Section (GS, GHQ), 75–77, 80–82, 84, 86, 89–91, 96, 98–100, 103, 107

goyo seito (kept-party), 38

"great-man" theory of leadership, 10–11

Gulf War, 213

haihan chiken (to abolish *han* and install *ken*), 23, 241n23

Hamaguchi Osachi, 56, 60
   Hamaguchi cabinet, 60, 233

hambatsu (provincial clique), 23–24, 30–35, 38, 43, 46–48, 155, 230

han (province), 17–20, 42–43

Hanai Hitoshi, 97

hanko (province school), 44

Hara Takashi, 42–43, 46, 48, 51, 57–58, 114, 141, 172

Haraguchi Kaname, 20

Haruko
   See Hatoyama Haruko

Hashimoto Daijiro, 168

Hashimoto Miyuki
   See Hatoyama Miyuki

Hashimoto Ryutaro, 168, 172, 178, 186–187, 221, 224
   Hashimoto coalition cabinet, 177–178, 198–199, 202–204, 221
   Hashimoto faction, 191

Hata Tsutomu, 167–168, 177, 184, 209–210
   Hata coalition cabinet, 167–168, 180–181, 193, 226

Hatoyama Emily, 160–161, 183, 185

Hatoyama Haruko, 25–28, 31, 33–34, 37, 39, 41–46, 49–53, 73, 143, 231, 235

Hatoyama Hideo, 1, 45, 49–51, 73, 158, 229

Hatoyama Ichiro, 1, 3–6, 19–20, 24, 27, 37, 41, 43–45, 48–75, 77–144, 146, 155, 158, 164, 172, 182, 215, 219, 222–223, 225, 229–230, 235, 246n19
   "Hatomander bill," 131–132, *see also* election law (HR)
   "Hatoyama boom," 125–126
   first Hatoyama cabinet, 124–125
   second Hatoyama cabinet, 126–129
   third Hatoyama cabinet, 129–130
   Hatoyama faction, 118–119, 147
   position on Japan's defense policy, 86, 113–114, 117–118, 130–131, *see also* constitutional revision

Hatoyama Iichiro, 1, 143–155, 161–165, 175, 221, 223, 229–230

Hatoyama Juemon Hirofusa, 17–18, 20–21

Hatoyama Jutaro, 18–19

Hatoyama kaikan (hall), ix, 155

Hatoyama Kaoru, 52–53, 66, 83–84, 125, 137, 143, 146–147, 151, 231, 235

Hatoyama Kazuko (Iichiro's daughter), 157

Hatoyama Kazuo, 1, 6, 17–48, 50–52, 57–58, 141, 153, 155, 157–158, 164, 219, 223–224, 229–230, 235
   "*bento* (lunch) speech," 29
   "Hatoyama speech incident," 25

Hatoyama Kikuko, 17–18

Hatoyama Kunio, 2, 6, 144–145, 155, 157–162, 165–166,

Jiyuto
  See Liberal Party
jochu naki Ampo
  See "U.S.–Japan Security Treaty
    without permanent stationing"
Johnson, Chalmers, 3, 108
Jutaro
  See Hatoyama Jutaro

Kades, Charles L., Colonel, 76, 86,
  89, 98, 103, 110
Kaiho-juku, 19
Kaishinto (Okuma, 1882)
  See Constitutional Progressive
    Party
Kaishinto (1952)
  See Progressive Party
Kaizo (political magazine), 65–66
Kajiyama Seiroku, 224
Kakushin Kurabu (Reform Club), 58
Kan Naoto, 3, 169–170, 173, 177,
  184–185, 197–204, 209–210,
  217, 219, 221, 223–224,
  227–228, 234
Kaneko Mitsuhiro, 160, 188
kangaku (governmental schools), 22,
  31–32
kanken (government police), 69
kanryo seijika (bureaucrats-turned-
  politicians), 4, 103, 123
Kanzaki Takanori, 208
Kaoru
  See Hatoyama Kaoru
karo (*han*'s high-ranking
  minister), 43
Karuizawa, 69–71, 73, 77, 97, 111,
  120, 143
Kataoka Tetsuya, 4, 49, 105,
  107–108, 110–111, 131, 135
Katayama Tetsu, 68
  Katayama cabinet, 106
Kato Koichi, 224, 228
Kato Takaaki, 24, 41, 56, 58
Kato Tomosaburo, 57

katsugareru hito (pepole who ride on
  the pedestal)
  See "pedestal rider"
katsugu hito (pepole who carry the
  pedestal)
  See "pedestal carrier"
Katsura Taro, 39–40, 54
  Keien age, 39–40
  second Katsura cabinet, 41, 43
  third Katsura cabinet, 44
Katsuyama-*han* (province), 17–18
Kazuko (Kazuo's daughter, her
  surname would be Miura),
  58–59, 243–244n21
Kazuko (Iichiro's daughter)
  See Hatoyama Kazuko
Kazuo
  See Hatoyama Kazuo
Keio Gijuku
  See Keio University
Keio University, 22, 32, 56
Kempo chosakai
  See Constitutional Research
    Council
Kennan, George F., 102, 108–110,
  116
Kennedy family, 2, 5, 52, 157,
  199, 233
Kenseihonto
  See Orthodox Constitutional
    Government Party
Kenseikai
  See Constitutional Government
    Association
Kenseito
  See Constitutional Government
    Party
kensetsuteki yato
  See "constructive opposition party"
kenzen yato
  See "wholesome opposition
    party"
Khrushchev, Nikita, 134–135
Kikuchi Takeo, 20–21

Poole, Richard, Lieutenant, 77, 110
"popular rights"
 See "freedom and popular rights movement"
Portsmouth Peace Treaty (1905), 43, 56
Potsdam Declaration, 75
prisoners of war (POWs), 134–136
Privy Council, 62
Progressive Party (Okuma, 1882)
 See Constitutional Progressive Party
Progressive Party (Okuma, 1896), 34
Progressive Party (1945)
 See Japan Progressive Party
Progressive Party (1952), 106–107, 118–120, 123
Progressives
 prewar Progressives, 6, 24, 32, 36
 postwar Progressives, 79, 81–82, 88–89, 91
proportional representation districts (PR districts)
 See election law (HR)
Public Peace Police Law, 38
"purge from public office," 80–81
P'u-yi, 60

Rangaku (the Dutch study), 19
Reischauer, Edwin O., 4
Renewal Party, 167
"reverse course," 107–110
Right, 139
right to collective self-defense, 214–216
right to individual self-defense, 214–216
right-wing, 65
Rikken Doshikai
 See Constitutional Fellow Thinkers' Association
Rikken Kaishinto (Okuma, 1882)
 See Constitutional Progressive Party

Rikken Kokuminto
 See Constitutional Nationalist Party
Rikken Minseito
 See Constitutional Democratic Government Party
Rikken Seiyukai (Friends of Constitutional Government Association)
 See Seiyukai
rito (government's party), 24, 32
Roosevelt dynasty, 5, 233
Roosevelt, Franklin, D., 74
Roosevelt, Theodore, 39, 43
Russo-Japanese War (1904–1905), 43, 59

Saegusa Saburo, 164
Saga-batsu, 25
 See also Hizen
Saigo Takamori, 23, 46
Saionji Kimmochi, 38–40, 42, 59, 61, 63–64, 73
 second Saionji cabinet, 43
Saito Makoto, 61–64
 Saito cabinet, 61–63, 65
Saito Shuichiro, 19–21
Saki Ryuzo, 136
sakoku (seclusion), 17
samurai (retainer), 17, 20, 25–26, 42–43, 52, 226
San Francisco Peace Treaty, 97, 110–111, 118, 133, 138
sangi (state councilors), 23
Sansha rengo (tripartite alliance among Ichiro, Miki, and Nakano), 69
Satcho-batsu (Satsuma-Choshu clique), 23–24, 30
Sato Eisaku, 106, 117, 119, 121–123, 129, 134, 143, 151
Sato Kanju, 231
Sato Tomoyasu, 1–2
Sato Tsunetami, 25